The Political Thought of Nineteenth-Century Spanish America

IVÁN JAKSIĆ
Stanford University

EDUARDO POSADA-CARBÓ
University of Oxford

CAMBRIDGE
UNIVERSITY PRESS

CAMBRIDGE UNIVERSITY PRESS

Shaftesbury Road, Cambridge CB2 8EA, United Kingdom

One Liberty Plaza, 20th Floor, New York, NY 10006, USA

477 Williamstown Road, Port Melbourne, VIC 3207, Australia

314–321, 3rd Floor, Plot 3, Splendor Forum, Jasola District Centre, New Delhi – 110025, India

Cambridge University Press is part of Cambridge University Press & Assessment, a department of the University of Cambridge.

We share the University's mission to contribute to society through the pursuit of education, learning and research at the highest international levels of excellence.

www.cambridge.org
Information on this title: www.cambridge.org/9781108491587

DOI: 10.1017/9781108868983

© Cambridge University Press 2026

This publication is in copyright. Subject to statutory exception and to the provisions of relevant collective licensing agreements, no reproduction of any part may take place without the written permission of Cambridge University Press & Assessment.

When citing this work, please include a reference to the
DOI 10.1017/9781108868983

First published 2026

A catalogue record for this publication is available from the British Library

A Cataloging-in-Publication data record for this book is available from the Library of Congress

ISBN 978-1-108-49158-7 Hardback
ISBN 978-1-108-79872-3 Paperback

Cambridge University Press & Assessment has no responsibility for the persistence or accuracy of URLs for external or third-party internet websites referred to in this publication and does not guarantee that any content on such websites is, or will remain, accurate or appropriate.

For EU product safety concerns, contact us at Calle de José Abascal, 56, 1°, 28003 Madrid, Spain, or email eugpsr@cambridge.org

CAMBRIDGE TEXTS IN THE
HISTORY OF POLITICAL THOUGHT

The Political Thought of Nineteenth-Century Spanish America

Throughout the nineteenth century, Spanish American writers and thinkers grappled with their unique circumstances of independence after three centuries of Spanish colonial rule. The emergence of a significant number of new polities that adopted representative institutions in an era when absolutism prevailed in Western Europe, their general adoption of republicanism, and their complex demographic composition, all posed serious challenges for the formation of national states in Spanish America. This volume explores how politically engaged Spanish American thinkers reflected on these issues, either in government or in opposition. Through a wide selection of texts, some previously unpublished in the English language, the volume demonstrates the multiplicity of voices across countries, perspectives, and social backgrounds. The texts included are organized around main themes reflecting central concerns including history; democracy, constitutionalism, and liberty; church, state, and religion; society; Spanish America and the World; and "Fin de siècle." This volume thus vividly demonstrates the significance of Latin America to the field of Global Intellectual History.

IVÁN JAKSIĆ directs the Stanford University Bing Overseas Studies Program in Santiago, Chile, and holds the Andrés Bello Chair at Adolfo Ibáñez University. A Guggenheim Fellow, he has received multiple awards, including the Chilean National History Award in 2020. He is the author of *Academic Rebels in Chile* (1989), *Andrés Bello* (2001), and *The Hispanic World and American Intellectual Life* (2007).

EDUARDO POSADA-CARBÓ is Professor of the History and Politics of Latin America in Oxford and William Golding Senior Research Fellow in Brasenose College. He recently co-edited (with Joanna Innes and Mark Philp) *Re-Imagining Democracy in Latin America and the Caribbean, 1780–1870* (2023). His work has been published in leading academic journals, including *Past & Present*, *Hispanic American Historical Review*, and *The Historical Journal*.

CAMBRIDGE TEXTS IN THE HISTORY OF POLITICAL THOUGHT

General editor
QUENTIN SKINNER
Queen Mary University of London

Editorial board
MICHAEL COOK
Princeton University

HANNAH DAWSON
King's College London

ADOM GETACHEW
University of Chicago

EMMA HUNTER
University of Edinburgh

GABRIEL PAQUETTE
University of Maine

ANDREW SARTORI
New York University

HILDE DE WEERDT
Leiden University

Cambridge Texts in the History of Political Thought is firmly established as the major student series of texts in political theory. It aims to make available all the most important texts in the history of political thought, from ancient Greece to the twentieth century, from throughout the world and from every political tradition. All the familiar classic texts are included, but the series seeks at the same time to enlarge the conventional canon through a global scope and by incorporating an extensive range of less well-known works and previously marginalised voices, many of them never before available in a modern English edition. Where possible, the texts are published in complete and unabridged form, and translations are specially commissioned for the series. However, where appropriate, abridged or tightly focused and thematic collections are offered instead. Each volume contains a critical introduction together with chronologies, biographical sketches, a guide to further reading and any necessary glossaries and textual apparatus. Overall, the series aims to provide the reader with an outline of the entire evolution of political thinking on a global scale.

For a list of titles published in the series, please see end of book

Contents

Acknowledgements	page vii
Introduction	viii
Note on Translation	xxxviii

PART I. ON HISTORY

1. José Victorino Lastarria, Investigations on the Social Influence of the Spanish Conquest and the Colonial System in Chile (1844) — 5
2. Lucas Alamán, History and Fiction (1844) — 16

PART II. DEMOCRACY, CONSTITUTIONALISM, AND LIBERTY

3. Bernardo Monteagudo, Memoir (1823) — 21
4. Anonymous, The Political Faith of a Colombian (1827) — 31
5. Esteban Echeverría, The Socialist Program (1838) — 44
6. Florentino González, The Suffrage (1871) — 62
7. Justo Arosemena, Constitutional Studies on the Governments of Latin America (1878) — 72

PART III. CHURCH, STATE, AND RELIGION

8. Vicente Rocafuerte, On Religious Toleration (1831) — 93
9. Francisco Bilbao, The Error, or Contradiction, under Which Spanish America Lives (1862) — 102

Contents

10. Miguel Antonio Caro, Freedom of Religion (1871–1872) — 109

PART IV. SOCIETY

11. Juan Francisco Manzano, Life of the Negro Poet Written by Himself (1840) — 127
12. Mariano Otero, Comments on the Social and Political Situation of the Mexican Republic in the Year 1847 (1847) — 136
13. José María Samper, Essay on the Political Revolutions and the Social Conditions of the Spanish American Republics (1861) — 146
14. Juana Manso, The Moral Emancipation and Education of Women (1854) — 155
15. Martina Barros, Prologue to *The Slavery of Women* (Critical Study by John Stuart Mill) (1872–1873) — 163

PART V. SPANISH AMERICA AND THE WORLD

16. Andrés Bello, International Intervention (1846–1847) — 177
17. José Antonio Saco, The Political Situation of Cuba (1851) — 189
18. Juan Bautista Alberdi, International Society (1870) — 205

PART VI. FIN DE SIÈCLE

19. Valentín Letelier, The Tyranny and the Revolution (1891) — 221
20. Manuel González Prada, Our Indigenous Peoples (1904) — 233
21. Andrés Molina Enríquez, The Secret of Porfirian Peace (1909) — 238
22. Francisco García Calderón, Latin American Democracies (1912) — 253
23. Carlos Arturo Torres, Idols of the Forum (1909) — 266

Selected Bibliography — 276

Index — 294

Acknowledgements

We would like to thank Gabriel Paquette for his encouragement in putting this project together, and for the support we received from the general editor and the editorial board of the Cambridge Texts in the History of Political Thought series. The reports from two anonymous referees were most helpful for deciding on the final shape of the volume. They all motivated us to advance a view on some of the key texts that contributed to a history of political thought from a Latin American perspective.

Most of the research undertaken for this book would not have been possible without the valuable assistance of a good number of librarians at the Bodleian Libraries in Oxford (including its Latin American Centre Library), the Bibliothèque Nationale de France, and the Biblioteca Nacional de Chile. Colleagues, too numerous to name, assisted us when we needed to look for texts, and understand the context and the language of the primary sources.

We felt fortunate to have the assistance of Julene Knox, who proved to be an exemplary copy-editor. Working with Ruth Boyes and Liz Friend-Smith, as with all the team at Cambridge University Press, has been a pleasure – indeed, a real treat for any author.

Iván Jaksić
Eduardo Posada-Carbó

Introduction

Iván Jaksić and Eduardo Posada-Carbó

This book offers a selection of key texts mostly written by leading figures in Spanish America during the first century of independence, who grappled with unique circumstances after three centuries of Spanish colonial rule. The emergence of a significant number of new polities that adopted representative institutions in an era when absolutism prevailed in Western Europe, their general adoption of republicanism, and their complex demographic composition all posed serious challenges for the formation of national states in Spanish America. Spanish American thinkers often reflected upon these and other related problems while being politically engaged, either in government or in opposition.

Long gone are the days when the history of political thought in the region was generally dismissed by scholars because of its "derivative" nature: Political thinkers were then considered just followers of mostly European theorists, lacking originality.[1] Subsequently, the field remained neglected while other areas of research attracted increasing attention. As Charles A. Hale noted, the "cultural and economic interpretations of Latin American History" predominant in the 1970s considered the nineteenth century "the century of imitation."[2] His own work on Mexico, together with that of other contemporary historians, served to make "the

---

[1] John D. Martz, "Characteristics of Latin American Political Thought," *Journal of Inter-American Studies* 8.1 (1966), 55, 73.
[2] Charles A. Hale, "The Reconstruction of Nineteenth-century Politics in Spanish America: A Case for the History of Ideas," *Latin American Research Review* 8.2 (1973), 53–73.

Introduction

case for the history of ideas" in nineteenth-century Spanish America, and inspired a new wave of scholarship on both sides of the Atlantic. Over the past few decades, the intellectual history of the region has expanded in extraordinary ways. We now have an impressive body of literature, covering a wide range of individual authors and their works as well as different schools of thought, in different periods, including the nineteenth century. The field has been the subject of intense debate, as scholars moved their attention from the history of ideas to that of language.[3]

Our edited collection is not a systematic history of political thought, but a selection of texts written by contemporaries, translated for an English audience. As such, it belongs to a particular genre with its own historiography, one that deserves more attention than the brief outline provided here. When in 1944 William Rex Crawford published *A Century of Latin American Thought*, the historiography of the subject in English hardly existed and very few Spanish Americans had seen their work translated into English. The picture has changed since then, thanks to several editorial initiatives.[4] Launched in the 1990s, for example, the Oxford University Press "Library of Latin America" has brought the work of individual authors such as José Victorino Lastarria, Andrés Bello, and Vicente Pérez Rosales to an English audience. Other collections have offered samples of the contributions of Spanish Americans to specific ideas, as shown in the volumes on liberalism in Mexico and Argentina, edited by José Antonio Aguilar, and Natalio Botana and Ezequiel Gallo respectively. The historiographical developments of some topics and periods have stimulated the translation of contemporary texts as a way of offering access to primary sources to students – as in the anthology on Latin American independence, compiled by Sarah Chambers and John C. Chasteen, or on nineteenth-century nation building by Janet Burke and Ted Humphrey. Writings by Spanish American thinkers have been included in some country readers, like the recent collection on Mexico edited by Gilbert M. Joseph and Timothy J. Henderson.

---

[3] Elías José Palti, "The Problem of 'Misplaced Ideas' Revisited: Beyond the 'History of Ideas' in Latin America," *Journal of the History of Ideas* 67.1 (2006): 149–179; Roberto Breña, "Tensions and Challenges of Intellectual History in Contemporary Latin America," *Contributions to the History of Concepts* 16.1 (2021): 89–115.
[4] We register here some examples in the English language. But there have been impressive editorial initiatives undertaken in the Hispanic world. Just consider the vast collection of the Biblioteca Ayacucho, launched in Venezuela in 1976.

Introduction

Our volume aims to contribute to this growing interest in the history of nineteenth-century Spanish American political thought. Following the remit of the editors of the Cambridge University Press series, our selection privileges lesser-known authors – that is, figures like Simón Bolívar, Domingo F. Sarmiento, and José Martí have not been included. The fact that some of our selected authors are less known today does not detract from their significance at the time. When we have included better-known thinkers, like Andrés Bello or Juan Bautista Alberdi, we have selected texts that are not as well known. Overall, we have highlighted the significance of texts over authors – thus the inclusion of some anonymous documents. We have proceeded by selecting, first, a set of subjects that we think were of primary concern among the political thinkers of the times and, then, samples of relevant documents. Space constraints compound further the inherent limitations that come from making any selection. In the rest of the introduction, we offer some historical context to our selected texts, following the order of our main umbrella themes: history; democracy, constitutionalism, and liberty; church, state, and religion; society; Spanish America and the World; and "Fin de siècle."

PART I. On History

The development of the discipline of history went hand in hand with the formation of independent nations in Spanish America. The field provided a central venue for political discussions on change and reform in the context of emancipation. Perhaps the richest debate concerning the wide-ranging scope of the discipline took place in Chile in the 1840s. It was triggered by the essay "Investigaciones sobre la influencia de la conquista y del sistema colonial de los españoles en Chile" that José Victorino Lastarria (1817–1888) presented before the University of Chile on September 22, 1844, whose excerpts open our selection.

In his speech, Lastarria invoked the name of Johann Gottfried Herder to the effect that history had both meaning and direction to be uncovered by research. "The essence of humanity is noble," Lastarria said, "and is destined to greater ends than those imagined by many who consider it stupidly tied to the laws of matter" (p. 8).[5] Humanity needed *lessons* to prevent

---

[5] Page numbers are given for quotations from the respective texts included later in this volume. (Editors' note)

Introduction

or combat social evils and secure "a happy future" for all. History provided those lessons and, consequently, Lastarria urged his audience not to reduce it to "a simple record of past events" (p. 9). Only a "philosophical" history, which he associated with "the light of divinity," could reveal the "fatal consequences of a past event ... the antisocial behaviors that persist ... [and] the inclinations and vices that take root in the heart of a people ... present[ing] a stubborn resistance to perfectibility" (p. 11). He then asked: "What is the history of our republic? What are the benefits of the study of history for the management of affairs in our current situation?" (p. 12).

According to Lastarria, the story of Chile was one of three centuries of colonial oppression and religious bigotry. It was a history of violence and hatred, and there would be no purpose in glorifying isolated events of heroic Indigenous resistance. Natives had succumbed to wretchedness, only to wake into sporadic bouts of deadly warfare and then repeat the cycle during the whole colonial rule. What colonial officials had not managed to do in the way of subjecting Chileans was accomplished by an intolerant church that promoted blind belief, superstitious practices, and conformity. In the end, "the Chilean people were profoundly debased, reduced to a state of complete numbness, and left without a single social virtue, ostensibly at least, because their political institutions were designed to make them slaves."[6] Such was the damning picture of the origins and formation of Chilean society at the time of independence: depressing yet terribly real. Drastic social, political, and cultural change was needed.

Lastarria's presentation elicited a strong rebuke from Venezuelan-born Andrés Bello (1781–1865). Change in post-independence Latin America, he stated, had to come in gradual ways. It was necessary to avoid the potentially destabilizing polemics that, in his view, were embedded in Lastarria's arguments. Any revival of the divisive passions that led to the independence struggle and continued afterwards, or any calls for the radical transformation of society, would threaten the carefully designed transition to the more liberal polity which Bello had in mind. Moderation, as the French Doctrinaires had recommended, was indispensable.

And yet, Lastarria's essay was of enormous significance at both the Chilean and Latin American levels. The polemic that followed defined the boundaries between "narrative" (meaning archive-driven research)

---

[6] "Investigaciones," chapter 4, in *Miscelánea histórica y literaria*, 3 vols. (Valparaíso, 1868), 1, 67.

and "philosophical" (purpose-bound) historiography. The debate had repercussions throughout Latin America, involving Argentine historians such as Bartolomé Mitre and Vicente Fidel López, or Lucas Alamán and José Fernando Ramírez from Mexico. Lastarria thus inaugurated a tradition of polemics regarding the political ramifications of historical inquiry in post-independence Latin America.

Lucas Alamán (1792–1853), in particular, advanced the opposite views in his *Disertaciones sobre la historia de la República Mexicana* (1844). History, he claimed, was characterized by a search for truth, meaning well-established facts based on verifiable records. Anything else was either fiction or deliberate distortions of known events for ideological purposes. As he stated in the selection for this volume, his work was intended "to confront new writings circulating about the Conquest which ignore historical facts and let the imagination run wild" (p. 18). This was a clear reference to the work of Carlos María de Bustamante, *Cuadro histórico de la revolución de la América Mexicana* (1823 and 1843–1846 editions), which Alamán regarded as a one-sided, anti-Spanish account of the independence of Mexico. Such polemics about the writing of history became fundamental components of the building of independent nations, with their respective pantheons of heroes and villains.

PART II. Democracy, Constitutionalism, and Liberty

Discussions about "democracy, constitutionalism, and liberty" sprung up with emancipation. Napoleon's usurpation of the Spanish crown in 1808 triggered a crisis of authority of transatlantic dimensions, leading to the establishment of eleven new republics in Spanish America by 1830. Their emergence was accompanied by intense debates on the type of government that would replace the imperial order. During these decades, the expression "democracy" still carried negative connotations in Europe and the United States, associated with memories of disorder in the ancient world and the terror of the French Revolution. Spanish America was no different in its cautiousness, reluctance, and hostility to embracing democracy as a form of government, although the term was sometimes used in opposition to "monarchy," or as a demand for equality against the privileged few and the remnants of the colonial aristocracy. What sets Spanish America apart is the variety of post-colonial experiences in a region populated by a highly heterogeneous population scattered in a vast territory. It was a huge laboratory of government, whose

Introduction

experiments were soon the subject of reflection by a wide range of protagonists, some in charge of designing and implementing the novel institutions, others fighting them from the ranks of the opposition.

Bernardo Monteagudo's *Memoir* (1823) epitomizes the nature of intellectual activity during the revolutionary period. It is also an extraordinary text that tackled some of the central questions concerning democracy and society. Monteagudo's trajectory illustrates the type of public intellectual who became notable at the time. Born in Tucumán (Argentina) in 1789, of relatively modest origins and mixed race, he participated in one of the earliest manifestations of the independence movement in 1809 in Chuquisaca (Bolivia), where he completed his university education. He moved to Buenos Aires, gaining notoriety for his contributions to the press and involvement in revolutionary politics. Political struggles forced him into exile between 1815 and 1817, when he visited Brazil, Europe, and the United States. On his return to South America, he joined the army of José de San Martín in both Chile and Peru. As he rose in the military ranks, Monteagudo secured San Martín's confidence due to his writing skills – he was in charge of the printing press that accompanied the liberation army. In 1821, when San Martín proclaimed the independence of Peru and made himself "Protector" of the new country, Monteagudo was appointed Defense Minister – he later added Foreign Affairs to his portfolio, becoming San Martín's "closest political associate and, effectively, his prime minister."[7]

Monteagudo's *Memoir* was written after he was expelled from Lima by his opponents, following popular riots against his rule. There he stated the "principles" that he claimed to have followed during his administration: secure Peruvian independence against the still dominant Spanish military presence; "restrict democratic ideas"; promote public education; and "prepare the opinion in Peru" for a constitutional rule with the strength to consolidate the state's independence. Our selected passages from his *Memoir* focus on Monteagudo's second principle: his reflections on democracy, more specifically on the reasons why democratic ideas were "absolutely unsuitable to Peru."[8] Monteagudo's intellectual journey, from his earlier republican "Jacobinism" to the monarchical autocratic project he helped to design under the Protectorate, was closely

---

[7] John Lynch, *San Martín: Argentine Soldier, American Hero* (New Haven, 2009), 141.
[8] Bernardo Monteagudo, "Memoria," in Monteagudo, *Escritos políticos* (Buenos Aires, 1916), 323.

xiii

tied to the wave of experimentations that the revolutionary governments undertook. He was repentant of his previous "frantic support" for democracy.[9] Monteagudo was less interested in "democracy" as an abstract concept than in the historical and socio-economic conditions required to establish a democratic government: the mores of the people, the state of their civilization, the distribution of wealth, and the interactions of the various classes forming society. Those conditions, he argued, were absent in Peru. Instead, the long colonial experience had debased the population to habits of subservience; the level of education was so low that there were few "capable men to manage the affairs of their country"; the concentration of wealth impeded individual liberty and freedom of action to make collective decisions, and above all, the ethnic hostilities threatened social coexistence. Monteagudo engaged systematically with democracy as a form of government at a time when the term did not have the ubiquity it gained in the Western world during the following decades. His skepticism regarding democracy was then common, but his thoughts on the topic, even if generally anchored in Montesquieu's *Esprit des lois*, were rather drawn from his own experience over a decade of involvement in the revolutions of independence.

While Monteagudo was facing the hostile opposition that overthrew him, San Martín was traveling to Guayaquil, where he met Simón Bolívar, who was heading south to fight the remaining royalist armies in Ecuador and Peru. After a legendary encounter between the two leaders, San Martín returned to polarized Lima, where he soon resigned his commanding position over the liberation of Peru, which now fell upon Bolívar. A congress in Lima gave the latter "supreme military authority" to carry on the war against the royalist forces, which were finally defeated in 1825 with the liberation of Upper Peru.

Independence was entangled with the intricate processes of recreating authority within the new boundaries of the emerging states. One such state was Bolivia (Upper Peru), for which Bolívar drew a constitution in 1826, also adopted by Peru, which included, among many other provisions, the figure of the presidency for life. Bolívar believed that his Bolivian Code could serve Colombia as well. The project alarmed liberal political circles that feared his dictatorial proclivities. Colombia was then governed under the 1821 constitution, which incorporated a representative

---

[9] Monteagudo, *Escritos políticos*, 326.

Introduction

form of government, based on the division of powers. Bolívar's proposal provoked debate on the nature of representative government and presidential power. By the time Bolívar returned to Bogota, after years of absence, in September 1827, a constitutional crisis threatened the existence of the republic, which he hoped to solve by convening a constitutional convention that met between April and June 1828. It is in this context that *The Political Faith of a Colombian*, the next text in our volume, ought to be read.

Published anonymously in Bogota in 1827, it was welcomed by *La Gaceta de Colombia*, the official newspaper edited by Vice-President Francisco de Paula Santander, who was in charge of the government while Bolívar led the military campaigns against the royalist forces. *The Political Faith* was clearly an anti-Bolivarian tract, though Bolívar's name was never mentioned – the tone of the text was impersonal, as its analysis focused on the central theme of the ills of absolute power in all its forms. It opened with a definition of the people (*pueblo*, in singular), in response to the sort of plebiscitarian calls from the various municipalities demanding a constitutional convention before the date stipulated by the constitution. By "people" *The Political Faith* understood the "universality" of the citizens. Equally crucial, the sovereignty of the people was limited and should be exercised by representatives. The notion of representative government was also in contradiction with any idea of the "omnipotence of parliament." Dictatorship, or any form of "liberal despotism," was explicitly rejected. Regular elections, the right of petition and freedom of the press were the best guarantors of representative government.

The Political Faith dealt with something that was still novel: presidential power in representative democracies. A major concern among the new republics was how to limit its potential abuses and tyrannical inclinations. For *The Political Faith* the remedy could be found in fixed, short terms of office. Bolívar convened the constitutional convention in Ocaña in April–June 1828 to address this issue, but its proceedings were dominated by his opponents. Two months later, he assumed temporary dictatorial powers until the meeting of a new constitutional convention should take place in January 1830. Unable again to control the assembly, Bolívar finally resigned as Colombia disintegrated while each of its components – Venezuela, New Granada, and Ecuador – parted ways.

In most of Spanish America, the late 1820s were years of serious challenges for the new representative institutions. Constitutional crises took different forms, followed by different outcomes. In the River Plate, after a

Introduction

decade of experimentations, including an expanding suffrage that in 1821 granted the vote in Buenos Aires to all free adult males, Juan Manuel de Rosas put on hold the very notion of constitutionalism as he assumed the governorship of the province. In 1835, he assumed the "sum of public power." His dictatorial regime lasted until 1852, becoming the symbol of *caudillo* rule, seen as the archetype in the region.

As Rosas rose to power, Esteban Echeverría returned from his years of study in France (1826–1830) to Buenos Aires, where he became "the leader of a new liberal awakening" in the Río de la Plata region.[10] This apparently paradoxical intellectual development under a despotic regime was relatively short-lived. Having helped create a literary salon and a Mazzinian youth association in 1837, his critical texts and other opposition activities forced him into exile, settling in Uruguay, where he remained until his death in 1851.

His *Socialist Program* (*Dogma socialista*), which is included in part in our collection, was published in Montevideo in 1838. "Democracy" rather than "socialism" would have been a more suitable title – as Mercedes Betria observed, "the whole of *Dogma socialista* is a text about democracy."[11] For Echeverría, democracy in Argentina was born with independence, but the country was still grappling with the obsolete traditions inherited from Spain. However, it was an unstoppable movement: The mission of his generation was to pave the way for democracy. Nevertheless, Echeverría warned that "democracy does not mean the absolute despotism of the masses, or the majority." He identified popular sovereignty with a "regime of reason" in a language that betrayed his familiarity with the French Doctrinaires. Echeverría's skepticism regarding universal suffrage was based on the Argentine experience with the wide suffrage adopted by Buenos Aires in 1821, which Rosas manipulated to "legitimize despotism."[12] He did not support restricting the suffrage to property owners or to levels of income and taxation. Instead, education and economic independence were the requirements for the exercise of popular sovereignty, and it was the task of the government to provide the necessary leveling conditions in the march toward democracy.

---

[10] Klaus Gallo, "Esteban Echeverría's Critique of Universal Suffrage: The Traumatic Development of Democracy in Argentina, 1821–1852," in C. A. Bayly and Eugenio F. Biagni, eds., *Giuseppe Mazzini and the Globalisation of Democratic Nationalism, 1830–1920* (Oxford and New York, 2008), 300.

[11] Mercedes Betria, "El concepto de democracia representativa en Esteban Echeverría," *Acta Sociológica* 71 (2016): 154.

[12] Echeverria, "Ojeada retrospectiva sobre el movimiento intelectual en el Plata desde el año 37", (first published in 1839), in Esteban Echeverría, *Dogma socialista* (Buenos Aires, 1988), 40

Introduction

The fall of Rosas in 1852 was followed by a congressional assembly that adopted a constitution in 1853, accepted by Buenos Aires in 1860 only after two brief military confrontations. Any qualms Echeverría's generation had about universal male suffrage were superseded by the wide notion of rights that prevailed in the new regime. Together with New Granada (1853) and Mexico (1857), Argentina was one of a handful of countries that took the lead in extending the vote to all adult males without any restrictions in the Americas, only a few years after France did so in 1848.

The notion of "universal suffrage," comprising both males and females, was defended by Florentino González (1805–1875), the first Chair of Constitutional Law at the University of Buenos Aires, in his *Lecciones de derecho constitutional* (Buenos Aires, 1869), whose selected passages on the topic are included in this volume. Born in New Granada, González had enjoyed a successful public career in his native country – notable for his free-trade policies as Minister of Finance, his prolific journalism, his work as a legislator, and his several electoral attempts to become president of the republic. In 1860, while on a diplomatic mission in Chile, a rebellion led by General Tomás Cipriano Mosquera, his political foe, toppled the constitutional government and forced him to stay in exile. From Chile, he moved to Buenos Aires in 1868 to assume the Chair in Constitutional Law. His *Lecciones* had continental repercussions: The same year as the first edition in Argentina (1869), the book was printed in Bogota; during the subsequent decade, it circulated in Chile, Central America, and Mexico, where another edition was published in 1879.

In his chapters on suffrage, González discussed two fundamental aspects of the subject: How could the franchise motivate citizens to advance the common good, and how could the vote most effectively represent the popular will? The former led him to oppose the notion of the suffrage as a "right" – instead, voting was a duty: Thus understood, its exercise moralized voters as they became accustomed to thinking about their electoral choices. This view led him to support universal suffrage. Here he took issue with John Stuart Mill, whose *Considerations on Representative Government* González translated while in Chile in 1865. He tackled Mill's argument for restricting the suffrage to literates. González turned around Mill's premise that universal education should precede universal suffrage: Since institutions were instruments of social change, universal suffrage would encourage citizens to appreciate the value of education. Although a relatively small portion of his *Lecciones*, his chapters on suffrage were nonetheless significant because he believed that "universal suffrage is the institution that can provide the most solid foundation for representative democracy" (pp. 70).

Estudios constitutionales sobre los gobiernos de la América Latina by Justo Arosemena (1817–1896), whose introduction and conclusion are included next in Part II, was first published in Paris in 1870, just about a year after González's *Lecciones*. Both shared some of the basic principles of representative democracy, but their approach to constitutionalism differed substantially. Arosemena's *Constitutional Studies* was a critique of abstract theories that invited the emulation of the "institutions of other countries" (p. 83). In contrast to González's *Lecciones*, Arosemena offered an examination of the constitutions of ten Latin American states, including sections on their respective historical antecedents. The colonial experience together with the revolution of independence posed great challenges to the creation of new political organizations, namely, that ignoring the past would lead to instability.

Arosemena was struck by how different the constitutions of these countries were, despite their similarities at the time of independence: All "political forms have been present in Latin America, from moderate monarchy in Brazil, to exaggerated republicanism in Colombia," the result, he thought, of following abstract theories rather than adjusting to actual conditions. Constitutions should "accommodate" the "social situations" of their respective countries, which required time and could be done through existing "enlightened means." However, he accepted some general constitutional principles: individual human rights should never be sacrificed; "clauses that facilitate arbitrariness and disorder" should be soundly rejected (pp. 85, 78, 88). Arosemena's *Constitutional Studies* has been considered the "first systematic work of constitutional law in Latin America."[13]

PART III. Church, State, and Religion

Among the ten countries whose constitutions were included in Arosemena's compilation (second edition, 1878), only Mexico, Colombia, and Haiti had accepted the separation of church and state. The rest proclaimed Catholicism as the official religion of the state although this was

---

[13] Miguel González Marcos, "Comparative Law at the Service of Democracy: A Reading of Arosemena's Constitutional Studies of the Latin American Governments," *Boston University International Law Journal* 21 (2003), 259, 322.

Introduction

stipulated in different ways in their respective constitutional texts. None reflected a fixed situation or was free of problems. Far from it, the relationship between the newly emerging states and the church was deeply conflictual and remained so throughout the nineteenth century. The issues at stake were all-embracing – from the more mundane aspects of the wealth of the church to the spirituality of citizens. At its core, this was a discussion about locating authority after the dismantling of the colonial order. Proponents of "religious tolerance" questioned centuries of dominance by the church, sparking a prolonged debate. The three texts selected for this part illustrate some of the terms of a highly complex discussion that cut across all levels of society.

Ensayo sobre tolerancia religiosa was published in Mexico in 1831 by the Ecuadorian Vicente Rocafuerte. Born in Guayaquil in 1783 into a wealthy family, he was representative of the generation of independence whose life had wider American and Atlantic dimensions. After receiving an education in Spain and France, he returned to Ecuador in 1807 and participated in the 1809 Quito insurrection. In 1814, he served as deputy to the Cortes in Cádiz and returned in 1820 on a mission to explore the possibilities of reconciliation between Spain and Spanish America. From the disappointing experience that followed, he became convinced of the inevitability of independence and the emergence of republics. In 1824, he was appointed to represent the Mexican government in London, where he stayed for the next six years. Recalled by Mexico in 1830 to answer questions about his activities in London, Rocafuerte became embroiled in the politics of the country until leaving for Ecuador in 1833.

Written during this latter period in Mexico, his essay on "religious tolerance" is best understood as part of his wider concern with the challenges of building a constitutional republic. "The most virtuous peoples," he stated in his *Ensayo político* in 1823, "are those where greater freedom of religion is observed."[14] He defended religious tolerance again in his criticism of an essay by Juan Egaña in 1826. His *Ensayo sobre tolerancia religiosa* opened with the puzzling question of why, after years of experiments with political liberty in Spanish America, "we are still unable to address the issue of religious toleration" (p. 94). The excerpts included in our volume illustrate Rocafuerte's more general reasoning in favor of separating the state from the religious sphere. His full text also examined

---

[14] Vicente Rocafuerte, *Ensayo político. El sistema colombiano. Popular, electivo, y representativo. Es el que más conviene a la América independiente* (New York, 1823), 31.

Introduction

the experiences of individual countries, in Europe and the Americas, to show the advantages of religious toleration, which included an extensive section on Mexico. There, economic and strategic reasons were paramount: to promote migration of industrious peoples from non-Catholic countries and, particularly, to encourage the colonization of Texas and the Californias. There, he suggested to first try the policy of religious toleration, as dictated by "prudence," an expression of his moderate approach toward religious reform, which he later undertook as Ecuadorian president in 1835–1839.

Francisco Bilbao (1823–1865), the author of the second text in Part III, belonged to a younger generation than Rocafuerte's, though they had much in common, including long years in exile and transatlantic connections; both were prosecuted for their publications on the religious question. But Bilbao's stand was far more radical. Born in Santiago, he grew up from his early adolescent years in Peru, where his family lived in exile because of his father's opposition to the Diego Portales regime. He returned to Chile in 1839 and enrolled as a law student at the Instituto Nacional. In 1844, Bilbao published "Sociabilidad chilena," a pamphlet that ignited the ire of the Catholic Church and the government. The trial that followed, on the grounds of violations of the extant 1828 press laws, gained him fame. Found guilty of "blasphemy and immorality," he avoided prison and moved to France. In Paris, he became personally acquainted with Félicité de Lamennais, earlier a liberal Catholic priest and thinker who had broken with the church by the time they met, and whose works, *De l'esclavage moderne* (1839) and *Du passé et de l'avenir du peuple* (1841), Bilbao had translated and published in Chile in 1843. He attended lectures at the Collège de France by the anti-clericals Edgar Quinet and Jules Michelet, whom he also met. Disillusioned by the outcome of the 1848 revolution in France, Bilbao returned in 1850 to Chile, where he was soon involved in the movement that led to the failed 1851 rebellion against the presidential candidacy of Manuel Montt. Forced again into exile, he first went to Lima, and then to various European cities and finally Buenos Aires, where he died at the age of forty-two in 1865.

"The Error or Contradiction, under Which Spanish America Lives," Bilbao's text in our selection, is part of *La América en peligro*, a book published in Buenos Aires in 1862. This was his answer to the French invasion of Mexico and the Spanish occupation of the Dominican Republic the previous year. Bilbao devoted most of his tract to examining why the

Introduction

region was so exposed to the foreign invaders: Material conditions may have mattered but the main cause of the problem was "intellectual." He pointed a finger at the church because the radical contradiction between Catholic dogma and republican principles was the main "cause of danger":[15] The French invasion was supported by the Mexican clergy, and Napoleon III was protecting Pope Pious IX in Rome. Bilbao did not trouble himself with developments on the ground, either in Mexico or in Europe. Instead, he dwelt on the "essential incompatibility"[16] between Catholicism and republicanism – the logic of the former was theocracy and that of the latter rationality. The public spirit was bound to perish wherever Catholic dogma prevailed, opening the door to absolutist rule. While his book concluded with a call for an American congress against the French invasion, this point was somewhat marginal to his overall concern with the "danger" posed by Catholicism to political and civil liberties. Bilbao's long-term remedy was to forge the "religion of the state," the reign of reason against the church.

In contrast to Rocafuerte and Bilbao, Miguel Antonio Caro (1843–1909) never left his native country. More significantly, Caro opposed the principle of "freedom of religion." Best known for his leading role in the "Regeneración" regime that restored the power of the Catholic Church in Colombia, which he himself led as acting-president from 1892 to 1898, Caro had an earlier career as scholar and publicist. He became notable for his work on Spanish grammar, his translation of Virgil, and, above all, his defense of the Catholic Church through his prolific writings. He welcomed Pious IX's *Syllabus of Errors*, which condemned liberalism; penned several tracts against utilitarianism, including his "Estudio sobre el utilitarismo" (1869), and his "Informe sobre los 'Elementos de la Ideología' de Tracy" (1870); in 1871, he founded the ultramontane newspaper *El Tradicionista*, whose pages were devoted to advocacy of the Catholic cause.

Caro's text in our volume was originally published in *El Tradicionista*, as part of a series of articles under the general title "Libertad de cultos." The first issue defended the rights of Colombian Catholics against the "despotism" of the liberal government, advocating a wider discussion about "political questions in relation to religious principles," which, he claimed, other Catholic newspapers rarely addressed.[17] In 1870, the

---

[15] Bilbao, *La América en peligro*, 7, 20–78.
[16] Bilbao, *La América en peligro*, 31.
[17] *El Tradicionista*, Bogota, November 7, 1871.

Colombian government issued a decree secularizing public elementary schools, the culmination of a series of measures against the church since 1849: the expulsion of the Jesuits; the adoption of freedom of religion and civil marriage; the separation of church and state; the expropriation of church property; and the forced exile of bishops and other members of the clergy. By the early 1870s, Caro had established himself as the leading voice of the Catholic opposition. His call was for action to restore the "Catholic republic."

PART IV. Society

The demand to recognize Catholicism as a state religion rested on the idea of homogeneous beliefs, shared by the vast majority of the population. It was a questionable if not altogether wrong assumption, but one that might have served to impose unity in what were highly heterogeneous societies – fragmented by race and geography, and deeply divided by wealth. This part offers passages from five documents that reflected upon those and other social differences.

The first document, *Life of the Negro Poet Written by Himself* (1840), highlights the struggles against an institution that marked more than any other the persistent inequalities in the region after independence: slavery. While slavery had been abolished in Chile and Mexico, in 1823 and 1829 respectively, and had been seriously weakened by various measures in most of the emerging Spanish American states that abolished it during the mid-nineteenth century, it long remained in Puerto Rico and Cuba – where it survived until 1886. *Life of the Negro Poet* was originally written in Spanish by the Cuban Juan Francisco Manzano (1797/8–1853), and translated into English by Richard R. Madden, an Irishman appointed by the British government as superintendent of liberated Africans in Havana from 1835 to 1839. Born into slavery, Manzano gained fame as a poet before obtaining his freedom in 1836, thanks to the help of Domingo del Monte, a "maecenas to the principal antislavery writers of the period."[18]

Manzano wrote his *Autobiografía* at the request of Del Monte with the aim of publicizing "the cause of abolition abroad."[19] The text was edited

---

[18] Edward J. Mullen, *The Life and Poems of a Cuban Slave: Juan Francisco Manzano, 1797–1854* (New York, 2014), 3.
[19] Sylvia Molloy, "From Serf to Self: The Autobiography of Juan Francisco Manzano," *Modern Language Notes* 104 (1989), 395.

Introduction

by a Cuban anti-slavery novelist,[20] before being translated by Madden, who published it in London in 1840 – it remained an anonymous document until its publication in Spanish in 1937.[21] *Life of the Negro Poet* has received a great deal of academic attention and has become the object of scholarly dispute. For some, in the act of editing and translating his *Autobiografía*, the document was not only "manipulated" but Manzano was "dispossessed" of his voice. For others, it should be considered a "networked text" of a "transatlantic nature."[22]

While Manzano's experience is best captured through his original manuscript, the English translation is itself a document of historical significance. Madden presented it to the British and Foreign Anti-Slavery Society in the same year as its publication, when he addressed the society's convention in London, attended by some 5,000 people. There, he challenged Tocqueville, who in an 1839 report to the French Chamber of Deputies, had claimed that in the Spanish colonies "slavery has always had ... a peculiar character of mildness."[23] According to Edward Mullen, "Madden's translation provided British abolitionists with the cultural capital to ensure a future beyond 1840." We know little about its wider impact, but some passages were published by the London *Christian Observer* in 1841, and the text seems to have been used by Scottish and French abolitionists – Victor Schoelcher worked on a French translation.[24] As the author of a text originally produced in Spanish America that was then used outside Cuba to fight slavery, Manzano's agency therefore acquired an international dimension. Historically, the *Life of the Negro Poet* is all the more significant since this is one of the few if not the only anti-slavery account written by an enslaved person in Spanish America.

The second abridged text in this section, *Comments on the Social and Political Situation of the Mexican Republic in the Year 1847*, was also published anonymously, undersigned by "several Mexicans." Unlike the *Life of the Negro Poet*, however, it is uncertain who the author of *Comments*

---

[20] Rodrigo Cánovas, "Juan Francisco Manzano, esclavo. Autobiografía (1835): reimpresiones de lectura," *Mapocho. Revista de Humanidades*, Santiago, 94 (2024), 72–73.
[21] *Autobiografía, cartas y versos de Juan Fco Manzano, con un estudio preliminar por José L. Franco* (Havana, 1937).
[22] Molloy, "From Serf to Self," 396; and Mullen, *The Life and Poems*, 25.
[23] Richard R. Madden, *Address on Slavery in Cuba* (London, 1840), 3.
[24] Mullen, *The Life and Poems*, 16, 20, 25, 28. Schoelcher referred to Manzano's poems and translated some of his verses in his book *Abolition de l'esclavage: examen critique du préjugé contre la couleur des Africans et des sang-mêlés* (Pagnerre, 1841), 89, 92. A brief review of *The Life and Poems* appeared in the *Freeman's Journal* in Dublin on February 16, 1841.

was. It has often been attributed to Mariano Otero (1817–1850), a jurist and politician, most renowned for his contribution to the Juicio de Amparo – a pioneering legal process to secure individual rights. The compilation edited by Jesús Reyes Heroles included the *Comments* as one of Otero's works. According to Reyes Heroles, the strong similarities with other texts written by Otero, in addition to the method he employed, offered sufficient evidence to attribute to him the authorship of *Comments*.[25]

Whether written by Otero, on his own or as co-author, or written by someone else, the document included here reflected deep concerns about the fate of Mexico after the war with the United States (1846–1848). Having lost Texas in 1836, Mexicans were filled with despair following a much larger territorial dispossession. The author argued that the causes of the country's defeat were rooted in the colonial past and decades of misgovernment after independence, whose outcome was a "society divided by the most opposite and conflicting interests."[26] What prevailed was therefore a lack of "national spirit" since there was "no nation" – a paradoxical denial of nationalism expressed with patriotic zeal in the hope of changing the trajectory of Mexico.

That wars and revolutions were considered "as proofs of incapacity that prevent any hopes for the future of our republics" (p. 153) was also the concern behind José María Samper's *Essay on the Political Revolutions and the Social Condition of the Spanish American Republics* (1861), whose selected passages are included in the third chapter of this Part IV. Samper (1828–1888), however, focused on civil rather than external wars. He offered some comparisons with Europe, just to show that the history of the old continent was filled with the horrors of war, "where extreme opulence coexists with extreme misery" (p. 152). Yet while Europeans found logical explanations for their violent past and trajectories, they judged Spanish America "in a most peculiar way" (p. 153). One of the main aims of the essay, Samper acknowledged, was to rectify the ignorance of Europeans, who were "more interested in our volcanoes than in our societies" (p. 159).

Samper's *Essay* covered a wide range of topics on the history of the region, but his core argument lay in the novelty of a society whose heterogeneity was leading to the formation of a new civilization emerging

---

[25] See Jesús Reyes Heroles' observations in Mariano Otero, *Obras* (Mexico City, 1967), 2, 95–96.
[26] Otero, 'Consideraciones….', in *Obras*, ed. by Jesús Reyes Heroles, 2 vols (Mexico City, 1967), 766.

Introduction

from the fusion of different races. The historical development of *mestizaje* could not be accommodated by the colonial regime: "hence its collapse."[27] Where miscegenation occurred, there was no place for aristocratic dominance: "democracy" was, therefore, the "natural government of *mestizo* societies."[28] Samper's ethnographic analysis has been criticized as "racist"– there is no doubt that his examination of the different ethnic categories adhered to a hierarchical racial order. But in contrast to the segregationist views propagated at the time in Europe and the United States, Samper was not only recognizing the merits of racial coexistence, but also visualizing a future of "harmony in diversity."

Like the anonymous Mexican pamphlet, Samper blamed the colonial legacy for the ills of Spanish America. The only way open to these new societies was the "democratic republic" but they were still "exploring unknown horizons." A prolific writer, Samper himself had been at the forefront of the generation that pressed for the radical liberal reforms that Colombia introduced after 1849. While Samper became disillusioned in later decades, his 1861 *Essay* reflected both the progressive hopes of his generation and the perceived need to defend the achievements of the "democratic republic," namely, to be treated as equals, with dignity, by Europe and the United States.

There were very few areas where the ills of the colonial legacy were more easily and repeatedly identified by contemporaries than in education, particularly among those like Juana Manso (1819–1875), who struggled for the emancipation of women, the theme of the next selection of texts in our volume. "Women in this America," Manso wrote to the American educational reformer Mary Mann in 1866, "are minors, without any influence. They are colonial offsprings."[29]

Considered today as the "first feminist intellectual in the River Plate,"[30] Manso embraced the cause of education with an almost unparalleled commitment in her lifetime, close to that of Domingo Faustino

---

[27] Samper, *Ensayo sobre las revoluciones políticas y la condición social de las repúblicas colombianas (Hispano-Americanas) con un apéndice sobre la orografía y la confederación granadina* (Paris, 1861), 101.
[28] Samper, *Ensayo sobre las revoluciones políticas*, 76–77.
[29] Manso to Mann, Buenos Aires, November 25, 1866, available at www.juanamanso.org/carta-de-juana-manso-a-mary-mann-1866-2/
[30] Catherine Davies, Claire Brewster, and Hilary Owen, "Juana Manso (1819–1875): Women in History," in Davies et al., *South American Independence: Gender, Politics, Text* (Liverpool, 2006), 245.

Introduction

Sarmiento, with whom she collaborated in several initiatives. Born and raised in Buenos Aires, she followed her father into exile from the Rosas regime in 1840, and spent the next fifteen years outside her country, living in Uruguay, Brazil, the United States, and Cuba. In Montevideo, she published some of her first poems and set up the Ateneo de Señoritas, a school for young women. Later in Brazil, in 1852, she established *O Jornal das Senhoras*,[31] in whose pages Manso first published *Los misterios del Plata*, a novel that narrated the "mystery" of "the atrocities of Rosas, and the sufferings of his victims," in a genre that "approximates *testimonio*, or documentary fiction."[32]

Manso returned to Buenos Aires in 1853, and further developed her interests with extraordinary zeal. Modeled on her Brazilian journal, she founded the *Album de Señoritas* – a short-lived yet significant experience. In 1859, Sarmiento appointed her to lead the Escuela de Ambos Sexos, a co-educational school, which she directed until 1865. She then became editor of the *Anales de la Educación Común*, a semi-official publication that, as noted by Julyan G. Peard, provided the "main platform" for her life-long educational reform agenda.[33] She was also directly involved in implementing and overseeing educational policies as a member of the Board of Public Instruction. Her activism defied the conventions of her times – certainly as a woman giving public lectures, inspecting schools, confronting her opponents (male and female alike), challenging the Catholic Church (she converted to Protestantism), and advocating for the emancipation of women.

As noted by Peard, "Manso raised nearly all of the demands that activist women took up at the end of the century (education, work, legal rights, suffrage)." Her approach to education and women was part of a wider conception of politics that merits further exploration. For Peard, Manso's work ought to be understood as part of her "mission" of "creating a nation."[34] Not any nation, but one that responded to the imperatives of the republic and representative government. A "common and universal

---

[31] *O Jornal das Senhoras*, January 1, 1852, cited in Stephen Basdeo and Luiz F. A. Guerra, "Juana Manso's Mistérios del Plata (1852) and a Global 'Mysteries' Tradition," *Victorian Popular Fictions* 4.2 (2022), 128, available at https://doi.org/10.46911/TCWH4587
[32] Davies et. al., "Juana Manso," 248.
[33] Julyan G. Peard, "Enchanted Edens and Nation-Making: Juana Manso, Education, Women and Trans-American Encounters in Nineteenth-Century Argentina," *Journal of Latin American Studies* 40.3 (2008), 463.
[34] Peard, "Enchanted Edens," 482, 479.

Introduction

education" was for Manso the basis for politics in this "democratic age." That was, however, the future against a dismal present: In a country where "class divisions are so profound ... where all is privilege and monopoly, democracy is a ghost."[35] The samples of her writings included in this volume, on the emancipation of women and on popular education, should be read within such a broader context.

Other women in the continent also stood out for their notable efforts in defense of women's rights. Martina Barros' essay included in our collection was published in 1872–1873, as a prologue to her translation of John Stuart Mill's *The Subjection of Women* – the second or third of the twenty-six non-English editions of Mill's work published between 1869 and 1928.

Barros (1850–1944) advanced women's emancipation in significant ways, advocating for suffrage, while offering a critical approach to current nineteenth-century thinking on gender distinctions. Born in a socially distinguished milieu, she encountered John Stuart Mill's *The Subjection of Women* (1869) at a young age and embarked on its translation by 1872. Enthusiastically received by leading liberals, her essay celebrated some aspects of Mill's work, but bemoaned others. She acknowledged the role of her husband, the liberal physician Augusto Orrego Luco, in the writing of the essay, but stressed in her autobiography that the ideas were her own.[36] Both had previously read Mill's *On Liberty* (1859), and shared his condemnation of the tyranny of customs, challenging gender traditions and participating actively in publications and intellectual circles in Santiago during the last quarter of the nineteenth century.

Barros' views, however, were far from radical. As she stated in her autobiography, "my aim in promoting the independence and culture of women was not to make them rivals of men, but rather their dignified companions."[37] She took a gradualist approach to reform, favoring social and civil over political rights for women, giving priority to access to education. It is not possible to assess the impact of her essay and Mill's translation, but they were published at a time when the debate on women's education and participation in politics seemed to intensify in Chile, reflected, indeed, in some significant practical ways: In 1875, some

---

[35] Juana Manso, "La iniciativa," *Anales de la Educación Común* 33 (March 31, 1866).
[36] Martina Barros de Orrego, *Recuerdos de mi vida* (Santiago, 2023).
[37] Barros de Orrego, *Recuerdos*, 217.

Introduction

women registered as qualified voters in the elections of that year; in 1877, women had access to university education.

PART V. Spanish America and the World

With Spanish American independence, a significant number of new states joined an international community dominated by empires. The consolidation of independence was a serious challenge on several fronts, domestic and external. For long Spain kept the hope to reestablish power over its former American dominions. Colonial expansion by other European powers as well posed constant threats to the sovereignty of the emerging republics, which also feared, and indeed suffered, the imperial aims of the United States. In addition, the formation of new states resulting from the sudden fragmentation of the Spanish empire raised questions of border definitions that led to conflict and war among the former colonies. This part offers abridged versions of three documents that addressed some of these challenges.

"International Intervention" (1846–1847), by Andrés Bello (1781–1865), dealt with the issue of states' interference in each other's affairs. One of the greatest intellectual figures of Spanish America, Bello's interests ranged widely, from philology to poetry, education, grammar, as well as civil and international law. Born in Caracas, Venezuela, he spent the longest part of his life (thirty-six years) in Chile, where he was a teacher, foreign relations official, founder and rector of the National University, senator of the republic, and author of the Civil Code. His thought was characterized by a search for balance between order and liberty; conciliation between tradition and change; and a conviction that the strength of republics rested on the rule of law and representative institutions.

Bello's essay included in this volume applies the central principles that he developed in Great Britain (1810–1829) when he was an official in the diplomatic legations of Chile and Gran Colombia, and then expanded upon in the three editions of his landmark *Principles of International Law* (1832, 1844, and 1864). Namely, that States were not entitled to intervene in the affairs of other States on the grounds of the justice of a cause, theoretical principles, or selfish interests. Bello was responding to a specific case, invoked by the Chilean newspaper *El Mercurio*, to the effect that the Chilean government should intervene regarding the news that former Ecuadorian president Juan José Flores was organizing a campaign (from Europe) to bring him back into power. That position, as stated by

El Mercurio, was that all Spanish American countries should not only condemn European support, but also unite against the campaign, should it materialize. Bello disagreed, arguing that intervention did more damage than good, and should never be invoked as a principle of international relations. Citing several examples from recent events (before and during the 1840s), Bello advanced the notion that the main role of international law was to establish the fundamental right of all States to self-determination. He disagreed that powerful States should determine what was a right or a wrong cause when it came to meddling in the politics of an emerging State. Any intervention, he argued, was unacceptable. Bello provided a realistic, if painful, statement to the effect that powerful nations acted according to their own best interests and used their strength to impose themselves. Such a tendency could only be countered by international agreements on the costs (primarily costs) of foreign intervention. Bello's ideas of non-intervention developed as independent countries in the Western Hemisphere found that the theory and practice of international law did not accord them the status of sovereign States in the aftermath of independence. In fact, Spain and its allies considered them insurgent colonies and did not grant recognition until 1836 (and only in the case of Mexico). Hence the need to establish the right of self-determination and the equality of nations regardless of their origin, size, or power. Establishing the legal status of newly independent nations was indeed one of the major concerns of Bello, and his ideas in this regard spread rapidly throughout Latin America.

The second text in this part, *The Political Situation of Cuba* (1851), was written by José Antonio Saco (1797–1879), one of the most notable Cuban intellectuals of the nineteenth century. Forced into exile in 1834, he spent the rest of his life abroad, except for a brief visit to his homeland in 1860–1861.[38] It is paradoxical, even intriguing, that despite his long exile, in permanent antagonism with the colonial regime, he remained loyal to Spain. His loyalty to the Iberian country was as vocal as his opposition to annexation, clearly expressed in a pamphlet that led to an intense debate, "Ideas sobre la incorporación de Cuba a los Estados Unidos" (1848). It is also paradoxical that such loyalty helped to lay the foundations of Cuban nationality, as Saco was "among the first intellectuals

---

[38] Wickie Burton Whalen, "José Antonio Saco, Cuban Reformer, 1797–1879," PhD thesis, University of Miami, 1970.

Introduction

to express their uniqueness as Cubans."[39] His conception of the Cuban nationality, however, was based on the views of white Spaniards.[40] His loyalty should be qualified as well: It was a critical loyalty since Saco opposed the despotism of Spanish rule in Cuba.

Saco's text included in our collection was published in the wake of a failed invasion of the island by Narciso López, a filibuster of Venezuelan origin, supported by US expansionist interests. In his pamphlet, Saco again warned Cubans about the "danger ... posed by the United States" (p. 190). To counter US ambitions regarding Cuba, he appealed to French and British protection, after criticizing the US policy of preventing "European powers from having a say in the Western Hemisphere" (p. 191). to some extent an unusual way of defying the Monroe doctrine by a Spanish American at the time. Most of the 1851 document, however, was devoted to another "danger" that threatened Cuba: the institutions imposed on the island by the colonial regime, which, in Saco's words, "are despotic in all branches of public administration" (p. 192). Cubans had been deprived of political rights by, ironically, the Spanish liberal constitution of 1837, which denied Cuban representation at the Cortes in Madrid.[41] While opposing Spanish tyrannical rule, Saco did not support independence since he thought "the island will quickly lose it" – Cuba "would fall victim to American rapacity" (p. 202). Saco's document serves to highlight the serious dilemmas and challenges Cubans faced, as the remaining Spanish colony, together with Puerto Rico, in the Americas.

"International Society," the last text in this part, is an abridged version of one of the chapters of *El crimen de la guerra*, written by Juan Bautista Alberdi (1810–1884), from Argentina. Of great renown for his *Bases* (1852), which set the foundations of the 1853 constitution that shaped the life of the country,[42] Alberdi started to write *El crimen de la guerra* in the early 1870s in exile in Europe. He wrote it in response to a call by the Societé des Amis de la Paix, offering a prize to the best book against war, an expression of a European movement to prevent future armed conflict

---

[39] Graciella Cruz-Taura, "Annexation and National Identity: Cuba's Mid-Nineteenth-Century Debate," *Cuban Studies* 27 (1998), 106.
[40] Christopher Schmidt-Nowara, *Empire and Antislavery: Spain, Cuba, and Puerto Rico, 1833–1874* (Pittsburgh, 1999), 19–20.
[41] Cruz-Taura, "Annexation," 91–92.
[42] Jeremy Adelman, "Between Order and Liberty: Juan Bautista Alberdi and the Intellectual Origins of Argentine Constitutionalism," *Latin American Research Review* 42.2 (2007), 86–110.

Introduction

after the end of the Franco-Prussian war (1870–1871). Nowadays *El crimen de la guerra* does not seem to stand out among Alberdi's prolific writings, although back in 1963 his biographer, Jorge M. Mayer, noted that it was Alberdi's "most commented and disseminated work after *Bases*."[43]

In one of his opening statements, Alberdi condemned the legality of war, as the largest possible scale of homicide, robbery, and destruction. There might be cases for "just wars," but these should be exceptional – as a rule, he made it clear that "war must be considered a crime" (p. 208). Alberdi had opposed the involvement of his country in the War of the Triple Alliance (1864–1870), launched by Argentina, Brazil, and Uruguay against Paraguay. His position, made public in a series of pamphlets, earned him the label of "traitor" in the eyes of his detractors. Alberdi returned to the Paraguayan conflict in *El crimen de la guerra*, although his main engagement here was with the wider topic of war in international law. At the core of his argument was the absence of a proper tribunal to arbitrate in conflicts among States. He saw in the organization of "the society of nations" a possible way of building a more humane future, but such an international society was not conceived as a league of States. Individuals were also international subjects. "When one or many members of a State see their international rights violated," Alberdi postulated, "they can, as members of human society, claim the protections of international law even against their own governments" (p. 206) – a proposition that, according to H. B. Jacobini, "anticipated one of the most momentous of twentieth century developments in the field of international law."[44]

All three authors demonstrate that Spanish America's engagement with the world was complex – not least because of their position of weakness due to the lateness of the recognition of independence – but inevitable. They may have differed in their emphases but agreed that either as fledgling republics or colonies (like Cuba and Puerto Rico), Spanish America needed to navigate the world of post-Napoleonic geopolitics. It is quite striking, although not often recognized, that Spanish American

---

[43] Jorge M. Mayer, *Alberdi y su tiempo* (Buenos Aires, 1963), 793. An English translation was published in London in 1913 – whatever its earlier diffusion, this edition was largely forgotten among English-speaking scholars by the 1960s. See Juan Bautista Alberdi, *The Crime of War*, trans. by C. J. MacConnell (London and Toronto, 1913). We thank Eduardo Zimmermann for drawing our attention to this translation. Mayer registered it in his *Alberdi y su tiempo*, 793, footnote 200.

[44] H. B. Jacobini, *A Study of the Philosophy of International Law as Seen in Works of Latin American Writers* (The Hague, 1954), 72.

thinkers contributed in significant ways to incorporating the independence experience into the larger discussion on the law of nations.

PART VI. Fin de Siècle

In 1898, the so-called Spanish-American war frustrated Cuban and Puerto Rican aspirations for independence, motivating further fears of US imperial expansion. From 1880, Argentina had started to enjoy relative political stability, material progress, and civil liberties. But the Argentine experience was hardly replicated. Elsewhere the prospect of civil war remained a constant concern. Where a degree of political stability was achieved, it often came at the cost of political freedoms. As Spanish America approached the centennial of independence in 1910, political thinkers used the opportunity to reflect about the past, present, and future in the region. The five texts in this final part illustrate how some of these issues were approached by leading intellectual figures of the times.

Valentín Letelier, the first author included here, offers a prime example of how positivism influenced social and political thought in Latin America, even though it was far from being a unified philosophical movement. There is a sharp division between "Comtean" early positivism, and the strand known as the "Religion of Humanity," which followed the French thinker's somewhat eccentric late religious ideas. While aligned with the former, Letelier departed from other Latin American positivists by embracing ideas of liberty over both "order" and "progress": Liberty resided in free associations and especially in political parties, essential for the functioning of democracy. He not only accepted but also welcomed the political confrontation of ideas.

Born in Chile in 1852, Letelier was educated at the prestigious Instituto Nacional, and subsequently at the University of Chile's School of Law. He received his core positivist (including anti-clerical) ideas from José Victorino Lastarria at the Academia de Bellas Artes in the 1870s. He served in the Congress as well as in the Chilean Foreign Service, occupying several key educational positions until his death in 1919. Had it not been for the revolution of 1891, which deposed the government of José Manuel Balmaceda, Letelier's views would have remained those of a typical "Comtean" positivist who shared the school's emphasis on the three-stage evolution of society, culminating in the "scientific" stage. Political liberty now became central to his thought, as he languished in prison because of his opposition to Balmaceda. He feared, as others did, dictatorial tendencies and advocated congressional prerogatives over the executive. The more orthodox Chilean positivists, who supported Balmaceda just as Comte had supported Napoleon III, reinforced his departure from the various expressions of positivist thought in the region. Solid political parties as well as the extension and transparency of the suffrage became central aspects of Letelier's proposals.

That Spanish American thinkers engaged, and often seriously, with positivism – be it that of Comte or Spencer – has been well documented. However, as the case of Letelier shows, not only did they interact with other currents of thought but, perhaps more significantly, their ideas were deeply rooted in their own reality and experiences. The second text in this part, by Manuel González Prada (1844–1918), from Peru, serves to further illustrate the point.

Born into a well-established conservative, Catholic family of colonial lineage, González Prada was called an "apostate" by the historian Jorge Basadre for his radical rejection of his family, Spanish ascendancy, and class background, while he attacked the church and the social hierarchies of Peruvian society.[45] González Prada's ideas were shaped by his direct involvement in the War of the Pacific (1879–1883), when Peru, allied with Bolivia, fought and lost against Chile. "With an army of disciplined Indians without freedom," he stated in the *Politeama* (public gathering site) speech that gained him fame in 1888, "Peru will always suffer defeat."[46] He pointed an accusing finger toward the long oppression of the Indigenous peoples, who "formed" the nation, for the failures of his country. His reiterated appeals to "science" to overcome Peruvian problems may induce scholars to identify positivist influences.[47] But by 1904, when "Nuestros indios" was written, he had turned to anarchism. The diagnosis in this text is similar to that of his 1888 speech, though expressed in stronger terms; his suggested course of action was now freedom from authority and the advocacy of rebellion. His was a form of liberal anarchism, with an emphasis on individual freedom from both state and

---

[45] Jorge Basadre, "Ubicación histórica de González Prada," in Basadre, *Perú: problema y posibilidad* (Lima, 1994), 101.
[46] Manuel González Prada, "Discurso en el Politeama," Casa de la Literatura Peruana, facsimile, Lima, 1888; available at https://repocaslit.minedu.gob.pe//handle/123456789/1018
[47] Thomas Butler Ward, "Manuel González Prada: Devoted Follower or Insubordinate Partisan of August Comte?" *Revista Hispánica Moderna* 44.2 (1991), 274–279.

church.⁴⁸ However, to the extent that he thought of "nuestros indios" as a collective, his text anticipated twentieth-century notions of Indigenismo that have not been sufficiently recognized in the literature.

The third text in this part is an abridged version of "El secreto de la paz porfiriana," a chapter of Andrés Molina Enríquez's *Los grandes problemas nacionales* (1909). Published just before the Mexican Revolution broke out, the book was hailed by Frank Tannenbaum in 1933 as "the most important single study of Mexican social problems."⁴⁹ Molina Enríquez (1868–1940) was born in a provincial town, studied law, and worked as a notary, gaining first-hand knowledge of the land-holding problems facing Indigenous peoples in rural Mexico. He developed an interest in ethnography and, after winning the prize for his entry in the contest to celebrate the centennial of Benito Juárez, he furthered his studies in the field while working at the National Museum. Out of that essay prize came his book *La reforma y Juárez: Estudio histórico* (1906), in which he advanced some of his ideas on race, land issues, and Mexican nationality that would later appear in *Los grandes problemas*.⁵⁰

Molina Enríquez is best known for his contribution to the agrarian reforms that followed the Mexican Revolution. At first sight, this would seem paradoxical for someone who has also been described as "the last Porfirian intellectual."⁵¹ Our selected text focuses specifically on his controversial theories of power and Mexican nationalism. The former was unabashed praise of personal, dictatorial power; the latter emerged from the *mestizo*, the emblematic new race that for Molina Enríquez established the Mexican nation. Consolidating the nation, however, required the integration of a highly heterogeneous society, divided by race and class – thus his overt defense of Porfirio Díaz, later turned into a defense of the nature of the semi-authoritarian regime that governed Mexico for so long.

---

⁴⁸ Bohdan Plaskacz, "Manuel González Prada and Prince Peter Kropotkin – Aristocrats Turned Anarchists," *Études Slaves et Est-Européennes/Slavic and East-European Studies* 15 (1970), 83–92.
⁴⁹ Cited in Stanley Frank Shadle, "Mexican Land Reformer: Andrés Molina Enríquez and the Mexican Revolution," PhD thesis, University of California, Santa Barbara, 1990, 3.
⁵⁰ Shadle, "Mexican Land Reformer," 6–67.
⁵¹ Mauricio Tenorio Trillo, "Del mestizaje a un siglo de Andrés Molina Enríquez," in Emilio Kourí, *En busca de Molina Enríquez. Cien años de Los grandes problemas nacionales* (Mexico City, 2009).

Introduction

Molina Enríquez's theory of political power was to some extent expanded to the whole of the continent by Francisco García Calderón's *Les democraties latines de l'Amerique*, whose selected passages are included next in our volume. Published first in French in 1912, translated into English and German the following year, the book appeared in Spanish only in 1979. Its slow diffusion in Spanish is in itself an editorial curiosity, given the prominence of the author – García Calderón (1883–1953) was considered to be one of the "most prestigious writers in [Spanish] America" by the end of the second decade of the twentieth century.[52] A scion of a distinguished family in Peru, García Calderón completed his studies at San Marcos University in Lima and then moved to Paris, where he resided for the rest of his life. There he joined a "contingent" of Spanish American intellectuals,[53] combining his literary and writing activities with his diplomatic roles as representative of his government in various delegations. *Les democraties* had important echoes in the region through articles in the press, while its French edition was available at least in bookshops in Mexico and Havana.

García Calderón's book was a long historical essay, covering the whole continent and predicting a hopeful future for the region. However, the republics of Spanish America were "tragically formed upon the ruins of Spanish power." Our version highlights the dominant role that García Calderón gave to the *caudillos* in this tragic history, as the "founders" of Latin American democracies. Tyrants, no doubt, *caudillos* were nonetheless representatives of the people against the oligarchy, and, for him, a genuine Latin American expression. In this, and in other aspects of what has been labeled "the sickness of the continent," García Calderón followed a long lineage of conservative thinkers. Very few, however, succeeded in creating a powerful narrative, first popularized in languages other than Spanish, that has endured and still prevails today.

Our volume closes with a shortened version of *Idola Fori*'s last chapter, written by the Colombian essayist and politician Carlos Arturo Torres (1867–1911). Originally published in 1909, his book offered a broad philosophical reflection against political fanaticism and tyranny. Far from a theoretical piece, Torres' essay was based on the experiences of his own

---

[52] *El Mercurio*, Santiago, November 15, 1918.
[53] See Beatriz Colombi, "Una ciudad letrada extraterritorial: escritores hispanoamericanos en París en el fin-de-siglo," in Pamela M. Graham, ed., *Migrations and Connections: Latin America and Europe in the Modern World* (New Orleans, 2012), 3–4.

country, torn apart by the War of the Thousand Days (1899–1902), a lengthy and bloody civil conflict between liberal rebels and the conservative government. A leading member of the Liberal Party, Torres opposed the war, favoring a reformist path through Congress. The outcome of the conflict was catastrophic, in terms of casualties and loss of territory, as Panama seceded from Colombia in 1903 with the help of the United States. The resulting sense of loss opened the way for compromise: Liberals regained representation and participation in government. Torres himself first held cabinet positions and, in 1905, was appointed consul in Liverpool, where he wrote *Idola Fori*.

Torres' text is best understood against the background of the civil conflict outlined above. "The direction of the age that is just beginning is that of reconciliation and agreement," he noted, while rejecting the extremes of revolution and reaction (p. 267). His message was one of "optimism," and "love of country" though explicitly distancing him from chauvinism. He saw the centennial of independence as an opportunity to reflect upon the past, present, and future of the republic. Torres envisioned a future where high notions of humanity would predominate over the deification of both the masses and providentialist leaders. *Idola Fori* was Torres' most accomplished work – he died shortly after its publication, in 1911. "Virtually unknown today," Shawn McDaniel observes, it was "one of the most valuable and influential intellectual documents of its time."[54]

All five authors have been commonly identified as "positivists." They all shared some enthusiasm for the intellectual trend that prevailed in the region during the last quarter of the nineteenth century. But they all differed in their approach to what, after all, was far from being a homogeneous body of thought. Molina Enríquez and García Calderón favored order over liberty, while Letelier and Torres defended freedom. If the former two sided with the *caudillos*, the latter wrote against them. González Prada departed from this dichotomy by advocating a more radical approach focusing on the predicament of Indigenous peoples. And whatever they took from positivism, or from any other foreign intellectual currents, they were aware of their limitations for capturing their own realities. As Stanley Frank Shadle noted, Molina Enríquez's theories of *mestizaje* had to turn social Darwinism and Spencer "on their heads."[55] Above

---

[54] Shawn McDaniel, "The Paradoxes of (anti) Imperialism: Race, Religion, and Resistance in the Latin American 'Arielista' Essay, 1898–1921," PhD thesis, City University of New York, 2013, 6.
[55] Shadle, "Mexican Land Reformer," 79.

Introduction

all, these thinkers, as the others included in this volume, were responding to the challenges and questions raised by their different societies.

***

We conclude this introduction with both an admission and a hope. We recognize that it is no longer possible to condense the history of Spanish American political thought into one single development, be it a "search for identity," a "transition from monarchy to republic," a struggle against the "colonial legacy," a "rise of the *caudillos*," a "centralist" or "liberal" tradition, or any other such effort to conceptualize Spanish American political thought with one overarching formula. Instead, it is best to identify the *issues* confronted by intellectuals in envisioning nations in highly heterogeneous societies. In some cases, it might be the proximity to aggressive empires, in others the location of power among competing institutions, and in yet others the cleavages separating race, class, and religion. We hope that such diversity will not deter the future student of political thought in Spanish America. On the contrary, that it will motivate further explorations into the deep connection between historical context and the emergence of new currents of political thought.

Note on Translation

The translators, who are also the editors of this volume, are fully aware that there is no substitute for reading texts in their original language. However, they also believe that important sources that have been missing in the discussions on political thought should be made available to those who may not have the time to acquire additional language skills. Even for the native speaker of Spanish, it is sometimes puzzling to encounter terms or concepts whose meanings have changed more or less drastically or vary from country to country. The grammar, the spelling, and a way of thinking closer to orality have also experienced substantial transformations since the nineteenth century. The translators have attempted to clarify and update the original Spanish, as well as correct errata that interfered with the proper understanding of some sentences.

A significant challenge has been to either maintain or update words and concepts that today might be offensive. Our choice has been to update terms that were blatantly racist or gender-biased in order to facilitate reading, even if they were in common use in the nineteenth century. Likewise, we must clarify that the term "American," which is today associated with the United States, was used by the authors to mean "Spanish American." Other terms in common use were "peninsular" and "*peninsulares*" to refer to Spain (or the Iberian Peninsula) and Spaniards (as distinct from "hispanoamericanos") respectively.

The translators have taken certain risks, primarily to make the readings accessible to the average English reader accustomed to shorter sentences. This has meant breaking up long Spanish phrases, sometimes lasting a whole paragraph. The main objective, always, has been clarity, even if at the cost of the flair that is apparent in the original writings. We have

Note on Translation

respected, however, the tendency to use three synonyms when one would have been enough, because they allow the authors to convey their meaning more precisely. What we have curbed, however, is the tendency to use metaphors that have no idiomatic equivalent in English.

To facilitate reading, we have omitted long digressions to retain the main arguments of each selection. Given the word limit we had for the volume, and the relatively large number of authors, we were not able to include the full version of all the texts presented here. Yet, when selecting the respective passages we took care to keep the unity and the spirit of the texts, as well as the fluidity of the narrative. The translators have edited silently, so as not to interrupt the reading with frequent marks to indicate elisions. We have, however, used square brackets in the text to add information that the authors took for granted, as is often the case with names, dates, or events that are no longer obvious. When explanations are somewhat longer, they have been placed in the notes.

Finally, most translations are original and appear in English for the first time. Some have been published in English before, such as the selected texts by Alberdi, Echeverría, García Calderón, and Otero, but the editors felt that they needed updating as well as a consistent style. The only English translation that we have maintained is Juan Francisco Manzano's, because that translation has its own history and significance in the context of the international movement for the abolition of slavery. We are mindful of the fact that these are only selections but hope that the core ideas that are represented here will one day achieve the recognition they deserve in a full publication of the sources.

Texts

Part 1.
On History

I

JOSÉ VICTORINO LASTARRIA

Investigations on the Social Influence of the Spanish Conquest and the Colonial System in Chile (1844)

José Victorino Lastarria (1817–1888) was a Chilean writer and politician closely aligned with the opposition to the three consecutive governments of Joaquín Prieto (1831–1841), Manuel Bulnes (1841–1851), and Manuel Montt (1851–1861).[1] A liberal, he later turned into a Comtean positivist. As a politician, he served in the Congress and later in government as diplomat and cabinet member. A prolific writer, he was the author of Recuerdos literarios *(1878), one of the best, if biased, accounts of Chilean intellectual life in the nineteenth century. He was also the author of* La América *(1865),* Lecciones de política positiva *(1874), and numerous contributions to the press. The fragment included here is the introduction to his work on the legacies of the colonial past, which he presented at the first anniversary of the inauguration of the University of Chile (1844). He promoted a view of history that saw in the past the guidance for shaping the present and future, meaning specifically the demolition of colonial institutions and ideas. This presentation became a part of a significant debate on the writing of history in the 1840s.*

---

[1] This essay appeared originally in four parts in the periodical *El Progreso* in 1844, and then in *Anales de la Universidad de Chile* 1 (1843–1844), 199–271, the source of the editors' translation. (Editors' note)

1. José Victorino Lastarria, Investigations (1844)

Gentlemen:
On this solemn occasion, the University [of Chile] convenes for the first time to report on its activities since the inauguration of the institution [1843]. This is something more than compliance with the statutes, however: this ceremony pays homage to the fatherland on the anniversary of that great day [September 18, 1810] when our political liberty first saw the light. The University has been charged with the promotion of knowledge and the development of civilization. Therefore, there is nothing more appropriate for the institution, as we celebrate the anniversary of the republic, than to give an account of its activities. Also, to highlight the merits of those who have devoted their efforts to addressing matters of true social importance. This is what the University expects from the scientific endeavors of its members.

I am honored to be asked to perform one of the most important duties that the law requires from the University: to present an essay on a notable chapter of Chilean history, using authentic documents, and developing its nature and significance with impartiality and truth.[2] But before I submit this work to your consideration, which is far from meeting my own expectations, let alone worthy of your approval, I will outline at least the principles that have guided my attempt to enter the sanctuary of the science of humanity.

History is to peoples what individual experience is to man. Just as he follows his path toward perfectibility by means of his recollections, the truths that have shaped his sensibility, and the observations that have emerged from the events surrounding him since childhood, in that same way society, in the various stages of its development, has sought the aid of history. The experience of mankind is recorded in history, that great mirror of all times where man and society go look at themselves. Nations are likely to be led astray if they blindly embrace the idea of inevitability [*fatalidad*], neglecting the moral laws that will ensure their well-being. Their existence would lack unity; their history would be little more than a succession of isolated facts. Their antecedents, then, would not contribute to an awareness of the true situation of nations, nor would they help predict the future because knowledge of the natural and necessary continuity between past and future would be lost. Their way to perfectibility would be slow and painful. Lost to the mercy of events,

---

[2] Article 28, law of November 19, 1842.

1. José Victorino Lastarria, Investigations (1844)

the road ahead will be as volatile and capricious as isolated events are; education would be left to chance, becoming contradictory and confusing because the experience and the spirit of the times will be lost with each generation. The lessons that humanity learns from the events that mark every century, with their particular character, will be lost as well.

It is true that one's spirit might be overwhelmed when contemplating, in the immense chaos of time, a superior and active power that regulates all things. It looks like a constant and powerful organic law of humanity. The prosperity, decadence, and ruin of empires obey this law. It presides over all societies, placing its unstoppable demands on them, destroying some and granting life and well-being to others. It is as if there was a wise and impressive harmony behind the anarchic confusion produced by the clash and dislocation of the components of the moral universe. It should not be surprising, then, that one's spirit might be fatigued to the point of abandoning analysis, judging that it is not only permissible, but also logically necessary, to believe in the inevitable and to embrace this regulating power of creation. It would be natural, as [Edgar Quinet] has said,

> to trust in the majestic order of time and to rest on the assurance that a power exists that knows how to manage empires and centuries, a power that has seen the days of Chaldea, Egypt, Phoenicia, Thebes of the hundred gates, heroic Saguntum, and implacable Rome, a power that knows how to manage the few instants that are left to man, as well as the fleeting movements that fill their duration.[3]

This reasoning is founded on error. It appears to be logical, but it unravels when we contemplate the greatness of humanity and focus on the freedom of action that the creator has given us. The succession of causes and moral effects which forms the great code that humankind follows, to be found in its very nature, is not so strictly fatalistic as to operate without the participation of man. Indeed, the effects of such causes disappear entirely if man does not promote them with his actions. He has such an important role in his own destiny that neither his misfortune nor his happiness comes about without his actions, that is, his liberty. Man thinks independently; his ideas are always the origin and foundation of his will. His spontaneous actions promote and accelerate the development of the natural causes that will result in either his happiness and improvement, or his complete decline. The wisest and most profound

---

[3] Quinet, introduction to Herder's *Idées sur la philosophie de l'histoire de l'humanité*.

philosopher-historian of the past [eighteenth] century teaches us this truth when he says that:

> The deity has in nowise bound their hands, farther than by what they were, by time, place, and their intrinsic powers. When they were guilty of faults, he extricated them not by miracles, but suffered these faults to produce their effects, that man might be better to know them ... The law of nature is not more simple, than it is worthy of God, consistent, and fertile in its consequences to mankind. Were man intended to be what he is, and to become what he was capable of becoming, he must preserve a spontaneity of nature, and be encompassed by a sphere of free actions, disturbed by no preternatural miracle. All inanimate substances, every species of living creatures that instinct guides, have remained what they were from the time of the creation: God made man a deity upon Earth; he implanted in him the principle of self-activity, and set this principle in motion from the beginning, by means of the internal and external wants of his nature. Man could not live and support himself, without learning to make use of his reason: no sooner, indeed, did he begin to make use of this, than the door was opened to a thousand errors and mistaken attempts; but at the same time, and even through these very mistakes and errors, the way was cleared to a better use of his reason. The more speedily he discerned his faults, the greater the promptitude and energy with which he applied to correct them: the farther he advanced, the more his humanity was formed; and this must be formed, or he must groan for ages beneath the burden of his mistakes.[4]

These observations, which are rigorously founded on facts, prove all too well that the essence of humanity is noble, and is destined to greater ends than those imagined by many who consider it stupidly tied to the laws of matter.

It is absurd as well as dangerous to think that human societies should passively submit to a law that arbitrarily destroys or improves them without having any role in their own well-being or misfortune. It is as absurd and dangerous as to decide that man should submit to a power other than nature, which has given him the means to make his own happiness. There

---

[4] Herder, *Idées sur la philosophie de l'histoire de l'humanité*, lib. XV, chap. 1. [Editors' note: We use the English edition of this work by Frank E. Manuel, ed., *Reflections on the Philosophy of the History of Mankind* (Chicago and London, 1968), 84–85.]

1. José Victorino Lastarria, Investigations (1844)

is no reason for man to submit to a fatalistic destiny which diminishes his active faculties to the level of inertia.

Society possesses the sovereignty of judgment and will that gives the individual the capacity to work for his own benefit and improvement, provided that he remains within the bounds of justice. Like man, society can do well or badly, either facilitating the course of the natural causes that will enhance its perfectibility, or doing violence to nature by making the mistakes that will cause its decadence or eternal ruin. In the latter case, only the memory of its name and vices will be retained.

I will not deny that weakness, ignorance, and other flaws are a part of the history of the world, and that they are very difficult to avoid. These flaws will spell the ruin of people even if they make every effort to prevent the blow that will destroy them. However, this consideration should convince us precisely of the urgent necessity, on the part of society, to take charge of its conservation and development. To do so, it can make use of its own resources, studying the lessons taught by humanity, either in the form of virtues, or aberrations and vices. This is how society can find the way to prevent evil, or at least neutralize its effects. Where is this experience to be found? Where are its teachings recorded if not in the sacred repository of history? This is the tabernacle that preserves both the splendor of bygone civilizations, and the sober wisdom that comes from the greatest calamities of humankind.

History is God's oracle. It is the means by which He reveals his wisdom to the world, the way He counsels and teaches people to secure a bright future for themselves. When history is considered as a simple record of past events, one's heart is dismayed and skepticism comes to prejudice the mind. A future of misery and disasters lies ahead, a future in which liberty and justice fight but ultimately succumb to the blows of despotism and wickedness. The most powerful and flourishing empires are shaken to the core. From one instant to the next, they turn into ruins that will astonish future generations, exposing the weaknesses and constant mutations of the works of man. He wanders everywhere bringing destruction, shedding blood and tears endlessly. Man appears to be in pursuit of an unknown end that he cannot reach without murdering his own brother. He himself perishes under the ax he wields against his fellow human beings.

How different history looks when we consider it as a science of facts! Only then philosophy can show us, beyond the interminable vicissitudes whereby humanity destroys itself, falling into an abyss of its own making,

1. José Victorino Lastarria, Investigations (1844)

the profound wisdom that the experience of centuries has taught us. This wisdom is infallible because it is based on the sacred precepts of the law that the omnipotent employed for the organization of the moral universe. Peoples must enter this august sanctuary with the light of philosophy in order to learn about the experiences that can guide them. Peoples and the men who lead them must stay away from the blind confidence in a fate that evades reason and numbs the faculties that nature has given them to achieve happiness.

Humankind has, in its own essence, the capacity for perfection. Man has all the elements to create his own happiness; he and no other has the ability to promote and direct his own development. The laws of his nature provide the key that he can use to produce harmonious results. In order to learn these laws and appreciate their effects, he must open the book of his own life. There he will find them written in indelible characters. There he will see that the constant alternation of good and evil that characterizes the centuries is not the inevitable work of a blind power that drives him from one event to another, nor the inevitable consequence of the demands of an arbitrary force. It is, rather, the natural effect of the laws and the conditions that surround his nature. He will see that in the physical universe, causes evolve spontaneously to become the laws that produce necessary results. However, the same does not occur in the moral universe, because man has the power to freely promote the development of these laws, or stop them, depending upon what is most conducive to his happiness. Such is the supreme wisdom of divine intelligence. Humanity has not been, and it is not today, what it could be due to the circumstances of time and place. It is what it had to be, given what the dominant leaders at the time made of the circumstances. Man has an active part in shaping his own destiny. If not, his liberty would be an insulting lie, his dignity would dissipate, and the idea of justice could not exist in this world.[5]

That is why, gentlemen, I have said that society must access the precious repository of experience provided by history to save us from misfortune. History is the light that can guide society through the darkness of the future. Only she can know the immutable laws of happiness and decadence, see the obstacles that must be overcome, the legacies of the

---

[5] I might be too bold in this regard because I distance myself from the brilliant theories of more than a few geniuses of modern times. I apologize for this, but may I be forgiven if this is a fault? I only ask to be able to exercise my freedom of thought. I do not believe in fatality, as some wise men do.

1. José Victorino Lastarria, Investigations (1844)

past that halt progress, and the errors that lead to ruin. In short, only history can show society the trajectory that it has followed, and the position it holds, in the larger world of nations. Public officials, on whom the joyful duty of leading a state falls, must for this reason know in depth the history of the people they have been entrusted to lead to happiness. According to [Simonde de] Sismondi, the constitution of a society, properly speaking, is essentially its form of existence, its very life, the sum of its laws and customs. If the basis of society is society itself, how can it be known, and its spirit followed, without studying history philosophically? Considering that the legislator must have a grasp of the present to prepare for the future, to promote reforms and accelerate progress, what, if not history, will guide him in the difficult path that he must follow in such a great endeavor? Without the light of divinity, how can the fatal consequences of a past event ever be known? What are the antisocial behaviors that persist? Which are the inclinations and the vices that take root in the heart of a people, and present a stubborn resistance to perfectibility?

I believe that those who love their country, and truly want it to be happy, will add to their knowledge of the social sciences the philosophical study of history. In that way they will avoid the mistakes that stop, or even set back, the advancement of societies. They either repeat actions that proved to be unfortunate or fatal in the past, or echo prejudices that, had they been detected early, would have been seen as infamies shameful to humanity, and destroyed accordingly. I hope with all my heart that the progress of civilization will lead us to a happier time when those degrading errors will disappear from the annals of civilized peoples; a time when the laws are so nearly perfect as to be able to punish those criminals who, in bad faith, seek to perpetuate error. Perhaps this hope will be regarded as utopian, but at least it is not based on chimeras that fascinate yet deceive the mind. This might be a naive hope, but not an impossible one.

I am convinced that these truths have the status of philosophical dogmas. I also think that the presentation of an episode in the history of our country, as mandated by the statutes of the University, is a wise policy that will render many happy results. The first of these presentations has been entrusted to me, perhaps the least apt for such a task. What I will present to you today will probably lack the quality that my more enlightened colleagues, who also have more talent and time than I do, possess to undertake historical investigations with the serious philosophical reflections needed to study remote and seemingly unconnected events. Please

1. José Victorino Lastarria, Investigations (1844)

believe me when I say that these are not mere rhetorical formulas to hide my vanity, but a true reflection of the feelings in my heart.

For the moment, please ignore the person who has the honor to address you on this solemn occasion, and let us proceed with the subject of my presentation.

What is the history of our republic? What are the benefits of the study of history for the management of [national] affairs in our current situation? These are the key questions for the discussion of such a vitally important matter.

The history of Chile is still the history of a young country that has lived through three centuries of a dark and motionless existence. It is the history of a past epoch that the philosopher can investigate without difficulty, as well as a new epoch that belongs to us because it is so very recent. The origin and early life of our society is within our sight; it is not yet lost in the darkness of time. To study it, we do not need the type of critique that confronts and rectifies past events in order to separate truth from falsehood. Instead, all it needs is to organize and evaluate known facts. Consequently, there are two turning points in our history: the Spanish Conquest, and the revolution of independence. These two great events encompass all the lesser ones that have contributed to the emergence of Chile. The simple narration of the first, as shown by the writers who present a lifeless chronicle pretending to pass as a history of Chile, has no interest for us, or is limited to the story of barbarians struggling to defend their independence from the domination of strangers. Much more interesting is the narration of the revolution, although it has been written without a unifying thread, or a philosophical understanding. The heroic actions of the war of independence, which so flatter our national pride, heralded the foundations of our political liberty; also, the origins of a collective happiness that is more deeply felt because the memories of the sufferings caused by despotism are still fresh. This is a philosophical conclusion we reach instinctively, without the help of a historian.

However, the events that led to the Conquest, resulting in the establishment of the Spanish domination in Chile, are worthy of serious study because they are not so isolated from, or independent of, our own time. We should not neglect their influence on the present state of the republic. When events are considered in their individuality, as historians who describe the wars of conquest do, paying no attention to the connection between events, they seem to be far removed in time. Also, from generations that are independent of, and distinct from, our own. Such a study

1. José Victorino Lastarria, Investigations (1844)

cannot add anything useful or beneficial to our contemporary society. It is difficult to see them as works that have a lesson for the future. That is why it is necessary to examine the relations between events to understand how they lead to the greatest events in our history, namely, the Conquest and the establishment of Spanish power in Chile. From this perspective we will easily arrive to the study of that greatest of events, which brings all the subordinate ones together. Only then will we philosophically apprehend the characteristics of that time and their influence on society. That is how we can truly understand its character and its prejudices. That is how we will, finally, accurately assess the power and the intensity of the upheaval that took place in 1810. Only then the study of the history of the Conquest will be useful for seeing our current situation in a true light, and direct our public affairs in a way that is conducive to improvement and happiness.

These are the principles that guide the investigations that I have the honor to present to you. My efforts have been directed to the characterization of the Conquest and its immediate result, namely, the establishment of the Spanish colonial system in our country. I do this to trace the influence of such a mighty historical event on the origins and formation of our society. I am assuming that the description of particular events, those that form the larger picture of the period, is already known. As Sismondi states, "before we inquire whether facts are beneficial or detrimental, we must first identify them."

I admit, gentlemen, that I would have preferred to give you an account of those heroic events, those brilliant episodes that form our history, to move your hearts with the enthusiasm of glory and admiration for the common sense of Colocolo, the prudence and fortitude of Caupolicán, the skill and boldness of Lautaro, and the speed and valor of Painenancu.[6] But, what good would come from such pleasing recollections? What social utility would result from focusing on an individual, as opposed to the larger context which demands a more rounded analysis? Also, and perhaps more appropriately, I could have focused on any of the important events of our glorious revolution. I have refrained from doing so, I admit, for fear of a lack of accuracy and impartiality in my investigations. Many of the heroes of those brilliant campaigns, and their witnesses, are still alive.

---

[6] These Indigenous leaders fought against the Spanish conquistadors in sixteenth-century Chile. (Editors' note)

1. José Victorino Lastarria, Investigations (1844)

Moreover, the accounts differ, and the simplest facts are contested about which influential factors led to the outcome of such a sublime epic. Hence, I do not dare to pronounce a judgment that condemns the testimony of some, and validates others, thereby stirring passions that should be extinct. My pronouncements in that case would be, if not offensive, at least opinionated and ultimately fruitless. As a young man, I do not have enough education or stature to reach the heights needed to judge events that I have not witnessed, or been able to study philosophically. Our revolution is still in the making. We are not, therefore, in a position to write a philosophical history of it. Instead, we must gather and discuss data so that we can pass it on, along with our research and opinions, to a generation that will possess a true historical criterion, and the necessary impartiality.

From these considerations I determined to conduct research on a period of our history that has not been studied, despite its intrinsic social interest. I do not present you with the narration of facts. Instead, I use them to show the history of their influence on society, making certain, however, that I am accurate and impartial in doing so. I neither celebrate nor condemn these facts, except when their character and consequences require it. Nor do I simply describe their influence without expressing my opinions, because I am not one of those historians who limit themselves to narrating events they consider to be inevitable, renouncing their examination because they consider them beyond the reach of human knowledge. In this matter, I follow a modern author who, speaking of the fatalists who write history, warns,

> stay away from me those who see in actions, whether good or evil, only a reflection of such and such a century, and who submit to a system that poisons humanity and ignore the cries of their own conscience. What is needed is for conscience to submit to higher moral and philosophical principles; to combat fanaticism whenever and wherever it is to be found; to fight sacrilegious impiety as another form of fanaticism; to wage war against despotism, iniquity, sedition, and indifference to the public good.[7]

Gentlemen, in this rough sketch you will not see a great nation calling the attention of the world because of its brilliant career, or a nation admirable for its mysterious origins, heroic youth, and remarkable maturity. What you will see is an unfortunate country chained from the start to the

---

[7] [Charles] Du Rozoir.

1. José Victorino Lastarria, Investigations (1844)

chariot of an arrogant conquistador. Ignorance and slavery have defined its existence for three centuries and continue to exercise their pernicious influence by spreading the prejudices and antisocial behavior that have accompanied us from infancy, and threaten to carry us to endless degradation. Nature, however, will not tolerate such abuse for long. It will take charge, restore dignity, and launch a new epoch of glory and happiness. Humiliated by slavery and ignorance for so long, our people will reclaim their rights and march toward a brilliant future.

Let us study our people, let us learn about their errors and prejudices so that we can understand the obstacles that prevent their movement toward perfection and happiness, as well as discover the elements that promote them. The heroes of our independence finished their arduous task: They destroyed the power that enslaved us, and started the social reaction that now occupies us against the past. It is now the responsibility of the present generation, and the public officials who are in charge of the state, to seize this reaction and lead it until the old Spanish system is completely vanished. This reaction started with a war to the death, and gathered momentum thanks to the enthusiasm of victory. But peace calmed it, and replaced burning enthusiasm with severe reasoning. The lingering influence of the Spanish system has taken advantage of the calm, and reappears from time to time to clash against the manifestations of our renewal. It tries to undermine it with the ill-inspired passions, the fanaticism, and the errors of the ignorant. The hatreds of the revolution reappear, creating and fomenting factions, pushing us to a true crisis. This is a shameless, hypocritical, and never-ending effort that invokes the interests of the nation as well as the truths of eternity in order to win. However, these attempts by the reactionary part of society reveal the last agonizing moments of the ominous Spanish influence. The day will come when we will have the opportunity to reflect on the combat between past and present, and to demonstrate the effects of this struggle. For the moment, we can only show the scene of the battle, and call on all Chileans of good will and enlightenment to take a part in it, even if it is only to take the side of civilization, and to recognize as criminals those who promote prejudice and deceive society into taking a step backwards!

2

LUCAS ALAMÁN

History and Fiction
(1844)

Lucas Alamán (1792–1853) was a Mexican intellectual and statesman born in Guanajuato, where he witnessed the massacre of Spaniards during Miguel Hidalgo's revolt in 1810, an event that would mark forever his conservative thinking.[1] *He studied at the Colegio de Minas in Mexico City, continuing his education in Freiburg and Göttingen. Alamán occupied several government positions, most importantly at the Ministry of Foreign Relations, until his death in 1853. He was the author of the* Disertaciones sobre la historia de la República Mexicana, *and* Historia de México desde los primeros movimientos que prepararon la Independencia en el año de 1808 hasta la época presente (1849–1852).

The aim of these dissertations is to examine the most important developments in our national history, beginning with the Spanish settlement. That is, the origins of the Mexican nation, through its diverse epochs, until the time when it became an independent nation. No study can be more important than that which helps us to understand our origins and the elements that constitute our society. This means the foundation of our ways and customs, our laws, our current religious, civil, and political

[1] This selection comes from the prologue and first chapter of Alamán's *Disertaciones sobre la historia de la República Mexicana desde la época de la conquista que los españoles hicieron a fines del siglo XV y principios del XVI de las islas y continente americano hasta la independencia* (Mexico City, 1844), I, vi–vii and 1–6. The chapter title has been provided by the editors of this volume. (Editors' note)

2. Lucas Alamán, History and Fiction (1844)

situation. Also, by what means have we arrived at the point where we are, and what obstacles have we had to overcome. If history, in general, is necessary to learn about nations and individuals, as well as guide us into the future hand in hand with past experience, the study of history is even more necessary when it is about ourselves and what has unfolded in the land we inhabit, when it is about our lives and all that pertains to us.

However, the very interest that leads us to seek knowledge about the past has been an obstacle preventing us from writing it impartially, under the light of both philosophy and a rigorous critical approach to fairly assess our actions and assign them their proper value. Foreigners who have studied our America have often done it with scant knowledge and usually under the influence of their own biases and national interests. As a result, they have issued rhetorical proclamations rather than history. I am not referring to either the judicious [William] Robertson or [Alexander von] Humboldt, whose work has given us the second discovery of the New World and is an obligatory source in all that relates to the records of our republic: such is the abundance and accuracy of the facts that it contains! Peninsular Spanish authors have obviously defended their government and their countrymen, although fairness demands to acknowledge that some of them, and especially Antonio de Herrera,[2] the father of Spanish American history, have covered events with such impartiality and truth that they help us to form an accurate assessment of the facts they describe. None, however, has approached the history in the way that I advance here: Their mere narration, or compilation, did not allow it. Only [Juan Bautista] Muñoz[3] has come close to my perspective, but his work remained incomplete, with only one published volume.

In Mexico, these matters have not been fully addressed because during the colonial period nothing but celebrations could be written about the Spanish authorities. When things went in the opposite direction, as it always happens when political change takes place, writers sought to highlight the evils that the former regime caused, hid, or minimized in order to utilize them as weapons (permitted during war time) promoting hatred as an opportunistic tool. The result has been total confusion and the proliferation of wrong ideas. That is why it is of absolute necessity to tell the

---

[2] Antonio de Herrera (1549–1625) was a Spanish chronicler who wrote the landmark *Historia general de los hechos de los castellanos en las Islas y tierra firme del mar océano* (1598). (Editors' note)

[3] Juan Bautista Muñoz (1745–1799), a Spanish historian, who was the author of *Historia del Nuevo-Mundo* (1791). (Editors' note)

2. Lucas Alamán, History and Fiction (1844)

citizens of the republic (including those whose level of education should have stayed away from error) what is, and has been, the nation they are part of: This knowledge is needed because losing it has led to evils that might still come back in an even bigger shape.

Now that heated passions have somewhat subsided, the time has come to examine these questions and to judge with impartiality the events of our history, from Conquest to Independence, even though we cannot make much progress because the obstacles that existed during the Spanish government are still with us today: There is still a fire under the deceiving ashes. That is why it will be wise to let this part of our history be addressed by a new generation. We should be content to compile well-established facts so that they can support their own conclusions.

What we will say about the three centuries from Conquest to Independence can nowhere be determined as freely and precisely as in our country. The authority that prevented us from speaking freely is gone, and we have all the facts to prove it. And yet, to proceed well we must completely shed our prejudices; we must assume the character of the philosopher who seeks the truth by applying the severity and rigor of methods that can help us find it. It is necessary to place ourselves at the time when the events took place; we must fully understand the ideas that prevailed then and how they were used; we must judge people according to the standards of the time when they lived. The most common error in history is to judge past events with the ideas of the present, as if it was possible for an individual to change at once the opinions, the prejudices, and the customs of his own time. This is not possible, not even for the most gifted man, because that can only happen with the passage of time, and with the successive passing of ideas for many generations.

It might perhaps be unnecessary to insist that the main principle guiding these dissertations is to present the truth as it emerges from valid historical records. I will not be silent about the crimes committed during the Conquest any more than I will be about the benefits it produced. This is probably the best way to confront new writings circulating about the Conquest which ignore historical facts and let the imagination run wild. These writings make errors that are easily identifiable by those who know the history of the time, but which fill the minds of those who do not with false ideas. As a result, and in a very short time, the romantic writing of history will make everything uncertain, so that we will be unable to distinguish fact from fiction, unless we consult those authors whose main purpose is to establish the truth.

Part II.
Democracy, Constitutionalism, and Liberty

3
BERNARDO MONTEAGUDO
Memoir
(1823)

Of humble origins and mixed race, Bernardo Monteagudo (1789–1825) was born in Tucumán, in the River Plate (Argentina today).[1] *Very little is known about his early years. He graduated in law from the University of Chuquisaca and soon became involved in the wars of independence against Spain, first in Upper Peru and then in Buenos Aires, where he stood out for his radical republicanism, which he originally displayed as a polemicist in newspapers. Embroiled in the internal conflicts of the revolutionary movement in the River Plate, he was forced into exile in 1815. In 1817, he joined the army of José de San Martín which drove the Spaniards out of Lima in 1821, when Peruvian independence was declared. Monteagudo became San Martín's right hand man and was practically in charge of governing Lima while San Martín continued the fight against the royalist forces elsewhere. Monteagudo's authoritarian rule provoked wide resentment and, following two days of riots, he was expelled from the city in 1822. Written a year later as a defense of his actions in government, his* Memoir *offered a systematic examination of the conditions that, in his view, made democracy unworkable in Peru.*[2]

---

[1] Selected passages from Bernardo Monteagudo's "Memoria sobre los principios políticos que seguí en la administración del Perú y acontecimientos posteriores a mi separación," *Quito*, March 17, 1823, in Monteagudo, *Escritos políticos* (Buenos Aires, 1916), 317–357. (Editors' note)

[2] See Carmen McEvoy, "El motín de las palabras: la caída de Bernardo Monteagudo y la forja de la cultura política limeña, 1821–1822," *Boletín del Instituto Riva-Agüero*, Lima, 23 (1996), 89–139. (Editors' note)

3. Bernardo Monteagudo, Memoir (1823)

Peru, like all the ancient Spanish possessions in the New World, suffered three centuries of the devastating regime established by the sword of inhuman adventurers. Until the end of the last [eighteenth] century, Spain needed no other force to keep the colonial order than the superstition and ignorance of the people. There were some partial rebellions from time to time but, rather than arousing concern in the metropolis, they provoked retaliation – although they were enough to warn politicians of the existence of a flammable mass in America that sooner or later could turn into the horrible spectacle of a universal fire around the globe.

The revolution of the English settlements in North America, together with the loud alarm echoed from France to the world, awoke the spirit of resistance among the Spanish colonies. Both nations sent an enthusiastic message to humankind, to join the age of major events, which made South Americans think about their own destiny. They then started to feel the oppression hitherto endured with superstitious patience.

Along with independence, general notions about the rights of man also began to be disseminated, but this was a language understood by very few. The science that teaches the rights and social duties is vast and complicated: It requires a long apprenticeship, and the history of all peoples, without exception, shows that nothing is so slow in the trajectory of humankind as the practical knowledge of what links governments and their subjects.

It was not expected that the American people would acquire new principles with the same speed that their feelings changed. Throughout the region, all inhabitants pledged to reject forever the Spanish domination and rather turn the fatherland into a dreadful desert than to depend on the heirs of Pizarro and Cortés – they did so without discussion and with the certainty of their rejection's significance. The war started with that aim, from the River Plate to the new California. None thought about anything else than to destroy the Spaniards, except some who, either with foresight or intellectual audacity, concocted constitutional plans applicable to their respective localities.

The American armies started to succeed. The pride that comes with victory exalted the imagination, and zeal turned into passion: Since then, men who had ignited hate against the Spanish thought that, to spread the love of freedom, it was necessary to disseminate principles that would intoxicate people with the hope of an absolute democracy. It was at that

3. Bernardo Monteagudo, Memoir (1823)

time an excusable fault, for there are "situations in which whatever we do can only lead to errors."[3]

From 1809 I became wholly devoted to the revolution.[4] I was by accident in the city of La Plata, when I took part in the first stirrings of rebellion among its heroic people. As the ideas I then had about the nature of governments were highly inaccurate, I embraced the democratic system with fanaticism. Even Rousseau's *The Social Contract* and other writings of that genre seemed to me favorable to despotism. I viewed it as a contradiction to be a patriot without being a zealous supporter of democracy. In 1819, I published *El Censor de la Revolución* in Chile, where I extricated myself from my earlier errors, a sort of mental fever which almost all of us have suffered.[5]

When the liberation army arrived in Peru, my ideas were shaped by twelve years of revolution. The horrors of the civil war, the delays on the road to independence, the ruin of a thousand families sacrificed by absurd principles – in short, all the vicissitudes that I had experienced as either spectator or victim – made me naturally think that it was necessary to prevent the causes of such gruesome effects. The democratic rage, and sometimes the adoption of the federal system, have been for the peoples of America a fatal Pandora's box.

Although Peru had the same motives as the rest of America to resent the peninsular government, nowhere else was the feeling stronger due to the larger number of Spaniards living in that territory and the magnitude of their assets, as well as other reasons peculiar to its population. In the

---

[3] Cardinal de Retz. Monteagudo was paraphrasing a maxim from the memoirs written by Jean François-Paul de Gondi, Cardinal de Retz (1613–1679), "one of the leaders of the aristocratic rebellion known as the Fronde (1648–53), whose memoirs remain a classic of 17th-century French literature" – www.britannica.com/biography/Jean-Francois-Paul-de-Gondi-cardinal-de-Retz. (Editors' note)

[4] During these early years, studies of Monteagudo refer to him as a "jacobin," "ultraliberal," "daring revolutionary [who] struggled for independence, for democracy, for public freedoms." See Alvaro Melián Lafinún, "Bernardo Monteagudo," in Monteagudo, *Escritos políticos*, 8; and Antonio Iñiguez Vicuña, *Vida de don Bernardo Monteagudo* (Santiago, 1867), 190. (Editors' note)

[5] In fact, the newspaper was launched on April 20, 1820. In its opening article, Monteagudo noted that "we know from experience the evils of despotism and the dangers of democracy." In the next edition, when he started to publish a series of articles about the "revolution," he acknowledged "past errors." These articles seem to have anticipated what he stated in his *Memoir*. See *El Censor de la Revolución*, Santiago, April 20, 1820, and its subsequent editions until July 10, 1820, in Museo Mitre, ed., *La prensa en la independencia del Perú* (Buenos Aires, 1910). (Editors' note)

3. Bernardo Monteagudo, Memoir (1823)

other countries, the revolution had mainly been caused by hatred against those who had brought so much affliction to the New World. This feeling needed to be generalized in Peru; indeed, to be turned into a popular passion for the cause of independence. That was the first principle behind my public conduct. I employed all the means at my disposal to ignite hate against the Spaniards.

The second principle I followed during my administration was to restrict democratic ideas. I was fully aware that to attract popular support all I needed was to promote them; but I wanted to pursue the dangerous experiment of suppressing at its source the cause that had produced so much evil elsewhere.

I will not cite the author of *The Spirit of the Laws*[6] to demonstrate that democratic ideas are unsuitable in Peru, nor will I look for similar arguments in the archives of humankind.

I think that, before deciding whether democratic ideas are appropriate for Peru, there is a need to examine the mores of the people, the state of its civilization, the distribution of wealth, and the relationships among the various classes that form society. These four principles contain what has been said by the best teachers of the science of government; in selecting them, I have followed my own observations without adopting any system as a model.

The mores of the inhabitants of Peru, considered in respect to the civil order, were those of a people enslaved until 1821 – who remain so in large parts of its territory. Among their main and most ancient habits were those of obedience, since they have never known the rule of law; subservience helped them to avoid violence and ameliorate their misery; [they are] all, in general, enslaved people, and tyrants at the same time.

A people that has just been subject to the calamity of being under such pernicious habits is incapable of being governed by democratic principles. Changing the language makes no difference while the feelings remain; to suddenly demand new mores is to put peoples in the position of confronting a monstrous mixture of opposing sentiments, leading to democratic arrogance and colonial debasement. Thus, the continuing struggle between the government and the people, who sometimes obey as enslaved people and on other occasions want to rule as tyrants: They are

---

[6] As in the United States, Montesquieu's book was one of the most cited works during the revolutionary years. For the prominence of Montesquieu in the US, see Donald S. Lutz, *The Origins of American Constitutionalism* (Baton Rouge, 1988), 140–144. (Editors' note)

3. Bernardo Monteagudo, Memoir (1823)

as eager to receive the reforms with veneration as to abolish them, thus displaying that legislative pride inherent to democracy. Each of their class strives to preserve the prerogatives and influences previously enjoyed and at the first cry of an ambitious demagogue they all demand equality, without understanding or wanting it; in short, the discontent, who form the largest number, denounce the rejection of their claims as an infringement of the rights of the people.

I now want to look at the sort of enlightenment required for a democratic government to be achievable. In a democratic government, each citizen is a civil servant: The difference is only found in the time and means of exercising that kind of mandate. The majority uses that right in the electoral assemblies and the rest in the stands. But the frequency of elections increases *ad nauseam* the number of candidates and requires an unfailing surplus of capable men to manage the affairs of their country. Unfortunately, most people in Peru lack the knowledge to perform such difficult tasks. The study of politics and law has hitherto been here as dangerous as futile. Economic science was in stark opposition to the colonial state. Diplomacy made no sense. I ask if the small number of people who have cultivated those sciences is enough to supply what is needed to bring about the democratic forms.

The distribution of national wealth also merits close attention, because next to enlightenment nothing determines the capacity of peoples to govern as much as wealth. When the general population of a country can live independently, from the yields of their capital, estates, and industry, everyone enjoys more freedom of action and is less exposed to giving up their rights, out of fear or bribery; this is how the powerful swindle the poor. It is true that those who live in abundance can sometimes be as corrupt as those who moan in misery, but it is unlikely that all who have a secure subsistence will sell their vote in the people's assemblies, betray the character of the national representation, search for jobs that they can use for their benefit, organize riots, and gather in the public space to yell with the resentment of the deprived. Those in possession of sufficient capital to satisfy their needs are only interested in order, the main condition for production. From the habit of thinking about what harms or favors their interests, they acquire exact notions of property rights. Where such conditions exist, it will not be difficult to establish democracy.

Let us examine the situation in Peru. It is certainly one of the richest countries on the planet in the eyes of the philosopher who looks at the extent of its territory and its fertility, and at what the three kingdoms of nature can produce. But if we consider its economic wealth by estimating its actual value currently in circulation, it is far from being able to match even mediocre states. The lack of statistics among peoples whose governments have ignored political arithmetic impedes the exact evaluation of wealth, although for my purposes it suffices to look at the largest proportion of its distribution. Rural and urban estates represent the largest value, particularly the former, given the yields of agriculture and the output of the few factories allowed by the Spanish government. Most of them are owned by a limited number of families or, even worse, are held in mortmain. The number of individual owners of real estate is too small in proportion to the size of the territory and the number of inhabitants. Most property owners are encumbered by obligations that benefit the monopolistic classes. In addition, since there is little demand for real estate given the lack of capital, the price of properties, and the rent they produce in the market is very low, few owners can make ends meet.

Capital in Peru is distributed among a low number of individuals, because the obstacles imposed on economic production have impeded its multiplication and diffusion. Money is scarce and in the hands of a few. As to industry, sadly while there are some "wise people" in Peru, they do not belong to that class of people required to invent and develop industrial products; the entrepreneurs are limited to their routines and to offering the most common goods in the market. As a result, the distribution of industrial capital in Peru does not guarantee the individual independence that the spirit of democratic institutions requires.

Democratic principles clash most strongly in Peruvian society when it comes to mutual relations among classes. The diversity of conditions and the multitude of *castas*,[7] the strong aversion that they have for each other, their opposing characters, in short, the differences in ideas, traditions, and mores, as well as the needs and means to satisfy them, leads to hostility and conflicting interests that threaten social coexistence, unless a wise and strong government is in place. Such a threat is more serious today because the habits that served to curb reciprocal animosities have now been relaxed. These animosities will be stronger and more harmful

---

[7] Generally, people of mixed race, although here Monteagudo seems to be referring to the many different races existing in Peru, excluding the white Spaniard (the term also excluded white criollos). (Editors' note)

as democratic ideas spread, and those who foster them will perhaps be their first victims.

Even men who think and can analyze the new principles they have adopted make frequent errors in their implementation, until forced to learn from experience. The diverse *castas* that form most of the population in Peru, far from being able to examine the simplest idea, barely exercise their intelligence, because Spain deployed a ferocious policy to extinguish it. In such circumstances and with no other criteria than those to which oppressed and insulted people are susceptible, they naturally believe that once liberty and equality have been proclaimed their duty to obey has ceased; that respect for magistrates is a favor dispensed to them rather than a duty to the authorities; that equality prevails in absolute terms, not just before the law, since the latter is a restriction that they do not understand except in the most absurd meaning of equality. Overall we must conclude that the relations between masters and those they enslave, among races that detest each other, and among men that form as many social subdivisions as they differ in their color are entirely incompatible with democratic ideas.

Having outlined the reasons I had to restrict such ideas, I will look at the third principle that I proposed to develop in my government: to promote public education and remove all the obstacles to it. I believe that the best way of being a liberal, and the only one that can serve as a guarantee for the new institutions, is to put the current generation on a level with its century, binding it to the enlightened world, to its ideas and thought, hitherto forbidden. This is the enterprise most worthy of zeal and perseverance by the true patriots: This is the way to prepare the people for those reforms. They will be beneficial if made at the right moment. Otherwise, they will be poisonous and destructive to society. This was the project that among my main tasks occupied me the most, despite the obstacles posed by war and the scarcity of resources.

The last principle that I proposed was to prepare opinion in Peru for a constitutional government that had the necessary vigor to defend the independence of the state and to consolidate the internal order without encroaching on the civil liberties of the people, considering the current political and moral circumstances. Peru, as any other newly established state, needs to supplement its novel institutions with a more vigorous executive power, which is called upon to defend the rights achieved by national independence. When a government begins to exist by itself, its situation with respect to those that have already been established is the most disadvantageous and unequal, both in peace and war. The old governments have more means available to wage war, more credit to enforce their claims, and less regard for nascent governments.

Only an eminently vigorous government will be able to balance such great disadvantages. But if in a conflict the new government is more concerned by the threats of democracy than by foreign hostilities; if the measures that need legislative approval are hindered by jealousy or frustrated by popular distrust; finally, if instead of finding support for its plans, the government is faced with demagogues fomenting an evil espionage to paralyze their course, it will find itself inferior in everything to other powers with which it must fight or negotiate.

The consolidation of the domestic order requires even greater levels of strength from the government to overcome the vehement and continuous resistance by the opposing forces of habit. After a dreadful revolution, whose end is not in sight, it is frightening to contemplate the situation of Peru when its territory is free of Spaniards and the passions that have been inflamed for so many years will have to be confronted. That will be the moment when the nefarious effects of the democratic spirit will finally be known; the hatred among the various races of the population will be displayed; strong provincial sentiments will manifest each against the other, exacerbated by complaints and resentments. And if the government is not sufficiently strong to prevail in such struggles, anarchy will set its throne on corpses, and the tyrant emerging from this situation will be welcomed as a gift from heaven, for that is the destiny of peoples who at certain times see happiness in the misfortunes that will save them from greater evils.

Peru will be a thousand times unhappier if, in the middle of these conflicts, it looks for its salvation in the federal system. As a member of human society, I wish that the country that this model comes from preserves and expands its prosperity; it may serve as a model with the passing of time, but hitherto it is a dangerous experiment, as observed by one of its best politicians: Forty years of duration are little proof of its stability. But if Peru wants to adopt the system of the United States, it will be ruined at the same speed as the masses of rock falling from the peak of the Andes. Those who believe that it is possible to implement in Peru the constitutional forms of the United States ignore or forget the origins of either country.

Peru and the United States differ in their circumstances just as England and Spain do. Were the peninsula to proclaim the constitution of

3. Bernardo Monteagudo, Memoir (1823)

Great Britain, the Spanish people would find themselves in a worse condition by adopting some of the general principles of that type of government. The same will happen in Peru regarding the federation. At the time of their emancipation, the United States had a less scattered and more independent population [than Peru], one that was accustomed to the exercise of legislative functions, however limited, and lived under a form of government that paved the way for their current constitutions. Peru has no other legislator than the sword of the conquerors; and the main colonies of the United States received their first laws from the most famous philosophers of that time. I conclude by reminding the federalists of the terrible misfortunes that befell the heroic country of Venezuela because of the Constitution of 1812.[8]

Whatever I have said about the mores, education, distribution of wealth, and the variety of social relations – to show that the democratic system is unworkable in Peru – does not contradict the idea of forming a constitutional government that reconciles freedom with independence. Under this form of government, mores will be transformed neither with violence nor with abuse from the reformers. The level of civilization that remained in Peru, following its separation from Spain, and the number of enlightened men that can be gathered, after all the provinces are liberated, will be sufficient to put in place a vigorous and moderate government. Once education is enhanced, its development will always contribute to the nature and needs of a constitutional government; but it would still be inadequate to sustain democratic institutions for a long time. National wealth, which always grows under governments that secure internal order and external respect, would be proportionally distributed, while the benefits of individual independence are extended. Finally, relations among the inhabitants of Peru would cease to be dangerous under a strong government, as their mutual passions come under control and their respective living conditions improve. The nobility would preserve its privileges with more luster; the clergy would obtain prerogatives more akin to its interest and attuned to the current state of civilization; and all the other

---

[8] He was surely referring to the 1811 Federal Constitution of Venezuela, to which Bolívar attributed the fall of the first republic: "what most weakened the government of Venezuela was the federal structure it adopted, embodying the exaggerated notion of the rights of man," in "The Cartagena Manifesto: Memorial Addressed to the Citizens of New Granada by a Citizen from Caracas" (1812), in David Bushnell, ed., *Simón Bolívar. El Libertador. Writings of Simón Bolívar* (Oxford, 2003), 6. (Editors' note)

classes would be able to aspire to happiness, knowing that their fortune would only depend on their abilities.

These are, in sum, the principles I have applied to the circumstances of Peru. I am fully aware that future generations might reverse what I have described. But until that happens, I believe that any other system will be unworkable and the cries of "freedom! freedom!" in popular assemblies will be useless. Unless freedom is moderated and adapted to the social conditions of those who claim it, it will only be a name for great crimes and a shield to cover their perpetrators. The trajectory of humankind toward the perfection of its institutions is slow and gradual;[9] no country can hasten it without consequences. Constitutional governments with relative breadth in the exercise of civil liberties shape the spirit of the current century. Democracy, feudalism, and absolute power all belong in the past.

The imminent danger of this century is not the fall into despotism, it is the abuse of liberal ideas and the assumption that all countries can enjoy the most perfect government, as if all have the same aptitudes. Today,[10] what is feared is ceding too much power to the rulers, as a philosopher (whose name cannot be objected to by the Democratic Party) used to say.[11] but in my view, it is the lack of obedience on the part of the governed that ought to be most feared. Unfortunately, not just among us but also in Europe, there is a great number of impassioned journalists who infuse the crowd with expectations that cannot be satisfied. Some go to the extreme of offering plans to reform the New World from the banks of the Thames or the Seine. The motives for their zeal may be reasonable, but their effect will never be helpful because they ignore our circumstances.

---

[9] "Le monde avec lenteur marche vers la sagésse": Voltaire.
[10] Monteagudo capitalizes this and the next sentence for emphasis.
[11] Franklin, lettre XCIV. A. M. le Velliard de Passy.

4
ANONYMOUS
The Political Faith of a Colombian (1827)

An anonymous and rarely cited text, Fe política de un colombiano[1] *was consulted by the editors at the John Carter Brown Library, whose catalogue[2] attributes it to Eloy Valenzuela (1756–1834), a Catholic priest from Santander, Colombia. However, it is highly unlikely that Valenzuela, who was close to Simón Bolívar at the time of publication, penned a pamphlet which appeared to be criticizing (though not in explicit terms) the Convención de Ocaña, convened by Bolívar to replace the existing 1821 Constitution. Indeed, the main message of the* Fe política *was one against the concentration of power in the executive, then perceived to be Bolívar's purpose in convening the Ocaña convention. On April 1, 1826, the* Gaceta de Colombia *registered its publication stating that "the author ... was born in one of the departments of the antigua Venezuela." There are reasons to believe that its author might have been Francisco Javier Yanes (1776–1846), particularly as in his* Manual político del Venezolano *Yanes used* Fe política *without attribution, in a book that is seemingly generous in acknowledging the work of others. But if the* Gaceta de Colombia *was right, this would rule out Yanes' authorship as he was not born in Venezuela but in Cuba.*

---

[1] The full title of this essay is *Fe política de un Colombiano, o tres cuestiones importantes para la política del día* (Bogota, 1827). It is important to note that "Colombian" in the context of this publication referred to citizens of what historians named Gran Colombia, the union of New Granada (which then included Panama), Venezuela, and Ecuador, which lasted from 1821 to 1830. (Editors' note)

[2] Available at https://archive.org/details/fepoliticadeuncooobogo (Editors' note).

4. Anonymous, The Political Faith of a Colombian (1827)

Introduction

At a time when the proclamations of political faith are as common as those of religious faith in the early centuries of Christianity, citizens today must have their own beliefs, and make them known, if they hope to place the government of the country on the firm bases of justice and public utility. Aside from this consideration, all who are politically aware must exercise their vote when the state faces a dangerous crisis. Posterity will then know who to blame for the misfortunes, or thank for the well-being, of the country: That is the purpose of the present essay.

Our readers will easily identify the reasons for addressing the important questions in terms of principles, with only a few references to the present circumstances. Our plan is to make our opinions as impartial as possible by abstracting them from specific people and issues: In this way the government policies that are recommended will have more force, and this force will double once the proposals are tested by actual experience.

We address this essay to all impartial people, whatever their opinions might be. We also dedicate it to those who have written frankly against our theories. But we do not address it to those who modify their actions or opinions depending on the victories or defeats of the parties involved; nor to those who have attacked those institutions founded with the approval of the nation. Such persons must be confronted with the force of events or challenged with their very same weapons. We want cold reason to be the judge, and reject the dictates of feverish passions.

On the People's Authority in a Constitutional System

The main question to be discussed here is on the essence of the representative system. That is, when and how a bad decision might damage or degrade the entire system. Such a simple thought helps us understand the importance of the point. Our desire is to ponder this issue with full clarity. Thus, we will begin by defining the term *people*, which is often misused or even abused. We will then explain the fundamental principle of all free governments, including those that are not free. That is, *that sovereignty resides in the people*. We will apply it to constitutional governments and determine the kind, and limits, of the authority of the population over the representative administration, paying due attention to the laws dictated by reason, and by the public interest. Those who know about these matters will excuse us from dwelling on well-known

4. Anonymous, The Political Faith of a Colombian (1827)

facts: The point is to make explicit the fundamental rights and responsibilities of a people who won their freedom after so many sacrifices. It is, however, true that, due to the colonial regime they endured for centuries, the people are not used to understanding either the almost imperceptible limits that separate freedom from license, or the distinction between the firm energy of a tutelary government, and the aggressive arrogance of a despotic one. Foreign nations have witnessed with admiration and respect the sacrifices we have made for the fatherland. And yet our commitment and persistence, which are true models for any country that wishes to break its chains, are due more to our hatred of despotism than the product of reflection concerning constitutional principles. These delicate questions are still too new in our political literature. Perhaps we could have saved ourselves much disquiet had our writers addressed such points from the moment we acquired a printing press. In order to develop a just and impartial judgment regarding all human affairs, but especially political affairs, it is important to have some knowledge of the principles involved. Only then can we avoid falling prey to the impressions of the moment. Perhaps this essay will arrive too late. However, we do believe that we will honor the national cause if we manage to motivate more fortunate intellects to look deeply into these matters to strengthen, through reasoning and experience, the receptive disposition of our compatriots.

What is the meaning of "people"? All the questions concerning the faculties of *people* are easily resolved once the word is well defined. "People" is the universality of the citizens. No population, no particular body, no union of individuals can appropriate the name *people* in order to exercise authority, and that is the only sense in which we use the term here. "People" means the entire society, the general mass of human beings who come together under certain conditions. When a particular group, a city, a corporation (however distinguished it might be) calls itself *the people*, it is not only uttering an absurd lie, but also committing a grievous injustice, for it excludes the rest of the citizens who form the immense majority of the nation. In a word, "people" is the nation. The people of Colombia are not the populations of Bogota, Caracas, or Quito; nor the military, nor the civil service, nor this or that corporation. The people of Colombia are the union of all Colombians. When the electoral districts of Paris burst into the capital, blinded by factions thirsty for blood and plunder, and gave themselves the name of *the people*, they perpetrated the atrocities that Europe has regretted and will regret for a long time to come. The origin of so many disasters was the misunderstanding and abuse of the word *people*. Grammar is a more important science than it is commonly believed.

It should be noted that in those periods of turbulence and fury, when a faction imposes the law, it generally does not invoke the name of the nation but rather that of *the people*. Either malice or instinct advises them to take such a step. When the Jacobins called for thousands of killings from the tribune, or from the galleries of the Convention, they did not call themselves *the French nation* – that absurdity would have been too obvious – but rather *the people*. This equivocal word, which really meant only a part of the population of Paris, was extended to the entire French people by simpletons who did not know how to reason. It is from those grounds that terror installed the bloody throne where Robespierre and Marat commanded a seat. Man is always the same, and he uses august and respectable words whenever he wishes to upset the established order.

If "people" means simply the entirety of the nation, it is clear that the authority that a particular faction appropriates for itself can only be an usurpation and a threat to liberty, whatever the name or the title under which it hides. It is also clear that, because the true and legitimate authority only exists in the collective, deliberations must take place to enforce the law. If ultimately such deliberations cannot take place, even when the necessity of a government and a legislature is patent, it is inevitable that the people should delegate their authority. That is what representative government means. If the question is asked, where is "the people" in constitutional countries? We shall not hesitate to respond: in the representatives of its will. The Congress is the nation insofar as legislative authority is concerned. We could even invoke higher principles and say that the people are present in all the powers created by the fundamental law that they approved. The authority of Congress is included in this principle, because the right to legislate, and the supervision and vigilance over the agents of the executive power, are given to the Congress by the constitution, from whose purview it cannot depart. This is so true that without doubting the power of the people to change the constitution, the Congress does not have the authority to propose or make changes without a special mandate from its constituents, according to the very provisions of the constitution. It is therefore evident that the authority of the people resides in all the powers they created with the adoption of the constitutional framework. It is also evident that this authority cannot be exercised in a manner different from that dictated, presented, and defined by the

4. Anonymous, The Political Faith of a Colombian (1827)

[constitutional] code. We can still say that, despite all this, the public will resides in the national Congress that has been entrusted with the most important mandate of that will, namely, to deliberate upon the laws, and exercise vigilance over any abuses of power.

Now that we fully understand the meaning of the word "people," and have pointed out the abuses that can be committed in their name, let us examine the principle of *sovereignty*: This is a scandalous topic for some (although very few), dangerous for others, and for most as abstract and useless as the unintelligible frivolities of the Aristotelians. Let us define this term. *Sovereignty* is the power superior to all other powers. Examined in its very roots, this term can only apply to the power that precedes all others, namely, the power that created the social pact, or constitution. No one doubts that this primary, inalienable, and independent power from all forms of government resides in the community. When the people accept the constitution, whichever it might be, they exercise sovereignty regardless of whether it is by express consent, or by spontaneous and frequent actions. It is in this sense that the principle of sovereignty as belonging to the nation must be understood. The prejudices inherited from slavery, and the designs of despotism, have tried to obscure this truth since the dawn of time, but they have never been able to destroy it. Even when cruelty and the use of force have done their part to consolidate the government of a despot, a conqueror, or a rebel, such a government has never been seen as legitimate until it has been implicitly or explicitly, but always *freely*, accepted by the community. This is the true sense of legitimacy, a subject on which much nonsense has been uttered in our day. If not, what is the source of legitimacy for the families that currently reign in Europe? Who will justify the usurpation of one, or the unjust conquest of another, or the imposition of a distantly related or bastard branch instead of one that is direct and legitimate? No one can. Acceptance or subsequent acquiescence can only come from nations. The most zealous defenders of absolute power must resort to this principle if they want to claim a valid origin or title. Indeed, nations that in centuries of ignominy or factionalism have adopted a despotic regime, or a feudal anarchy that is perhaps even worse, such a pernicious government (or rather lack of it) has not come into being or been consolidated without the acceptance of its victims. Centuries pass, enlightenment increases, people come to their senses. And thus, they return to the rights of sovereignty, which, however abolished in the books or in the institutions, still lurks in the indestructible instinct of people who want, and want justly, to modify the social pact.

4. Anonymous, The Political Faith of a Colombian (1827)

Who will deny them that right? Who will dare deny the right of a people to reform its fundamental laws? Even when absolute power attempts to prevent it through the use of force, or the threat of the gallows, public opinion secretly takes hold, a segment of the larger association takes the initiative, and the entire community follows. When this happens, the idol falls on the ruins of its own altar. This is where we are in Colombia today.[3]

Let us suppose that the government of a people is already established according to constitutional principles. Let us assume as well that the representative pact is widely accepted and consolidated. What part, then, remains of the radical and original sovereignty? None other than the ability to revise and modify the pact. The truly liberal constitutions always devote some articles to this sound procedure. Our code [the Cúcuta Constitution of 1821] establishes a term of ten years, and the nation's explicit approval, for the undertaking of revisions. Our prudent constitution-makers estimated that experience might call for the implementation of some reforms and wanted them to be informed by constitutional procedures in order to avoid any political turmoil caused by the inconvenience of some articles. When that situation obtains, the Colombian people exercise their original sovereign right by naming deputies who have a special mandate for this important purpose, and by accepting the changes that the wisdom of the time judges as appropriate.

Besides this case, we do not know of any representative system where the people must exercise a primary or constituent sovereignty. Indeed, once the powers that the nation regards as convenient for its government are in place, it ceases to be the sovereign and becomes subject to the very authority it established. This is the case even in unlimited democracies, because there the people are slaves to the law. If a community is to have a government, and if the administration must have fixed rules, then it is imperative that citizens honor the pact to which they have sworn allegiance. What security, what order will a nation have if the people, always present, always dictating, has the liberty to alter or modify at any time the fundamental principles of the constitution? Let us not mention the unrest caused by individual corporations: We have already said that they are not the people, and that it is an abominable usurpation, as well as a pernicious example, when innovations are introduced by particular segments of the society. The nation has a legal method of representation: It has

---

[3] It should be kept in mind, as observed above, that the Colombia referred to here included present-day Colombia, Ecuador, Panama, and Venezuela. (Editors' note)

4. Anonymous, The Political Faith of a Colombian (1827)

legal procedures to modify its system of government. It would be the greatest of all evils to bestow popular representation to the first adventurer who claimed to speak in the name of the fatherland.

Let us now address the question of *actual* or practical sovereignty. In a constitutionally organized system, where does governmental sovereignty reside? In contrast to the last question, this is not an easy one to answer because when powers are divided, the constitutional pact is the only instance to decide where the supreme power resides. In places where the head of state has complete control of the executive, as well as the appointment of judges and the unlimited support of the laws, there is no doubt that he has been entrusted with the sovereign power. This is the case regardless of which laws bind him and his agents to the exercise of the sovereign power, which will be restricted depending on the nature of the constitution. This is why all the monarchs of Europe call themselves sovereigns, even if there is a great difference between the king of England and the emperor of Russia. The question of actual sovereignty does not seem to be as important as the radical or primary sovereignty in a republican state. It could be said that the law is the true actual sovereign in any good government, especially where the law is supported by the political conscience of every citizen. There, the law is stronger than any human inclination, and even physical force. This is the solution to all disputes.

From the preceding observations it can be inferred that in every government the primary sovereignty or constituent power belongs to the nation; and that in a representative government the exercise of sovereignty, or the *actual* sovereignty, resides wherever the constitution has placed the supreme power. According to the Colombian constitution the actual sovereignty resides in the president, in the Congress, and to some degree in the Supreme Court of Justice. In the president, because he is the supreme head of the executive power and authorizes the law; in the Congress, because after a certain period of time this branch can assume that the laws it has proposed have been approved, or when one of the chambers clears certain appointments, or when it assumes the role of a great jury that dismisses public employees and penalizes them for either misusing their positions or compromising the social order. Finally, in the high court because this body exercises the supreme functions of the judiciary. In England the king is undoubtedly the actual sovereign because he is the center of all powers, and exercises over them, in all cases, a true supremacy.

4. Anonymous, The Political Faith of a Colombian (1827)

Ultimately, it is a principle of the representative regime that the exercise of sovereignty does not reside in the nation, but rather in the persons to whom the nation has delegated it. This principle is of the utmost importance because otherwise there would be two powers working simultaneously: that of the total mass, and that of the representatives. In a word, there would be two governments: one democratic, and the other representative. All the evils of the French Revolution came from ignoring this principle.

The objections that frenzy or ill intent usually present against this theory are simply despicable. *The nation*, they say, *must watch both its agents and its representatives*. There is no doubt about this, and that is why the nation, in a constitutional system, does not submit to any other authority than that created by itself. That is why any authority not emerging from the nation's code is intrusive and invasive. *The nation is omnipotent, faultless, and it can do no wrong.* Its physical power is not in doubt; its moral power can and must be subject to certain laws, because the most important priority of the people is to be governed. Those who claim that the nation can neither err nor sin are flatterers: That is the same as saying that the nation has no duties. A single glance at history shows the inconsistencies, evils, and perfidies committed by the people. The harshness and cruelty of the Lacedaemonians, the blatant judicial assassinations of Socrates and Phocion, the bloody conquests of the Romans, were they anything other than national injustices? Different peoples can err and sin like individuals because societies are composed of individuals prone to error and sin. Those who so speak should know that there is a higher power that rests on the very nature of man and which is above the omnipotent will of the people: *public utility*. It was public utility that united families in the primeval forests; established governments; turned man from being a tyrant, or a slave to force, into a moral being either protected or destroyed by the immense power of association, whenever he obeyed or broke the original pact. Let us not exalt, then, the power, the wisdom, and the virtue of the people beyond what is just. Let us not replicate the flattery due to the monarchs. Let us simply pay attention to the utility involved in legislative operations and let us not forget that the universal clamor of all centuries, and of all peoples for the institution of government, proves that people would rather resign a portion of their liberty, and their rights, for the sake of order and tranquility. If this is true of all governments, would it not be even more the case with representative government? That is, the type of government where a clever invention, a tribute to the human spirit,

4. Anonymous, The Political Faith of a Colombian (1827)

puts the general will of the association in the hands of a small number of representatives?

Therefore, the nation is a slave to the powers that it has formed. No: It is only a subject, or, if you will, a slave to the law, not to men.

What if men abuse the law and use it for oppression? What if they turn their weapons and power against the fatherland that entrusted them to defend the law? Nothing proves the excellence of the constitutional regime better than the legal mechanisms that protect the people against the abuses of power. Even after people have divested themselves of their *actual* sovereignty to accept the pact, they still have three great powers available to them. Unfortunately, Europe does not want national governments, but rather privileged ones, and looks upon the authority of both people and reason with hatred. However, the friends of liberty can trust that these three guarantees, if used well, can by themselves preserve liberty. It must be apparent by now that we refer to the electoral power, the right of petition, and above all the freedom of the press. The constitution leaves these three powers in the hands of the people: He who denies that these are true powers does not know the century in which he lives.

The right to elect representatives is so embedded in the minds of people that it cannot be taken away without delegitimizing the entire representative system. It is only prudent, however, that representation be attached to property for both the voter and the elected official. The legislative body must always come from the people. The theory, the experience, the humanity, plus the agents who exercise some influence over the human heart all demonstrate that *man cannot be bound to any other laws than those he imposes on himself, and that he should not provide more help than what he himself accepts.* Citizens cede to the authorities the monopoly of force, the implementation of the laws, and, most importantly, the power to check immoderate desires and stop the naturally democratic impetus of popular organizations. But precisely because they cede so much power, they require keepers of their confidence who watch the actions of the government, and who deliberate and discuss all matters of public interest. To abolish or obstruct electoral rights is to deprive the nation of the advantages of a constitutional regime or, to put it more clearly, to destroy liberty. There cannot be public trust, or true responsibility on the part of the functionaries of the government, if the legislative body is not freely elected by the people. This, because the legal fiction which assumes that members of Congress represent the will of the nation would

4. Anonymous, The Political Faith of a Colombian (1827)

otherwise lose all foundations, or become entirely absurd, the moment the people no longer elected their representatives. This is what always happens when elections are not free. An independent and free electoral power is the principal guarantee that the laws will be good, and that the government will be moderate and just.

If the right of suffrage is an important guarantee for the people, the right of petition plays the same role for individual citizens. Violations of the constitution, abuses of power, vexations inflicted by government agents, can all be denounced at the temple of the laws by any individual or corporation. In the same way, all useful projects and ideas to improve administration in all its branches can be proposed. One should not fear that petitions will go unattended: These are mandates from the people to those that receive them and who have a stake in upholding constitutional principles. Attending to them dignifies the difficult role of the legislators. Petitions make the current needs of the people known to the Congress; they protect them from trespasses, which, if repeated, could become generalized and erode the foundations of liberty. Ultimately, the power to address petitions to the nation (meaning its representatives) gives citizens the right to monitor public affairs. However, woe to the people whose representatives cannot confront the abuses of power with all the rigor of the law! Woe to the people whose various components, far from using the law to punish criminals, instead grant impunity to those who attack their rights, and undermine those individuals chosen to be guardians of their liberty, all in order to supposedly protect its violation! Such people deserve their chains.

Even after we examine all constitutional powers, we find that none has more vitality, especially in a century of enlightenment, than thought. *The world*, Rousseau stated, is *governed by books*. The reason is clear: Human beings do not make use of their powers except to fulfill desires: They are constantly driven by what they understand as good. Hence, there is no power comparable to that of thought, which is the power that reveals what is truly good. That is why a wise writer [Cicero in *De Oratore*] has called both enlightenment and knowledge the *magistracy that teaches* [*Magistra vitae*]. Thought creates and nurtures society, promotes new customs and habits, and establishes the laws. It is the whole of man: To think is to exist. In truth, thought is not supported by power: In fact, it does not need it. Thought is the most absolute of despots: It overthrows tyranny, tames the wild savagery of barbarians, triumphs over the most entrenched prejudices, chains the most ferocious passions, and destroys the most invincible

4. Anonymous, The Political Faith of a Colombian (1827)

armies. Its aid is time; its destiny, to submit the universe to the victorious power of reason.

This immense power residing in the constitutional system is available to the people via freedom of the press. We will, in another place, discuss the precious fruits of this freedom when it is regarded as a right. We will now consider it as a power. The nation happy enough to possess this power has nothing to complain about: It will be protected from the assaults of the executive power and from the betrayals of its rulers. The power of thought is eminently national, that is, it belongs to all citizens. This is the case not because everyone can put their thoughts in writing, but because public opinion, once established by informed deliberation, spreads to the people all the truths that can be obtained through debate. As these truths become a part of the reservoir of national knowledge, they cannot be alienated, nor will there be an authority that dares to attack them. Freedom of the press enshrines reason and this, we believe, is the greatest contribution of the constitutional system.

These three guarantees, however, being so essential for the conservation of liberty, have rules in all constitutional countries. Among us, the electoral power is not exercised directly by the people, but rather through the mediation of municipal and provincial electors. Each voter must have property or income that should be larger for aldermen, representatives, and senators. The right of petition has limits because the alteration of a decree based on the law can only be approved by the executive. The reform of a law can only be asked of the Congress that originated them. Redress for the innocent in a criminal case can only be adjudicated by the courts, which are the bodies with the capacity to judge. Petitions, in a word, must be addressed to the authorities that are relevant to the object pursued. Freedom of the press also has some restrictions: One may not slander under the guise of denouncing; nor should order in society be subverted in the name of reform.

Some might still say: *The laws that spell out the procedures for the exercise of the three guarantees were established during times of peace; but under extraordinary circumstances any procedure obtains, especially with regards to the election of authority; and finally, in such cases ordinary laws should not apply.* Should there be a law for each circumstance, we would have to say, along with Madame de Staël, that legislation is like a good woman, who can be helpful in the management of the household during workdays but who should not be present on solemn occasions. Still, she adds, it is on those occasions when passions run high that the stern demeanor of the

4. Anonymous, The Political Faith of a Colombian (1827)

laws is more necessary than ever. Absolutist governments are prone to dictate circumstantial laws; in a constitutional system, those that are fixed and permanent are both natural and essential to it.

In sum, these three guarantees are sufficient for containing and punishing those who abuse the law to oppress others, as well as those who use their power and weapons against the same fatherland that gave it to them for the purposes of defense.

Let us then refrain from granting the people, *when gathered in a crowd*, the right to intervene in the actions of the government, push it to do something, obstruct its initiative, and tumultuously censor its operations. Let us refrain, also, from granting it the power to deliberate, *again as a crowd*, on matters entertained by the Congress, and above all on matters that the constitution itself has determined as falling outside the powers of the representatives of the nation. If the people can, out of the sheer power of their numbers, take over legislative deliberations and governmental decrees, then it will also be able to demand from, or intimidate, judges into issuing the sentences that favor them, even if they run contrary to the law. We cannot find any reason why the people should have the right to do the first and the second, but not the third, when it comes to crafting the laws, implementing and applying them. Would there be any personal security? What would the courts be about? Where would the laws be? And liberty?

These rights might have been legitimate and easy to implement in the ancient republics. However, in modern nations with large territories it is nearly impossible to bring everybody together. Popular deliberations might be justified in extraordinary circumstances, such as the need to overthrow an arbitrary government, or establish the rights of man and the citizen. But they should never be permitted in a constitutional regime. There, rights are guaranteed, and people understand and have the legal means to secure both liberty and good government, be it in the form of the distribution of powers, rights of suffrage and petition, or freedom of the press. Tumultuous meetings where factions rather than people participate were considered illegal in ancient democracies. There is no discussion in such gatherings but rather vociferous threats and expressions of political passions that barely conceal selfish interests. Some who join such meetings only seek to either manifest their rancor or exact private retributions. What better occasion to unleash such malice than the absence of the law, and the power that upholds it?

4. Anonymous, *The Political Faith of a Colombian (1827)*

It is necessary for people to understand that, when they consented to the constitutional pact, they renounced the direct exercise of sovereignty. They have no other faculties than those assigned by the constitution, because those provisions are sufficient to guarantee their rights. They should know that insistence, apart from being unfair and illegitimate, will not add more security to the possession of their rights. Instead, it will upset both [the public] order and the representative system, impeding governmental actions in the process, and replacing them with the brute force of conflicting passions. That is the road to slavery. Nations will then follow an inevitable course: from liberty to license, and from license to servitude.

5
ESTEBAN ECHEVERRÍA
The Socialist Program (1838)

Esteban Echeverría (1805–1851) was born in Buenos Aires before the May 25, 1810, revolution, but was educated in the liberal environment of Bernardino Rivadavia's government, which sent him to Paris to further his education.[1] Upon return in 1830, he saw the rise of Juan Manuel de Rosas and became an opponent of his regime in both a literary and a political sense. He along with others founded the Asociación de Mayo in 1837, which caused his exile in Montevideo, where he wrote the compelling "El matadero" (The Slaughterhouse) and published the Dogma socialista, *from which the current selection is taken. The "socialism" of the title might be somewhat deceiving, in that Echeverría's program contained the standard tenets of liberal democracy. His thoughts on the rule of law, while not entirely original, became a powerful weapon against dictatorship, one that was seen as applicable well beyond his native land and became a classic of Spanish American political thought.*

Association

Society is a fact recorded in the pages of history. It is also the condition that God imposed on humanity for the free exercise and full development of the individual faculties. Society is the vast scenery where humanity

[1] From *Dogma socialista de la Asociación Mayo, precedido de una ojeada retrospectiva sobre el movimiento intelectual en la Plata desde el año 1837*, in *Obras completas de D. Esteban Echeverría* (Buenos Aires, 1873–1874), IV, 119–126, 158–170, and 175–180. (Editors' note)

5. Esteban Echeverría, The Socialist Program (1838)

expands, intelligence thrives, and ceaseless activity produces concrete results.

Without association there is no progress. Indeed, association is the necessary condition for civilization and progress.

To work for the dissemination of the spirit of association among all social classes is to work for the progress and civilization of our fatherland [*patria*].

There cannot be a true association without equality. Inequalities produce hatred and passions that suffocate the sense of community and weaken the social bonds.

To expand the scope of association, and at the same time strengthen and tighten it, it is necessary to level social differences, or make every effort to achieve equality.

In order for association to achieve these goals, it is necessary to organize it in such a way that social and individual interests do not collide. Instead, the social element and the individual element, the fatherland and the independence of the citizen, should always be combined. It is in the alliance and harmony of these two principles that the fundamental challenge of the science of society resides.

Both individual rights and the rights of association are equally legitimate.

The efforts of politics should be directed to ensure, via association, that each citizen enjoys liberty and individuality.

Society must protect the individual independence of each member, to the same degree that all individuals must contribute to the good of the fatherland.

Society should not overpower the individual, or demand the absolute sacrifice of his individuality. Likewise, individual interests should not prevail over the social. Otherwise society would dissolve, because members would have no bonds uniting them.

The will of the people, or the majority, cannot dictate any mandate that injures individual rights, because there is no absolute authority on earth; because no authority represents supreme justice; and because the laws of conscience and reason are above human laws.

No legitimate authority rules except in the name of law, justice, and truth. It is the national will, the true public conscience, that interprets and decides what is just, true, and mandatory – this is the realm of positive law. But beyond this law, and in a higher sphere, there are individual rights that are the measure and the essential condition of the social order. These rights are above and beyond positive law.

No majority, party, or assembly has the right to dictate a law that infringes upon natural law and the principles that hold society together, or that subordinates the security, liberty, and life of all to the arbitrary will of one individual.

A people that inflicts such an assault is either insane, or stupid, because it exercises a right that it does not have, and because it trades with something it does not own, namely, the freedom of others. It is as if an individual decided to sell himself into slavery: He cannot do this because the laws of God and nature have made him free.

The will of the people can never determine as just what is essentially unjust.

To invoke reasons of state in order to violate fundamental rights is an act of Machiavellianism; it means subjecting human beings to the disastrous rule of force and arbitrariness.

The well-being of a people depends on the rigorous and incorruptible respect for the rights of each individual.

Society, in order to exercise its own rights over the members, must deliver justice, equal protection, and laws that ensure an individual's selfhood, property, and liberty. Society is obligated to protect members from injustice and violence; to check the passions of the members so that they do not hurt one another; and to provide them with the means to work without obstacles for their own benefit, although without obstructing the work of others. Society must protect everyone so that each person can peacefully enjoy his property, and anything he has acquired through work, industry, or talent.

A social power that divides rather than unites; that sows mistrust and resentment; that exacerbates factionalism and retribution; that encourages perfidy, espionage, and betrayal; that turns society into a wasp's nest of informers, executioners, and victims, that is an iniquitous, immoral, and abominable power.

A government is helpful, moral, and necessary to the extent that it guarantees all citizens their inviolable rights and, principally, their liberty.

An association's excellence is directly related to the freedom of each member. To achieve it, it must promote fraternity, generosity, and selflessness among the members. All must work so that each individual's efforts, far from isolating them, or making them selfish, simultaneously unite to achieve a single aim: the progress and greatness of the nation.

The prevalence of individualism has hurt us. Egotistical passions have sown the seeds of anarchy in the soil of liberty, and spoiled their fruits. That is where the weakening of social bonds comes from. Selfishness is embedded in every heart, and shows its twisted and ominous appearance everywhere. Hearts do not throb anymore at the sound of the same words, or at the sight of the same symbols. Minds are no longer united by the same belief in fatherland, equality, fraternity, and liberty.

How can we revive a society that is in the throes of dissolution? What can we do to bring back the sociable element in the human heart, and save both the fatherland and civilization? The remedy can only be found in the spirit of association.

Association, progress, liberty, equality, and fraternity are all related concepts in the great social and humanitarian synthesis. They are the divine signs of the promising future for both different peoples, and humanity.

Liberty can only be accomplished by means of equality, and equality can only be achieved by means of association, namely, the combination of all individual forces to reach a single objective: continuous progress. This is the fundamental philosophical orientation of the nineteenth century.

The best social organization will be the one that offers the strongest guarantees for the development of equality and liberty, as well as the greatest expansion of the free and harmonious exercise of the human faculties. The best government will be the one closest to our customs and social situation.

The road to liberty is equality. Equality and liberty are the foundational principles of democracy.

Democracy is, therefore, the type of regime best suited to our needs, and the only one realistically available to us.

Our mission is to provide the grounds for the organization of a democracy that already exists, albeit in embryonic form, in our society.

The provisional organization of the Association of Young Argentina heralds the future nation. Its mission is essentially preparation. It will seek to disseminate both its spirit and doctrine; extend the scope of its progressive tendencies; gather support for the great national association by uniting opinion in favor of the fatherland, as well as the principles of equality, liberty, and fraternity.

The Association will strive to bring together the citizen and the fatherland, the individual and society, and establish the foundations of an Argentine nationality based on the democratic principle.

Once established, the Association will seek to reconcile the two fundamental ideas of the age: fatherland and humanity. It will also try to make the progressive movement of the nation march in step with the progressive movement of the great human association.

Independence from the Retrograde Traditions That Keep Us Bound to the Old Regime

There are two ideas that always appear in the landscape of revolutions: First, the stationary idea that wishes to maintain the status quo, and stick to the traditions of the past. Second, the reformist and progressive idea. That is, the old regime and the modern spirit, respectively. Each of these ideas has its own representatives and partisans. Their struggle and mutual rejection beget war and the disasters of revolution.

For us the triumph of revolution means the victory of the new and progressive idea: It is the triumph of the sacred cause of liberty for both the individual and the collective. However, this victory is not yet complete, because these two ideas continue their hostility, and because the new spirit has yet to annihilate the old spirit of darkness.

The Spanish American generation carries the habits and inclinations of the past generation in its blood. It shows the scars of slavery even if it is no longer enslaved.

The body is free but the mind is not.

One could say that revolutionary Spanish America is free from the paws of the Spanish lion but remains paralyzed by its gaze and omnipotence.

Independent Spanish America retains the signs of imperial vassalage and continues to wear the moth-ridden gown of its former master.

What an incongruous sight: a young and strong person covered with rags, like a democracy wearing the medals of monarchy and the powdered wigs of the aristocracy; a new century saddled with the remains of the old; a youth walking like a decrepit; a corpse and a living human being covered by the same shroud; a revolutionary Spanish America wearing diapers fastened by a former stepmother.

Two dreadful legacies from Spain obstruct the progressive movement of the Spanish American revolution: customs and legislation.

5. Esteban Echeverría, The Socialist Program (1838)

A new political order requires new constituent parts.

Customs based on class inequalities will never be compatible with the principles of democratic equality.

We inherited from Spain a culture of inertia, which in the moral order means the abdication of the right of critical examination and choice. That is, it means the suicide of reason. In the physical order, it means following the same trodden path, the lack of innovation, and the use of the same old pattern to confront new realities. But democracy requires new actions, more innovation, and the constant exercise of all human faculties, because movement is the essence of life.

Spain imposed on us the blind respect for both tradition and the infallible authority of some doctrines, while modern philosophy proclaims the independence of reason and does not recognize any other authority than its own, nor any criterion to choose principles or doctrines other than the uniform consent of humanity.

Spain demanded respect and deference for the opinion of grey-haired men. But grey hair is an indicator of age, not of intelligence or reason.

Spain taught us to be obedient and superstitious, but democracy wants us to be submissive to the law, to religion, and the embracing of citizenship.

Spain educated us to be colonial vassals, but our fatherland requires us to acquire knowledge consistent with the dignity of free human beings.

Spain divided society into corporations, hierarchies, professions, and gilds. The laws treated clergy, nobility, common people, and anonymous crowds differently. Democracy, for its part, levels all conditions: It tells us that there are no hierarchies beyond those established by law for the government of society; that the judge is just one more citizen outside his bench; that the priest, the soldier, the lawyer, the merchant, the artisan, the rich, and the poor are all one; that the poorest is the same as all others in terms of rights and dignity; that only probity, talent, and ingenuity generate superiority; that the most humble artisan, if he has virtue and capacity, is in no lower a position than the priest, the lawyer, or anyone who uses his faculties for the practice of any profession; that there are no occupations that are more noble than others, because nobility does not consist in wearing a cape, or displaying a title, but rather it is found in actions; and, in sum, that in a democratic society only those who contribute to the common good and the prosperity of the country are dignified, wise, virtuous, and worthy of consideration.

5. Esteban Echeverría, The Socialist Program (1838)

To destroy these noxious germs, and achieve complete emancipation from such stale traditions, we need to reform our customs radically, by means of education and laws.

A semi-barbarous legislation promulgated during tenebrous times by the arbitrary will of one man who protected the interests and domination of a particular class; a legislation made, not to meet the needs of our society but rather to strengthen the tyranny of the metropolis; a legislation for colonial vassals rather than citizens; a legislation that perpetuated disputes, causing the ruin of individuals and the state; that opened a wide field for abuses and bad faith; and that permits to this day the continuation of an obscure and vacillating jurisprudence plagued with scholastic subtleties. That legislation, in sum, has no roots in the collective intelligence of the nation, and undermines the principles of equality and democratic freedom. That legislation will never be appropriate for independent Spanish America.

Our legislation must be the product of the customs and intelligence of the nation.

The education and moderation of the people should be the very basis of a legislation appropriate for the needs and the state of our society.

The work of legislation is slow, because customs cannot be changed at once.

The laws have a major role in the improvement of customs. When the laws are bad, customs are corrupted; when they are good, they improve.

The vices of a people are almost invariably rooted in their legislation. Spanish America is a demonstration of this. Spanish American customs are the offspring of the laws of Spain.

Our positive laws must be compatible with the principles of natural law. *Jus privatum latet sub tutela juris publici.*[2] Just like reason is the foundation of all rights, natural law is the origin and first rule of all other laws.

The laws could either be personal or obligatory for everyone. The power of the law resides in being applied to all.

The laws will define the limits of the rights and duties of the citizen. They will teach what is useful or detrimental to either individual or collective interests.

---

[2] Echeverría appears to take this quote from Francis Bacon. The Roman aphorism is often quoted as *Sub tutela juris publici latet jus privatum*: "bajo la tutela del derecho público se halla latente el derecho privado." (Editors' note)

If the law applies to all, no civil, military, or religious class can have its own special laws. All are subject to the same law.

A complete body of Spanish American laws, informed by the gradual progress of democracy, will be the foundation of the emancipation of the Spanish American spirit.

The Emancipation of the Spanish American Spirit

The great goal of the revolution is yet to be accomplished. We are independent but not free. The arms of Spain are no longer oppressing us, but its traditions are. Counterrevolution has emerged from the depths of anarchy.

The stationary idea, namely, the Spanish idea, has reemerged from its disgusting den and triumphantly rears its ugly head, spewing insults against the reformist and progressive spirit.

Fortunately, its triumph will be short-lived. God has willed, and the history of humanity proves it, that the ideas and actions that once existed will disappear from the face of the earth, and plunge forever into the abyss of the past, just like generations disappear one after the other. God has willed that today has no resemblance to yesterday; that our century is not a monotonous repetition of the last; that what once was shall not return, and that the moral and the physical world, just like the life of both the individual and peoples, advances and improves in an unceasing, continuous movement.

The counterrevolution is little more than the slow agony of an obsolete century, the retrograde traditions of the old regime, and of the ideas that completed their lifecycle in history. Who, violating the laws of God, in a delirium, can revive a shrouded specter already in its grave? Will the impotent efforts of a few recalcitrant spirits do that? What a chimera!

Revolution roars in the innermost corners of our society. It is waiting to show itself as a star that will illuminate our fatherland. It sharpens its weapons in the dark, and prepares itself in the prisons where it is gagged and oppressed. It kindles the patriotic heart; it nurtures its reformist plans in silence, and gains power and intelligence while it waits.

The revolution advances, but in chains. It is the duty of the young generation to break these shackles and take the initiative in that great work of emancipation of the Spanish American spirit, which consists of both political liberty and social emancipation.

5. Esteban Echeverría, The Socialist Program (1838)

The former has been accomplished, but not the latter.

The liberty of the fatherland depends on social emancipation.

The Spanish American social emancipation can only be accomplished when we repudiate the legacies of Spain, and join all our efforts to create a new Spanish American sociability.

The sociability of a people is formed by all the elements of civilization: politics, philosophy, religion, science, art, and industry.

Spanish American politics will seek to organize democracy along the lines of equality and liberty, assuring everyone, by means of appropriate laws, the widest and freest exercise of their natural faculties. It will recognize the principles of independence and sovereignty for each country, inscribing in gold characters, at the top of the Andes, and under each [Spanish American] flag, the following divine mandate: Nationality is sacred. Nationality will dictate the rules of international relations within Spanish America, and with the rest of the world.

Philosophy recognizes individual reason as the only judge in everything related to the human person. It also recognizes collective reason or general consensus as the supreme arbiter in all matters concerning society.

Philosophy will facilitate a pact of alliance between individual reason and collective reason, namely, between the citizen and the fatherland.

Philosophy illuminates faith and explains religion while subordinating it to the laws of progress.

Philosophy seeks the laws that explain inanimate nature as well as the laws that explain the transformation of all living creatures. In history, it seeks the thread of the progressive traditions of each people, and of humanity. Consequently, it looks for the designs of Providence. In art, it searches for individual and social expressions, which it then compares and explains. In metaphysical terms, it looks for the harmonious expression of finite and contingent life, as well as the infinite and absolute life.

Philosophy provides rational laws for industry, and for the physical work of individuals.

Philosophy, in sum, is the science of life in all its forms, from the rock to the plant, from the plant to the insect, from the insect to the human, and from the human to God.

Philosophy is the intelligent eye that examines and interprets the laws that rule the moral and physical world, as well as the universe.

Religion is the moral foundation of society, the divine balm for the heart, the pure fountain of our hopes for the future, and the mystical stairway the leads us from earth to heaven.

5. Esteban Echeverría, The Socialist Program (1838)

Science teaches human beings to know themselves, to understand the mysteries of nature, turn their thoughts to the Creator, and find the means for the improvement and perfectibility of both individual and society.

Art encompasses, through its divine inspirations, all the moral and affectionate elements of humanity: the good, the just, the true, the beautiful, the sublime, and the divine; the individual and the social, the finite and the infinite; love, the expectations and the visions of the soul, and the most uncertain and mysterious intuitions of the mind. The prophetic spirit of Art penetrates and comprehends everything; sees all through the brilliant lens of the imagination; gives it light and fire through its foundational work; gives it beauty through the bright colors in its painter's palette; and translates it into sublime and ineffable verse. Art sings of heroism and liberty, gives solemn luster to the great occasions, both internal and external, in the life of nations.

Industry provides human beings with the instruments to control the forces of nature, ensure their well-being, and master the power of creation.

Politics, philosophy, science, religion, art, and industry should all lead to democracy, support it, and cooperate actively to both strengthen and consolidate it.

The natural, harmonious, and complete development of all these elements address the problem of the emancipation of the Spanish American spirit.

The Democratic Organization of the Fatherland

Equality and liberty are the two main components of democracy.

Democracy springs from a necessity, namely, social equality, and advances with a sure step toward the conquest of the realm of freedom; that is, individual, civil, and political freedom.

Democracy is not just another form of government, but rather the essence of all republican governments as well as those established for the good of the community and the [political] association.

Democracy is the regime of liberty founded on the equality of conditions.

All modern political associations tend to establish class equality and, on the basis of the progressive movement of European and American nations, it can be established that "the gradual development of the equality of conditions is ... a providential fact, and it possesses all the characteristics of a divine decree: it is universal, it is durable, it constantly eludes all human interference, and all events as well as men contribute to its progress" (Alexis de Tocqueville).[3]

Democracy is the government of the majority. It represents the uniform consent of the reason of all, to create the laws and to decide on everything that concerns the Association.

This general and uniform consent constitutes the sovereignty of the people.

The sovereignty of the people has no limits in anything that involves society: politics, philosophy, and religion. But people are not sovereign when it comes to individual conscience, property, life, and freedom.

The Association has been established for the good of all. It is the foundation of all individual interests, the living symbol of the strength and intelligence of each one.

The aim of the Association is the organization of democracy, to assure each and every member the widest and freest exercise of their natural rights, as well as the widest and freest exercise of their faculties.

Therefore, the sovereign people, or majority, cannot violate individual rights, or obstruct the exercise of individual faculties, because such rights are at once the origin, the linkage, the condition, and the goal of the Association.

The moment those rights are violated, the pact is broken, the association dissolves, and each individual becomes the absolute master of his will and actions, making rights dependent on individual power.

It can be concluded from this that the limits of collective reason are in the law; and that the limits of individual reason are in the sovereignty of the people's reason.

The rights of the individual precede the rights of association. By the laws of God and humanity, the individual is the exclusive master of his life, property, conscience, and freedom. His life is a gift from God; his property is the product of his labor; his conscience is the window to his soul as well as the intimate judge of his actions. His freedom is the necessary condition for the development of the faculties granted by God to enjoy happiness, which is the very essence of life. Life without liberty is death.

---

[3] Passage taken from the introduction to volume 1 of *Democracy in America* (1835). Translated by Henry Reeve. (Editors' note)

5. Esteban Echeverría, The Socialist Program (1838)

The right of association is therefore circumscribed by the sphere of individual rights.

The sovereign, the people, the majority promulgate positive social and political laws in order to protect the primary law, that is, the natural law of the individual. When an individual joins society, he does not resign a part of his liberty or rights. In fact, he joins the Association in order to preserve and expand them.

If the positive law of the sovereign is truly bound by natural law, its right is legitimate, and all should obey it, lest they be punished as offenders. If the sovereign violates natural law, sovereignty becomes illegitimate and tyrannical, and thus no one is obligated to obey it.

The right of the individual to contest the tyrannical decisions of the sovereign people, or majority, is therefore legitimate, as is the right to meet force with force, and punish the thief or murderer who assaults our property, or our lives, because such a right emerges from the very conditions of the social pact.

First principle: The sovereignty of the people is unlimited insofar as it respects the rights of the individual.

Second principle: The sovereignty of the people is absolute to the extent that it is guided by reason.

Only collective reason, not will, is sovereign. The will is blind, arbitrary, and irrational. The will demands, while reason examines, ponders, and then decides.

From here it follows that popular sovereignty can only reside in the people's reason, and that it can only be exercised by the rational and moderate part of the social community.

The ignorant part must remain under the tutelage and vigilance of the laws dictated by the uniform consent of rational people.

Democracy, then, does not mean the absolute despotism of the masses, or the majority; it means the regime of reason.

Sovereignty is the greatest and most solemn manifestation of reason in a free population. How could people who do not recognize its importance participate in this manifestation? Could those who lack the understanding to discern between good and evil in public affairs? Or those who, not understanding what is appropriate to all, lack their own opinions and are therefore prepared to follow those of the ill-intentioned? Or those who, by voting imprudently, compromise the liberty of the country and the survival of society? I insist: How could the blind see, the cripple walk, the

5. Esteban Echeverría, The Socialist Program (1838)

mute speak, or he who has no capacity or independence, participate in the acts of sovereignty?

Another requirement for the exercise of sovereignty is industriousness. The lazy, the vagabond, the untrained in any skill cannot play the role of the sovereign. Having no bonds to society's interests, he will yield his suffrage when threatened, or bribed.

He whose welfare depends on the will of someone else, or does not have personal independence, cannot enjoy the benefits of sovereignty, because he will not sacrifice his interests to the independence of reason.

It is therefore necessary to keep the ignorant, the vagabond, and anyone who does not have personal independence under tutelage. The law will not prevent them from exercising sovereign rights, except while they remain under tutelage. The law does not deprive them of rights but imposes a condition for their possession: the condition of emancipation.

However, the people, the masses, do not always have the means to achieve emancipation. Society, or the government that represents it, should make those means available.

The government will promote industry, remove fiscal obstacles, lower taxation, and allow the free exercise of industrious activities.

The government will disseminate knowledge in every segment of society, and will help the poor and the disadvantaged. It will seek to elevate the proletarian class to the level of the higher classes by first emancipating their bodies, and then emancipating their minds.

To emancipate the ignorant masses and give them access to sovereignty one must educate them. Masses only have instincts: They are more impulsive than rational; they want the good but do not know how to find it; they want liberty but cannot see the road to freedom.

The education of the masses must be systematized.

Once the masses are moralized, religion will open their hearts to let the seeds of good customs grow.

Elementary instruction will prepare the masses to acquire higher knowledge, so that one day they will understand the rights and duties required by citizenship.

Even if temporarily deprived of the exercise of sovereignty and political liberty, the ignorant masses are fully entitled to individual freedoms. As in the case of every member of the Association, their natural rights cannot be violated: Civil liberty applies to them. The same civil, penal, and constitutional laws, as dictated by the sovereign, protect their lives,

5. Esteban Echeverría, The Socialist Program (1838)

property, conscience, and freedoms. They can be indicted if they break the law, and then either sentenced or absolved.

They cannot participate in the writing of the laws that define the rights and duties of the members of the Association for as long as they remain under tutelage. However, the same law provides for the means of emancipation, and guarantees their protection in the meanwhile.

Democracy leads to the leveling of classes, namely, the equality of conditions.

Third principle: Class equality requires individual liberty, civil liberty, and political freedom. When all members of the Association are in full and absolute possession of these liberties, and when together they exercise sovereignty, democracy will have been definitely established on the firm basis of equality.

Up to this point, we have identified the spirit of democracy and defined the limits of popular sovereignty. Let us now inquire into how the sovereign acts, namely, to identify both the visible shape of the sovereign's decisions, and the ways in which it organizes a democratic government.

The sovereign delegates the writing of the laws, but keeps the power of sanction to itself.

The delegate represents the reason and the interests of the sovereign.

The legislator exercises a limited and temporary sovereignty, and must be guided by reason.

The legislator promulgates the organic law. There, he spells the rights and duties of the citizen, as well as the conditions of the pact of association.

The legislator divides power into three branches, defining the limits and the attributes of each. These three branches represent the symbolic unity of democratic sovereignty.

The legislature represents popular reason; the judiciary, justice; and the executive, action or will. The first crafts the law, the second adjudicates it, and the third implements it. The first votes on expenditures and taxes, and also conveys the needs and wishes of the population. The second is the mechanism for social justice, as manifested by the law. The last is the tireless administrator of the social interest.

These three powers are independent, but not isolated or immobilized. They balance each other out in order to maintain an equilibrium. They move harmoniously in the same direction: the achievement of social progress. Their power will result from the three combined forces; they will constitute one will. Just like reason, sentiment and will constitute the moral unity of the individual, the three powers will form the unity of democracy and constitute the legitimate organ of sovereignty. Their union is destined to decide in a peremptory manner on all questions concerning the Association.

The conditions of the pact are written; the foundational stone of the social edifice is in place; the government has been organized and is enlivened by the spirit of the fundamental law. The legislator presents it to the people; and the people will approve it if it represents the living symbol of reason.

Then the work of the constituent legislator will have concluded.

The organic law must be the manifestation of public reason as proclaimed by its legitimate representatives. They must include, in the law, the opinions and interests of the electorate. They must make every effort to understand their thoughts. If the legislators do not do that, betraying their mission and the needs of the people, they will become shameless plagiarists who take from here and there the articles of foreign constitutions. They should write one that has live roots in the popular conscience. Otherwise, it will be like an aborted monster, a lifeless body, an ephemeral and impotent law that will never pass the public test.

The legislator will have betrayed the trust of the electorate. The legislator who does that is an imbecile.

If on the contrary the legislator completely satisfies the public reason, his work will be great, sublime, and similar to God's.

In that case, neither the people, nor the legislator, nor any social power will be able to bring a sacrilegious hand to touch this sanctuary where the supreme and inviolable law is written in divine letters. This is the law of laws which all have recognized, proclaimed, and sworn to respect before God and humanity.

Sovereignty, in a manner of speaking, becomes flesh with this law: that is where reason and popular consent reside; that is where order, justice, and liberty are; that is where democracy is safe.

This law can be revised, improved over time, and made to coincide with the progress of public reason by an assembly appointed by the sovereign. But until the time comes to change it, the power of the law is omnipotent; its will predominates over all others; its reason shall prevail over any other reason.

No majority, no party, and no assembly can violate the law. Should they attempt to do so, they will be declared usurpers and tyrants.

5. Esteban Echeverría, The Socialist Program (1838)

This law is the foundation of all other laws. Its light illuminates them all. All thoughts and actions by the social body and the established powers emerge from it and gravitate around its center. The law is the force that gives them motion and sets their orbits, much like the stars around the sun, or the elements that define democracy. They all move in the same direction.

In a democracy so constituted, popular sovereignty starts from the law and follows an unlimited and unceasing course, albeit always in a predetermined orbit. Its power goes no further.

Representative democracy makes and unmakes the laws, introduces constant innovations, takes its constant activity everywhere, and provides an unceasing movement as well as the gradual transformation of the social body.

Each of democracy's actions is a new creation; each decision made by its reasoning is progress.

Democracy examines, processes, judges, and sentences everything: politics, religion, philosophy, art, and industry – the voice of the people is the voice of God.

From here it follows that if the people lack knowledge and morality, the task of organization cannot be accomplished. The ideas of a constitution must be rooted in customs, feelings, memories, and traditions. The legislator cannot create an organic law or acclimate the constitution of another country into his own, without knowing the instincts, needs, interests, and everything else that forms the intellectual, moral, and physical life of the people he represents, much less craft them and turn them into law. Only those who have the highest capacities and virtues, and a complete knowledge of the needs and spirit of the nation, can or should be legislators.

From here it also follows that before inquiring into the most preferable form of government, the legislator must (if he is true to his duty) inquire if the people are in a position to be ruled by a constitution. If that is the case, the legislator should offer, not the best or even the perfect constitution, but one that is appropriate to the situation of the population.

Solon said that he had given the Athenians, not the best laws, but those they were prepared to receive.

In sum, we can infer from this the need to prepare the legislator before we entrust him with the writing of a constitution.

The legislator cannot be prepared if the population is not. Could he work for the good if the people do not know him? Or if they do not appreciate the advantages of freedom? Or if they prefer inertia instead of activity? Or if they would rather stick to their habits than innovate? Or if they esteem what they know and can touch rather than what is unknown and appears remote?

It is absolutely necessary, therefore, to prepare both the people and the legislator. That is, to prepare the grounds that are the objective of the law, to disseminate the ideas that legislators should embrace, and include in the law. Such ideas must circulate, become common knowledge, and be a part of the public spirit.

It is imperative, in a word, to illuminate the understanding of both the people and the legislator before we start building a nation.

Only then will we be able to accomplish what we most keenly want: that a legislator appears, or else some other form of national representation, that is capable of understanding and fixing the problems of society, satisfying the people's needs, and establishing an unassailable and permanent social order.

Until the public spirit reaches the necessary level of maturity, constitutions will do little more than foment anarchy and animosity toward the law, justice, and the most sacred principles.

Democracy being a form of self-government, it requires the constant activity of all human faculties. It cannot be established without the aid of knowledge and morality.

Starting with the principles of class equality, democracy seeks to be anchored in the ideas, customs, and feelings of the people. Democracy crafts the laws and institutions that can extend and consolidate its own prevalence.

All the efforts of our governments and our legislators must be directed to the accomplishment of the goals of democracy.

The Association of Young Argentina believes that democracy exists as a fledgling idea in our society. Its mission is to preach it, disseminate its spirit, and devote all its faculties so that democracy can one day be firmly established in the Republic.

The Association understands the obstacles it will encounter from several sources: aristocratic resistance, retrograde traditions, laws, and the lack of both knowledge and morality.

The Association knows that the organization of democracy cannot be accomplished in a day; that constitutions cannot be improvised; that liberty requires a solid foundation in knowledge and customs; that society cannot be enlightened and moralized at once; that the reason of all who aspire to be free needs to be nurtured. Having faith in the future, and

5. Esteban Echeverría, *The Socialist Program* (1838)

believing that the high aims of the revolution are not confined to demolishing the old order, but rather building a new one, it will concentrate all its efforts to provide the new generations with better tools to organize and establish Argentine society on the strong foundations of democratic equality and liberty.

6
FLORENTINO GONZÁLEZ

The Suffrage
(1871)

Florentino González (1805–1875) was one of the "founders" of classical liberalism in nineteenth-century Colombia.[1] *His early life was marked by the experience of independence since his family, close to the patriotic cause, was forced to move from their home by the loyalists when he was still a child. He completed his studies in jurisprudence in Bogota in 1825. As Gran Colombia tore apart, González participated in the plot to assassinate Bolívar in 1828, and subsequently suffered prison and exile. He was back in Bogota shortly after Bolívar's death and became actively involved in politics and journalism for the next two decades, when he held a succession of important posts, including elected member of Congress and State Secretary of Finance. Throughout his life, González also became notable for his intellectual production. In 1840, he published* Elementos de ciencia administrativa, *a two-volume treatise about public administration, a subject he then taught at the university in Bogota. He authored a significant number of essays, some of them in the newspapers he edited. González's life and work had a significant continental dimension. Appointed to a diplomatic mission that took him to Lima and Santiago de Chile, he resigned it in 1861 and remained in exile until the end of his life, first in Chile and later in Argentina. In Chile, he wrote on Andrés Bello's civil code and translated John Stuart Mill's* On Representative Government *(1864). In Argentina, he also translated the works of Frederick Grimke (*Ciencia y derecho constitucional. Naturaleza y tendencia de las instituciones libres, *1870), and*

[1] Selected passages from chapters XI and XII of Florentino González, *Lecciones de derecho constitucional*, 2nd edition (Paris, 1871), 107–125. (Editors' note)

6. Florentino González, The Suffrage (1871)

*Francis Lieber (*La libertad civil y el gobierno propio, *1872). He authored other works during his Argentine residence, including a tract on* El juicio por jurados, *his memoirs, published in the* Revista del Río de la Plata, *and his* Lecciones de derecho constitucional *(1869), the result of his lectures as the first Chair in Constitutional Law at the University of Buenos Aires.*

A good electoral system is undoubtedly one that can give popular opinion its due influence on government, understood in the widest sense, because that system can place the most able people in public positions. To the extent that the electoral system ensures complete liberty of suffrage to all individuals entrusted by society to elect officials in the various departments of government, that is the extent to which there will be confidence in the competent people who will exercise power. The majority that elect these officials will be on the receiving end of authority, and thus they are likely to support those individuals who inspire enough confidence to act for the good of the community.

A good electoral system is, therefore, one that most efficiently ensures the participation of the people in the election of public officials. It is a system that provides the means to ensure that the majority vote prevails, while at the same time it gives the minority the space to make itself heard. However, in order to establish the principles that will help us achieve such a system we need to ask some questions. Principally, what is the nature of suffrage?

If we are to follow what most political philosophers say, and include the laws that have been written in accordance with their ideas, suffrage is the right of a citizen to elect the individuals who will exercise the public power to govern the community.

Is this notion of suffrage correct?

No, it is certainly not.

There is no question that the ability to elect persons with the power to rule the nation only resides in the sovereign, which is the social body, meaning the entire people. If the sovereign, as defined by the constitution, gives the ability to elect only to some individuals who have certain qualifications, and not to the larger population, that sovereign entrusts those individuals with a public duty of the first magnitude in order to exercise power. It does not grant them a right that they can use as they wish, or according to their particular convenience. Suffrage is not an individual right, like property or liberty, which persons can use as they want, but

6. Florentino González, The Suffrage (1871)

rather a public duty. This is the duty that the citizen must assume, along with all other duties assigned by the constitution, in order to advance the best interests of the community. Should he not honor this charge, society will be left without government. This is the obvious consequence of not choosing the appropriate persons. One can conclude from this that suffrage is a duty that the citizen cannot refuse without a just cause. Once the citizen has been granted the ability to cast a vote, suffrage becomes truly and really a public duty. It cannot be considered a right, except in the sense that he who has this constitutional mandate has the right to call any public official to perform his duty.

Even though legislators have, up to the present day, declared suffrage to be a right, it would appear that they see it as something different from other rights. That might be the reason why the laws punish those who sell their vote, and take precautions so that the exercise of the franchise is always in the interest of the community, as is the case with any public employment. The laws regulate suffrage not in the interests of the individual, but for the good of the people. Suffrage, then, ought to be considered under the true light of a duty rather than as a right.

Elective governments, in order to meet the goals of the political community, must make certain that the election of officials is truly representative of the popular will. In this way, there will be at least the possibility that those called upon to assume public duties will have the necessary commitment to serving the interests of the community. The guarantee that this will happen depends on the interest of the electorate in choosing the appropriate persons, and the responsibility of the latter to serving the former. The larger the electorate, the more security there will be that the popular will is implemented, because it will be closer to the actual size of the population, and less likely to be distorted. Therefore, the best system is that which entrusts elections to all individuals capable of understanding the true interests of society.

Most political philosophers are clear about this, but differ on the qualities that demonstrate the abilities necessary to exercise the vote. Some say property proves the possession of such abilities, because owners of it are most likely to elect those who understand the importance of property. Others believe that it is the quality of intelligence that makes the electorate choose those individuals most likely to understand the importance of their duty.

There is no doubt that educated people should always be in charge of ruling. One could assume that an intelligent electorate will be inclined to

6. Florentino González, The Suffrage (1871)

elect those who possess an advanced level of education. One could furthermore assume that a certain degree of education should be required of those who exercise the vote. There should then be no need of property qualifications, because it is assumed that an individual who has a certain degree of instruction has, by the same token, some property, although there might be some exceptions to this rule. From this it could also be assumed, as a logical consequence, that suffrage should be extended to those who possess a degree of intellectual culture demonstrated, for example, by literacy. This view is held by many of the most enlightened statesmen.

> I regard it as wholly inadmissible, says Mr. [John Stuart] Mill,[2] that any person should participate in the suffrage without being able to read, write, and, I will add, perform the common operations of arithmetic. Justice demands, even when the suffrage does not depend on it, that the means of attaining these elementary requirements should be within the reach of every person, either gratuitously, or at an expense not exceeding what the poorest who earn their own living can afford. If this were really the case, people would no more think of giving the suffrage to a man who could not read, than of giving it to a child who could not speak; and it would not be society that would exclude him, but his own laziness. When society has not performed its duty, by rendering this amount of instruction accessible to all, there is some hardship in the case, but it is a hardship that ought to be borne. If society has neglected to discharge two solemn obligations, the more important and more fundamental of the two must be fulfilled first: universal teaching must precede universal enfranchisement. No one but those in whom an a priori theory has silenced common sense will maintain that power over others, over the whole community, should be imparted to people who have not acquired the commonest and most essential requisites for taking care of themselves; for pursuing intelligently their own interests, and those of the persons most nearly allied to them.

When this work on representative government was published, the Duke of Ayen criticized the views of Mill in a notable essay published by a prestigious journal in continental Europe.[3] There he presented solid arguments in favor of universal suffrage. Before him, the American Frederick Grimke, in his *Considerations Upon the Nature of Free Institutions* [1846],

---

[2] *On Representative Government*, chap. VIII.
[3] *Revue des Deux Mondes*, July 1863.

6. Florentino González, The Suffrage (1871)

presented many wise arguments in favor of the widest extension of the suffrage. I greatly respect the opinion of Mr. Mill, but I must say that the arguments of the French and American writers in favor of universal suffrage are more convincing than Mill's arguments to restrict it.

Mr. Mill has been the first to say that suffrage is a duty, not a right. He has also said that representative government is the ideal form of government because it can most efficiently cultivate the individual qualities that contribute to the intellectual, moral, and material progress of society. He has in addition demonstrated that free institutions are the most conducive means for the cultivation of such qualities. Of course, it is necessary that the individual participates actively in the work of free institutions in order to develop those qualities. Otherwise, the influence of free institutions will be so indirect and slow that it could hardly have an impact. Influence could only come from direct contact with those who take an active part in free institutions, but they will not always be disposed to share the benefits of education. It is quite possible that those who have the privilege will keep the right to vote to themselves, and be less than enthusiastic to extend it to those who do not have the means to acquire it. It is easy to say that society must provide them with the means, in the form of education. However, I do not think that this is the best solution; namely, that of providing the right to elect representatives only to those who have an education, because they will probably develop an interest in keeping those who do not have it in a state of ignorance, rather than providing them with the instruction that would enable them to vote.

If on the contrary the constitution establishes that suffrage is a duty that society entrusts to all adults able to care for themselves, without parents or tutors, to elect those who are to govern, and that this duty is mandatory, then every citizen will have a genuine understanding of suffrage, will be obligated to exercise it, and will appreciate its importance.

As Grimke has stated, individuals will thus acquire the habit of reflection, which will contribute not only to the citizens' appropriate performance of their political duties, but also to the good management of their private affairs. It is to this habit, acquired in the practice of free institutions, that Grimke attributes the superiority of his compatriots, compared to the rest of the world, in the performance of public and private affairs. This is the effect of universal suffrage, adopted in almost every State of the Union, because the qualifications required of the electorate are so few that nearly all possess them.

6. Florentino González, The Suffrage (1871)

The United States has been the stage of the most notable political experiments in the last eighty years. This is proof that it is not necessary to wait until education is widespread enough to give people the widest participation in public affairs. This participation makes them understand, in a short time, the need to expand education. The system of public schools, which is today ubiquitous in the entire Union, was limited, during the first fifty years of independence, to the states of New England, and others in the North and East. It was only later introduced in the Mid-Western, Southern, and Western states. The few educated inhabitants of these latter states, having experienced free institutions and having voted in municipal and national elections, acquired the habit of thinking about public matters. They realized that further education would help them to better manage public affairs. The experience of fifty years of free institutions made this rough population amenable to introducing educational improvements, because they had acquired the habit of appreciating the importance of education.[4]

Property has generally been seen as the most important qualification for suffrage. England insists on requiring it, although less emphatically than in the past. Initially, Great Britain summoned the representatives of the people only to vote on matters of taxation. Naturally, those who paid them constituted the electorate. Today, however, the representatives of the people have more to do than vote on taxes: They must address the concerns of the community, whatever they are. It is important, therefore, to grant participation in elections to all those who are interested in public issues. In this manner, all social classes will be represented – be they property owners or not – and the country will be governed according to the national will, considering the interests of all.

If property qualifications for suffrage cannot be required of the electorate for reasons that justified them in the past, and that the very nature of the democratic representative government is against these requisites, they could be justified on the grounds that they would encourage individuals to try to become property owners, which would be a good thing for society. Experience, however, has proven the contrary. On the basis of statistical data, Grimke has noted that wherever suffrage is restricted by

---

[4] Mr. Grimke makes some valuable comments on this point. I recommend them to students who wish to delve deeper into how participation in public affairs can enhance an individual's education.

6. Florentino González, *The Suffrage (1871)*

property, the number of property owners is actually smaller than in countries that do not require this qualification. This is an important practical reason, and in my view decisive, against the restriction.

It could be objected that if no educational qualifications are required of the electorate, there would be great inconveniences for the exercise of the franchise. But these inconveniences would disappear if the electorate was already educated.

The vote, it is said, should be either secret, in the form of a written ballot deposited in a box, or pronounced publicly.

If the voter is illiterate, he will not be able to vote secretly, or might need to ask someone else to deposit his written choice. This latter person might cheat him, casting the vote for another candidate. There is no guarantee, then, of an independent vote.

It should be noted that this objection is made by those who are already convinced that literacy qualifications should be mandatory, because they believe that this is the legitimate way of exercising the franchise. They get what they want, namely, that only the literate population votes in elections. However, illiterates still think about the importance of suffrage. Many will fully understand the advantage of writing down and casting the ballot themselves, with complete independence, and will seek to acquire the skills for it in the future. They will become interested in the establishment of schools, thus guaranteeing that society will see education as a duty. If people are barred from participation in elections, they will remain uninterested in public affairs, and will not seek the qualifications that would empower them. Society thus loses one of the great benefits of representative government – the education of the people.

When the vote is cast publicly, it makes no difference whether the voter is literate or not, as the choice is expressed aloud. Fraud can only come from those who hear the vote and write it down in the register. This can be avoided by taking the necessary precautions.

Government is established to care for the needs of everyone, including the educated and the uneducated. It is therefore important that they all participate in the election of public officials. Illiterates should vote, as the Duke of Ayen argues, if only to know what they say and want.

There are two scenarios that an elective government may face: 1) The great majority is literate, in which case there is no question that the majority must have an influence on elections; the illiterate minority is left to find other ways to be heard, which might play a role in majority decisions. 2) Only a minority have the literacy qualifications, in which case

6. Florentino González, The Suffrage (1871)

the majority could not be excluded without serious damage to both the representative system and the principle of popular sovereignty. Sovereignty resides in the political community, which manifests itself through the vote of the majority. If only literates are counted (although in the first case they would be the majority), illiterates will be deprived of a voice. In the second case, the constitution would be a true oligarchy, albeit in democratic dress.

All things considered, the best option to ensure that the elected officials are representative of all social classes is to extend the franchise to all able and self-sufficient adults, because they have reached an age when their reason and faculties have so fully developed as to act on their own, rather than under the tutelage of others.

It is true that the development of human faculties depends greatly on education. Individuals are considered to have reached their full development at age twenty-five, although education might lower that age. Taking this into account, qualifications for voting could vary, for instance by extending the franchise to individuals who, by the age of twenty, are fully literate. Those who are not must wait until the age of twenty-five.

The partisans of uniformity, who prefer that all members of society be placed on a level of equality, will probably dislike the notion of a differential age for voting. However, this objection does not make the idea any less rational or well-founded. What is natural and well-founded in the principle of popular sovereignty is that the active members of the community (meaning all those who are self-sufficient, and not under the control of parents or tutors) play a part in public affairs. If it is true that the qualifications needed to be considered as such vary according to the level of individual commitment, it is clear that there are many good reasons to establish a difference in terms of age.

Grimke has good reasons to say that one of the principal obstacles for the progress of the science of government is the complexity of political societies.[5] They make it difficult to generalize on the basis of particular cases. That is why it is not advisable to use a single system to organize the elements of a constitution, simply because they have had certain results in specific situations. They cannot be the basis for the establishment of general principles because the elements that make governments work reside in human beings and their faculties, and they vary as much as individual

---

[5] *The Nature and Tendency of Free Institutions*, book I, chap. I.

physiognomies do. One should not classify such elements according to the capacity for contributing to the goals of government. However, this does not mean that we should not make some distinctions. For instance, the one I made between the educated and the uneducated, which seems to me to identify the two great categories of the social body, and might lead us to productively analyze the elements that compose each of them.

In the current conditions, universal suffrage is the institution that can provide the most solid foundation for representative democracy. It could perhaps be corrupted or turned into an instrument for capturing power or territory, but in the long term the institution will demonstrate its vitality and efficiency for the safeguarding of liberty. It should, however, be true to its aim, namely, the election of those who will be temporarily entrusted with the exercise of power. To use it for plebiscites, which are presented for the approval of the people after the fact, giving voters no other alternative, is contrary to the very nature of suffrage. Such use of the franchise is as questionable as pure democracy. Suffrage is indisputably more apt, however, to elect those who represent public opinion, especially after what has just taken place in France: The imperial government had the electorate caught in a web of administrative rules and had powerful means to influence voters. And yet, voters made their voice heard in the last elections, and forced the author [Louis-Napoleon Bonaparte] of the coup on December 2 [1851] to end his personalistic government.[6]

There is one other question that is assuming increasing importance in the political world: Must suffrage be extended to women?

Suffrage can be considered a duty, or something else, but it is always the case that it is extended to an individual who is capable of expressing the general will and takes part in public affairs. If women are as capable as men (and of this there is no doubt), there is no reason to exclude them from participation in public affairs.

We need not go as far back as the times of Nineveh and Babylon to speak of Semiramis (who is most likely a myth). Modern history shows how women are endowed with the necessary genius, energy, and determination to rule political society with as much or greater ability as men. The reigns of Elizabeth, Anne, and the incomparable Victoria are among the most glorious in English history; Elizabeth and Catherine II are among

---

[6] On this matter I recommend the interesting article by M. A. Cochut published in the *Revue des Deux Mondes*, July 15, 1869.

6. Florentino González, The Suffrage (1871)

the ablest autocrats of Russia. All nations that do not have a Salic law have regarded women as capable of ruling. The Spanish government approved Columbus' project, and helped consolidate the sense of nationality, thanks to the ability and prudence of Isabella. Without her intelligent cooperation, Ferdinand of Aragon could have hardly been able to accomplish the latter endeavor of consolidation. It might be that another queen of the same name [Isabella II] has abused her power to push Spain back to the Middle Ages, and has driven the Spanish people to overthrow her, but this is not because she lacked the capacity to govern. It was rather because of the perverse instincts of the ominous dynasty to which she belongs that made her use power to do evil. Her uncle Carlos, or any of her cousins, would have done the same, or worse.

There is no doubt about the ability of women to address the concerns of society. There is even less doubt about their interest in such concerns, as can be seen in their commitment and service, inspired solely by sentiments of care, to the social institutions in which they participate. We can see many examples of the role they play in beneficent societies, as well as in sisters of charity organizations.

Mr. Mill believes that women who have certain qualifications ought to be extended the franchise, and he further believes that they can exercise it with as much skill as men. During the parliamentary reform discussions [Mill] argued strongly in favor of extending the suffrage to women. The Duke of Ayen thinks differently, but he offers no other reason than the convenience of keeping women in the private sphere, by exempting them from political responsibilities. I do not understand why the duke, after arguing in favor of extending the suffrage to all adult males on the grounds of the convenience of their participation in the representative system, would not extend it to women, who form one half of the population. Just like men, women have business and interests in society that must be acknowledged by the government. It is just and appropriate that they should have a role in the election of those who are to occupy positions of power.

7
JUSTO AROSEMENA

Constitutional Studies on the Governments of Latin America (1878)

Justo Arosemena (1817–1896), better known today as the "father of Panamanian nationalism," was one of the most notable constitutionalist jurists in nineteenth-century Spanish America.¹ He was born in Panama City, where he grew up, before moving first to Bogota and then to Cartagena to pursue his studies in jurisprudence, completed in 1837. In 1855, Arosemena published Estado Federal de Panamá *at a time when New Granada (Colombia today), of which Panama was part, was following a radical federalist trajectory – that year, he was elected as the first president of the Federal State of Panama. As a leading figure from one of the nine states that formed the Estados Unidos de Colombia in 1863, Arosemena's voice carried weight. But he earlier rose to national prominence through his various publications, including his* Apuntamientos para la introducción a las ciencias morales y políticas por un joven americano *(1840)*, Principios de moral política *(1849), and his work on the codification of Colombian legislation in the fields of civil and criminal law. Arosemena was a significant contributor to the constitutions adopted by the liberal regimes of the mid-nineteenth century – although a moderate, he presided over the deliberations of the assembly that issued the radical constitution of Rionegro in 1863. In the following years, he was appointed to several diplomatic*

---

¹ From Justo Arosemena, *Estudios constitucionales sobre los gobiernos de la América Latina*, 2 vols. (Paris, 1878). The editors of this volume use selections from the introduction, I, v–xxii, and from the conclusion, II, 504–513. (Editors' note)

7. Justo Arosemena, Constitutional Studies (1878)

posts to represent Colombia in the United States and in other Latin American countries – he supported regional integration, a theme he elaborated in his Estudio sobre la idea de una liga americana *(1864). His credentials as a constitutionalist of hemispheric dimensions were marked by the publication of his* Constituciones políticas de la América Meridional *(1870), expanded and reedited in 1878 as* Estudios constitucionales sobre los gobiernos de América Latina, *from which we have selected the passages for our volume.*

Politics considered as an art, namely, as the set of rules that organizes society and directs the government, has always been a subject of study and teaching. One could say that politics was born before science, if that was indeed a possibility in the processes of the mind. Science was still inchoate when, especially in the imagination of philosophers and public servants, plans were laid out for political organization and government.

There is no science without the demonstration of facts. Those of political science are complex, and many. It is not easy to observe them and then classify and explain them. That is why, for a long time, politics was not considered a science but rather the art of governing people. It is only in modern times that all arts have been shown to emerge from science. No legislative plan, or executive and judicial administration, could be conceived without a prior understanding of the nature of society, the way government is created, and the different forms and specialties that have an impact on the collective fate.

Many commentators believed themselves to be writing science when in fact they were only attempting to understand the art by using their imaginations, or their limited and confused knowledge of society, rather than relying on evidence to justify their conclusions. All socialists, from Plato to Fourier, belong to this group. Close to them are Aristotle, Thomas Aquinas, Bodin, Hobbes, Locke, and Montesquieu. They have examined the facts, but only partially, according to their individual inclinations, epoch, social relations, education, and interests. They have done a great service to science, clarifying some questions whose solution science was developing, and separating truth from error.

There are a few recent writers, like Tocqueville and [Richard] Hildreth, who have examined how facts, seen as a harmonious totality, can provide the basis for a rigorous political science. They have avoided preconceived notions on the origins of government, or the superiority of some types over others. Instead, they have patiently examined the facts related to the nature and effects of political institutions, extending their sharp focus to the study of human nature as well. However competent, the immensity of the subject has not permitted these thinkers to give us more than a preview of science. But they have opened a path that others can follow. Now scholars can apply the rigorous analysis found in one of the principal parts of *Democracy in America*, which expands on the brief comments made by the author of the *Theory of Politics*.

Art will not attain perfection until science pronounces the last word. However, science is still far from being fully formed: Its true foundations are just beginning to be established. This is the reason why modern nations get trapped into interminable debates when they seek to establish or change their constitutional laws. Also, the reason why France in 1789, and the new Spanish American republics, are constantly looking for treatises, or examples of successful governmental institutions, to cull political notions that, in the end, do not yield the expected results. They forget or are unaware of what science has been able to contribute. They get mired in a maze of ideal or imaginary politics, relying more on inspiration than on facts.

The principal and most serious mistake that sentimental politicians make is to build plans of social and governmental organization based on an imperfect understanding of human nature, incomplete knowledge of history, and disregard for the customs of the people to whom they address their essays. That is, they do not consult science, which consists precisely of these three elements.

The first steps in the government of society must have been instinctive, based exclusively on the natural tendencies of man. As a social being, he needed the preservation of society. Because he is also unjust due to either ignorance, or an unbalanced mind, the establishment of supreme reason, or justice, was necessary to prevail over individual instincts. Primitive contracts have been imagined justifying some conclusions about *political society*, and *government*. This is an entirely useless exercise, because the natural laws of the human mind can better explain such origins. Man could not have evolved or even lived without society. This social tendency is not the result of calculation, but rather of an irresistible instinct, as is the case with numerous other animals. Wherever there have been human beings, however savage, they have lived in some form of society. Today this is a well-established truth, although it was not always so.

In any group of individuals, there has always been a common regime, or government. It was initially in an embryonic patriarchal stage, but became more diversified and complex due to the expansion of learning,

7. Justo Arosemena, Constitutional Studies (1878)

wealth, and interests of all kinds. This original government was not preceded by a contract at all, based as it was on natural laws as compelling as those of society itself. The human mind has faculties or dispositions to either dominate or obey. These two elementary laws are the foundations of all government. There is a third inclination to oppose oppression, and that is the principle of liberty. The first two, by themselves, lead to an irremediable despotism.

All forms of government, division of powers, ideas of political balance, and even revolutions derive from the same primitive laws in association with mental faculties. As societies grew, so did inequality, which means domination by the wealthy. By then war had organized and trained military forces, created *caudillaje*,[2] and secured the predominance of valor and force. Religion emerged as well, bringing fanaticism, superstition, clericalism, and arrogance in the mediation between the Creator and his creatures.

In truth, instinct, sentiment, and all faculties of the human mind are laws active and influential in politics to different degrees. Science must make use of this foundation, helping to illuminate the controversial issues that occupy the philosophers who study this branch of human knowledge. "Mindology" [*mentología*] today is little more than an aspiration among phrenologists against the old dogma of the undivided individual self. Could political science exist without showing the same foundations as all the other social sciences? One cannot understand politics without considering the primitive laws of imperiousness, veneration, and self-esteem. In the same manner, one cannot have morality without acknowledging the sentiments underlying social relations, the human *will*, or the nature and malleability of all mental faculties.

Along with the laws of the mind, which vary depending upon race, the special characteristics (topography, climate) of each population contribute to the establishment of government. With the passage of time, myriad circumstances produce change and give a special character to the country and its government. Political evolution, and specialization, are subject to laws that history elucidates, and serve as sources for the scholar. Already by the time of Aristotle there were numerous constitutions for the philosopher to compare. They served him well to prepare his famous work, which we still admire: He classified governments, divisions of power, and

---

[2] This word derives from *caudillo*, or warlord who operates outside any consistent framework of law and institutions. (Editors' note)

other abstract ideas. However, we also see with regret that he shared the prejudices of his time: the acceptance of slavery, and the contempt for industry.

One cause of delay in the development of a science of politics is the inclination on the part of some practitioners to observe phenomena through the deceptive lens of their individual perspectives, or the circumstances that surround them. If it is true that a historian should have no country, religion, or trade, the political scholar should be an eminent person; have a well-developed mind, neither too excessive nor deficient; have experience observing the customs and laws of different peoples; have a free and just conscience, and a spirit free of prejudice, so as to serve only the truth. At any rate, it is necessary to pay attention to the students of politics, even if they do not have all these qualities.

It is the history of government in general that concerns us here, with due consideration of place and time. We will scrutinize the writings that study the science of experimental politics, as opposed to sentimental exhortations that do not consider the past and its lessons. In particular, those of Aristotle and Cicero in Greek and Latin antiquity, respectively, Bodin in the early modern age, Auguste Comte, Guizot, Stuart Mill, Laboulaye, and many others in our day, who have made numerous and valuable contributions to the science of sciences.

Man is both actor and spectator in the great theater of politics. As an actor, he exercises or resists domination; participates in government or follows its policies; and prevents or supports revolutions. As a spectator, he observes how mental faculties influence public affairs in the development of societies; studies the creation of governments, their nature, the way they change, and the prosperity or decadence of society. This dual character presents an obstacle to the scholar. If he could only observe and present the facts of history, he would proceed just like a scientist who studies any of the physical sciences impartially, that is, detached from the subject of observation. He cannot produce facts at will, except in a very limited fashion, and in most cases not at all. He is not responsible for even the facts he could produce, unless they fall into the area of morality. That is not the case of the politician when, presenting the laws of his field, he assesses general results; praises or condemns human conduct; highlights or belittles the actions of both government and the governed, and influences how they proceed. The spectator we have mentioned is influenced by the same actors he brings to the stage, and in turn influences the actors who follow his script.

7. Justo Arosemena, Constitutional Studies (1878)

Apart from ephemeral screeds published during times of unrest that fire the passions of parties and incite persecutions on one side, and revolutions on the other, some books have been written for all times. They slowly shape profound convictions and bring out passions to the degree that they fuel repression, or drive individuals into resistance or rebellion. That is how Rousseau's *Social Contract* exaggerated democracy, Hobbes' *Leviathan* flattered despotism, and Machiavelli's *Prince* corrupted heads of state.

This political literature has certainly not created a new instinct or sentiment that was not already present in the human mind. They could, given the circumstances, produce analogous results. Imperiousness can push patient veneration to limits determined by self-esteem. The latter, especially in Asia, is condemned to an interminable night of abject despondence. In the same manner, following a law that applies to both political and physical science, human beings anywhere who feel the sting of personal dignity, or invoke the joys of a liberty once lost, will throw themselves into the perilous path of revolutionary salvation.

A most difficult problem is that of the reason, right, opportunity, and justification for a violent political revolution. They all receive some support, or rejection, depending on individual perspectives. History tells us loudly and clearly that they all cost enormous sacrifices. That they all conquer a space for liberty and rights, or eliminate a restriction or abuse, is something unquestionable if we impartially examine their antecedents and consequences. However, at what point is it justifiable to stir the natural sentiments that trigger these revolutions? How can we measure and weigh, beforehand, the sacrifices and gains, the costs and the benefits of a political cataclysm? It is true that nothing can stop a reaction that has been set in motion by centuries of oppression, just like it is impossible to identify its immediate cause. It is in the most common cases, those of day-to-day politics, that the difficulty increases. In such cases neither prudence can be so extreme, nor moderation too excessive, if it manages to avert the horrors of a fratricidal war, whereby the benefits can be as easily measured as in a commercial transaction. Political passion is always inclined to exaggerate the magnitude of the gains, especially when the future consequences cannot be seen clearly. In such cases, the political spectator must help the fanatical actor, save him from himself, as well as society from unnecessary pain.

When society has reached a certain degree of civilization, there is much that can be done to advance the cause of various peoples through the enlightened means at their disposal, to show in a calm and timely way the dangers that are intrinsic to situations of tension. Such is the harmony of social interests: No one needs to sacrifice anything when justice is delivered to all. This is the harmony that, by exposing the blindness and error of abusive interests, can make the universal and justifiable interests to prevail. What must never be accepted is the sacrifice of individual rights, which are the very conditions for the life and development of human beings. Such rights must be elevated from a weak aspiration to the rank of guarantees. This is the reasonable objective of the laws that must be implemented by the *government*. The entire edifice of politics rests on the need to materialize the rights that nature has given us as an essential condition of our being.

One of the most notable revolutions of the modern age is the independence of the American continent from Spain and Portugal. Inspired by a notion of rights, stimulated by the example of British America, and seizing the opportunity provided by the situation of peninsular Spain at the beginning of the [nineteenth] century, Spanish America embarked on a struggle that in fifteen years broke the bonds that tied the continent to a dark, despotic, and stagnant past. Once in control, and after the efforts and sacrifices of that great war, the no less difficult task of creating a new political organization began. It was entrusted to the very offspring of those Spaniards who knew nothing better than their colonial system.

To fully appreciate the demands of the new situation, one should start by considering the Spanish conquest of the New World. Many of the observations are applicable to Portugal and its main colony in the region.

Shortly after Spain placed its flag on the Alhambra, Columbus gave the monarchs evidence of the existence of a rich land, which his genius had discovered for the benefit of the emerging monarchy.

After the conquest of Granada, a swarm of ignorant adventurers, greedy entrepreneurs, and fanatics were idle. It was only natural that they would want to go to the new sources of gold and silver, where precious metals were in the hands of *infidels*. The latter were looked upon as inferior beings and, therefore, as enslaved people. History tells us how the conquistadors treated the Indigenous peoples: They dispossessed them first, and then enslaved them, oppressing and offending them from then on. Inspired by Christian rulers, the Spanish legislation did not condone the harsh treatment imposed on the Indigenous peoples. But the law was only exceptionally applied, and was in addition implemented selectively by greedy and cruel agents, very much in the spirit of the first conquistadors.

7. Justo Arosemena, Constitutional Studies (1878)

The conscience of the invaders was satisfied with the propagation, not of morality, but of their Christian dogmas and rites. It was enough for them that the frightened natives proclaimed their faith in the Catholic, apostolic, and Roman religion of the Spaniards. It did not matter that they pillaged and killed the Indigenous peoples for as long as they saved their souls. That is how the Conquest reconciled greed, ferocity, and fanaticism with the interest in bringing together the two races. Another strange reconciliation, but not atypical of the times, was advanced by Fr. Bartolomé de Las Casas. Out of compassion for the *Indians* who died working in the mines, he recommended the introduction of enslaved people from Africa. From here emerged an active trade conducted in conjunction with the British and the Dutch. But the relief for the Indigenous people was only partial, because they were distributed by the thousands in *encomiendas*[3] to work as serfs.

Soon, there was an important change in the composition of the European race in Ibero-American society. The criollos, or descendants of Europeans, saw the land of their birth as their *patria*, while the Spanish and Portuguese often saw it as the place where they could make their fortunes and then return to their native land. Many of the peninsular Spaniards who came to the New World were often ignorant men who were placed very low in the social scale of the metropolis. But their Spanish American descendants received some education, both because of the natural tendency to progress, and the better financial situation of their parents.

The various races, and their mix, did not get along. What they had in common was superstition and a lack of interest in industry. They established themselves in a huge area of habitable land, well irrigated, separated by mountains, fertile, rich in minerals, and hospitable to the penniless. The Conquest was brief, followed by a colonization that, due to its vicious origin, was not conducive to the creation of a truly industrious society, or a fraternal spirit, sense of justice, elevation of the soul, or dignity that could have rejected oppression and inspired a desire for individual and political liberty.

---

[3] Simon Collier offers a simple definition: "it was a grant of a number of Indians to a Spanish settler, who was expected to Christianize and civilize his charges, and in return to exact labor services or tribute from them"; From *Cortés to Castro: An introduction to the History of Latin America, 1492–1973* (London, 1974), 107. (Editors' note)

7. Justo Arosemena, Constitutional Studies (1878)

It followed that the colonies of Spain and Portugal were governed according to the dominant ideas of their respective metropolises. In addition to being homogeneous, they were characterized by an official church, an arrogant clergy, religious intolerance, hatred and persecution of anything foreign; a preference for ephemeral enterprises rather than stable industry; centralized administration, corrupt employment practices, authoritarian government without a trace of popular participation; slow, expensive, and prejudiced justice plagued with useless procedures; a severe and even cruel penal system; and, lastly, industrial restrictions and monopolies, in addition to numerous, inequitable, and abusive taxes.

Once transferred to the New World, the political systems of Spain and Portugal had to adjust to the new circumstances. The immigrant population was ignorant, but audacious and enterprising; however poor, it was representative of the great majority. That is how the foundations of democracy were established, countered weakly by an imported aristocracy. This aristocracy was small, experiencing great changes in a world where landownership meant little, and where public office was not necessarily their birthright. In addition, the colonies did not have to suffer militarism or the presence of large permanent armies, as they did after independence.

However, many of the vices of peninsular administration were exacerbated in the New World, in part because of distance and the immensity of the territory, which impeded a thorough knowledge of the localities and their needs. In part, also, because of the wealth of the colonies, which the metropolis wanted for itself, and the alleged inferiority of the races that made up the majority of the population. The laws of the Indies, as well as numerous licenses, ordinances, resolutions, and regulations issued for the government of the colonies (mostly municipal) showed a deplorable ignorance about the character and needs of the larger population. It would have been impossible to correct these blunders without changing the entire system of political organization, or without decentralizing a colonial government which, in legislative matters, rested on the monarch and his immediate advisors.

There were other vices that increased greatly in the New World. Social inequality, which in the metropolis was based on lineage and depended more on laws than on custom, in the Indies was based on race. Already lacking in unity, race was regarded in different ways by the dominators. There were laws that protected both Indigenous peoples and free people of color. However, both Spaniards and Portuguese had nothing but contempt for them, making legal protections meaningless. What was most hateful, and became a powerful influence on the independence of the colonies, was the systematic exclusion of the criollos (who actually wanted to avoid independence) from nearly all public positions of importance. This exclusion was not based on any law, but on the discretion of the rulers, which is greater in a semi-absolutist monarchy than in any other form of government.

The system of education and public instruction was even more defective than in the metropolis. Higher education was controlled by the government, and consisted of some elements of psychology, theology and canonical studies, and civil law (Roman and Spanish). Most sciences, but especially political economy, as well as constitutional and international law, inspired serious alarm among the rulers of the Ibero-American world, who thought that they could obstruct the course of the natural and eternal laws of politics, in the same manner that Joshua once obstructed the laws of the planetary system. Primary education was limited to basic skills taught in a few private schools funded by wealthy parents. Even so, more than a few Spanish Americans were educated in Europe, or even in the New World (despite many obstacles), thus achieving a higher level of enlightenment. They cultivated their minds by reading the few books that eluded censorship.

One of the areas of social activity where the metropolis displayed a considerable myopia was commerce. Trade with other nations was strictly prohibited, and capital punishment was meted out to foreigners who came to our shores without permission. Some peninsular ports reexported products from Great Britain, France, and Italy as if they were national, and then sold them at inflated prices. In return, Latin America exported goods necessary for manufactures that the region was not allowed to produce locally. Several articles, like tobacco, salt, liquor, gunpowder, and playing cards were government monopolies, providing one of the main sources of revenue.

In addition, taxes were applied to merchandise, contracts, Indigenous tribute, government-stamped paper, and several other items that impacted production, transport, and consumption of the few colonial products, as well as the imports controlled by privileged commercial agents. They were all indirect, and in violation of sound economic doctrines that were scarcely known even in nations more advanced than Spain and Portugal.

Those Spanish Americans who acquired an education, despite many obstacles, concluded that they should neither be condemned to endure

7. Justo Arosemena, Constitutional Studies (1878)

in perpetuity the absurd colonial system, nor expect anything from their authorities. However, to shake off their yoke and replace it with a progressive government based on the rule of law was a titanic task. Some impatient spirits took some premature steps, causing the alarm and suspicion of the authorities.

The events of 1808 in the peninsula determined the timing of an independence that had already been conceived in philosophical terms. Once Napoleon invaded Spain and Portugal, the latter's court had the good sense to escape to the New World, thus avoiding humiliation and a possible civil war. Much less smart was the court of Madrid, which, ignoring the advice of the Prince of the Peace [Manuel Godoy], trusted the great conqueror of modern times [Napoleon]. The crown was made captive without a fight, abandoned its vast territories, and provided the opportunity for the establishment of provisional governments in Spain. The colonies followed the model of these governments, placing power in the hands of creoles, thus raising awareness of their aptitudes, and offering the means to secure their rights.

Even though the colonies claimed to govern in the name of Ferdinand, Spaniards rejected the transfer of authority. They immediately took up arms, thus beginning the war between father and son even before the war between Spanish Americans and peninsulars started. Old hatreds confronted each other. The arrogance of the oppressor ignored the just aspirations and the dignity of the oppressed. Anticipating the direction of the colonial movement, and protecting the rights of their master, Spaniards did not wait for the approval of the captive king to wage war against the colonial innovators.

After Ferdinand VII was restored to the throne, war became a recognized reality: Colonials no longer had a reason or even a pretext to delay the open manifestation of their true intent. Spanish America became independent after fifteen years of hard and bloody struggle. Power was now in the hands of the natives. They had removed the few aristocratic groups that sided with the metropolis. *Royalist* ferocity unleashed a most profound hatred of the monarchy, which no longer had a place, or roots, in Spanish America. The republican model emerged spontaneously from this situation. Democracy saw the end of its powerful enemies. However, a new foe appeared before the fires of combat were extinguished, which would present a formidable obstacle to the definitive organization of the new societies. An assortment of warlords cynically invoked liberty, which they credited to themselves, but this was in fact an insulting claim.

7. Justo Arosemena, Constitutional Studies (1878)

The most bastard ambitions occupied the place of legitimate aspirations. Thus, the establishment of republican democracy and the rule of law were delayed. Be that as it may, nations still emerged from the former colonies. They tried to organize themselves from the moment they assumed a political identity. There is still agitation in that open field of influences and opinions, making it hard to predict when the period of experimentation will end.

The problem of organization facing the Spanish American heads of state was quite complicated. On the one hand, the abstract science of politics could have revealed to them the nature of the mind as well as the general lessons taught by the history of government. On the other hand, the practical science of politics showed them a present born from both colonialism and the bloodbath of revolution, providing them with the means to modify the principles derived from the abstract science of politics. The latter can be studied like zoology, chemistry, or botany. Political reality, however, contains such diverse, and even opposite, elements that no one can claim to know it in depth.

Therefore, we should not be surprised about the instability of constitutional principles in Spanish America. I refer to those who have only followed the abstract theories of writers who in turn followed their own imaginations; those who imitated the institutions of other countries without considering their applicability to our own; and those who created original systems based on the belief in political perfectibility. These various attempts have ignored the two most important forces at play: colonialism and revolution. Reality provided both a basis and an obstacle. As a basis, it gave facts the attention they require in light of a long and complex history. The obstacle should have been removed in the name of progress. But how, and under what conditions? Many assumed, and this was their mistake, that one could change institutions and customs as one could change clothes. And yet, even fashion evolves slowly, sometimes taking centuries. The revolution, for its part, destroyed the institutions that opposed its path or provoked its fury. There is nothing more difficult than reconciling the past with a new situation that announces and makes inroads into the future. British Americans solved the problem. That is not the case in Spanish America.

A country may adopt a form of government, but this does not mean that it is thereby fully organized. Between 1791 and 1852, France adopted fifteen constitutions but has not succeeded in consolidating a system. The current one is fifteen years old [as of 1867], but it is still considered transitional. For a constitution to be regarded as the political system of a country it must be firmly based on customs and have roots in each individual spirit; it must inspire the love of the citizenry; it must be defended by everyone as if it were their property and the guarantee of their protection, and, in sum, be identified with love of country. The ephemeral rules that each revolution has dictated in Spanish America are only a reflection of the actions of those who have assumed power by trampling on the rights of everyone else, and drowning the national will in blood. They might invoke popular sovereignty, but they are only imposing its mortal enemy, the sovereignty of the sword. Therefore, to confirm that a state is properly constituted, it is necessary to establish whether its political institutions are a reflection of society, and whether they are sustained by the free will of the citizenry. Also, whether they contain the fundamental principles that are acclaimed, professed, and ardently defended by those who obey them. This is the only system that forms the true political constitution of a state.

A country that has endured strong commotions for many years; a country that has faced hard and bloody situations in order to destroy, if not an entire past, at least its foundations and reason for being, cannot and probably will not find the definitive formula for political organization. It might in the future, after many attempts, when a system is produced with sincerity and with more knowledge of complexity; when it does not seek to impose the will of the triumphant party, or when, as the genuine expression of the popular will, it is better equipped to understand the interests of the population. This is the aspiration of all honest people in Spanish America, even if the fate of each country differs substantially from the other.

In any case, the political institutions of Spanish America are worthy of study. I have examined ten states, namely, Brazil, Paraguay, Argentina, Uruguay, Chile, Bolivia, Peru, Ecuador, Colombia, and Venezuela.[4] I have gathered, not without effort, their current constitutions, and commented on them according to the current standards of science. Two objectives have guided my inquiry: First, to apply a political criterion for the understanding of the various materials that illustrate the still

---

[4] Arosemena seems to have left unchanged his introduction to the second edition of his work (which we are using here), because he had added six more countries to his examination in the second edition: Mexico, Guatemala, Salvador, Nicaragua, Costa Rica, and Haiti. (Editors' note)

contested principles of science. Second, to compare these diverse materials to identify the discrepancies in opinions and goals. Spanish America appears destined to union, though not under a single government, or even a league of nations for offensive or defensive purposes. It will be more of a union through trade, letters, international law, and legislation. It could be extended to political institutions, to the degree that this is acceptable to the particular characteristics of each state. There is reason to believe that Mexico and Central America will follow a different path, given the geographic distances that separate them from the regions to the south. Still, why not consider that a citizen of one country could well be the citizen of all? Could they not share some political principles such as the naturalization of foreigners, individual rights, political liberties, and the same organization of governmental powers?

Today, Spanish American countries with common borders barely know each other. The chorography, history, literature, and the institutions of each country are practically unknown to the others. Let us try to bring them closer together so that they study, understand, love one another, and *unite* in one fraternal embrace. They should come together to combat the enemies of humankind, along with error and injustice.

Conclusion

When we consider the similarities in Spanish America at the time of independence, both in terms of antecedents and current situation, we might conclude that the natural political evolution, and its institutions, should have followed the same path. However, the constitutions of the various states differ considerably. In fact, if we exclude the two extremes of the spectrum – Russian autocracy and Swiss republicanism – all political forms have been present in Latin America, from moderate monarchy in Brazil, to exaggerated republicanism in Colombia. This is the result of ignoring evolution, following instead theories based on the imagination of politicians who are strangers to a science that, we must admit, is still in the process of formation.

What results have the Latin American states obtained from their institutions? With the exception of Brazil and Chile, none has accomplished, and many are far from it, the great combination of liberty and order. The Republic of Argentina is probably closer to this enviable situation.

Some special factors favored the organization of Brazil: Independence was more of a son's farewell to his supportive parents, than the obstinate

7. Justo Arosemena, Constitutional Studies (1878)

opposition of a robust but bad-mannered young man who violently breaks away from parental control. A liberal monarchy was established so easily in Brazil that it is hard to see where, or how, opposition to it would have emerged. There was no war of independence leading to disorder. The Portuguese character, in addition, though analogous, is not the same as the Spanish character.

The fate of the Spanish American countries was very different. The hereditary transmission of certain qualities among individuals and races has been mentioned before, but it is only today that it has been studied in depth, as science has demonstrated the nature and extent of the inheritance. Consequently, to say that the descendants of peninsular Spaniards share some of the same mental traits is to say nothing new. However, it is true that just a few years ago hereditary transmission was viewed as little more than a metaphor, while today the phenomenon is examined in a rigorously scientific way.

The Spanish American population, then, has the characteristics of the Spanish race, plus those of the Indigenous and African races. Some individuals (certainly the majority) descend from two or all three of these races. We will not attempt, nor could we competently do so, to conduct an ethnological study of these races. For our current purposes, it will be sufficient to call attention to their most distinctive characteristics for sociology, and government.

When considered together, the most salient characteristics of these races are the prevalence of sentiment over reason, and of imagination over the study of facts. Hence the vindictive, warlike, and contentious spirit; the intolerance, sophistry, and inclination to fraud. In short, if we examine their degree of civilization in relation to mentality,[5] the Iberian race, and even more the Spanish American, are behind other European races.

Let us recall how Spanish American independence was accomplished, the long war to the death, and the hatreds that developed between peninsulars and colonials. The war had two fatal effects for peace and the rule of law: First, the victory of the rebels against the government; second, the animosities between the contending parties did not disappear – they simply adjusted to new situations. Once the original legitimacy was lost, and the principle was established that a victory in war inaugurated a new

---

[5] I mean this term in the broadest sense, namely, as encompassing all mental faculties, including intellectual faculties.

legitimacy, military *caudillos*, driven by ambition and knowledge of the roads to power, made no difference between the old government and the new. They turned against the latter just as they had done against the former, confirming the French saying "c'est le premier pas qui coûte" [it is only the first step that costs]. Hardened by disrespect for law and government, insurrections multiplied, passing the contagion from the military to the larger population. Willingly or unwillingly, society was militarized.

Lacking enough time to establish themselves in order to protect liberty, the new independent governments resorted to all forms of violence, provoking new insurrections that served as the cause or pretext for endless conflict. This is the vicious circle in which the new Spanish American republics consume their energies. It could be argued that not all countries needed to wage a war of independence, because they already faced internal revolts. I will respond by saying that only Central America and Paraguay belong in that category. Both went through the break with colonialism. The former had the bad examples of Mexico and Colombia, while the latter, exceptional because of its isolation, escaped the contagion of anarchy only to fall into the most degrading despotism.

British Americans also fought a war of independence against Great Britain, but they did not acquire the nefarious habit of rebelling against the government. Here I confirm the principle of race and political education under colonialism. Anglo-Saxons do not embrace passion over reasoning, as Spanish Americans do. Nor were they in the lamentable state of political education in which the descendants of Iberians found themselves. On the contrary, those who left Great Britain were precisely those who disagreed with the politics and religion of the metropolis. Compared to Spain, Great Britain was far more advanced on matters of liberty and order, thus providing the strongest base for the creation of a true and vast republic which admirably combines liberty and order.

Brazil has done better than the Spanish American republics in achieving the proper balance between order and liberty, regardless of its form of government.[6] Chile, like other republics, endured a period of disturbances, but enjoys special circumstances that facilitate the work of government with respect to order. Once order is fully established, and barring an unpropitious climate, the seeds of liberty will flourish.

---

[6] Slavery is still a stain on the empire, but it will be gradually abolished, following the law of 1872.

7. Justo Arosemena, Constitutional Studies (1878)

The Argentine Republic, though not formally organized until much later than Chile, has made great progress toward political civilization.

These two republics have factors conducive to civilization: climate, which not only has an influence on passions (compared to the tropical regions) but also attracts a European population that improves the local in matters political, moral, and industrial. In any case, these two republics are in a better position than the rest, although I speak more from the wish that they reach a higher stage in the not-too-distant future, than from actual evidence.

My main point is that the political situation of these republics, despite their many different institutions, is very similar. This demonstrates that if the written constitutions do not adjust to the social situation their function will be compromised. Such constitutions, which the British call *paper* constitutions, produce effects unintended by their authors. They have the fate of all inadequate laws, namely, noncompliance.

Once the constitution adjusts to the social situation, it must avoid clauses that facilitate arbitrariness and disorder. In this respect, as in all secondary legislation, Bentham's maxim concerning the need to prevent crimes is applicable ["To avoid furnishing encouragement to crimes"]. Examples are those clauses that authorize the use of extraordinary faculties, or those that, after creating a powerful executive, organize elections in such a way that electoral struggles become battlefields.

Lately, we have identified principles and powers that induce the most deplorable abuses. That is why they should be established with the utmost parsimony, and all due precautions. Here we include the corrupt practice of firing public employees, and the granting of amnesties for political crimes that have been virtually erased from the penal code. Some of them are savage attempts against persons and property that leave a trail of desolation and ruin.

In truth, there is no constitutional article free of potential abuse, nor any constitution that can fully protect the population, if political morality is not profound enough to become the supreme rule of conduct. Let us not forget that moral sanction is the manifestation of uniform, correct, and rigorous public opinion. Clever constitutional experiments that are not supported by a public opinion of such characteristics are like the machines invented to achieve perpetual motion. That is, the power of motion, in physics as in morality, has to come from outside. That is why it is so difficult, not to say impossible, to provide for one's education without assistance. Likewise, it is difficult to achieve progress in morality and public affairs in the Spanish American republics when passion obstructs the emergence of an impartial and mentoring public opinion. A party that approves whatever followers say, and attacks adversaries without examination and proper judgment, is incapable of fomenting an impartial public opinion.

Related as they are, the sciences, especially those that belong to the same order, encounter morality in all discussions on politics. In fact, any comment on the constitution of a country would be incomplete without showing how the absence of political morality can frustrate the aims of institutions that depend on it. Governments could be placed in one of the following politico-moral stages:

1st. Laws are not obeyed. They are, therefore, hypocritical or impotent because they lack the support of public opinion. This situation results from either the negligence or moral lassitude that characterizes despotism, or the proliferation of races and factions that prevent the formation of a uniform national opinion on the few matters that concern everyone without distinctions.

2nd. Laws are obeyed in the abstract, but when they challenge the interests of parties or factions they are twisted in such a way as to favor the dominant interests, or they are openly violated on the grounds of higher necessity, or they are fraudulently evaded while faking compliance.

3rd. The law applies in the vast political space covered by public administration, but there is great freedom of action. The letter of the law is observed, but clumsily or in order to favor individuals, businesses, factions, parties, or localities, thus sacrificing the common interest.

The Latin American states have already left the first stage, except for the observance of laws that are difficult to implement, or have been superseded by popular custom. These states are currently immersed in the other two stages, although in different degrees depending on their respective situations. I will not enter into this discussion now, but I will make a general observation, and express my fervent desire to see the different countries take the only sound road for both individuals and nations – the path of morality, agreed upon beforehand, practiced without hesitation, and imposed on all destabilizing inclinations or interests.

Unfortunately, this is not a matter that can be solved by a simple wish. The stairs of civilization must be climbed step by step: Even a well-intended impatience will not accelerate the ascent. Happy are those countries that have already overcome stagnation, and perhaps even conquest from abroad! Will the tropical regions suffer the same fate as similar regions in the Old World? When I contemplate such an unfortunate scenario, my spirit darkens and my heart is oppressed. May God allow us to see, before our eyes are closed for eternity, some incontrovertible facts that will drive our sad thoughts away.

Part III.
Church, State, and Religion

8
VICENTE ROCAFUERTE

On Religious Toleration
(1831)

Vicente Rocafuerte (1783–1847) was born in Guayaquil, in today's Ecuador.[1] Educated in Spain and France, he entered politics early, serving first in his native land as a local magistrate. While in Europe (since 1812) he was elected as one of the Spanish American representatives to the Spanish Cortes. In Madrid in 1814 he witnessed the demise of the parliament after the restoration of Ferdinand VII, devoting himself from then on to the service of some of the emerging nations of Spanish America. As an advocate of republicanism, he opposed the Mexican empire of Agustín de Iturbide and served as Mexico's representative in Great Britain and Europe. Back in Guayaquil in 1833, he opposed the regime of Juan José Flores, becoming president of Ecuador between 1835 and 1839, and serving later as president of the Senate. He died in Lima in 1847, while on a diplomatic mission to Peru. The current selection was written while in Mexico in 1830 and represents one of the earliest Spanish American arguments for religious toleration. Rocafuerte was by no means an atheist but opposed the establishment of an official religion for the emerging states.

In many parts of the American continent, winter begins on June 21; on that very day, summer begins in Europe: The seasons are reversed. Could this difference, so clear in the physical world, be seen in the moral world? Let us compare what we see beyond the Pillars of Hercules with our own

---

[1] This translation is based on a reprint of Rocafuerte's *Ensayo sobre la tolerancia religiosa* (Mexico City, 1831). The editors use selections from the introduction. (Editors' note)

8. Vicente Rocafuerte, On Religious Toleration (1831)

situation. The rebirth of the arts and sciences in Italy fostered a spirit of inquiry, doubt, and analysis that the Germans applied to uncover the abuses of the Roman Church. That is how freedom of thought came about, which in turn led to political liberty. We have followed exactly the opposite path. We have first established political liberty, which should lead to religious toleration. Let us hope that, by different means, we will arrive at the same stage of civilization as the Europeans. The federal system we have adopted [in Mexico] will help emancipate our minds from the Gothic education we have inherited.[2] It will also spread the ideas of independence of thought, as well as examine and remove the errors that surround the truth. Everything leads to unity in our century, which justly merits the name of the positive century. Everything is discussed in our parliaments. Everything leads us to identify the facts, prevent abuses, and improve our social existence. This is how human reason is gradually developed by the progress of civilization, which is constantly fighting superstition and despotism. Superstition corrupts man by turning error into truth; despotism degrades him by shackling him with chains and misfortunes.

Just as fanaticism and tyranny are connected, so are liberalism and religious toleration. After we threw off the Spanish yoke, we were no longer enslaved people. However, we have not yet learned to be free. Nor will we ever be free without virtue and good customs. Such is my objective here. I consider religious toleration as the most efficient means to achieve this aim. I know very well that many of my compatriots, who are wise and virtuous, and as patriotic as I am, do not believe that public opinion is sufficiently informed, or that enlightenment is sufficiently spread, to promote this cause and to present sublime Christianity under the light of divinely inspired toleration. Only an excess of timidity that borders on indifference to public morality could keep silent on the crucial question of religious freedom. The principle of toleration is a logical consequence of our system of political liberty. Hence, it is not in anyone's hands to obstruct or contradict it, because it comes from the very nature of our institutions. Would it not be prudent, then, to prepare ourselves for this inevitable change? After ten years of independence [in 1821], and several experiments in political liberty, we are still unable to address the issue of religious toleration. How much longer will we wait to address this most

---

[2] His reference to the "federal system" was surely about the Mexican Constitution of 1824. (Editors' note)

8. Vicente Rocafuerte, On Religious Toleration (1831)

important problem? Let us discuss it with the calm that is required, with the spirit of truth, benevolence, and charity that Christianity expects, and the ghosts that haunt us will vanish. Some twenty years ago, when I declared myself in favor of independence, my friends and relatives thought I was insane. Furthermore, they said that I would not see the fulfillment of that project in my lifetime. And yet, time has shown that the principle of independence triumphed. So will the principle of religious toleration. Let us now plant the seeds that in forty or fifty years will yield the fruits of virtue and morality. Time will do the rest, by improving public education, shedding light on the darkness of error, revealing the truth, and proclaiming the following axiom: "political liberty, religious freedom, and commercial liberty are the three main elements of modern civilization. They form the pedestal that sustains our national glory. Standing by it, people will enjoy peace, virtue, industry, commerce, and prosperity."

I know very well that an emerging country should not introduce innovations that are not supported by public opinion as well as favorable circumstances. To replace old practices with new ones, however infinitely superior they might be, is to provoke resistance to reform and mobilize the ignorance that provides the basis for prejudice. The introduction of any political or religious reform requires prudence: To ensure success, the ground must be prepared so that everyone is convinced, persuaded, and well-informed. This is my hope and my motivation in promoting and establishing religious toleration in the future. Now, because of the power of superstition and ignorance, we are unable to enjoy the priceless benefits that it brings. The doctrine of toleration can be traced to the early Christians persecuted by the pagans, as well as the Jews and Muslims during the times of Ferdinand and Isabella. This is the doctrine that both enlightenment and civilization demand today. The first martyrs showed the injustice of their persecution, because their new religion had no connections with politics. They demonstrated that the former is concerned with heaven, and the latter with earthly matters. Both must be independent from each other; the distance between them must be comparable to the distance between the universe and our planet. They insisted on the divorce between religion and the state when they declared – and insisted – that the kingdom of Our Lord Jesus Christ is not of this world. For as long as they paid their taxes as citizens, and gave to Caesar what belonged to Caesar, civil authorities had no right to interfere with the free exercise of their religion. This sublime truth, obscured later by ignorance and the length of the barbarian centuries, has returned much stronger in our times. It is the new triumph of the enlightenment in our century. The separation of religion and state improves public morality and facilitates social prosperity. It adapts admirably well to the physical and moral constitution of man, and it gives Christianity itself a proof of its sublime origin. Because these are abstract ideas that require some explanation, I will seek help from the philosophy of [Victor] Cousin to present them in a clear and organized fashion.[3]

The Industrial World

When man is exposed to heat, cold, insalubrious swamps, lightning storms, earthquakes, tigers, venomous snakes, and wild animals, he finds himself in a hostile foreign world. The laws and phenomena of such a world appear to conspire against his existence and to contradict his very nature. If he is still standing, if he lives and breathes for more than two minutes, it is because he can understand such phenomena and laws. He would be destroyed unless he learned how to study, observe, measure, and calculate these phenomena and laws. He can know and command this world by means of a developed and well-directed intelligence. Thanks to his freedom, he can modify, master, and submit nature to his will. This is how he turns deserts into fertile lands, overcomes mountains, widens the rivers, levels the fields, and introduces, through the centuries, such miracles that would astonish us, were we not accustomed to the possession of the happy consequences of our power.

The first person to measure the space around him, to count the objects in sight, observe their properties and actions, that was the person who launched the physical and mathematical sciences. The first one to craft a bow, or a hook, or wear animal skins, that is the person who started industry. Let this industrial seed germinate and grow over the centuries by means of the activity of several and diverse generations, and we will see all the wonders that surround us and that we take for granted. The physical and mathematical sciences represent the triumph of the mind over the secrets of nature. Industry represents the conquest by liberty of the forces of nature. The world was foreign to man, but the physical

---

[3] Victor Cousin (1792–1867) was one of the most influential philosophers in nineteenth-century Spanish America. In Rocafuerte's time the most widely known work by Cousin was the *Cours de l'histoire de la philosophie* (1827). (Editors' note)

and mathematical sciences, followed by industry, have made the world friendly to man. He has shaped the world according to his own image.

Human intelligence is either weakened or degraded in different places. Nature, for its part, only produces things, matter without value. Man transforms them, gives them shape, and imprints his personality on them. Thus, he brings them nearer to liberty and intelligence, and gives them the greatest part of the value they have. The material world is little more than matter that man works to make it shine with the touches of intelligence and liberty. The field of political economy explains how work generates wealth, and how the products of industry are directly related to the contributions of the exact sciences. Mathematics, physics, industry, and political economy all help to meet our needs and establish utility as the main objective. Is utility, however, the only need in our nature; the only idea that condenses the many others present in our mind; the only way in which man considers things? Certainly not. Beyond utility there is justice, which emerges from the very nature of human relations. Justice brings results as tangible as those of utility, making them even more admirable.

The Political World

The idea of justice is one of the most glorious in human nature. Man recognizes it at first sight, although it appears to him as lightning coursing through the dark night of primitive passions. He sees it covered by clouds and eclipsed from one moment to the other by the disorder of impetuous desires and contradictory interests. What is called natural society is a state of war where the right of the strong, pride, and cruelty prevail. It is a state where passion always overwhelms and sacrifices justice. Once conceived, man's idea of the just stirs and drives the human mind, compelling its realization. In the same manner in which man had changed nature through the idea of utility, he now turns natural or primitive society, where everything is disorder, confusion, and crime, into a new society based on the idea of justice. The state is basically justice established. The mission of the state is to impose the observance of the law by force; not only to prevent injustice, but to punish it. This is how a new order of society comes about. Civil and political society means the exercise of justice by the legal order represented by the state.

The state is not concerned with the infinite variety of human elements that thrive on the confusion and chaos of natural society. It is not concerned with the whole of man. The state only considers him in light of the relations between the just and the unjust. That is, man is considered capable of committing or suffering an injustice, committing or becoming a victim of fraud or violence in the free exercise of his voluntary activity. This is the source of all legal rights and obligations. The most important legal right is the right to be respected in the peaceful exercise of liberty. The only legal obligation (in civil terms) is the duty to respect the liberty of others. This is what is called justice. Its object is to keep and maintain the right balance between liberties. The state does not limit freedom, as it is often assumed. On the contrary, it develops, secures, and gives higher legal latitude to liberty. This is a major improvement from primitive society, where a higher level of inequality exists among human beings because of the differences in needs and feelings, as well as physical, intellectual, and moral faculties. In a civilized state all inequalities disappear before the law. Thus, it can be said that the fundamental attribute of liberty, that is, equality, forms the basis of both the legal order and the political world. That is the greatest creation of human ingenuity, greater even than the scientific, economic, and industrial worlds, compared with the primitive realm of nature.

The World of Art

The mind is not limited to the idea of the useful or the pernicious, the just or the unjust: It extends to the consideration of the beautiful and the ugly. The idea of beauty is as natural to man as the ideas of utility and justice. The idea of beauty comes from nature itself: the impression made on our senses by the bright colors of dawn, the reflection of the moon on the vast expanses of the ocean, or the sight of great pristine and snow-capped mountains. It also comes from the presence of human beings, like the smiling face of an innocent child, the elegant silhouette of a young woman, the gallantry of the soldier, or the enthusiasm raised by heroic patriotism. Once man captures the idea of beauty he improves on it, just like he did in the physical world through science and industry, or when he made the chaotic primitive society yield to justice and virtue. In the same manner, he rescued beauty from a world of forms surrounded by mystery. He reshaped the objects that inspired his sense of beauty and turned them into a triumph of splendor. There is nothing perfect on earth: The sun has dark spots, the most beautiful face has moles, and even heroism, perhaps the greatest and purest of all beauties, is exposed to a thousand human miseries, should one look at them closely and impartially. And yet, man can ignore such imperfections and search with ingenuity for what is beautiful and perfect in all things. He brings them together, combines them, and makes a whole out of the parts. In this way, he creates an artificial nature that is superior to the primitive. Is there a greater beauty than Phidias' Venus of Medici? Is there a human form comparable to the Belvedere Apollo? The ideal of beauty is the creation of a new nature that is more alive, more luminous, and more sublime than primitive nature. The artistic world, then, is as true and positive as the political and the industrial. However, it is the work of intelligence and liberty applied to raw beauty. In that sense, it differs from the work of industry over rebellious nature, or the work of politics over indomitable passions.

The Religious World

Man has not only shaped nature to his likeness, organized society on the principle of justice, and introduced beauty through art. His mind has also gone far beyond to identify a primary force, a power superior to his own and that of nature, a magnificent power that is manifested in concrete works, a power that is unlimited because of its superior essence and absolute omnipotence. Man, chained as he is to the limits of the planet, sees everything in earthly terms. Because of this worldly perspective, man irresistibly assumes that there is something, a substance, a cause, a model for everything. He sees it in himself and in the world. In a word, beyond the industrial, the political, and the artistic realms he sees God. The God of humanity is neither on this earth nor separate from it. It embraces everything. This God gives life, energy, and joy to the entire universe. A God without a world would not exist for man. It would be an inexplicable enigma to his mind, and an enormous burden to his heart.

The intuition of God, distinct from the world, yet patently manifest in it, is what I call natural religion. In the same manner that man superseded the primitive world, rudimentary society, and raw beauty, it follows that he also wanted to improve natural religion. This religion represents only a vague understanding of divinity, a marvelous but fleeting ray of light that travels through the darkness of ignorance and blinds the savage's imagination. Christianity came to our aid, and God himself reorganized

8. Vicente Rocafuerte, On Religious Toleration (1831)

the religious world. He taught us how to apply intelligence and liberty to the ideas of sanctity, placing them in harmony with those of utility, justice, and beauty. Hence, Christianity is in harmony with the industrial, political, and artistic worlds, and with all the elements of modern civilization. Christianity can be regarded as the complement to all the fundamental needs of society, and as the most powerful instrument to secure public peace through good customs. As an intellectual pursuit, the study of Christianity develops and nurtures the mind. As an eminently peaceful and tolerant tradition it promotes ideas of order and liberty. It adapts perfectly well to the physical and moral organization of man. The state, as we have seen, does not encompass all that is human; it limits itself to man's relations to justice or injustice, to civil matters, and to the material aspects of social happiness. When it goes beyond those limits, the state contradicts the very reason for its establishment. It is limited to the industrial, political, and artistic worlds. It has nothing to do with the religious world.

Religion does not encompass all that is human, either: It is concerned with his spiritual side, his relations with God, his conduct, and the virtues that will secure his future happiness. Both institutions [the state and religion] are indispensable to man. Both want his happiness, one on earth, and the other in eternity. One is in command of the body, the other in command of the soul. Just like the latter is invisible and manifests its existence through the effects of the will on the body, religion must be separate from both the government and the constitution. It should only be recognized for its influence on morality and good customs, for the dignity of its rites, and for the virtue of its ministers. It should replicate the order of heaven on earth, just like the sun rises daily to fill us with joy. The political absence of the clergy in the state, or the clear separation between them and public affairs, will enhance the moral appearance of sublime Christianity, as well as facilitate the high spiritual role of the priesthood. Modern man is so clear about these truths that he has separated the interests of the government from those of religion. He has proclaimed the absolute independence of one from the other, and established as a principle of social necessity that a free government must be tolerant, and should allow freedom of religion without protecting any creed in particular. The modern vocabulary no longer recognizes the words "State Religion," or any theories about "Altar and Throne."

8. Vicente Rocafuerte, On Religious Toleration (1831)

All Dominant Religions Are Oppressive

Dominant religions not only oppress, but also persecute other religions. The Romans persecuted the early Christians, as the Turks and the Algerians do today. The Mufti and the Ulema, the Rabbis, and the Brahmins are as intolerant as the inquisitors of Spain and Portugal. The intolerant egotism of the Protestant bishops and clergy of England is insufferable. They were in a continuous fight against the Irish Catholics until the spirit of toleration and justice of the century overcame their throne-backed power. It has at last liberated the Catholics of Ireland from the yoke that choked them ever since the Treaty of Limerick, until the year 1828. To proclaim a dominant religion is the same as establishing a monopoly of religious opinions. It only benefits the legal interpreters of heaven to the detriment of society. The enormous wealth of the Protestant clergy in England comes from this source, as it does in the case of the Catholic clergy in Spain, the Ulema of Turkey, and the Brahmins of Hindustan. The religious monopoly is as damaging to morality and thought as commercial monopolies are to the expansion of trade and the prosperity of national industry. That is why the combination of political, religious, and commercial liberty must be the creed of modern societies.

9
FRANCISCO BILBAO
The Error, or Contradiction, under Which Spanish America Lives (1862)

Francisco Bilbao (1823–1865) was a Chilean writer and political activist educated at the Instituto Nacional.[1] He rose to notoriety when he published an essay, the "Sociabilidad chilena" (1844), condemning the role of both the Catholic Church and the legacies of colonialism in Chile. He was brought to trial for violating the laws regulating press freedoms. As a result, he left Chile for Europe, where he established contact with Edgar Quinet and Hugues-Félicité Robert de Lamennais and witnessed the European revolutions of 1848. Returning to Chile, he founded the Society of Equality in 1850 and participated in the uprising of April 1851, which led to his exile in Peru, Europe, and Argentina, where he died. His principal works, in addition to "Sociabilidad" are La América en peligro (1862), and El evangelio americano (1864). The essay included here is representative of his views regarding the radical contradiction between Catholicism and republicanism, which was in turn an expression of his views on the struggle between despotism and freedom.

Freedom and Catholicism are two radically contradictory terms
Lamennais

---

[1] This selection is taken from *La América en peligro*, published in Buenos Aires in 1862. It is included in Francisco Bilbao, *El evangelio americano*, ed. by Alejandro Witker (Caracas, 1988), 204–209. (Editors' note)

9. Francisco Bilbao, The Contradiction of Spanish America (1862)

The predominant religion in Spanish America is Catholic.
The political principle of Spanish America is republican.
Is the dogma true? Is the principle true?
I state the truth of the principle. I will not argue with whoever denies it.
The principle being true, it must be the legitimate result of a true dogma.
Can the republican principle logically derive from the Catholic dogma? That is impossible. Therefore, this dogma is false.
Is it possible that the republican principle will lead to the Catholic dogma? That is impossible.
The logical political consequence of Catholicism is theocracy: the papacy.
The logical consequence of the republican principle is RATIONALISM.
Rationalism and Catholicism are mutually exclusive. Catholicism anathematizes rationalism; the latter annihilates Catholicism.
This is the central contradiction. A world that lives with contradiction will eventually destroy itself if it does not suppress one of the contrarian elements. That is the price of salvation.
I respect the sincere Catholic. I will not discuss his dogmas at the moment, but a sincere Catholic will deny my own right to free thought. He will deny the sovereignty of reason and will subject reason to the authority of the church. According to him I cannot be a sovereign person, a free citizen, or an independent man. I will endure the *capitis diminutio*, the decapitation of my personhood, whose essence and substance are reason, free reason, the light I have received directly from the Creator.
Catholic beliefs rest on the notion of miracle. That is the starting point, and its own proof. WITHOUT MIRACLES THERE IS NO CATHOLICISM. This is the equivalent of another statement: THERE IS NO CATHOLICISM WITHOUT ABSURDITY.
The Catholic religion imposes the notion of miracle.
Faith in the miracle is the condition for salvation. This is the same as saying: Belief in the absurd, faith in the absurd, is the fundamental condition for salvation.
What is the meaning of the authoritarian imposition of blind faith, miracles, and absurdity? That we should not trust independent reason, that we should believe in the opposite of reason.

9. Francisco Bilbao, *The Contradiction of Spanish America (1862)*

What can result from a world educated in that absurdity?

Stupid and repressive fanaticism, absolute doubt, and a radical contradiction.

Catholicism destroys the authority of reason, unsettles the mind to the point of making man "a cane in the hands of the old," as Ignatius of Loyola said and tested. Catholicism deprives man of his sovereignty, undermines his person, and delivers him "as a corpse" to anyone who wants to control him. Can there be republics, or republicans, with that kind of education?

What do republics fight against? The Catholic religion and its induced fanaticism; the infallible church with its unquenching thirst for power and wealth; the political despotism that rests on religious dogma; the authority of the church; the power of the clergy, and the ignorance of the masses whose fanaticism it exploits. The portrait of [Juan Manuel de] Rosas placed in a Catholic temple!

What progress have the republics made?

They have taken away, little by little, the lands of the church.

Freedom of religion, mixed marriages, elimination of censorship, freedom of the press, the institution of patronage, abolition of perpetual vows, teaching institutions informed by philosophy, and freedom of education (which the Catholic suppresses in countries where Catholicism dominates; demands or proclaims where it does not). In Chile, Peru, Rome, Naples, and Austria, the Catholic demands exclusive rights, or the prevalence of Catholic education, censorship of books, appointment of teachers, etc. In Russia, Poland, Turkey, Great Britain, and the United States, the Catholic demands freedom of education with mean hypocrisy.

What has been the fate of those republics that have clung to Catholicism? Death, as in Venice, Florence, Paraguay, etc.

What has been the vital principle of the Catholic republics of Italy? As Edgar Quinet has proven, it is *terror*. I quote him because one cannot talk about Italy without citing him.

Have Catholic nations been able to prosper? Only by renouncing Catholicism. Everything that is free, strong, splendid, and advanced on earth belongs to nations that have detached themselves from Catholicism. Germany, Holland, Scandinavia, Switzerland, England, and the United States.

Can people who are under *the shadow of death* (Rome) be revived?

9. Francisco Bilbao, The Contradiction of Spanish America (1862)

Denying Rome, seeking the light that reaches the catacombs of liberty.

How has science advanced? By offering martyrs to the persecutions of the church.

How has the law advanced? By rejecting canon law and the barbaric penalties imposed by the Catholic codes.

Who lit the fires of the Inquisition, lately legitimized by [Juan] Donoso Cortés in Spain, and Canon Piñero in Buenos Aires? The Catholic Church.

Who extinguished the fires that ravaged the Andes, in Mexico and Peru, the Apennine Mountains, the Pyrenees, and the Sierra Nevada? Philosophy.

Who established the *divine power* of kings? Many, from [the Apostle] Paul, who legitimized slavery, and [Jacques-Bénigne] Bossuet, who incited that monstrous crowned pheasant Louis XIV to impose his *divine power*, to Pius IX, who called the Polish executioner, in a letter to the archbishop of Warsaw in 1862, "the illustrious king of Poland." Who did? Catholicism!

Who abolished torture and other barbaric punishments, and seeks to abolish the death penalty? Philosophy. Who has used firing squads for political reasons in the Pontifical States? Pope Pius IX.

Who has abolished slavery? Philosophy.

To whom did the last *serfs* of France belong? To the Catholic Church.

Catholicism has legitimized the permanent threat to the rule of law, as well as the horrific crimes and butchery recorded by history: that of St. Bartholomew was approved and organized by the church. Likewise, the extermination of the Waldensians, Albigensians, and Hussites was blessed and is still celebrated by the church.

Who covered with corpses the forests of the Low Countries, and burned 20,000 heretics in the Seville Inquisition alone?

And what about the Conquest of the New World?

Mexico and Peru were both empires burned to the ground with their temples, books, and the greater part of the population.

Let us stop, then, the lies about [the Catholic Church's] past, history, and essence, which is intolerance; about its substance, which is absurdity; about its tendency, which is despotism; and about its logical and fatal consequences, which are backwardness, fanaticism, corruption, misery, and the brutal servitude of the ignorant masses. They should serve as examples to all enemies of despotic domination. The dogma, the principles,

9. Francisco Bilbao, The Contradiction of Spanish America (1862)

the history, the facts, the logic, and the experience all demonstrate that there is an essential and radical incompatibility between Catholicism and republicanism.

Why, by God, shall we not see the day when people of different beliefs engage in a sincere debate? It would be a noble sight, indeed, to see a believer holding his views with conviction, without fear or diffidence, against opposite arguments. But the spectacle of the sophist, the Jesuit, the man who is insincere, who betrays his principles, who throws a veil over the consequences of his doctrine, who denies or hides the facts that unmask him, who believes to be authorized by Ignatius of Loyola to call *white* what is *black* (for the greater glory of God),[2] that is the closest thing to the putrefaction that comes with death.

I believe in [Joseph] de Maistre's sincerity. He is the strongest champion of Catholicism in modern times: He promotes theocracy as a system of government and gives the role of executioner to the prime minister of a prince.

I believe in the sincerity of [François-René de] Chateaubriand, who varnished the Catholic edifice with the honey of his style and brilliant fantasy. He said, in opposition to the emergence of the South American republics: "We have enough with one republic in the world."

I believe in the sincerity of Donoso Cortés when he sings the praises of the Inquisition, and presents despotism as the salvation of society.

I believe in the sincerity of Canon [Bartolomé] Herrera in Peru, when he rejects and insults the principle of *popular sovereignty* in the name of Catholicism.

I believe in the sincerity of the Peruvian church when they persecuted me for proclaiming the freedom of religion. I admire the impudence of a canon, and member of Congress, who thundered his opposition to that freedom:

"God is the foremost intolerant."

I believe in the sincerity of the Archbishop of Santiago [Chile] when he ordered that families be spied upon and denounced for any heresy, and to accuse people who did not profess the Catholic religion.

I believe, finally, in the sincerity of Pope Pius IX when he entered Rome, his "beloved city," thanks to foreign intervention and support, and

---

[2] This is a paraphrase of Loyola's "What seems to me white, I will believe black if the hierarchical Church so defines," in *The Spiritual Exercises of St. Ignatius*, trans. by Louis J. Puhl (1951). (Editors' note)

9. Francisco Bilbao, The Contradiction of Spanish America (1862)

called the butcher of Poland, the foreigner who oppresses the country, "the illustrious king of Poland."

All of this is clear, sincere, and logical. We can see the enemy's face, unmasked.

And yet, what is to be said of the Catholic who denies the authority of reason and states that Catholicism is liberal? What is to be said of the Catholic who proclaims the infallibility of the church and the pope, and affirms that reason is Catholic?

What is one to think of the Catholic who hides his beliefs, reneges or momentarily silences his dogmas in order to show only one side of his doctrine? Why does he not accept his responsibility and openly proclaim the entire body of his dogmas and principles? Why not repeat the words of Paul and ask about democracy: All power comes from God? – "Slaves, obey your earthly masters" [Ephesians 6:5].

Why do Catholics not say what they think or believe about humanity's immense non-Catholic majority, that which is born and dies without baptism? As Bossuet implies, those millions of human beings, including the newly born, will be forever and ever condemned to suffer in limbo, purgatory, or hell. For what? To pay for an original sin that Catholics invented?

Ah, sincerity! The day we see you shut the sophist's mouth, we believers of all religions will be closer to embracing each other and uniting under one vision of truth! Error separates us, but interest, the selfish considerations of social position, hypocrisy, cowardice, sophistry, indifference, and sectarian hatred are the principal obstacles to the enlightenment of the spirit and the fraternity of all souls.

How to convince those who seek a career as teacher, judge, minister, envoy, governor, or president in a Catholic society?

How to convince those who live off the income of convents, or administer the funds of religious communities?

How to convince those who need the approval or the influence of the clergy, or their allies, to administer this or that enterprise, or lead a financial institution?

How to convince those who live off testaments, inheritances, or pious funds devoted to the care of bygone souls?

How to convince those who, fearful of eternal flames, tremble at the thought of contact with heresy?

To conclude, how to convince those who see their social position compromised, their future sacrificed, their names cursed, their souls excommunicated, their beliefs anathematized, their persons persecuted and

9. Francisco Bilbao, *The Contradiction of Spanish America (1862)*

slandered? How? I hope that the obstacles to the victory of light can be fully understood.

Opinion, society, women in particular, politics, administration, and the church, all united and conspiring against reason and liberty, on the one hand. Reason and liberty, advancing and winning every day, on the other. This is the *miracle*, Catholics! This is the law of truth, rationalists!

10

MIGUEL ANTONIO CARO

Freedom of Religion (1871–1872)

Miguel Antonio Caro (1843–1909) was notable among the most systematic conservative thinkers in Spanish America.[1] He was born in Bogota in a socially prestigious and politically influential family (his father was one of the founders of the Conservative Party in 1848), but of modest economic means. Caro rose to prominence for his scholarly work on grammar, his translations of Virgil, and, above all, for his defense of the Catholic Church and his critical stand against the radical governments that ruled the country after 1861. A staunch defender of the papacy, he subscribed to Pius IX's Syllabus and his condemnation of liberalism. He was appointed to his first public post in 1880, as director of the National Library, by the then president Rafael Núñez, a liberal who broke with the radicals to lead the Regeneración movement in Colombia. Caro became the closest ally of Núñez, and one of the main architects of the 1886 Constitution, which provided the institutional framework for the new regime's devolution of power to the church after decades of liberal persecution. Caro succeeded Núñez after his death (1894) in the presidency of the country. His vast intellectual production, however, preceded his rise to power, including a critical study of Bentham's utilitarianism. In 1871, he founded El Tradicionista, *a newspaper whose pages advocated the protection of the Catholic Church by the Colombian state, and where his series of articles against religious tolerance, the basis of Caro's piece in our volume, were first published.*

[1] "Libertad de cultos" by Miguel Antonio Caro first appeared in the Colombian periodical *El Tradicionista* on November 4, 6, and December 8, 1871, and January 2, 1872. The editors use selections from the modern edition of *Obras*, ed. by Carlos Valderrama Andrade (Bogota, 1962), 1, 761–809. (Editors' note)

10. Miguel Antonio Caro, Freedom of Religion (1871–1872)

Between the absolute freedom of religion, and absolute intolerance, there are countless layers. In the first case, we have a government that is absolutely and practically indifferent when it comes to religion. In the second case, we are talking about a government that is absolutely and practically intolerant of any religion, either privately or publicly observed, unless it has chosen one as its own. There is a long series, a gradual scale, of restrictions that go from absolute liberty to absolute intolerance. The first legal restriction that can be placed on freedom of religion is the adoption of one religion by the civil authorities, even when it does not prohibit the private practice of other religions. I say that this is in effect a restriction because 1) such an adoption is by itself a preference that invalidates the equality of all religions, and 2) because such a preference, coming from the government, signals that other religions are tolerated rather than absolutely free. Once a religion is adopted by the government, the second restriction imposed on those excluded consists in allowing the private, but not public, practice of religion, as is the case in Portugal. This private liberty is founded on *freedom of conscience*. The final restriction consists in prohibiting even the private practice of religions other than the official. At this point, we come close to absolute religious intolerance. The wars of religion in Europe show how various governments established the principle of intolerance.

These three restrictions can be severe, and hence the different gradations that I have mentioned. In the current state of civilization, and in order to clearly address what is important here, that is, freedom of religion, we must distinguish three stages, or situations. Two of them are often lumped together, when they are in fact very different:

1. *Absolute freedom of religion*, or, simply *freedom of religion*: The government is indifferent, treats all religions the same, and gives perfect equality to all religions to practice and disseminate their beliefs.
2. *Religious toleration*: The government adopts a particular religion, treats all others as false, but allows them a higher or lesser degree of manifestation and dissemination. Toleration applies to a higher or lesser degree, but freedom of conscience is always respected.
3. *Intolerance*: The government protects one religion and inhibits any opposition to it.

To elucidate these issues, it is important above all to define the terms. They must be defined according to etymology and usage. When a philosophical debate takes place, whether etymology or usage are followed or not, what is important to the consistency of ideas is that once a term is

10. Miguel Antonio Caro, Freedom of Religion (1871–1872)

understood in a certain sense, it should be permanently understood in the same sense. This is my aim when I propose to define the terms "freedom" and "toleration." In this essay, I will maintain the sense in which I define them. If anyone wishes to contest my views, I beg him to keep these definitions in mind for the sake of both a productive discussion, and clarity.

The first question that arises is this: Of the three stages mentioned, "freedom," "toleration," and "intolerance," which one is better and more convenient for society? Since "intolerance" is unanimously rejected by educated and sympathetic people, the question narrows down to the terms "freedom," and "toleration."

Because this is not only a philosophical but also a juridical question, the first aspect that must be considered is about applicability: Is "toleration" possible? Yes, it is, and we see it legally applied, in one sense or another, in all enlightened countries. Is "freedom," meaning absolute freedom of religion, possible? I do not believe it is: Enlightened reason demonstrates it; the facts prove it.

Indeed, the absolute freedom of religion depends, firstly, upon the existence of an absolutely indifferent government. But a government cannot be absolutely indifferent without ceasing to exist. The notions of government and absolute indifference are incompatible. To govern is to educate. Education presupposes moral and religious principles. He who professes such principles has, in consequence, a faith, a belief. He who believes is not indifferent.

Secondly, the notion of freedom of religion consists in the perfect equality of all religions before the government. However, what is religion? How does a government know whether a set of beliefs and practices can be considered a religion? What are the criteria it will follow to make the distinction? To establish a difference between what is, and what is not, a religion, a government must have some moral and religious views to be able to say what principles are sufficiently religious to be *tolerated* as constituting a religion. Likewise, it must have such views in order to say what principles are *intolerable* for qualification as a religion. Otherwise, anyone would have the right to say, "I so declare to be the founder of a religion whose main articles of faith are the following: 'Man is a monkey,' 'polygamy is a right,' and 'property is theft.'" A government that proclaims to be indifferent and respectful of freedom of religion would have to recognize that this self-appointed founder has a right. Consequently, this government would be compelled to allow his practices and propaganda, and thus his errors and vices under the guise of religion.

10. Miguel Antonio Caro, Freedom of Religion (1871–1872)

All branches of public administration constantly encounter issues of morality and religion. It is after all men who fill these offices, and their distinctive character as human beings is both religious and moral. It is imperative that in all circumstances the government acts either in favor of or in opposition to religious principles: It has an obligation, even though it could decide not to honor it. If it does, why? Because religion compels man to honor his word. The government educates. Why? Because there is a religion which says that these and not others are the only moral truths. The government punishes, especially crimes. Why? Because, following religion, it knows what are, or are not, crimes, and because having a religious conscience, it has the right to punish. Without religion, education and punishment are mere acts of violence that might be explained as necessities of a material order, but in no wise as rights of the moral order. It is for this reason that an atheistic government, even if it calls itself liberal, is a thousand times more threatening than an absolutist government that professes a particular religion: Even if false, it has a religious conscience, while the former does not. A human entity without a religious conscience is a blind and ferocious entity.

The impossibility of an absolute freedom of religion is also proven by experience. Countries that are most boastful of their freedom of religion do not in fact have it. In some mixed societies the restrictions on freedom are sometimes supported by general opinion, and sometimes they are entirely capricious. In the United States the Mormons have been persecuted as *religious bandits* for interpreting the Bible in an unusual way. Their leader, [Joseph] Smith, was murdered. In Catholic countries where freedom of religion is legal, punishment does not come from the Catholic majority but rather from an agnostic, audacious, and privileged minority: The same minority that seeks to impose violent restrictions against Catholicism. In Colombia we have seen the pillaging of churches, the exile of priests and prelates, and the multifaceted persecution of the religion of most Colombians, all in the name of freedom of religion. The same has happened in Belgium, Spain, Italy, and in other Catholic countries that have proclaimed the illusory freedom of religion, or an excessively extensive toleration.

Common sense and experience show that freedom, the absolute freedom of religion as I have defined it, is an unreachable ideal. But if this is the case, some could ask, why does freedom of religion exist in some countries? It might exist legally, but no country *really* practices it to the full extent that is essential to the notion. Without such latitude, freedom

10. Miguel Antonio Caro, Freedom of Religion (1871–1872)

is not absolute freedom but simply toleration: And it is more arbitrary than legal. It means that restrictions do not come from the law, but from capriciousness, or a random combination of interests.

Now, if freedom of religion is impossible, is it just or convenient that the laws should proclaim such a liberty? No. The laws must, first and foremost, be consistent with the nature of things. Second, they must be consistent with the circumstances and customs of the country that issues them. But because the impossibility of the freedom of religion resides in the nature of things, the law cannot dictate such a freedom without trampling upon it. Since there is no country whose circumstances and customs can dispense with religious beliefs, the law cannot ignore this constitutionally essential and formative element. If it does, it harms or abandons the principle to the mercy of opportunistic interests. Therefore, it is neither just nor convenient to legislate without religion.

Official irreligion, then, is an absurdity. Therefore, the freedom of religion that follows from this official irreligion is impossible. Freedom of religion without legal restrictions, it can be concluded, means freedom of religion *with* unjust and fearsome extralegal restrictions. Hence, confronted with "liberty" and "toleration," a sensible person must opt for the second if only because "freedom" is impossible, and "toleration" necessary.

And yet, the exclusion of liberty, it might be argued, poses grave difficulties. It does not really matter: Such difficulties are still in the future. For the moment, let us escape the impossible and the absurd. Being a good person is difficult, yes, but must we then stop trying to do good? It is difficult to be knowledgeable, but should that be a reason to stop learning? If we are sure that a step to the left will land us in a hole, clearly we should take a step to the right even if that means following a dark and difficult path. The argument of "difficulty" is made by those who, not understanding God, deny him. This is the argument of the lazy and the bad. In good logic, when facing a dilemma between the absurd and the difficult, we must choose the latter.

The difficulty – and this is the core question once the issue of liberty is removed – resides in how to establish and implement toleration. Toleration presupposes knowledge of the truth: Toleration is for error, not for truth; it is for dissidents, not for the faithful. However, what is the truth? Everyone fights everybody else in the name of the truth. Who can judge?

This is, undoubtedly, the difficulty. As I once stated while fighting official atheism:

10. Miguel Antonio Caro, Freedom of Religion (1871–1872)

We are facing a difficulty and a danger: that the state chooses as national a false religion. And yet, the difficulty poses an interesting question for anyone seeking the truth. We are all exposed to error, but does this excuse us from seeking and choosing the truth? Certainly not. It only means that we are doing our duty when we seek and follow in good faith what we judge to be the truth. We risk error all the more when we ignore this duty. Indifference is an even greater danger: the danger of death. He who proceeds in good faith in these matters will undoubtedly embrace Catholicism.

This difficulty arises only in mixed societies, because that is where belief and jurisprudence collide. In other words, the question of how to know the truth when all disagree, and also the question about whether the government can officially adopt a religion when everyone holds different beliefs. This difficulty is the product of an evil: the plurality of beliefs. We can see it in the United States, where a public conscience has not yet been formed. Thus, the government cannot say: "Catholicism and Protestantism exist in the public conscience and, therefore, as the representative of the people, I will convey such a conscience through my actions." There, freedom of religion cannot be limited by law. Instead, restrictions will develop apace with the progress of the nation in a peaceful religious struggle, which is part of the effort to form a conscience. When Catholicism triumphs in the United States, the state will be essentially Catholic. In Colombia, this problem does not exist. However inferior to the United States in some respects, the country is far superior in terms of religious unity. As this advantage exists in reality, it should be present in the laws: a toleration rigorously established from the Catholic perspective.

Why? Why should we be discussing a matter so obvious? Because Colombia follows the logic of imitation and, as Mr. Soto has stated, it lost its sense of good logic.[2] Medication is actually poison, so that it can only be regarded as a relative good. Colombia has administered a medication called "freedom of religion" without suffering the illness, that grave sickness called "plurality of beliefs." We shall see the consequences of this insane procedure.

The plurality of beliefs is an evil that obstructs unity and progress. A nation of multiple creeds is as inferior as that with only one, just like the

---

[2] A footnote from the editor of the collection, Carlos Valderrama Andrade, says that "he must be referring to doctor Francisco Soto, author of some Memoirs of 1827"; in Caro, *Obras*. (Editors' note)

10. Miguel Antonio Caro, Freedom of Religion (1871–1872)

man plagued with doubts when compared with a man of fixed ideas. If the latter admits to having some doubts, they come from toleration, exactly as a government tolerates dissident religions. The United States does not have a national literature because it does not have a national religion. Had it been a completely Catholic nation, one could venture to say that the country would not have destroyed itself as it did in the Civil War. It resembles a robust man who suffers a serious illness.

In largely Catholic countries like Colombia the difficulties and inconveniences already noted emerge not naturally but rather artificially, due to inept politicians or audacious minorities of agnostics. The nation is Catholic; Catholicism is part of the national conscience. Is there a compelling need that prevents the government from loyally, frankly, and tolerantly representing the religious sentiments of the nation? Is there a reason for the government to officially embrace atheism? Religious unity, and such conditions for peace, like the strength of family and society, that cost other countries enormous efforts and long wars, we Spanish Americans have inherited without conflict. Unfortunately, our situation is similar to a man who, born rich, allows subordinate administrators to dilapidate his fortune. We have foolishly abandoned our title as a Catholic nation. The church has barely managed to be tolerated like any other religion, and even this is considered an excessive concession. Some agitators propose to launch new persecutions against the church in the name of "national sovereignty"!

The example of the United States is the only model that can be invoked to introduce freedom of religion in our country. Such a statement falls apart when we consider that we already have a religious conscience. We are in peaceful possession of our heritage. The United States wages a religious war, bloodless perhaps, but still a war that we do not want. There is also a huge difference between their public officials and our own. There they are afflicted by the proliferation of creeds that is the legacy of English Protestantism, however much they know it and seek a remedy for it. Having such a multiplicity of religious beliefs, and lacking a public conscience, they allow freedom of religion *pro bono pacis*. The law does not incline one way or the other, but common law prepares the way for positive law in this matter. Magistrates officially and respectfully invoke the name of God. It is agreed that Christianity has more rights to influence public affairs than other religions. For example, the great majority of Christian communities condemn polygamy, and hence Mormons have been persecuted. In some states, the local government protects the

10. Miguel Antonio Caro, Freedom of Religion (1871–1872)

dominant religion in a particular locality. Religious questions are debated with the aim of reaching the truth through the unity of Christian communities; Catholicism gains ground; there is an aspiration for unity, and a road in that direction. Here in Colombia we do the opposite: We have unity but do not love it; our laws protect liberty, but since liberty cannot exist absolutely, restrictions do not come from fixed constitutional principles but rather from the arbitrary actions of the government. In sum, the law ignores the conscience of the nation, and in practice it is barely tolerated. We face the constant threat of persecution.

From this presentation I conclude that in those countries where religions proliferate without adding up to a public conscience, legislators are compelled, out of painful necessity, to approve the freedom of religion. But this freedom, impossible as it is in an absolute way, is susceptible to restrictions, hopefully prudent but always dangerous because they do not originate from established constitutional principles. The law in those countries must respond to the movement to establish a public conscience with a progressive spirit. However, in Catholic countries that owe their strength and identity to Catholicism, the people's religion ought to be adopted by the civil government. Should that be the case, the law must clearly and amicably settle the boundaries of their power, including the type of toleration granted to foreign dissidents so that they enjoy safety within the limits of the law. The United States belongs to the first set of countries, and Spanish America to the second.

The Inconveniences of Liberty

The first inconvenience presented by the absolute freedom of religion is the arbitrary action of the civil government. A government that does not recognize a divine law superior to its own is essentially despotic. How can a society free itself from this yoke? One can easily demonstrate that there are no human means to accomplish this aim. Governments cannot be destroyed because society cannot exist without authority. The attempt to make it moral by only changing its form is a materialistic pretension bound to fail. An atheist monarch, and an atheist popular assembly, are two sides of the same Proteus: two forms of an always dangerous impiety.

The belief that despotism is only to be found in personalistic governments is wrong because, first, despotism comes not from the one or the many, but from the injustice and the absence of charity that exists in either an individual or in a larger body. Second, however popular a

10. Miguel Antonio Caro, Freedom of Religion (1871–1872)

government might seem to be, it still has a strong personal element. Populations are unable to govern themselves: They are governed by representatives or delegates who, lacking religion, will always try to avoid the wishes of the community for selfish motives that are detrimental to the common good. Moreover, representatives gathered in a congress cannot think collectively. They will rely on a more limited circle, which is in turn dominated by a single person. It is important, for the happiness of the people, that this person be inspired by a wise and religious conscience. Otherwise, his leadership of the administration will be a faceless despotism that will invade all agencies of government and, in the end, oppress the entire society.

There is no bigger threat to society than a parliament that assumes the divine attributes of infallibility and omnipotence. It does so when, denying them to God, it pretends to have received them from the people. It was not long ago that the Congress of Colombia believed it had the right to impose utilitarianism and sensualism in public schools. Did the people who elected that Congress believe in such doctrines? No, but just as people exercise the right to vote, representatives exercise the power to make decisions. Society not always has the means to call to account men who, lacking the fear of God, lack any human fear as well. This is where atheistic parliamentarianism comes from, which is no less fearsome or ferocious than the rule of the pagan Caesars.

Official atheism is, by its very nature, a despotism. It can be either violent, or tame, but it is always alarming. It cannot be rectified by human means and thus it is necessary to appeal to a higher authority, a law respected by all, that can guarantee the observance of justice and the enjoyment of peace. Hence the bold but significant sentence by an impious writer: "If God did not exist, it would be necessary to invent him" [Voltaire].

The primary duty of government is to avoid tyranny, and as atheism and tyranny are synonymous, it is clear that the civil government must be religious. Governments that adopt a false religion start with the right aim but use the wrong means. Clever pagans understood this need for religion and appealed to a natural one that was insufficient for both the individual and the government. Other governments have resorted to a national religion, which is as insufficient as a personal religion is to an individual. A religion that emerges from the will of the people, or the individual, ceases for that very reason to be a religion and turns into an opinion like any other, in the case of a person, or results in an *establishment* in the case of society, as England shows. Some conclude in this regard that "it is not convenient for the government to be religious." This is a great mistake, like confusing the end with the means. If a hungry man bites a stone in error, this does not mean that he should stop eating. That the government should be religious is an inescapable need for society, but neither natural law alone, nor an ecclesiastical establishment, can satisfy this need. Therefore, we must look elsewhere for fulfillment.

Freedom of religion in mixed societies can be regarded as a lesser evil, according to some, or a means to achieve unity by letting different doctrines oppose one another publicly as equals, until one is validated by general opinion as victorious. In the opposite case, countries that have achieved the cherished Catholic unity will return to freedom of religion only by violent means, and be kept that way only by force. The reason is clear: Freedom of religion in a Catholic country is not the work of the majority, because it is a Catholic principle that the plurality of beliefs is evil, and the unity of truth the ultimate good. How could this majority, then, contradict its own principles? It is the dissident minorities, the apostate, that impose freedom of religion in Catholic countries. By making all religions nominally equal, they introduce the "religion of impiety" as the official religion. Is this not demonstrated by contemporary [i.e., nineteenth-century] history? Here [in Colombia], have we not seen the persecutions conducted by this horrible religion of impiety? This is the case because freedom of religion presupposes a government with no moral compass for leading society. In Catholic countries where freedom of religion is in place, the government's arbitrariness is manifested in the form of anti-Catholic fanaticism. In this arbitrariness and fanaticism, the evil consequences of the so-called freedom of religion is to be found.

The Situation Created by Liberty

Colombia has a popular representative system. One might expect, then, that what the law sanctions as obligatory reflects what the majority of citizens regard as just and appropriate. Based on this principle, the advocates of a particular social program should cultivate public opinion in order to obtain the majority of the vote. If this is the case, little else needs to be done: Victory is assured for as long as the majority remains in favor of the program. In sum, in a republic, opinion should preside over the formation of the laws, and the administration of public affairs.

10. Miguel Antonio Caro, Freedom of Religion (1871–1872)

However, experience often shows exactly the contrary. The people of Colombia, with rare individual exceptions, are Catholic. And yet, the constitution is atheist and hostile to the Catholic Church. Our electoral system assumes that the people will elect those who will represent the general opinion, but we see everyday examples to the contrary. This is an extraordinary case, as worthy of study as it is discouraging to all honest citizens.

If this system was true in practice, we would not be analyzing the means to restore Catholic unity: The system would mirror the Catholic principles that guide Colombians. The people are Catholic, and they cast votes. And yet, they do not manage to bring Catholicism to the laws of the nation. The same happens in other countries. Therefore, it is not enough to have a majority; it is necessary to find the peaceful means to make Catholic principles prevail. It is not enough to have an electoral system: We must prevent fraud through peaceful means. This is the key question in a Catholic republic.

The Means to Restore Unity

The means to restore Catholic unity in the civil order require that those who are in favor of the restoration be in the majority, and that their energy be equal to their faith. Now, the vitality of opinion requires the same characteristics of human life: intelligence, will, and activity. To know, to want, and to be active are the prerogatives of a rational being. The same applies to the view that aspires to receive the blessings of Providence.

Consequently, those of us who wish to see Catholic unity restored in Colombia, that same unity which is present with more or less force in other Spanish American republics, we must make the effort to advance unity by informing opinion with the vital elements of *knowledge, strength,* and *activity*.

Collective opinion, just like individual opinion, consists of *ideas* and *feelings*. The idea represents truth; feeling represents loyalty. In a well-organized army, the idea is in the head of the commander, and the feeling is in the hearts of obedient soldiers. But neither should the leaders who possess the truth be deprived of enthusiasm, nor the loyal followers lack an understanding of the plans for a campaign. Something similar occurs in Catholic societies where the educated classes, the men destined to govern church and state, are obligated to acquire a solid theological learning. In the same manner, the common citizen is required to respect the righteous dictates of church and state.

10. Miguel Antonio Caro, Freedom of Religion (1871–1872)

To *educate* general opinion means to expand both ideas and sentiments, and to teach individuals the reasons for the rational obedience. It means to teach citizens the foundations of their religion, and to promote knowledge of their rights and duties. This is a labor of the highest importance given the nature of our political regime: Without a class specifically entrusted with governing, and given the eligibility of all citizens to positions of authority, it follows that all classes should be sufficiently educated. The goal is that the citizens who will oversee public administration understand the public good and govern with the support of the majority.

It is therefore important to expand domestic and popular education, instilling from infancy exact but not detailed notions about the church and its rights; about the relations between the ecclesiastical authority and the earthly powers; about the dangers of modern liberalism, and about the need to restore Catholic unity. Such notions, clearly and simply explained, will give people the tools to unmask the sophistry of those anti-Catholic screeds that ill-intentioned writers use to deceive the masses. A people of honest sentiments, but no principles, will always be exposed to the seductions of ornate language and euphonic words. How many painful experiences have our people endured to overcome the hallucinations provoked by the word *liberty*? Even today, insidious words and phrases circulate to excite the passions of the people. An educated public will not listen to empty words; they will examine their meaning as well as their purpose from the perspective of religious principles and true science.

A common requisite for access to public posts is the study of political science. However, this field, as studied in Colombia, is an anti-Catholic instrument. This explains the liberals' tenacity to control public secondary education, and how hard they work to monopolize primary instruction to influence the secondary. This also explains, at least in part, why Catholic electoral victories have not translated into a change of the laws. Why? Because while sentiment drives both the individual vote and the larger electoral results, it is the elected representative, already corrupted by liberalism, who governs and legislates.

There are two factors that led the teaching of political science astray, namely, the hatred of religion, and a servile as well as imitative spirit in the realm of intellectual activity. Those who introduced the works of [Jeremy] Bentham and [Destutt de] Tracy in secondary schools believed that these authors had two main merits: that they were prohibited by the church and were new as well as foreign. One of the characteristics

10. Miguel Antonio Caro, Freedom of Religion (1871–1872)

has faded with time. Those writers are now relatively old, but the other two remain: irreligion and the allure of foreign models. The latter demonstrates the liberal spirit of servile imitation. It is imperative that our Catholic thinkers protest against this ignominious yoke which oppresses us all, and break it.

Different peoples share specific interests, a role in the life of humanity, and a providential mission. Colombia must have a vocation like any other people, but it should not be identical. Colombia belongs to the Catholic world, to Spanish America, and to the nineteenth century. Bentham and Tracy belong to the revolution, to demoralizing France, and to the eighteenth century. They cannot tell us what we are or what we should be. We must determine that on our own. Our teachers of political science ought to study the field and present it under the light of Catholic principles and contemporary circumstances. The people of Spanish America share the same religion: not any religion, but one, the Catholic; the same customs, and the same language. Will public officials look at such important commonalities with indifference? In case of yet another – likely – revolution in Europe, and a new wave of immigration, should we not enact laws to receive such potential immigration without a threat to our character and national mission? Once we are in a position to determine our future, should we not establish the basis of national unity?

In the process of informing general opinion, either verbally or through the printing press, we must seek to *strengthen* and *exercise* speech with all the means that prudence dictates and which are within the realm of both natural and national law. The following are the individual rights guaranteed by the constitution:

1. "Freedom of the press." Let us make use of this freedom by disseminating our opinions and supporting, either as readers or writers, the legitimate representatives of our ideas. Also, let us withdraw any support to publications that *slander* and *persecute* us.
2. "Freedom to receive and impart education." Let us teach our doctrines and withdraw support from those teachers who promote contrary ideas. Let us also bring our protests against the laws that violate this guarantee before public opinion and the courts.
3. "The right to obtain prompt resolution of written petitions to public functionaries." Let us never tire of elevating our just demands to these employees, forcing them to pay attention to the matters that impact the interests of our Catholic community.

10. Miguel Antonio Caro, Freedom of Religion (1871–1872)

4. "Freedom of peaceful association." Let us then gather together peacefully. Let us establish and expand our Catholic associations, no matter how much the intolerant liberal press attacks us.

The constitution also guarantees the rights of suffrage and representation. We shall exercise these rights: Let us consequently assemble to agree on candidates and to submit petitions. It is true that the right of representation reflects the opinion of people more clearly than the right of suffrage. We do have the support of the majority and should convey it to both public opinion and the Congress.

We must study the constitution to determine the extent to which it empowers functionaries to favor or protect the sentiments of [Catholic] unity. The spirit of our constitution is evidently atheist, as demonstrated by the absence (with one exception) of the name of God. In addition, it includes hostile statements against the Catholic Church. However, if we set aside this general spirit, which does not add up to a law, and those specific statements, the constitution, due to its excessive federalism, permits that which is not prohibited, could not be prohibited, and cannot be considered as prohibited without detriment to the larger interest. Neither former legislators nor current interpreters of the law consented to regard as illicit, or outside the range of public powers, the latitude to permit.

"All matters of government," the constitution declares, "that have not been manifestly, specifically, and deliberately delegated to the [federal] government are the exclusive responsibility of the states." Since church–state relations have not been delegated to the government, it follows that the states have the power to legislate on the matter in any way they wish, for as long as they do not violate other elements of the constitution. Therefore, any state can adopt the Catholic religion as the official religion, albeit without prohibiting the public or private exercise of another religion, because this right is protected by article 15, item 16, of the constitution. In the same manner, the right of any state to declare an official religion is implicitly guaranteed by the same article.

The general [federal] government cannot establish unity because it does not have the tools to do so. The matter gets more complicated because the government exercises enormous powers with regards to public instruction. That the government should teach, as evidently it does when it opens schools and universities, can be considered unconstitutional. But once it does, it becomes less unconstitutional to impart a Catholic rather than an anti-Catholic, or indifferent, education.

10. Miguel Antonio Caro, Freedom of Religion (1871–1872)

The former reflects the public sentiment while the latter denigrates and opposes it. Good hermeneutics suggests that a constitution promulgated in the name of the people should honor the interests and aspirations of the people instead of denigrating and opposing them.

The freedom of religion guaranteed by the constitution is another barrier to the government adopting and protecting the Catholic religion. The freedoms of teaching and industry are in the same situation. If the government cannot interfere with such liberties, then it cannot promote instruction, industry, or belief. However, if these liberties are not opposed (as liberal papers like the *Diario de Cundinamarca* argues) to the role of government in advancing them, neither should the protection of public beliefs be opposed. If the government has the right to build roads, and prefers this or that route, it should also have the right to support the interests of religion by preferring one doctrine over the other. But there is a difference: When the government makes the choice to build a road, it defers to a competent engineer. In choosing a Catholic system for the organization of public instruction, a choice that is either constitutional or unconstitutional, the government will satisfy the demands and needs of the entire nation.

If we use all our energies, within the framework of the constitution, our victories will be so evident that our adversaries will be compelled to step aside or remain in contempt of the adopted system, thereby showing their dictatorial tendencies openly. For the sake of our rights, this is the decisive choice that we must force upon them.

Part IV.
Society

11
JUAN FRANCISCO MANZANO
Life of the Negro Poet Written by Himself (1840)

Juan Francisco Manzano (1797/8?–1853) was born and grew up as an enslaved person in the province of Matanzas, Cuba.¹ He taught himself to write despite being forbidden to do so by his masters: "when everybody went to bed, I used to light a piece of candle, and then at my leisure I copied the best verses, thinking that if I could imitate these, I would become a poet."² He published a first selection of his poems in 1821, still under slavery. His work attracted the attention of literary circles in Havana, and the favour of Domingo del Monte (1804–1853), "a wealthy intellectual, leader and patriot who ... mentored a generation of young writers."³ It was thanks to del Monte's efforts that Manzano was able to buy his freedom in 1836. Del Monte also persuaded Manzano to write his autobiography narrating his sufferings under slavery, which he started to write in 1835. Richard Madden (1798–1886), an abolitionist who had been in Cuba for three years, understood the importance and significance of the account. When he returned to London in 1839 he brought an edited copy of Manzano's manuscript, which he translated and published with Thomas Ward and Co. in London (1840) and presented it to the Anti-Slavery Society. Our selected passages are taken from this edition, which came to light anonymously under the title Poems by a Slave in the Island

---

¹ Selected passages from "Life of the Negro Poet," in *Poems by a Slave in the Island of Cuba, Recently Liberated; Translated from the Spanish by R. R. Madden, MD, with the History of the Early Life of the Negro Poet Written by Himself* (London: Thomas Ward & Co, 1840). (Editors' note)
² In *Poems by a Slave*, 79. (Editors' note)
³ Ivan A. Schulman, "Introduction," in Juan Francisco Manzano, *Autobiography of a Slave/Autobiografía de un esclavo* (Detroit, 1996), 13. (Editors' note)

11. Juan Francisco Manzano, Life of the Negro Poet (1840)

of Cuba, Recently Liberated; Translated from the Spanish by R. R. Madden, MD, with the History of the Early Life of the Negro Poet Written by Himself.

The Senora Donna Beatrice, the wife of Don Juan M____ took pleasure every time she went to her beautiful estate, the Molino, to make choice of the finest Creole children about the age of ten or eleven years, and carry them to town, where she gave them instruction comfortable to their new condition. Her house was always filled with these young slaves instructed in everything necessary to her service. One of the favourite young slaves was Maria____, my mother, who was greatly esteemed for her intelligence, and her occupation was to wait on the Senora Marquesa of J. in her advanced age. This lady was accustomed when she was pleased with her attendants to give them their liberty when they were about to marry, if it were some mechanic likewise free; providing them with all things necessary, as if they had been her own children, without depriving them after their marriage of the favour and protection of her house, which extended even to their children and husbands; of which conduct there are many notable examples, amongst those who were not even born in the house. Various changes, however, taking place in the service, Maria became the chief waiting-woman of the Marquesa. In this situation she married Toribio de Castro, and in due time, I was ushered into the world.

It would be tedious to detail the particulars of my childhood, treated by my mistress with great kindness that I deserved, and whom I was accustomed to call "my mother." At six years of age, on account, perhaps, of too much vivacity, more than anything else, I was sent to school to my godmother every day at noon; and every evening I was brought to the house, that my mistress might see me, who seldom went out without seeing me, for if she did, I roared and cried, and so disturbed the house, that sometimes it was necessary to send for the whip, which nobody dared to lay on me, for not even my parents were authorized to flog me. And I knowing this, often took advantage of it.

But passing over much of my early history, in which there was nothing but happiness, I must not omit the circumstances which happened at my baptism; my mistress desiring to solemnize that day with one of her noble traits of generosity, in part liberated my parents by "*coartación*,"[4] giving them the power at any time of purchasing their liberty at the sum of three hundred dollars each.

---

[4] A practice that allowed enslaved people to purchase their freedom. (Editors' note)

11. Juan Francisco Manzano, Life of the Negro Poet (1840)

I had already at the age of twelve years composed some verses in memory, because my godfather did not wish me to learn to write. From this age, I passed on without many changes in my lot to my fourteenth year; but the important part of my history began when I was about eighteen, when fortune's bitterest enmity was turned on me.

For the slightest crime of boyhood, it was the custom to shut me up in a place for charcoal, for four-and-twenty hours at a time. I was timid in the extreme, and my prison, which still may be seen, was so obscure, that at mid-day no object could be distinguished in it without a candle. Here after being flogged I was placed, with orders to the slaves, under threats of the greatest punishment, to abstain from giving me a drop of water. What I suffered from hunger and thirst, tormented with fear, in a place so dismal and distant from the house, and almost suffocated with the vapours arising from the common sink, that was so close to my dungeon, and constantly terrified by the rats that passed over me and about me, may be easily imagined. My head was filled with frightful fancies, with all the monstrous tales I had ever heard of ghosts and apparitions, and sorcery; and often when a troop of rats would arouse me with their noise, I would imagine I was surrounded by evil spirits, and I would roar aloud and pray for mercy; and then I would be taken out and almost flayed alive, again shut up, and the key taken away. This kind of punishment was so frequent that there was not a week that I did not suffer it twice or thrice.

My ordinary crimes were – not to hear the first time I was called; or if at the time of getting a buffet, I uttered a word of complaint; and I led a life of such misery, daily receiving blows on the face, that often made the blood spout from my nostrils; no sooner would I hear myself called than I would begin to shiver, so that I could hardly keep on my legs, but supposing this to be only shamming on my part, frequently would I receive from a stout negro lashes in abundance.

At night I had to go to sleep at twelve or one o'clock, some ten or twelve squares of buildings distant, where my mother lived (in the negro *barracones* [rudimentary sleeping (or living) quarters]). Being extremely timid, it was a serious matter to me to pass to this place in the wettest nights. With these troubles, and other treatment something worse, my character became every day more grave and melancholy, and my only comfort was to fly to the arms of my mother, for my father was of a sterner nature.

We were returning from the town late one night, when the *volante* [a horse-drawn light carriage] was going very fast, and I was seated as usual,

11. Juan Francisco Manzano, Life of the Negro Poet (1840)

with one hand holding the bar, and having the lanthorn in the other, I fell asleep, and it fell out of my hand; on awaking, I missed the lanthorn, and jumped down to get it, but such was my terror, I was unable to come up with the *volante*. I followed, well knowing what was to come, but when I came close to the house, I was seized by Don Sylvester, the young mayoral. Leading me to the stocks, we met my mother, who giving way to the impulses of her heart, came up to complete my misfortunes. On seeing me, she attempted to inquire what I had done, but the mayoral ordered her to be silent, and treated her as one raising a disturbance. Without regard to her entreaties, and being irritated at being called up at that hour, he raised his hand, and struck my mother with a whip. I felt the blow in my own heart! To utter a loud cry, and from a downcast boy, with the timidity of one as meek as a lamb, to become all at once like a raging lion, was a thing of a moment – with all my strength I fell on him with teeth and hands, and it may be imagined how many cuffs, kicks, and blows were given in the struggle that ensued.

My mother and myself were carried off and shut up in the same place. Scarcely it dawned, when the mayoral, with two negroes acting under him, took hold of me and my mother, and led us as victims to the place of sacrifice. I suffered more punishment than was ordered, in consequence of my attack on the mayoral. But who can describe the powers of the laws of nature on mothers? The fault of my mother was, that seeing they were going to kill me, as she thought, she inquired what I had done, and this was sufficient to receive a blow and to be further chastised. At beholding my mother in this situation, overwhelmed with grief and trembling, I asked them to have pity on her for God's sake; but at the sound of the first lash, infuriated like a tiger, I flew at the mayoral, and was near losing my life in his hands; but let us throw a veil over the rest of this doleful scene.

The second time that I was at Matanzas, there never passed a day without bringing some trouble to me; no, I cannot relate the incredible hardships of my life, a life full of sorrows! My heart sickened through sufferings, once after having received many blows on the face, and that happened almost daily; my mistress said, "I will make an end of you before you are of age;" these words left such an impression on my mind, that I asked my mother the meaning of them, who quite astonished said, "my son, God is more powerful than the devil." On another occasion, going to be chastised, for I do not remember what trifle, a gentleman, always kind to me, interceded for me; but my mistress said to him, "mind, Señor, this boy will be one day worse than Rousseau or Voltaire, remember my words." These strange names, and the way that my mistress expressed herself made me very anxious to know what sort of people they were; but when I found out, that they were enemies of God, I became more uneasy, for since my infancy I was taught to love and fear God.

Although oppressed with so many sufferings, sometimes I gave way to the impulses of my naturally cheerful character. Whenever I went to Señor Estorino's house, I used to draw decorations on paper, figures on cards or pasteboards, and scenes from Chinese shades, then making frames of wild canes, for puppet shows, with a penknife, the puppets seemed to dance by themselves.

Sometime after this, we went to Havana, where I was appointed to the service of young Nicolas, who esteemed me not as a slave, but as a son, notwithstanding his youth. In his company the sadness of my soul began to disappear. I was now kindly treated, and never was without pocket money. My business was to take care of his wardrobe, to clean his shoes, and wait upon him. As soon as day dawned, I used to get up, prepare his table, armchair and books, and I adapted myself so well to his customs, and manners that I began to give myself up to study. From his book of rhetoric I learnt by heart a lesson every day, which I used to recite like a parrot, without knowing the meaning; but being tired of it, I determined to do something more useful, and that was to learn to write: but here was a difficulty, I did not know how to begin, nor did I know how to mend a pen; however, I bought ink, pens, and penknife, and some very fine paper; then taking some of the bits of written paper thrown away by my master, I put a piece of them between one of my fine sheets, and traced the character underneath, in order to accustom my hand to make letters; with the stratagem, at the end of the month I could write almost the same hand as my master's. Extremely pleased with myself, I employed the hours from five to ten every evening, exercising my hand to write. My master was told how I employed the evenings, and once he surprised me with all my writing apparatus, but he only advised me to drop that pastime, as not adapted to my situation in life, and that it would be more useful to me to employ my time in needlework. In vain was I forbidden to write, for when everybody went to bed, I used to light a piece of candle, and then at my leisure I copied the best verses, thinking that if I could imitate these, I would become a poet. But this happiness lasted only about three years, when my former mistress of Matanzas, hearing reports so favourable of me, resolved to take me into her own service again.

11. Juan Francisco Manzano, Life of the Negro Poet (1840)

My former mistress arrived, and intimated very kindly to me her intention to take me back. Early next morning I ventured to ask paper and ink, in order to advertise for a new master. This quite astonished my mistress, and saying that she took me back for my own sake, and that I had better stop with her till she made some other arrangements, and when she turned her back I was sorry for having given her this uneasiness. At dinner time, she mentioned my boldness to her sister the Countess, and, with an angry tone, said to me before all the company, "this is the return you intend to make for all the care I took in your education; did I ever put my hands on you?" I was very near saying, yes, many a time, but better to say, no. After prayers in the afternoon, I was sent for by the Countess and Donna Maria Pizarro, who both tried to persuade me to desist from my intention. I plainly told them that I was afraid of my mistress's fiery temper; this conversation ended by the Countess advising me to stop with my mistress till she thought proper to give me my liberty.

Some time after this we left for Matanzas, stopping at the Molino. Here they pointed out to me my new duties, and I acquitted myself so much to their satisfaction, that in a short time I was the head servant of the house. When I was about nineteen years of age, I had some pride in acquitting myself of my duties, so much to the satisfaction of my mistress, and never waited to be ordered twice; at this time I could not bear to be scolded for trifles; but the propensity to humble the self-love of those who are in the good graces of their masters is a contagious disease in all rich families. Such was the case with a person, who without any cause or provocation on my part, began to treat me badly, calling me bad names, all of which I suffered, till he called my mother out of her name: then I retorted on him a similar expression, he gave me a blow, which I could not avoid, and I returned it. When [my mistress] was told of what happened; I excused myself, saying, that I could not suffer my mother to be called so bad a name; "So," said she, "if he repeats it again, you will not respect my house?" At the third day we went to breakfast to the Molino: meanwhile I was uneasy, I had before me all the vicissitudes of my life, and was apprehensive of what was to come. Soon after our arrival, I saw the mayoral coming towards the house; I escaped through the garden, and hid myself: In the afternoon I went to town, to the Count of G., who gave me shelter and protection; I was still uneasy, I wept bitterly when I remembered the kindness I was treated with by other masters in Havana. Scarcely was I there five days, when for a trifling fault they sent for a commissary of police, who secured me with a rope, and took me to the public

11. Juan Francisco Manzano, Life of the Negro Poet (1840)

prison in the middle of the day; at four o'clock, there came a white man from the country, who demanded me, and I was delivered to him; he put on me the coarse linen dress, he tied my arms with a rope, and led me towards the Molino which I desired never to see again. At the Molino, Don Saturnino Carrias, the mayoral at this time, examined me, I told the truth, and he sent me to work at the fields without any chastisement or fetters. I was there about nine days, when my mistress coming at the Molino to breakfast, sent for me, gave me a fine suit of clothes, and took me to town again in the volante. I was known at this time under the name of the Chinito, or the little Mulatto of the Marquesa.

Some time past on without any novelty, when my mother died suddenly. I was made acquainted with this accident soon afterwards, when my mistress gave me three dollars to have prayers for her. A few days later she gave me leave to go to the Molino, to see what my mother had left. The mayoral gave me the key of the house, where I only found a very large old box empty: as there was a secret in it, which I knew, I pulled the spring, and found there some trinkets of pure gold, but the most worthy were three ancient bracelets, near two inches broad and very thick, two strings of bead, one of gold, the other coral and gold: I found also a bundle of papers, in which were some accounts of debts due to us, one of 200 and odd dollars, another of 400, payable by my mistress, and some other small sums. I returned to my mistress, and gave an account of what I found. At the end of five or six days, I asked her if she had examined the bills; she answered calmly, "not yet;" and I went to inform the Creole, Rosa Brinsiz, who had the care of my sister, Maria del Rosario. Rosa was continually urging me not to lose any opportunity of asking my mistress about it, as she wanted my sister's share, to repay herself the expenses of nursing and keeping her, and as I was the eldest, it was my duty, she said, to look after the money. Teased by her, I ventured to mention it again to my mistress; but what was my astonishment, when instead of money, she said, "You are in a great hurry for your inheritance, do you not know that I am the lawful heir of my slaves? If you speak to me again about it, I will send you where you will never see the sun or the moon again; go and clean the furniture." The following day I made Rosa acquainted with this answer, and some days after she came herself to speak to my mistress, with whom she was a long time; when she came out I gave her two of the three bracelets, and all the beads. My mistress, who was always watching me, came near us, and intimated to Rosa, that she disliked her to have any communication with me, or any of the servants, and Rosa went away, and never came there any more.

As for me, from the moment that I lost my hopes, I ceased to be a faithful slave; from an humble, submissive being, I turned the most discontented of mankind: I wished to have wings to fly from that place, and go to Havana; and from that day my only thoughts were in planning how to escape and run away. Since the idea of freedom took possession in my mind, I endeavoured to learn everything useful to me; I invented many fancy things in my leisure hours, though these were few, I took sheets of paper, and doubling them in different shapes and forms, I turned them in various shapes of flowers, pine-apples, shells, fans, epaulettes, and many more things, for which I was praised by everybody. I began to be as comfortable as ever; in a word, I thought myself already free, and waited only to be of age; this hope encouraged me to learn many useful things, so that I should not be a slave I should earn a honest livelihood. At this time I wrote a great many sonnets. Poetry requires an object, but I had none to enflame my breast, this was the cause of my verses being nothing else than poor imitations. I was very anxious to read every book or paper that fell in my way, either at home or in the streets, and if I met with any poetry I learnt it by heart, in consequence of this, I could recite many things in poetry.

My mistress was continually threatening me with the Molino and with Don Saturnino and I had no wish to pay him another visit. With the belief that if I could go to Havana I would have my liberty I inquired the distance, and was told twelve leagues, which I could not reach on foot in one night. One day my mistress ordered my shoes to be taken off and my head shaved, after which I was commanded to carry water for the use of the house, with a large barrel upon my head; the brook was distant thirty yards with a declivity towards it from the side of the house. I was returning up the little hill, when my foot missed, and down I went upon my knee, the barrel falling a little forward came rolling down, struck against my chest, and down both tumbled in the brook. My mistress said, "that is the trick of your's to evade work," she threatened me with the Molino and Don Saturnino, which name had a magic effect on me, and I began to think seriously about escaping to Havana. The following morning when all the people were at church, a free servant called me aside, and in a whisper said to me "my friend, if you suffer it is your fault; you are treated worse than the meanest slave; make your escape, and present yourself before the Captain-General at Havana, state your ill treatment to him, and he will do you justice;" at the same time showing me the road to Havana.

At eleven o'clock, I saw Don Saturnino arrive at the house; from this moment my heart beat violently, my blood was agitated, and I could not rest, I trembled like a leaf, my only comfort at that moment was the solitude of my room, there I went; and there I heard the servants talking together, one was inquiring of the other the reason of the coming of Don Saturnino. "Why," said the other, "to take away Juan F." This was more than I could endure, a general trembling took possession of my limbs, and my head ached very much. I fancied myself already in the hands of Don Saturnino, leading me away tied like the greatest criminal – from this moment I determined on my escape. I left the room with this determination, when I met again the same servant, who said to me, "Man take out that horse from the stable, and leave him outside, here are the spurs, take them, and there is the saddle, and so you will know where to find every thing." And then he gave me such a look as quite convinced me that, he advised me to take the opportunity, and not lose it. I was hesitating, yet I did not like to leave behind me my brothers, and then I was afraid to travel a whole night through roads unknown to me, and alone. And in danger of falling in with any commissary of police; but what was my surprise, when after supper, as I was sitting on a bench by myself, meditating about what to do, Don Saturnino came to me, and asked, "Where do you sleep?" I pointed to him the place and he went away; this entirely determined me to make my escape – he might have made the inquiry with good intention, but I could not consider it but with great suspicion. I remembered at that moment the fate of one of my uncles, who in a case like mine, took the same determination of escaping to Havana and was brought back again like a wild beast – but for all that I resolved to venture on my escape, and in case of detection, to suffer for something. I waited till twelve o'clock. That night everybody retired early, it being very cold and rainy. I saddled the horse for the first time in my life, put on the bridle, but with such trembling that I hardly knew what I was about, after that I knelt down, said a prayer, and mounted on the horse. When I was going away, I heard the sound of a voice saying, "God bless you, make haste." I thought that nobody saw me, but as I knew afterwards, I was seen by several of the negroes, but nobody offered any impediment to my flight.

Juan____

12
MARIANO OTERO

Comments on the Social and Political Situation of the Mexican Republic in the Year 1847 (1847)

Mariano Otero (1817–1850) was born in Guadalajara, Mexico.[1] A lawyer by training, Otero made early choices in favor of liberalism, advocating a return to the federalism embodied in the Constitution of 1824, although with some alterations which included the separation of the clergy from politics. He was also concerned about the political instability of the post-independence period. He participated in the liberal revolt of 1846, was part of the Constituent Assembly of 1847, and was one of the members of Congress who opposed the Treaty of Guadalupe Hidalgo on the grounds that the conflict was an illegitimate war of conquest. He became Minister of Foreign Relations in the government of José Joaquín de Herrera in 1848. His premature death was due to the cholera epidemic of 1850. In this selection, which he wrote during the Mexican–American War, he tried to explain the causes that led to defeat, tracing them back to the colonial and independence periods, but eloquently rejecting any justifications based on race.

A foreign army of ten to twelve thousand soldiers has occupied Veracruz and marched into the capital of the republic. With the exception of the bombardment of the port, the engagement at Cerro Gordo, and the smaller clashes with Mexican troops near the capital city, the invading army did not encounter much resistance on their way across three of the

[1] This abridged versión is based on Mariano Otero's *Consideraciones sobre la situación política y social de la República Mexicana, en el año 1847* (Mexico City, 1848), 3–56. (Editors' note)

12. Mariano Otero, *The Mexican Republic (1847)*

most important – and populous – states of the Mexican Federation, an area inhabited by more than two million people. An event of this magnitude demands the most serious reflections.[2]

Shallow individuals who only look at the facts, rather than at the causes that produce them, often make enormous mistakes. It is not surprising, then, that foreign newspapers call the Mexican people "an effeminate people, a degenerate race that does not know how to govern or defend themselves."[3]

A thoughtful individual, on the contrary, is not satisfied with mere effects and seeks to establish their antecedents. That individual will easily identify the true motives whereby the Mexican people have not taken an active part in the war, and remain distant spectators. Once the motives are identified, only the blindest of partialities can insist that these are the inherent defects of the Mexican race, rather than the consequence of very specific causes.

The purpose of this essay is to identify as clearly as possible the heterogeneous and corrupt elements present in Mexican society. This is, undoubtedly, the only way to show the true and specific causes that have put Mexican society in the current state of decadence and prostration. With this approach, I believe we can dispel the errors that even educated people make when they attribute to the Mexican race defects that are, in fact, common to the human species.

It is rather sad to describe the state of society in our republic. The task is uncomfortable, especially for a Mexican, when there is nothing pleasant to say. But I am writing in Mexico, with thousands of witnesses before me. Not only do I not fear to be contradicted, but I can also state that the picture of our unfortunate situation is even darker. I would be happy to be proven wrong, because I am Mexican and wish to see my country happy and respected by the world. But I do not entertain any illusions. The picture that I paint of our society is truthful, and can be seen with

---

[2] The Mexican–American War (1846–1848) resulted from the annexation of Texas by the United States in 1845. Mexico was occupied from the north by the troops of General Zachary Taylor (who subsequently became the twelfth president of the United States), and attacked from Veracruz by General Winfield Scott, who entered Mexico City on September 14, 1847. The conflict ended with the Treaty of Guadalupe Hidalgo (February 2, 1848), which ceded nearly a half of Mexican territory to the United States. (Editors' note)

[3] In *The Dead March: A History of the Mexican-American War* (Cambridge, Mass., 2017), 113–121, Peter Guardino examines the generalized views among volunteers in the US Army during the war depicting Mexican people as racially inferior. (Editors' note)

12. Mariano Otero, The Mexican Republic (1847)

all clarity by those who look at it dispassionately and without distorting the reality of things.

Therefore, it seems futile that foreign writers should attribute to "effeminacy" or "degradation of the Mexican race" the indifference shown by the nation during the present war. Likewise, it is ridiculous for Mexicans to blame each other for what has happened. For my part, I believe that the following words explain it all: "In Mexico there is no national spirit because there is no nation." That is, Mexico cannot properly be called a nation until it has all the elements to create internal happiness and well-being, and to attain external respect.

The Mexican Republic has a territory of 120,000 leagues. It is bathed by two oceans, has many navigable rivers, as well as different climates where products from all over the world thrive. It has fertile virgin lands that yield over 100 percent of what is sown, and great mountains rich in mineral wealth. These factors prove that the country has all the natural elements to become a great and happy nation. In time, the people of this land will form one of the richest and most powerful nations in the world. Nevertheless, for as long as fanaticism, ignorance, and laziness continue to be the basis of our education, and for as long as we lack an enlightened and energetic government that improves society, it will be a weak and unfortunate country. It might be abundant in gold and silver, but will continue to offer the contemptible spectacle of a beggar who is exhausted by hunger and misery, and who covers himself with rags. He will inhabit a palace filled with gold and all kinds of wealth, but without knowing how to use it even for his own benefit and happiness.

A nation is nothing but a great family. To become strong and powerful, all individuals must be united by the ties of interest, and the bonds of affection. To confirm that this unity is not possible in Mexico, it is enough to look at the different classes that compose our unfortunate society. Moreover, the ceaseless civil war that has raged for thirty-seven years [since 1810] has demoralized all classes and destroyed the only element of order that our country had on the eve of independence. That is, the respect and obedience to authority that was the foundation of the colonial system. Such respect and obedience have been replaced by the most scandalous license and disorder. Freedom of the press, which should be established everywhere to enlighten the people, here it has only served to demoralize and diminish the population. Instead of exposing abuse and prejudice, promoting knowledge of the vital needs of society, and seeking with frankness, loyalty, and good faith the necessary improvements for the good and

12. Mariano Otero, *The Mexican Republic (1847)*

prosperity of the country, the periodical press exacerbates the lowest passions and cultivates hatred. Moreover, it misleads public opinion by serving the interests of the very class that thrives on the ignorance of the people.

In addition, the countless governments of the last twenty-six years,[4] and the leaders of the different parties that have been part of them, have shown their incompetence, or their evil intent. The people no longer respect the authorities because they cannot find examples of wisdom and virtue: only vices and weaknesses. The result has been hatred and contempt, because there is not a single man who can inspire trust. Everyone in authority has mishandled our numerous domestic affairs, and lost what little prestige they had either because of their perfidy or their incompetence to solve the numerous ills that afflict the republic. Obviously, the generalized and permanent disgust of society has generated profound hatreds among individuals. Classes are divided into factions whose political principles lead them to claim that their adversaries are the sole cause of what is wrong with the nation. Their views are so tenaciously held that they would rather see the collapse of the country before accepting the triumph of any party other than their own. Truth has disappeared in this hurricane of passions, where words no longer convey their true meaning, having been replaced by the most despicable nonsense. Each person has their own plan for shaping the happiness of the country. In this racket, the Mexican Republic presents a most curious spectacle: Everyone speaks the same language, but fail to understand each other. The only ones to take advantage of this situation are those who, having no political opinions, make a living out of the generalized disorder.

For all these reasons, Mexicans are farther apart in understanding one another than the inhabitants of St. Petersburg are from those of Cape Horn. There are no two persons who share the same political opinions. Even if they agree on this or that end, they still disagree on the means to achieve them. What kind of resistance can a people in such a state of dissolution present? Most certainly, none. It is utterly in vain to seek the causes of this misfortune in any racial defects, because the true cause is none other than a dismal education and even worse political organization. Mexico will go the same way that all peoples have gone, and will go, when they are badly educated and governed. There are too many examples of

---

[4] Mexican independence is often traced back to Fr. Miguel Hidalgo's rebellion in September 1810. Otero here refers to the events following the fall of the Spanish viceregal government, and the initiation of Agustín de Iturbide's rule in September 1821. (Editors' note)

12. Mariano Otero, The Mexican Republic (1847)

this truth in the history of the world, and now the current misfortune in Mexico provides yet another lesson for all nations. I hope that other Spanish American nations will steer away from this path, for we are all similar in terms of origin, education, and even social defects.

Some say that it is a shame that after twenty-six years of independence Mexico has not yet constituted itself as a stable nation. Moreover, that far from achieving self-government, Mexico appears before the eyes of the world as poorer, more divided, and therefore weaker than it was by the end of colonialism.

This evaluation is not without foundation. That is why we often hear about the inability of Mexicans to govern themselves. In fact, not a few claim that this inability is beyond repair because it comes, according to some, from the influence of climate, or, according to others, from defects inherent in our nature. We adamantly reject such absurd claims because we are convinced that what has occurred in Mexico since independence is exactly what had to happen, without race having anything to do with it. If one agrees to look impartially at society at the time of independence, one must conclude that any other country, sharing similar social conditions, would have offered the same bloody and horrific spectacle.

We still hear repeated, almost like a prophecy, the statement made by judge [Miguel] Bataller at the time of independence: "One cannot think about a more severe punishment than condemning Mexicans to govern themselves." He did not have to think very hard to pronounce this terrible sentence, because a simple glance at the population of New Spain is enough to predict that, left to their own devices, Mexicans will be unhappy for as long as it takes to remove the vices and prejudices so deeply rooted in their education and customs.

What was the state of society at the time of independence? Apart from the four million or more semi-savage Indians who can hardly be considered members of society, what were the customs and education of the so-called enlightened class? In the first place, it should be said that of the more or less three million Europeans and mixed-race population, eighteen out of twenty did not know how to read and write. This fact alone shows that Mexico and its population did not belong to the civilized world. The clergy were dominant in this society, lacking in either education or virtue, but sufficiently shrewd and avaricious to own, in the course of 300 years, the greatest portion of land in the country. In addition to the influence they enjoyed on account of wealth, the clergy monopolized the education of the young through the schools, the pulpit, and the confessionary.

12. Mariano Otero, *The Mexican Republic* (1847)

From these positions, they disseminated ideas designed to consolidate their power. If this was not enough, they insinuated themselves into the private life of families, to observe and direct their actions. They became the censors of all family activities, abusing their trust in order to commit acts contrary to morality and religion. This is a clergy that believed it had a right to influence and even intervene in public affairs. They also presumed to be independent of the government, and of the nation itself, because their *divine* mission on earth placed them beyond any human power. A country saddled with such a monstrous institution, it is easy to see, has more than enough to be unhappy about for quite a long time. The power of this privileged class, founded on the ignorance and the prejudices of the people, is an enormous power that can only be driven away by enlightenment. However, to reeducate the people, and to change their customs, will take a long time, especially as the clergy work incessantly to prevent such an occurrence.

Under the influence of the clergy, Mexicans learned to see religion not as the simple practice of virtue, but as the practice of externalities: They started to believe that to be good, men or women must attend religious services frequently, even if this meant neglecting their households and their families. The man who filled his house with countless images of saints, attended mass daily, confessed and took communion often was considered exemplary even if in private he engaged in the most vicious and shameful practices. This is how hypocrisy became the most important virtue, and how honesty was punished as a vice. The clergy, fearing that civilization would bring down their power, fostered a most profound hatred of foreigners, declaring them to be heretics. They were so successful in this regard that the population, at the time of independence, thought that being heretics and witches, foreigners had tails.

In the principal cities of the republic, the people lived in the most horrible poverty as a result of the abject situation in which they were held. Accustomed to laziness and a wandering life, their favorite pastimes were bullfights, religious processions, novenas, gambling, and drinking. A people devoted to such practices is a miserable and degraded people, always lacking the means not only to feed themselves, but even to cover their nakedness. And yet, they constituted three quarters of the population of the large cities at the time of independence.

The higher classes of the country, composed of counts, marquises, other titled nobles, property owners, large landowners, and merchants, did not have a very good education. It could be said that they only differed

12. Mariano Otero, The Mexican Republic (1847)

from the larger population in the way they dressed, and in reading, writing, and counting with relative ease. They read no other books than those related to their businesses, the calendar, the catechism by father [Jerónimo Martínez de] Ripalda, the *Christian Year*, and a devotionary. Above all, what was called the *Mexican nobility* was characterized by their notorious ignorance, even in the context of the generalized ignorance, so that the titles of count, marquis, and *mayorazgo* were synonyms of ignorant and fool.

This level of ignorance should not be entirely surprising, because in the monotonous colonial life it was useless to know anything. This was especially the case in Mexico, where leadership positions, and most public employments, were occupied by peninsular Spaniards. Consequently, all that Mexicans needed to learn was how to obey, keep out of politics, and, especially, avoid discussion of religious matters. As the saying goes: "about king and Inquisition, say nothing!" In such a vegetative lifestyle, education and knowledge were useless. The important thing was to have enough money to purchase the greater goods of material life.

The Spaniards who came to settle in the colonies were generally honest and hard-working, but ignorant and bigoted. Consequently, they passed the same attitudes to their children. It would have been better to pass their good customs and their love of work, but they had the stupid mania of educating their children to become gentlemen, putting them in schools, buying them a military commission, or placing them in a government position, so that they would not have to work as their parents did. From these mistaken ideas, transmitted through education, comes the contempt that most Mexicans feel for the *decent* class, for commerce, for agriculture, and for the useful arts. From these same ideas come the groundless ambition and desire for public employment that has caused, and will continue to cause, the ills of our society.

The educated class in Mexico was composed of lawyers, physicians, and other professionals, but they were still far from being enlightened. To the lack of instruction, we must add that the example of Spain was not so good with respect to morality in business and public affairs. The scandals of the court in Madrid were well-known in Mexico: Gold or influence guaranteed employment and special considerations. This should not be ignored, because many unqualified individuals came to Mexico to occupy positions of importance.

It is easy to understand how, in a country like this, where laziness, vice, fanaticism, prejudice, and ignorance are the only learned "science," many

12. Mariano Otero, The Mexican Republic (1847)

years must pass before proper national organization can be established. It is clear that abuse, founded on the ignorance of the people, will fight fiercely to stay, and will present a formidable obstacle to any new, normal, and enlightened order of things. Could Mexicans be blamed, with justice, for the state in which they are?

The work of independence – namely, the overthrow of the viceroyalty by force – was the easy part because it only required the use of weapons: All it required was audacity and valor in combat. The most difficult work, however – the political regeneration of society – was still pending. It could not be done except by organizing a government whose aim was the well-being and prosperity of the nation. It needed to take all the necessary measures to educate and moralize the population; remove or destroy the abuses and privileges inherited from the colonial period; remove all the obstacles to commerce and agriculture, the true sources of wealth, power, and enlightenment. Also, open the door to all the industrious people from abroad who wish to live with us. In fact, the most important goal of this underpopulated country should be to attract an active and industrious population that can develop the resources that the Creator of nature has given us. Our situation would be entirely different. However, we must agree that in order to launch the necessary reforms we need leaders who are knowledgeable, and free from prejudice. They should have the courage and determination that can only come from a genuine interest in the happiness and greatness of the fatherland. This means that they will not be deterred by any individual or corporate interests. Such leaders could not have existed during colonial times. Some have attempted, at different times, to introduce important reforms. They have been unsuccessful, however, because the interests of the privileged class, as well as all sorts of passions supported by the generalized ignorance of the people, have managed to prevent them. Consequently, the country has marched toward inevitable ruin and annihilation.

Our description of the education and customs of the people of New Spain should not be construed as an offense to either the people of Spain, or their government. Our only point has been to provide an accurate idea of what Mexico was like at the time of independence, and continues to be today, to show the reasons why it has been unable to govern itself, or defend itself during the current war with the United States. I trust that this concise assessment will reach its objective: The causes of Mexican misfortune, when looked at impartially, call for the understanding rather than the contempt of other nations. Mexico should inspire noble

12. Mariano Otero, The Mexican Republic (1847)

sentiments when it is understood that its misfortunes do not come from race but from a host of negative circumstances that have reduced society to the sorry state in which it finds itself.

I feel no animosity toward the Spaniards, and have always considered the insults exchanged between Mexicans and peninsular Spaniards, in the last twenty-six years, ridiculous nonsense. In my view, the latter have no reason to dislike Mexico because of independence. The desire for independence is inherent in human nature, and thus there is no reason to consider it a crime. Mexicans, for their part, have no reason to hate Spain for the bad education and customs they inherited. It is a universal principle of justice that no one should be required to give more than one can. Spaniards brought to America nothing less than the same education and customs that predominated in the peninsula since the times of Philip II. That is why I completely dismiss the statements by some Madrid periodicals that claim that the victories of the US Army in Mexico, and the feeble resistance to it, made Spaniards *ashamed of having anything in common with Mexicans*. I believe that it makes more sense to say that *all who are part of the Spanish family feel ashamed of the backwardness and unhappiness that pervades all regions that speak the beautiful Spanish language. Instead of trading insults that lead nowhere, we should in good faith seek to remove ignorance, fanaticism, and the remains of barbarianism that are still with us.*[5]

In light of the painful situation in which Mexico finds itself, prostrated and without the will to fight; with an invading army in control of the ports, the proceeds from customs, and even the capital city; with a government on the run that, lacking resources and stature, is unable to defend the honor and rights of the nation, it is easy to conclude that the only way out of this tragedy is a peace treaty. It can also be predicted that such a treaty would be highly detrimental and shameful for Mexico: We will lose a great part of our territory in order to compensate for the expenses of a war that the victorious enemy brought to us in the first place. Once signed, it is also certain that our national independence will not only become an empty word, but also a bitter sarcasm. After the spectacle we have made of our weakness, or rather impotence, our political life as a nation will grow even more precarious and insubstantial.

On the basis of this sad conviction, I only wish that the despoliation and pain we have endured during this war will provide us with a salutary

---

[5] Italics in the original, probably as a means of emphasis. (Editors' note)

12. Mariano Otero, The Mexican Republic (1847)

skepticism. Most especially, that the people who have an influence on society, and consequently on public affairs, become convinced that we must change course because the one we have followed will inevitably bring us to another abyss. If we do change course, the war, though so devastating at present, will in the long term do us some good. At the very least, we could have the hope that our country, despite the loss of territory, will preside over a government of liberty and enlightenment that will be seen by civilized nations under a very different light. In the future, our children, and perhaps ourselves, will no longer be ashamed to be Mexicans when we visit other countries. We could then be proud of the name of our fatherland.

I do fear, however, that we will not learn from the hard lessons of the war. Should we go on as before; should the crass interests of individuals or corporations prevail over the true interests of the country; should the army, or public officials, continue to be tyrants and executioners instead of servants of society; should the clergy continue to influence politics to keep the country stagnant; should the government continue to live day by day without thinking about tomorrow; should the administration of justice continue to act as always, allowing criminals to circulate freely; should commerce and industry continue to be burdened with heavy and unfair taxes to support a crowd of lazy idlers; should public debt continue to be an element of chaos, instead of order and prosperity, to satisfy the greed of selfish speculators; should our petty ideas about foreigners remain, so they can never settle among us to help us improve our country; finally, should we continue with our military coups, overthrowing and replacing governments every three months to please malcontents who thrive on disorder, and whose numbers increase in the same proportion as the impunity that the disturbers of the peace enjoy, then it is of the utmost necessity that all sensible Mexicans who have something to lose shall become fully aware of the truth, no matter how sad it might be: Namely, that we will not be able to function as a nation, at least for some years, without the support or the armed intervention of a foreign country Once we are persuaded of this truth, the only question is whether that support will come from the democratic United States, or monarchical Europe. May heaven grant us, after all these calamities, the necessary good judgment to avoid this humiliating extreme as the only means of salvation!

Mexico, December 1847

13
JOSÉ MARÍA SAMPER

Essay on the Political Revolutions and the Social Conditions of the Spanish American Republics (1861)

José María Samper (1828–1888) was born in the provincial town of Honda, Colombia.[1] *A prolific author (his intellectual foe Miguel Antonio Caro mocked him by stating that Samper "did not have time to write short pieces"), he combined his writing activities with politics, journalism, and teaching. In his earlier career, Samper became prominent within a young generation of radical liberals who advocated universal and direct suffrage, the separation of church and state, and the abolition of the standing army. In 1855, in what was perhaps one of the first usages of the expression "Latin American," Samper proposed the formation of a federation of Spanish American republics to defend their emerging "democracies" and their interests from the ambitions of the European monarchies, the Brazilian empire, and US expansionism (*Reflexiones sobre la federación colombiana, 1855; *"Colombia" was the name Samper gave to his proposed union; at the time he wrote, the name of the country we know as Colombia today was Confederación Granadina). Later in his life, however, Samper tempered the radicalism of his youth and moved closer to the Conservative Party. Yet in the convention that adopted the 1886 centralist, "conservative" constitution, Samper's interventions revealed that he continued defending key liberal principles. Samper's selected passages in our volume come from his earlier liberal phase.*

[1] This selection is based on Samper's introduction to *Ensayo sobre las revoluciones políticas y la condición social de las repúblicas colombianas (Hispano-Americanas)* (Paris, 1861), 1–13. (Editors' note)

13. José María Samper, Spanish American Republics (1861)

The Spanish American republics are a complete mystery to Europe, particularly with regards to politics and society. They represent perhaps something worse than a mystery, indeed something closer to a deformed fifteen-headed monster sitting at the top of the Andes Mountains, in between two oceans, and occupying a vast continent. The nobility of the words that are spoken, the beautiful images that are created, and the good deeds that are accomplished in Spanish America seem to have never reached Europe. On the contrary, what arrives there are the loud and confusing echoes of our political tempests, the pictures of our military or clerical dictators, the murderous or ridiculous proclamations by equally disloyal chiefs of insurrections or reactions. Because Europe does not know us except through these images, it has formed an opinion about Spanish America that can, without exaggeration, be summarized like this: "Spanish America is a permanent scandal to civilization: It is made up of fifteen disorganized republics."

These strange aberrations are often incurred by civilized societies when they study, ponder, or judge peoples they consider inferior. Europe has had enough sense to send capable scientists to the New World to study the physical nature of our continent: [Alexander von] Humboldt and [Aimé] Bonpland (not to mention many important eighteenth-century travelers), [Jean-Baptiste] Boussingault and [François Désiré] Roulin, [Alcide] D'Orbigny, and a hundred more who have conducted studies of the highest importance. Europeans know, more or less, our colossal mountains and formidable rivers, plains and wilderness, glaciers and volcanoes, gulfs and harbors, flora and fauna, as well as geology and meteorology. They may know less about some curious details in our Spanish American natural environment, but they know enough about its general shape. Some characteristics are no longer a mystery to educated Europeans.

Something similar happens in the economic realm. The merchants of London and Liverpool, Hamburg and Amsterdam, the Havre and Marseille, Genoa and Trieste, Barcelona and Cádiz, all know how to obtain silver and cochineal in Mexico; indigo and coffee in Central America; gold, tobacco, and dyes in New Granada; coffee and cacao in Venezuela; straw hats and cacao in Ecuador; guano and silver in Peru; copper in Chile; quinine and silver in Bolivia; hides in Buenos Aires; coffee in Montevideo, etc. Those same European merchants also know to which of our markets they can send their cotton and woolen fabrics, linens and silks, wines and other beverages, metals and hardware, and a thousand other manufactures.

13. José María Samper, Spanish American Republics (1861)

What else? Does Europe know any more about the continent or about Spanish America? No. What for? Does it matter to Europe to know more? Judging by the facts, the answer seems to be, no. European societies know that we have volcanoes, earthquakes, savage Indians, caimans, huge rivers, immense mountains, extreme heat and fevers on the coasts and wetlands, boa constrictors and a thousand snakes, black people and mestizos, and endless insurrections and reactions. They also know that we produce gold and silver, quinine bark and tobacco, as well as numerous other articles of commerce. That's about it. Do they know about our colonial history, the nature of our revolutions, our racial background, the structure of our institutions, the sources of our customs, the external influences that impact us, the international treatment we receive, the aspirations that drive us, the character of our literature, our journalism, and our human relationships? No, none of that. Europeans are more interested in our volcanoes than in our societies. They know more about our insects than about our literature, and are more interested in the reptiles of our rivers than in the policies of our statesmen. They are much more knowledgeable about the cutting of bark or the salting of hides in Buenos Aires, than about the vibrancy of our young democracies.

This contrast is rather sad and embarrassing, although somewhat more so for European societies than for our own. We could cite the names of a hundred naturalists who have come to explore and study our natural world during this [nineteenth] century, but not one (other than the admirable Humboldt, a man of universal genius) who has come to study our society carefully. [Gaspard-Théodore] Mollien did not intend to study Spanish America, but did collect a series of ridiculous tales, publishing nothing but platitudes and absurdities. The majority of visitors, many of whom did not venture beyond the coast, visited some cities for a few days, and talked selectively to some people. They then returned to Europe to spread errors, incomplete or exaggerated notions, and extravagant views that cause laughter among Spanish Americans. It is a fact that Europe is profoundly ignorant of the social, political, and historical conditions of Spanish America.

Who is responsible for this ignorance? Europeans? Spanish Americans? Both, although to different degrees. In the case of Europeans, the commercial drive, and the materialism of governments, have looked at Spanish America as mere markets for their products, have searched for gold and silver to fill their banks and their treasuries, and have established naval stations as bases for the control of the seas and places to launch

13. José María Samper, Spanish American Republics (1861)

political intrigues and schemes of enrichment. That is why it has not been necessary for them to understand our societies, which are treated by Europeans as little different from Berber societies. This approach has been terribly wrong because it ignores the fundamental basis of all commerce and international influence: knowledge of people. However mistaken, this is the approach that has guided European policy toward Spanish America.

In addition, Europeans have been dismally wrong in their approach, especially during the first quarter of the nineteenth century, to the Spanish American revolutions of 1810. They have treated them with fear and loathing. Some who do not understand the laws that inform the establishment of governments and institutions have feared that Spanish American democracy, by making great progress and becoming more secure, could sooner or later influence Europe and destroy, or at least undermine, their monarchies, aristocracies, and institutions. Hence the obstinate war of antipathies, disdain, and usurpation that some European governments have waged against Spanish American democracy since 1810. This, without considering the enormous difference in the social conditions of the two worlds, greater even than the distance that nature established between the shores of the [Atlantic] Ocean.

Others have not feared Spanish American democracy, but many have ignored it to such an extent that they fail to recognize its vitality, which is irreversible, logical, and unstoppable, like the equilibrium required by civilization by the [social] and economic worlds. This is a democracy that cannot be eliminated without causing the total ruin of Spanish American societies. Those who have treated our democracies with contempt have been short-sighted, but nevertheless logical. When they viewed the revolutions of 1810 as a sudden and inexplicable movement, apparently without a cause, and when they considered the failure of the European democratic revolutions (a view which we are far from accepting), they concluded that in Spanish America everything was temporary and shallow; that it was a mere change of names: president instead of viceroy, parliament instead of the dictatorship of the *audiencias* [courts], the dictatorship of the many instead of dictatorship of one, the monarch. They thought that the new situation was a mere fact, not an emerging idea; that the revolution was not profoundly social, but simply political; that the civilized world had no interest in respecting or supporting the revolution, or at least allowing it to develop freely, accepting it as the starting point for a great and needed transformation. In short, they thought that this

13. José María Samper, Spanish American Republics (1861)

republican revolution could, in time, turn into a constitutional monarchy that would reinforce European traditions, or turn into a chaos that would make European intervention necessary, thus allowing for the exploitation and division of spoils that European powers had for a long time wanted from Spain's envied domination of the New World.

This colossal mistake in the way of understanding the transformations of Spanish America has made Europeans hostile to our societies. Their hostility has not stopped at causing conflicts and embarrassments, or inflicting numerous humiliations for ridiculous reasons. They have done something worse than that: They have ignored us, exempting themselves from the duty of understanding us, disdaining our own efforts to make ourselves known, and in the process wasting precious time for the advancement of civilization.

There was, however, a powerful motive for European prejudice: the situation in Spain. Had this noble country of our ancestors conquered liberty as we did, it could have, since 1812, become a major European power. The enjoyment of free institutions could have inspired feelings of intelligent benevolence, assuming from early on our emancipation as a promising and irreversible event, which could yield enormous benefits. Then, a great social confederation between Spain and the former colonies could have emerged, founded on the principles of liberty, independence, constitutionalism, literature, history, religion, language, race, etc., as well as a mutual collaboration in terms of agreements and shared benefits. Spain could have then gained an enormous influence, based on the support of a whole [Spanish American] continent, and we, supported in turn by Spanish prestige, could have consolidated, in a shorter time, a peaceful, hospitable, noble and progressive democracy, thanks to the respect of the European world.

Alas, things did not proceed this way. After heroic efforts to achieve independence, and to save the throne of Ferdinand VII, Spain was put back in chains. Soon thereafter, the same country [France] that had caused the misfortunes of Spain, launched an iniquitous campaign to reestablish the temporarily defeated despotism. This third fall [in 1823, after the Napoleonic invasion of 1808, and the restoration of Ferdinand VII in 1814] initiated a decade of bloody and devastating civil war. Spain, once the constitutional regime was reestablished, has not been able to do much beyond recovering from disaster and resisting the absolutist reaction. Until 1833, therefore, the Spanish government, under the circumstances, was in no mood to make peace with Spanish America, or enter

13. José María Samper, Spanish American Republics (1861)

into an alliance that could have elevated our [Latin] race to the first rank. After 1833, however, Spain has had neither the time nor the moral strength to achieve this goal. That is why we Spanish Americans have felt the burden of the European disdain. That is why Europe has had less interest in studying, understanding, and treating our people as would be appropriate for the advancement of civilization.

And yet, we have also done our part, as peoples and governments, to obscure and delay a more profound knowledge of our situation. It is not the case that we have neglected the cultivation of letters and sciences to the point that there are no grounds to evaluate us. Aside from our literature, which thrives in Caracas, Bogota, Santiago, and Buenos Aires, closely followed by Mexico, Quito, Lima, and other capitals, there are also journalists, historians, geographers, writers, economists, and jurists who have published notable works on the true historical, social, political, economic, and ethnographic conditions of our countries. To prove this point, it will be enough to cite the names of [Rafael] Baralt, [José Domingo] Díaz, Toro, Rojas, García de Quevedo, and many more (not forgetting the heroic and indefatigable [Agustín] Codazzi) in Venezuela; Vergara, Pinzón, [José Manuel] Restrepo, [Joaquín] Acosta, Plaza, [Manuel] Ancízar, Royo, Uricoechea, and a hundred more in New Granada; [José Joaquín] Olmedo and Villavicencio in Ecuador; the illustrious and eminent [Andrés] Bello, the prolific [José Victorino] Lastarria, [Miguel Luis and Victor] Amunátegui, [Benjamín] Vicuña Mackenna, [Domingo Faustino] Sarmiento, [Francisco] Bilbao, La Fragua, Magariños Cervantes, and a great many writers of merit in Chile, Peru, Buenos Aires, and other republics of Spanish America.

However, the work of these distinguished writers has not had a good reception in Europe: Our turmoil and political tempests have prevented a close European reading of the discoveries and manifestations of the Spanish American mind. This is the part we ourselves play in the neglect, unjust treatment, and partiality of Europe.

Still, are the Spanish American revolutions as shocking and scandalous as some Europeans would have us believe? Let us engage for a moment in a bit of comparison. Today, nothing attracts more attention than the Italian Revolution – an admirable revolution considering its timing, specific events, and meaning. Why is it being followed so attentively? It is not only because the solution to significant problems is at stake, and that the hopes of Europe are fixed on that revolution. It is also because the historical

13. José María Samper, Spanish American Republics (1861)

value of Italy, being the mother and cradle of modern civilization, elicits more attention, respect, sympathy, and admiration from the world.

And yet, what is the spectacle offered by this great people? There is nothing as sad, bloody, and terrifying as the social and political history of Italy from the times of Odoacer until 1858 or 1859. What a procession, fourteen centuries long, of popes and anti-popes, emperors and anti-emperors, kings and princes, bishops and feudal lords, dux and consuls, free cities and republics, condottieri and aristocrats, all acting in an endless drama, ranging from sublime virtues and harrowing crimes, rebellions and reactions, to somber despotism and murderous demagoguery! The history of Italy summarizes all the greatness, as well as all the horrors of humanity in this perpetual search for progress and renewal.

Beyond Italy, what do we see when we examine the history of various countries up until recent times? The history of the revolutions in Germany, England, France, and Spain sends shudders down a reader's spine. It has not been long since Russia, that pretentious great power, settled all dynastic matters with poison, daggers, and military conspiracies. In Paris, just twelve years ago [the 1848 revolution], candles were lit on the skulls of the victims of fighting. In Ireland, Catholic Ireland, assassinations and all kinds of violence are permanent. Are more examples needed, when the truth is so evident? And yet, this civilized Europe, heir to the Greeks and Romans, continues to destroy itself in horrendous wars, or undermines peace with suspicion and preparations for war; this is the Europe where extreme opulence coexists with extreme misery, and where people live under the threat of communism and the official organization of socialism (under the guise of strong, central, and defense-ready government); this is a Europe agitated by the nightmarish problems of Italy, the East, Germany, Hungary, etc.; a Europe that is far from consolidation or free from the dangers of the future; a Europe that is old, yet lives in the turmoil of new trials and experiences, and is satisfied with nothing. However, this Europe has the support of ancient traditions, and the light and strength provided by eighteen centuries since the foundation of Christianity.

Europeans believe that everything that happens to them is explicable, natural, and logical. But when it comes to the Spanish American republics the criterion changes. A society barely formed in the sixteenth, seventeenth, and eighteenth centuries, composed of heterogeneous and badly combined elements; that only has had a half-century of independent existence; whose population of twenty-six million is scattered over

13. José María Samper, Spanish American Republics (1861)

a continent two or three times the size of Europe, a region of 300 million inhabitants; this Spanish America, which is an emerging society overwhelmed by the challenges of its own creation, is judged in a most peculiar way. Europeans see the Spanish American revolutions not as the awkward first steps of a child, or as enduring the agitations that go with the search for progress, or as going through the typical phases of any social and political transition. No, they see these revolutions as crimes, as signs of corruption, as proofs of incapacity that prevent any hopes for the future of our republics. Europe has been humiliated and dishonored by the likes of Ferdinand [VII], [Joseph] Radetzky, and many others, but they are seen as exceptions. Spanish America, however, is viewed in an entirely different light: [Juan Manuel de] Rosas is our epitome; [Antonio López de] Santa Anna, [Manuel Isidoro] Belzú, [José Tadeo and José Gregorio] Monagas, and other terrible characters are seen as the rule. This is the logic that has guided European opinion regarding the Spanish American republics.

Not much attention has been paid to the need for the profound studies required to write the history of civilization. Perhaps sooner rather than later a dedicated and knowledgeable person will conduct such studies and write a history. This is one of the greatest needs of universal civilization, given the immense importance and novelty of Spanish America, and the fact that both the conquest and the independence of our continent are the most transcendental events in the history of humanity since the invention of the printing press. But until a qualified person appears, who has the necessary energy to carry out this work, it is the duty of every Spanish American who loves truth and progress to contribute to this task, however obscure his name might be in Europe.

The objective of this essay is to provide an overview of the elements and conditions of the conquest and colonization of Spanish America; define the characteristics of the colonial regime that ruled until 1810; analyze the spirit of the revolution of independence and the subsequent formation of our republics; determine with accuracy the elements of the current situation, and identify the true tendencies of our society. We will say what we think is true with frankness, sincerity, and candor. We will not point any fingers, or use flattery, both of which are repugnant to us. Our only aim is to invite the governments and the thinking persons of Europe to closely examine the life of our societies, setting aside the disdain with which they observe us. This attitude is detrimental not only to Europeans, but also to us, and to the general progress of civilization.

13. José María Samper, Spanish American Republics (1861)

We must refer to many events in the history of Spain and Spanish America. We know we will be read by people from both areas – after all, we are siblings by race, traditions, and many other ties – thus I hope that some references to the past will not be taken badly. It will be equally ridiculous and unjust for Spanish Americans to remain resentful for the oppression we suffered, and for Spaniards to hate us because of our emancipation. The resentment of the former has dissipated just as much as the hatred of the latter. We Spanish Americans have recognized that our oppression did not come from the Spanish people (who were themselves oppressed to an even higher degree) but rather from a corrupt time and civilization. Spaniards, for their part, have understood that our revolution of independence did not come from hatred, but was rather the inevitable result of the laws of progress, and the logic of both facts and principles. There is nothing, then, to prevent us from having a frank and calm discussion about the social and historical conditions of the Spanish American republics.

14
JUANA MANSO

The Moral Emancipation and Education of Women (1854)

Juana Manso (1819–1875) has been described as "the first woman to be appointed to an official government position and arguably the most radical feminist in nineteenth century Argentina."[1] *Indeed, her contributions to the cause of women's rights were extraordinary, through her writings, editorial and educational activities, and public speeches. Born in Argentina, she left the country with her family in 1840, after her father was exiled by the Rosas regime, and moved first to Uruguay, then to Brazil, Philadelphia, and Cuba. When she returned to Buenos Aires in 1853, she was already an experienced educator, author, and editor – her novel* Los misterios del Plata *had been published, serialized, in* O Jornal das Senhoras, *a woman's journal she set up in Brazil.*

The latter was somewhat replicated in the Album de Señoritas, *established by Manso in 1854, which only lasted for about a year. In 1859, Domingo Faustino Sarmiento, then head of the Elementary Schools Department, appointed her as director of the Escuela de Ambos Sexos, the first co-educational school in Buenos Aires, and editor of the educational journal* Anales de la Educación Común. *As Argentine president, Sarmiento appointed her to the Board of Public Instruction in 1871. Manso not only advocated for women's education but also for popular education more widely – her selected passages in our volume, originally published*

---

[1] Julyan G. Peard, "Enchanted Edens and Nation-Making: Juan Manso, Education, Women and Trans-American Encounters in Nineteenth-Century Argentina," *Journal of Latin American Studies* 40.3 (2008), 454. (Editors' note)

in the Album de Señoritas, *serve to illustrate her most passionate interests in these causes. She also favored civil marriage and non-religious education, positions that led her to clash with the Catholic Church; she converted to Anglicanism in 1865.*

The Moral Emancipation of Women

To address an issue of this magnitude – the moral emancipation of women – requires a great deal of circumspection. Also, that we give the greatest vigor, moral force, and solid ground to the new doctrines concerning women.[2]

Such doctrines are new to South America. In Europe and the United States, the emancipation of women is an established fact. Just a few months ago, British legislation has provided incentives to advocates who revise the old laws (iniquitous, to say the least) and propose new ones that *protect women*. As a result, in August of this year,[3] a husband who beat his wife was sentenced to two months in prison. Apparently, he thought that he still lived in those happy times when he could physically abuse her, put a rope around her neck and sell her in the market.

A great nation like England, the freest in the world, which has a thousand philanthropic institutions, and which has gifted humanity with the ending of the commerce in human flesh, suppressing the slave trade, could not continue the monstrosity of keeping women in the degrading state of slavery.

Human progress, that huge locomotive that runs over the customs and laws of countries, had already abolished such awful practices. However, the written law remained as an awkward, old, and twisted monument amidst the clean, graceful, and elegant buildings of the age.

Thus, England tore the yellowing and unintelligible page from the code of Romulus, which may have not killed the body, but did assassinate the soul. England called upon lawyers to write the articles that protect women from the brutal despotism that burdened them. By recognizing her intellectual capacity, it also guaranteed her personal dignity, rescuing her from the oppression and ignominy that surrounded her in the unequal contest between the weak and the strong. It thus righted the wrong

---

[2] This article was published in *Album de Señoritas: Periódico de Literatura, Modas, Bellas Artes y Teatros*, 1.1, Buenos Aires, January 1, 1854. (Editors' note)

[3] Because the issue of the periodical was published on January 1, 1854, "this year" certainly means 1853. (Editors' note)

14. Juana Manso, Moral Emancipation and Education (1854)

that dishonored her and stood out like an evident and awful stain in the fabric of other glorious institutions characterized by the wisdom of their philosophical spirit.

Society was created by men. Man alone has written the laws and, consequently, reserved the supremacy for himself. He has drawn a very tight and impassable circle around her. What is a crime in a woman, it is only human weakness in a man. And so, women are isolated within their own families, the same family of which God made her an integral part. She has been segregated from all the vital questions of humanity because she is considered weak. And yet, she is obligated to be strong while men, when it comes to temptations, are excused because of their individual failings.

Despite the inconveniences of her position, subordinated to a perpetual tutor who is sometimes full of vices and stupidity, women must still lower their heads without a word; she must tell her mind, do not think; to her heart, do not bleed; to her eyes, do not cry, and to her lips, do not complain.

Why? indeed, why this long torment which begins and ends with the life of a woman?

Why is her intelligence confined to the sense and perpetual darkness of ignorance?

Why, since youth, has her heart been deprived of the awareness of her individuality, of her dignity as a human being who lives, thinks, and feels? She is told repeatedly: You are not in possession of yourself, you are a thing, not a woman.

Why should she be reduced to a childbearing being whose only purpose is to perpetuate the species?

Why deny her access to science, art, industry, and even work, leaving her with more misery than nourishment, or the thousand-times more terrible meal of infamy?

Without a complete emancipation from aberration and prejudice, woman will never rise to the heights of her mission and the duties that come with it. Despite her perspicacity, she will fall into an absurd position: She will mistake one thing with another and will never achieve her goals, or advance the education of her children, because she does not know herself. Without knowing herself, she will not be able to know the hearts of others. Even if she defeats barbarianism and is guided by a beautiful maternal instinct, she might still take the wrong path: because without knowledge of the true moral instruction she will fall into absurdity, or

14. Juana Manso, Moral Emancipation and Education (1854)

empty generalizations that grow parasitically in the heart of children, removing them from access to enlightenment and becoming stationary, thus rejecting the moral spirit of justice and reason.

The upper classes have an easier time keeping the reign of error away. But the poorer classes, mired in barbarianism and prostitution, will not be able to escape that situation without much more work and perseverance.

At this solemn time in our *patria*, when progress and liberty are imminent, we call on the authorities to address the education of the poor. There are no improvements yet, and to build from the wreckage of the past will take us nowhere: It does not meet the needs of the present and, much less, those of the future.

We will return to this matter later, though without reflections and reasoning alone. Instead, we will disseminate sciences and knowledge that were confined to the realm of mystery. This is the knowledge that will accomplish the moral emancipation of women in our country. There will be no reason to envy the American women of the north.

With regards to the poor, we will point to the concrete ways to advance their education, by applying the means that we have seen to work elsewhere.

The Education of Women

A distinguished Portuguese poet has written that women "are the link to the chain that unites man and heaven."[4] Another no less illustrious poet has written, in a rich imaginative poem called "The Bard's Jealousies": "Oh, if a wretched race of poisonous snakes / could all be brought into a single bark / and I be the pilot!"

I believe that this last Lusitanian poet wanted nothing less than the extermination of all descendants of Eve. It would be curious indeed to see what men could do without women in all inhabited worlds. What sadness, what late regret! Woman! what mystery, either for good or ill, virtue or crime do you embody! Man hates you or adores you, insults you or celebrates you, but is always around you, like a butterfly around a flame! ... the delicate wings of the latter emit a gentle sound before it dies, a victim of imprudence. But man, how it screams for your attention or curses your alleged cruelty. Either warriors or poets, merchants or physicians, lawyers

---

[4] This article appeared in *Album de Señoritas*, no. 8, February 17, 1854. (Editors' note)

14. Juana Manso, Moral Emancipation and Education (1854)

or bankers, artisans or farmers, erudite or ignorant, scientists or laymen, they all ask you to make them happy, as if God had placed their joy in the hands of women!

Be that as it may! despite the pride and egotism that makes you [men] take away all our rights as sensitive, intelligent, and free souls, in the end you are the blind instruments of our will.

You might feel like a monarch, but the lowest of the creatures upsets you. The weakest of all human beings, those you despise and call "women" as an insult, are nevertheless a constant pain in your side, whether you adore or oppress us. God has given us the power of a master over a slave.

Angels in shape, but demons of malice, women will always be a mystery to you. You have solved the most difficult problems of algebra and mathematics; you have conquered the seas, scrutinized the heavens with your telescopes, and unearthed cities buried by the dust of centuries, or the lava of volcanoes, for the benefit of archeology. In your laboratories you have triumphed over nature, dividing it in parts or uniting them at will. Experimental physics is no longer a challenge for you. Natural history tells you about the instincts and behavior of animals; botany, the life of plants. Even the human soul has been placed on the operating table for analysis. Anatomy, physiology, phrenology, philosophy have all given you the data and the notions to study the internal and the external, the material and the immaterial worlds. But you have failed to understand women except in momentary flashes of inspiration. Calm abandons you at this point: Love or hate clouds your judgment, and you can only murmur praise or spit insults.

The sage and the philosopher disappear and only the man is left, facing that cause of his good or his evil. The slave is now in front of his master.

What fatality!

But this is how you want it. You are blind to the light of truth and deaf to the voice of reason. You have turned an angel into a demon. You have taken all the divine elements from her heart, and instead you have made her a hypocrite, an invidious being, a traitor. You have stolen her intelligence. Without a noble goal, she turns against you with a vengeance. You oppress her will, chain her freedom to either the father or the husband, and thus you force her to lie, to deceive you, to betray you. She will play with your weaknesses and lead you like a halter.

You take everything away from women! Everything that could give a noble aim to her intelligence, her sensitivity, and her free will. Instead, you flatter her vanity and make her love luxury. Your blind love of her beauty becomes an incentive for corruption, for what value will she give

14. Juana Manso, Moral Emancipation and Education (1854)

to her soul if she does not know it? What is conscience, honor, and dignity to a woman? Who speaks to her about it? Conscience? He defines it for her. She fears the world. But who teaches her to fear herself, and be ashamed of herself? Honor? Why would a woman want it when no one trusts her? What is honor to her? If single, the honor she safekeeps is that of the father or the brother; if married, that of the husband. Fools! how do you expect someone to care more for the good of others instead of their own? Freedom? Yes, the freedom to follow fashion, not the freedom given by God to the character of her soul. Women become slaves of their appearance, of their husbands, of error, and prejudice. Their motions are controlled, their steps counted: One inch outside and what has she become? A mix with no name, a monster, an oddity. What do you think will come out of this? Because man is weak and unable to undo the work of God, life will go on: Oppression results in deception, lies, and illicit means. And the less moral authority, sense of duty, or respect for the link between the human and the divine there is, the more common these are. Conscience becomes mute, and if it says something, it will be *do not chain me, do not oppress me!* When personal dignity, honor, and conscience are fully enlightened we understand that another's wrong does not justify our own. No one is responsible for our faults, not before God, or the severe tribunal of morality, because shame shall fall on those who deserve it. In this world we must carry our cross, be it heavy or light, as determined by the will of God.

That is why education will always be the foundation of a solid moral edifice. Erroneous notions and stale prejudices distort the education of women and turn into a demon she who came to this world to become an angel. This vicious circle is one of your own making, and it turns against you! You say that women are vain, voluble, and have a weakness for clothing and jewelry. Furthermore, that men should not marry because they will be ruined. You in the upper class, why do you not educate her instead of preparing her for a life of dissipation? And you, the poor, why do you close the door to work and industry, and place her in the position of choosing between prostitution and misery?

Women must be educated according to the moral and intellectual imperatives of the human soul. They must be educated as sensitive, intelligent, and free souls. Let them use and exercise the moral and intellectual faculties that God has granted them. They will then become symbols of the good for man, and not the target of angry and wrong vituperations.

14. Juana Manso, Moral Emancipation and Education (1854)

On Popular Education

The news that the budget for the schools has been increased represents a great victory. However, I wish I had the means to double or triple it.[5] Also, that the money thus spent be seen not only as the best investment there is for the nation, but also that good books are regarded as important. It is time to realize that the material aspects of education will not by themselves achieve the moral development of youth. The education of the heart not only leads to moral improvement but it also promotes intellectual development as well as the surest and fastest advancement of the masses.

It is vitally important to educate our people both physically and morally. We must defeat the laziness that undermines and corrupts them; we must replace the clothing of the Pampas with that of civilization; we must change the embarrassingly ferocious and uncouth language that so horrifies the foreigners who come to our shores; and we must purge those vices that mire our people in the mud. These aims cannot be accomplished with police decrees alone. That is a feeble containment that people easily break, just like a young horse ejects the rider that spurs him for the first time, and then runs wild and free in the plains.

The budget increase is a great step, perhaps the truest and safest road to progress. But it will be incomplete if, as we have insisted, the methods, the regulations, and the appropriate books are not provided. This, because learning to read, write, and count is not sufficient to educate a people who have little regard for the rule of law, and for whom barbarianism and throat-cutting are normal; a people completely left to their own devices; the blind instrument of hatred and fratricidal wars, whose heart has no mercy or feeling; a people whose children have grown amidst slaughter and human butchery, children who talk of blood and stabbings with precocious malice and without any awareness of guilt.

Therefore, there are moral needs for the youth that we intend to educate. And yet, we must ask ourselves, is there a book, a single book, that can meet those needs? The answer is no, and it is urgent to write one.

We should not confuse simple *instruction* with *education*. Today, both need to be in place. When we have a people who are poor and yet as moral, industrious, and moderate as that of the United States, then there will be no need of the teaching gospel that we desire, because children will learn

---

[5] This article appeared in "Educación popular," *Album de Señoritas*, no. 7, February 12, 1854. (Editors' note)

14. Juana Manso, Moral Emancipation and Education (1854)

the best moral education from their parents, which is the education by example that is learned without effort. Today, our primary education is insufficient; something more is needed. I fear being labeled a *visionary* if I say that in Buenos Aires we need temperance societies, as well as other institutions that seek to improve and moralize the poor. In the United States, such institutions are common because there is no reluctance to turn theory into practice. But that is not our case: We leave it all up to Providence, which knows best!

And yet, how much more could be done, and how much precious time we waste!

We took one step: We allocated a million pesos (which is a great sum) to popular education. That is quite enough!

Books? Ah, those we have are good. They could be better, but we have time. Now we are too busy. Perhaps tomorrow. Later! There is no expiration date!

All could be so much easier with just a bit of good will. Unhappily, nothing goes beyond the project stage. The [newspaper] *El Nacional* called for a school for artisans, without success. It called for an educational establishment sponsored by the government, a sort of refuge that we have insistently asked for, also without success. And yet, already having the space, not much effort is needed to make the establishment possible. Perhaps one day it may happen. It will always be a piece of good news.

Regardless, we congratulate ourselves, the government, and the people of Buenos Aires. It is our hope that some smart approach will take advantage of the resources made available, as well as these times of peace, to set the foundations for our future and our greatness.

What I have written in this regard may or may not be the most intelligent plan, but it represents at least my sincere hope for the good of my country.

I have articulated the ideas that I thought most appropriate. However, my voice does not reach the privileged circle of those who can do something about it. I have nothing, I am worthless. I can only offer useless proposals.

15
MARTINA BARROS

Prologue to *The Slavery of Women* (Critical Study by John Stuart Mill) (1872–1873)

Martina Barros Borgoño (1850–1944) was a pioneering Chilean who advanced women's rights in significant ways, not least in terms of advocating for suffrage, but also in terms of a critical approach to nineteenth-century thinking on gender distinctions. Born in a socially distinguished milieu (she was related to independence hero José Manuel Borgoño and to historian Diego Barros Arana, his uncle and mentor), Martina Barros encountered John Stuart Mill's The Subjection of Women *(1869) at a young age and embarked on the translation and commentary of the source by 1872.*[1] *Enthusiastically received by such leading liberal lights as Benjamín Vicuña Mackenna and Miguel Luis Amunátegui, Barros' prologue celebrated some aspects of Mill's work, but bemoaned others. She acknowledged the role of her husband, the liberal physician Augusto Orrego Luco, in the writing of the prologue, but affirmed that the ideas were her own in her autobiography.*[2] *Both had previously read Mill's* On Liberty *(1859), and shared his condemnation of the tyranny of customs, challenging gender traditions and participating actively in publications and intellectual circles in Santiago during the last quarter of the nineteenth century. Her views, however, were far from radical. As she stated in her*

---

[1] Martina Barros, *Prólogo a la esclavitud de la mujer (Estudio crítico por Stuart Mill)*, ed. by Alejandra Castillo (Santiago, 2009), 37–69. (Editors' note)
[2] Martina Barros de Orrego, *Recuerdos de mi vida* (Santiago, 2023), 104. (Editors' note)

15. Martina Barros, Mill's The Slavery of Women (1872–1873)

autobiography, "my aim in promoting the independence and culture of women was not to make them rivals of men, but rather their dignified companions."[3]

The title of [Mill's] book may suggest a seditious element it does not have, a heated call for an absurd rebellion, or a revolutionary proclamation intending to destroy the pleasant happiness of the home. However, next to the title of the book there is the name of the author: a serene and high-minded thinker who, like all those who seek the truth, may at some point be led astray. But it is far from his objectives to yield to the vulgar purpose of upholding strange and dangerous paradoxes: I mean those who might be applauded for their novelty, or fascinate because of their audacity, until time and good sense expose their tinsel and reduce them to their real value. This book is a study of women, a study that when conducted on the basis of careful observation and quiet reflection is far from the celebratory courtesy that constitutes the generous ideal of a poetically minded spirit. It is also far from being a repetition of those vague ideas that provide a sorry refuge for mediocre spirits and which make no sense in either life or science. When women are studied on the basis of nebulous metaphysics, the subject becomes interminable and its conclusions perennially absurd. When an observer judges a woman based on his own experience, he might be attaching to the nature of women what is exclusively and peculiarly limited to his own experience. This is the cause of significant error.

Now, is there anyone alive who has not experienced the happy (or unfortunate) influence of a mother, wife, or sister? A woman in each, or all, of these roles has entered universal life by giving man his shape, his developing self, and his inner harmony. If the influence has been unfortunate, he who studies it with the miserable logic of his personal disappointments will no doubt color his pen with the ink of resentment and will draw an ungrateful and cruel portrait. If on the contrary the influence has been favorable, his conclusions will be colored by an easily understandable enthusiasm that will appear in his written page idealized by his feelings and transformed by his poetic reveries.

Here is another cause of error, which can happen when women become indifferent to the observer, something that is inconceivable in human nature or, if it could be conceived, monstrous. Under this completely personal point of view one can only err, neither understanding women nor being able to work for the improvement of their condition.

---

[3] Barros de Orrego, *Recuerdos*, 217. (Editors' note)

15. Martina Barros, Mill's The Slavery of Women *(1872–1873)*

[John] Stuart Mill studies women from the perspective of experimental science, thereby suppressing the feelings and affections that women could awake in him. There are objects like pots, scales, eyeglasses that cannot feel anything. The reality of nature becomes overwhelming: It confuses vision with sleep, truth with whim, and woman with ghost. Mother, wife, and sister disappear; all that is left is a material being, an object of study that can be taken apart, analyzed, and defined just like any other object. This type of study is not entirely new: It is simply the subordination of a particular case to a general system. Indeed, here and there one can find numerous applications of this system to different aspects of womanhood. The principal merit of Mill's work is that it encompasses all such aspects and others yet to be studied. This system is susceptible to a critique that is not without value. One can easily see, as I have just pointed out, that a woman seen in this fashion will be deprived of her moral personality. She will no longer be considered as a sensible being and will be primarily examined as an object, just like a chemist examines a precious stone or a naturalist a flower. In this fashion she will be seen for what she is but not for what could be seen in her. We will only see a dead woman, not the life that animates her, or the feelings that give her beauty.

Let us suppose that all of this is true, even though it is far from having been demonstrated. But even accepting the existence of this cold science, would it be wrong to acquire it? When a physician examines a patient, he does not proceed by examining his father, his brother, or his sons. He lays a cadaver on the marble table of an amphitheater, and from that cold corpse and marble he extracts the mysteries of nature, opening up the secret compartments where pain and illness hide. This is what the corpse reveals and that is all the doctor needs to know. Women in our century are ill. The malady that torments a woman is as undefined as herself; she has an understudied sickness. What she now needs is not a poet who sings of her beauty and turns her into a divine being: She suffers and she needs a doctor who will remove her suffering. The doctor should work like the physician he is. Unfortunately, the author of this book has not followed such a rigorous method of examination: He lets himself be swept up by the reasoning of a superficial truth; he has ignored the study of facts, taking as truths general statements that though widely accepted are far from being exact. This is how big the influence of error can be seen even in the most superior spirits! Taking the slavery of women as his starting point and considering the obstacles they face in expressing their complaints, Mill has looked at the oppression of women

15. Martina Barros, Mill's The Slavery of Women (1872–1873)

only at the point when the tight bonds that brought down and degraded women have relaxed somewhat. A mere glance at the literature could have told him that this supposed fact is far from accurate. The complaints of women have been voiced ever since the printed book made an entrance into the world. The Venetian Lucrezia Marinella published *The Nobility and Excellence of Women and the Defects and Vices of Men* [1601] by the middle of the sixteenth century [sic]. Earlier, Modesta di Pozzo made a no less enthusiastic defense of her sex; a little later Margarita de Navarra brought to light a work with the same purpose. Similar works in the seventeenth century are not rare at all, and a tedious listing of them would be unnecessary after those already cited.

Before I proceed I will describe yet another mistake that originates when, as in the previous case, the neglect of facts leads to the glittering mirages of reason. Mill tries to convince us that society's domination of women is the result of the brutal abuse of power. However, to the extent that the rule of the strong declines and is replaced by the rule of reason and law, women will emerge from their low situation to occupy a place more in harmony with the needs of their bodies and the aspirations of their souls. From here the assumption follows, naturally and logically, that the position of women in our [nineteenth] century is vastly superior to that of the past, and that the rights to which they are entitled are exercised in a wider sphere than the limited circle that they occupied in previous times. Such a conclusion involves a willful forgetting of the rights that feudal society conceded to women, as for example an heiress who presided over civil and criminal cases, recruited troops, coined money, etc. Such a conclusion would erase from history an unquestionable fact: the many Renaissance controversies where women of talent and eloquence left an enduring legacy in the fields of philosophy and social science.

I.

I will now leave this troubling line of criticism to present the ideas developed in Mill's book. In doing so I experience, along with a pleasant feeling, a sad one. Our century has erased the distinctions between master and slave, as well as those of race and color, but it is still considered reckless, imprudent, and even dangerous to ask for the ending of the ill-conceived distinction between man and woman, that odious separation of the sexes.

15. Martina Barros, Mill's The Slavery of Women *(1872–1873)*

How does this remnant of those times that did not see the fraternal rise of Christianity, nor the emergence of legal science, continue to be alive today? Once the separation of the sexes was established by force, its continuation has been perpetuated by a vicious education that makes men consider themselves, from their birth, as superior to women. From their earliest years they are exposed at home to this capricious inequality. He is granted a freedom that keeps increasing to the same extent that a woman's is curtailed. In this way, a prejudice becomes second nature even though it cannot resist even the most basic criticism. By the same token, a woman is taught to see as sacred the arbitrary principles established by custom. This is how she is subjected to a system of education that rests on a notion of inferiority: It settles in her spirit, takes over her heart, and invades her entire life.

This is perhaps the only case, in our time, that a class (women) born in a Christian society is prevented, by the simple fact of their birth, from ever achieving the positions to which their character, spiritual tendencies, and inclinations entitle them. Society makes matrimony her only destiny, declaring her unable to be anything other than wife and mother in the name of a certain difference established between the natures of men and women. And yet, neglecting logic, women are denied rights by virtue of a nature arbitrarily attributed to them, even when they are extended without question to a woman destined to the throne. It is an inconceivable aberration that it should be seen as natural, logical, and simple that a queen should preside over the supreme court of a great nation, while it is seen as ridiculous and grotesque that a woman should administer a court in a small neighborhood.

Such blatant inconsistencies can be attributed to the false ideas about the character and nature of women that circulate freely and unexamined in the intellectual world. The most notable, and without a doubt the most original, part of Mill's book is devoted to the study of such false ideas.

> Standing on the ground of common sense and the constitution of the human mind I deny that any one knows, or can know, the nature of the two sexes, as long as they have only been seen in their present relation to one another. If men had ever been found in society without women, or women without men, or if there had been a society of men and women in which women were not under the control of the men, something might have been positively known about the mental and moral influences which may be inherent in the nature of each. What is now called the nature of women is an eminently artificial thing – the result of forced repression in some directions, unnatural stimulation

15. Martina Barros, Mill's The Slavery of Women *(1872–1873)*

in others. It may be asserted without scruple, that no other class of dependents have had their character so entirely distorted from its natural proportions by their relation with their masters; for, if conquered and slave races have been, in some respects, more forcibly repressed, whatever in them has not been crushed down by an iron heel has generally been let alone, and if left with any liberty of development, it has developed according to its own laws; but in the case of women, a hot-house and stove cultivation has always been carried on of some of the capabilities of their nature, for the benefit and pleasure of their masters. Then, because certain products of the general vital force sprout luxuriantly and reach a great development in this heated atmosphere and under this active nurture and watering, while other shoots from the same root, which are left outside in the wintry air, with ice purposely heaped all round them, have a stunted growth, and some are burnt off with fire and disappear; men, with that inability to recognize their own work which distinguished the unanalytic mind, indolently believe that the tree grows of itself in the way they have made it grow, and that it would die if one half of it were not kept in a vapour bath and the other half in the snow.

"Hence," he states later,

In regard to that most difficult question, what are the natural differences between the two sexes – a subject on which it is impossible in the present state of society to obtain complete and correct knowledge – while almost everybody dogmatizes upon it, almost all neglect and make light of the only means by which any partial insight can be obtained into it. This is, an analytic study of the most important department of psychology, the laws of the influence of circumstances on character. For, however great and apparently ineradicable the moral and intellectual differences between men and women might be, the evidence of their being natural differences could only be negative. Those only could be inferred to be natural which could not possibly be artificial – the residuum, after deducting every characteristic of either sex which can admit of being explained from education or external circumstances.[4]

There is as much force as accurate observation in these reflections. It is sufficient to present them to establish the facts with indestructible solidity. What cannot be accepted without reservations, however, are the conclusions the author extracts from these facts. What has been proven thus

---

[4] John Stuart Mill, *The Subjection of Women* (London, 1869), 39 and 42. (Editors' note)

15. Martina Barros, Mill's The Slavery of Women *(1872–1873)*

far is simply how serious the difficulties are when examining the character and nature of women based on their relations to men, as they currently exist. What is not proven is the assumption that what can be said about the subject should necessarily rest on slippery conjectures. There is simply no consideration of the two methods for examining the problem that could lead us to an appropriate solution. Nothing is said about the powerful resource represented by the natural sciences. Even if these sciences have not given a clear and precise solution to the problem, they at the very least provide a solid base for conclusions that are far from premature hypotheses.

The study of both the brain and the central nervous system, and, to say it all, the study of the comparative physiology of men and women show differences between the sexes that are entirely independent of the social position in which they are placed. There should be no leveling or confusion between sexes that nature has separated so profoundly.

Nothing is said either about studies that are based on conclusions from the natural sciences and the history of human intelligence, which have positively established the division between men and women regarding their ways of knowing, thus highlighting the characteristics of their respective intellects.

To fill this void, it would be necessary to develop an argument that is beyond the space constraints of a prologue. It will be enough to state some general conclusions emerging from these studies.

The most notable of those published up to date, in the opinion of critics, belongs to the fine and thorough writings of the late [Henry Thomas] Buckle. These are his main conclusions:

Due to the natural formation of her brain, the evolution of her central nervous system, and her greater facility to react to any stimulus, a woman can quickly form ideas, reason with speed, and allow herself to be dominated by whatever impresses her heart with some degree of vehemence. This is why her normal system of thought is deductive, a system that is in line with the nature of her faculties, a system that arrives at truth via intuition.

Man is more patient and less lively when it comes to impressions due to the lower development of his central nervous system. Compared to women, he follows an inductive method that requires careful investigation and an abundance of facts to support them.

This evidence suggests that there is a moral and intellectual difference between men and women. Although this difference prevents the

15. Martina Barros, Mill's The Slavery of Women (1872–1873)

application of any notion of equality, it still does not follow that one is superior to the other. To each his or her own sphere: Man walks the difficult path of careful analysis, as well as rigorous and detailed investigation; woman, the brilliant yet perilous road of a system as delicate and utopian as she herself.

II.

[John] Stuart Mill's conclusions, although rejecting the blurring of sex differences and failing at the same time to recognize their equal standing, are my own but coming from a completely different standpoint. Indeed, what is it that he wants with this book? He wants to return to nature, place society at its starting point, bring men together around the rustic hearth of those primeval times when they prepared their simple meals and gave way to the first delicate affections. Mill seeks to examine the moment when society first organized, revealing the first abuses of power, as well as the origin of the prejudices and failures of humanity. He then seeks to bring that social situation into our present but removing its barbarity and preserving its freedom. His is a work of demolition as well as construction: He dismantles society. Faced with this situation, what shall we do? We should give women the same freedom that man enjoys so that she can use her faculties as best she sees fit. That is, the freedom to acquire an education and to make use of her knowledge. In the process of explaining the advantages represented to society by an education that does not differentiate between men and women, Mill shows how the number of qualified persons would increase in occupations currently reserved for men. He shows how the latter would find great stimulation by the need to justify the superiority men claim over women. Moreover, education will make women more influential in their roles as mothers and wives.

The cultivation of women's intellectual faculties will bring even greater advantages. Taking Buckle's view of the moral difference between men and women into consideration, we can also assume that the education of women is not simply for increasing the number of people useful to humanity: It also means gaining access to faculties that men do not spontaneously possess and which are nevertheless of incalculable benefit to the sciences. It is worth noting that the discoveries that most distinguish the human spirit, those that mark the greatest periods of civilization, are those that follow the deductive method, a method that all agree can be attributed to women. Columbus, Galileo, and Newton owe to this method the high place they enjoy in the gratitude, renown, and respect of all peoples. The education of women will develop those same faculties on grounds that flourish the more easily, and with better results, because they are natural to women. If we focus on the home, that space that appears so small and yet contains such infinite horizons for those who believe that the future of humanity rests in that place, the education of women would bring vast improvements. Trust and respect will thrive in a home where women can find in their husbands companions who will guide them with tenderness and respect; men for their part will find in their wives confidantes who are at their level of intelligence, and can help support them in times of uncertainty, when doubt chills the souls of even the strongest men. Women will contribute the enthusiasm of their optimistic souls, and the audacity that will give life to the projects of their eager husbands. Women will contribute the strengths of their sex as well as their ability to confront the reversals of life when misfortune threatens the future of their families. What woman who has a heart does not dream of such a future? And yet, that future might be frustrated by the insufficiencies of her education, or because her husband, unable to think as she does, refuses to help her rise to his level.

The husband, would he not be happier if he has a wife with an intelligence as cultivated as his, who helps him in his efforts, understands his purposes, and is loved for who he is rather than for simply being a husband? We would then see something that is generally not seen today, as Mill so justly observes, when so many young men, who had such promising futures, stop seeking advancement for the lack of stimulation when they marry women lacking the necessary instruction to engage them, and which they used to have in other types of relations. The education of women, from any perspective, can only be considered a decisive step toward justice and civilization. Only narrow and mean spirits can be opposed to this. It is utterly unnecessary to try to justify the right of women to access such knowledge with the same freedom as men. It is often claimed that women are incapable, due to their abilities and constitution, to perform a serious employment that requires sustained effort. Even if one entertains the lowest expectations regarding women's intellectual capacities or consider that they will never rise to the level of genius, that is still not a reason to deny them access to employments and professions which men, even the least able of them, occupy after tests that could equally be administered to women. If her nature makes her truly unable to assume certain tasks, she will still not need the help of man, or society's mandate, to seek them. What will those who deny women the right to freely choose their lives' path have to say?

III.

The main obstacle to the solution of this problem comes from seeing it through the distorted lens of politics. Some believe that granting social rights to women means extending them political rights as well. That assumption introduces the fear that progress and public prosperity will be compromised, especially if it goes to a social class unprepared to handle them, thus becoming the dangerous instrument of decadence. Fear has made them unfair. What women demand are social rights. It hurts them to see their political rights denied because an appeal is made to clever arguments that offend women without convincing them. If the intention is to deny them such rights because women are seen as incapable of exercising them; if they are told that their education and intelligence are insufficient to claim the right to elect representatives who can lead them to achieve the political objectives of their country, women will only see injustice and inconsequence behind that hurtful view. Women will feel offended rather than convinced. They will see the inconsistency of those who recognize in them the necessary aptitude to choose the husband who will represent and direct them during their entire life. And yet they are denied the same aptitude to make a much less serious and transcendental choice. If they are denied those rights because they are believed to only be able to become a mindless instrument of an external will, women will only see offense and a lack of logic in such a feeble reasoning. If their opinion will always be but the echo of a man's opinion, does it make any difference to have them? It would be the same as a man voicing his opinion twice.

The true reason for this injustice, the sheer stubbornness of denying women the aptitudes that everyone knows they have, is in the end more honorable to women than the intended offense. The true reason is fear. The fear not so much of seeing the family divided, or the husband and wife disagreeing with one another over politics. What is feared is that the majority of men and women will come to support unpalatable ideas. Women are not demanding political rights. What they are asking for are not political but rather social rights. They can be recognized without excluding the others. In no civilized legislation is intellectual capacity the measure of political capacity. The requirement for suffrage is income, not intelligence or aptitudes. Women are therefore entitled to claim that

15. Martina Barros, Mill's The Slavery of Women *(1872–1873)*

they are being denied political rights for the same reasons that England denied them to Newton. Injustice then may not appear so dishonorable to women. But if they are generous enough to forgive such usurpation, should the denial of social rights be in any way justified? Why deny her the rights that nature itself has given to women? Why deny them rights that would make women enjoy the happiness of a home in which men and women love and respect each other as two equal hearts and minds? Why not exercise such faculties that today are numbed by ignorance or destroyed by neglect? Justice, happiness, and progress all demand a moral emancipation that will only arrive when the reign of inconsistency will finally be defeated.

Part V.
Spanish America and the World

16
ANDRÉS BELLO
International Intervention (1846–1847)

Andrés Bello (1781–1865) was born in Caracas, Venezuela. Early in his career he occupied various administrative positions in the government of the Captaincy General, including the board that administered the vaccination against smallpox, and the editorship of the Gaceta de Caracas.[1] *In 1810, the newly inaugurated Junta of Caracas appointed him secretary of the commission sent to Great Britain to request support for the new government. He remained in London for nineteen years, before accepting a position in Chile in 1829. He lived in Santiago for the remaining thirty-six years of his life, serving as government official, senator, and rector of the University of Chile. He was in addition a poet, a literary critic, and a jurist. His most important works include* Principios de derecho de jentes *(1832),* Gramática de la lengua castellana *(1847), and the* Codigo Civil de la Republica de Chile *(1855). A towering intellectual figure in Spanish America, he has only recently been translated into English. The* Derecho de jentes *is mostly unknown in English, except for some translated passages and fragments. The current selection concerns a specific development in Ecuador but involves a central principle of international relations where Bello took a strong position against foreign intervention, especially coming from emerging states that sought the political and military assistance of stronger ones. The polemical tone of the article is typical of the press debates in Chile in the 1840s and beyond.*

---

[1] This essay was originally published in three parts in the Chilean periodical *El Araucano* on December 18, 1846, January 8, 1847, and February 5, 1847. The editors used the second Caracas edition of Bello's *Obras completas*, 26 vols. (Caracas, 1981–1984), X, 509–526. (Editors' note)

16. Andrés Bello, International Intervention (1846–1847)

I.

According to *El Mercurio* (December 12, 1846) the actions of the government of Chile concerning the expedition of [Juan José] Flores illustrate a principle, and that principle is *intervention*. Intervention to oppose the governments of Europe that support the former president of Ecuador. Or, intervention to oppose the same former president in case he, with his own resources, invaded the country at the head of a foreign legion in order to take the supreme power by force. This, by virtue of his personal legitimacy, or link between the government and his person.

We disagree that the principle of intervention is the preeminent principle of the age, or that it is a sacred and Christian principle, as *El Mercurio* claims. Anyone who consults the historical record will see that there has never been more distrust of this presumed principle than today. Its application is seen with great animosity and disapproval. The involvement of one government in the affairs of another, or others, is not a rule but rather an exception. Such involvement is illegitimate and threatens the independence of states. It can only be justified in particularly grave circumstances of present and imminent danger. If General Flores, heading a force against Ecuador, attempted to overthrow the government of the country and sit again in the presidential chair, we believe that our [Chilean] government would take no part in the matter. It would wait until the conflict is over, or the will of the Ecuadorean people prevails. But this is not the case: General Flores is gathering troops and securing the means for the invasion in a European country. Let us suppose that he is successful. What would be the consequences? From then on, any exile would have the certainty of finding similar help, especially in Europe, where an impoverished mass of people, a class of men accustomed to political agitation, and many who are hungry for booty will follow any banner that promises gain. The profits made by the capitalists who invest in the Flores campaign would encourage others to invest in similar ventures. In that case, the Spanish American republics will see no end to alarm, conflict, and devastating wars. It is not just the institutions of Ecuador that will be threatened by the presumed personal legitimacy of the invader or the linkage between the government and his person. All South American societies will be in danger. We must prevent such a lethal threat because if it extends (as will undoubtedly happen), it will lead our civilization, our institutions, and our existence to untimely ruin. This is assuming that Flores, or Flores and [Andrés de] Santa Cruz, are

16. Andrés Bello, International Intervention (1846–1847)

only planning a private enterprise funded by their own resources. But the danger will be no less consequential for all the South American republics, including Chile, if Flores is the instrument of a European government that has its own designs in supporting his plans.

We could make a more definitive judgment on this last point, but for the moment let us save it for the sake of caution. One observation is in order, however. *El Mercurio* states that "[Spanish] America would be right to assume an attack against its independence, because Flores has no legal claims that European justice could support." According to this, a European state would be qualified to judge as just or unjust the intentions of Flores. Should it find them just, they could aid him with all the force of its system of justice. Is this not giving a foreign power the right to pronounce a judgment on all our political conflicts, and decide on who to favor by force of arms? Is this the Christian and sacred rule that nineteenth-century civilization was destined to uphold? Who has ever given the principle of intervention such a dreadful latitude? What other pretext would be more desirable for a powerful state seeking to dominate, oppress, and tyrannize a weaker one?

II.

Regarding intervention, we have read some bold opinions, but none as wild as that of *El Mercurio*. According to this paper, the principle of intervention allows any foreign power to get involved in the domestic conflicts of a state and support the party that it considers just. This principle is supposedly illustrative of the wisdom of our century, although the paper could also have said, with equal authority, the wisdom of the year 1846. If, for example, a foreign power intervened in Ecuador today to support Flores, *El Mercurio* would reproach such an action not because of the meddling in the internal affairs of the country, but because it would support injustice.

To fully understand the monstrosity of such an unheard doctrine, it is important not to confuse the presumed right of intervention with that of war. One state might attack another to defend or vindicate its own rights. As it often happens when a state becomes the judge of its own cause, it will in good or bad faith claim rights it does not have and use force to get them. When it does, the principle invoked is that of its own conservation and security, which it uses to recover or retain what it claims by force.

What has been said about a state also applies to a league of states. The point of an alliance is to make the cause of one the cause of all, either in general terms, or within the limits predefined by the alliance.

16. Andrés Bello, International Intervention (1846–1847)

Beyond this point, the right of war ceases. It is illegal to wage it to force another country to change its religion or government; to return a prince or magistrate to their respective thrones or presidencies, however justly they might have been deposed; to force the opening of ports to commerce if, by virtue of a previous treaty, a country has not contracted the obligation to do so, etc. The injury that has been inflicted, or attempted, on me or my allies (when by virtue of the pact of alliance I have made a commitment to defend them) is the foundation of my right to disturb the peace and declare war.

Where the right of war ends, the right of intervention, if it exists, begins. According to it, a state takes on the role of an armed referee to adjudicate on its own authority, the rights of others. This is the principle that *El Mercurio* defends. The right to armed arbitration is the modern invention that *El Mercurio* proclaims as beneficial to humanity, as well as precious and sacred. We, on the contrary, see it as one of the most dangerous weapons that could be handed to powerful states against weaker ones. Does one state want to extract from another that has a weaker force an important concession? All it must do is intervene. This is the order of things that *El Mercurio* envisions as the condition for the existence of nations and would be happy to see it established around the world.

It could be said that *El Mercurio* does not see intervention as a general and absolute right. It only accepts it when *legitimized by powerful motives or guided by important interests*. But who is to determine how powerful the motives are? Who is to measure the magnitude of such interests? The interventionist nation, of course. Who is to guarantee that this nation will not consider great its own interests, or powerful such motives as are beneficial to itself?

The principle proclaimed by *El Mercurio* is so mistaken and potentially deadly, so hateful its nature, so alarming and threatening to the security of nations, that not even those states that have used it in practice dare to proclaim it openly. Those powers that have intervened in the affairs of others pretended to justify their actions not because of a general right, but rather on particular and exceptional circumstances. Like the Holy Alliance, they have limited themselves to the defense of monarchical institutions threatened by the revolutionary upheavals of neighboring nations. In other words, they have limited themselves to a particular and exceptional objective. "Change your form of government," the Holy Alliance said to Spain, Portugal, and Naples, "or you will endanger our own." England, Russia, and France intervened in Greece to end the

16. Andrés Bello, International Intervention (1846–1847)

brutal domination of Turkey over a Christian people, following the universal clamor of all Christian nations. Therefore, even when nations have made use of it, intervention does not exist as a rule. It only has a place in extremely rare situations, when there is no other means to confront an imminent danger (claimed by the Holy Alliance without any foundation) or promote interests that are not just great but involve a large portion of humankind. Even in those cases, European powers have shown a circumspection worth noting. Is there a cause more important, more sacred, more Christian for humanity than the abolition of the cursed slave trade? If there is ever a legitimate cause for intervention, this is it. And yet, Great Britain did not assume to be authorized to employ, by itself, force against traffickers caught in the act. Great Britain appears to be unaware of the great discovery made by *El Mercurio*.

We are sorry to say that there is a great distance between the opinions of *El Mercurio* and our own. One consideration will be enough to show the extent of the difference. Assuming that a European government had aided Flores' campaign, *El Mercurio* would have disapproved of such an act on the grounds not of intervention but of injustice. Had Flores justice on his side, then, *El Mercurio* would see nothing wrong with the intervention. Now, if the restoration of a president in one of the South American republics (which matter very little in the larger world), placed as they are so far from Europe, constituted, as *El Mercurio* claims, one of the *powerful means*, and *great interests*, would that legitimize intervention (and justify it)? What conflict between persons or factions would not offer similar or even greater incentives?

The consequences of such an unheard principle of international law are evident. Were we to grant sufficient discernment on the part of the interventionist power to support only a just cause (and this is conceding a lot) and granting also that it is incapable of deceiving itself (which is beyond possibility or even belief) even so intervention, as understood by *El Mercurio*, would subject the South American republics, and other states in the same category, to a humiliating dependence on more powerful nations. No matter what precautions their governments take, there will always be some means involving Europe. We would have to recognize, in our domestic policy, as many courts as there are states powerful enough to impose their justice on us. Once we submit to their arbitration we would also have to pay for it. This is assuming that there are infallible and impartial judges who would not take advantage of the opportunity to favor, not the just cause, but the one most likely to benefit them. What if

16. Andrés Bello, International Intervention (1846–1847)

the opposite is the case, as lamentably the experience of humankind has shown for centuries on end? Would ambition and greed lack pretexts to advance wickedness, should they be looking for them? Such arbitrations and armed interventions have up to now been seen as abuses of power. But according to *El Mercurio* they are simply the legitimate exercise of a sacred right.

El Mercurio gives us a catalogue of interventions to justify its views, but almost all are imagined cases where interventions have either not taken place, or the presumed interventionist has merely defended its rights. When, for example, did Great Britain intervene during the Spanish American revolt against the metropolis? Is it not evident that it refused to recognize any of the agents of the new republics, or sign any treaties with them, until the fortunes of war had decided the question in favor of Spanish America? Even then, what did it say? That it recognized them only as *de facto* governments; that Spain was free to use any means to bring them back into submission; that as an impartial observer of the conflict, its recognition was limited to establishing communications with the Spanish American states to protect British persons and property. These are facts recorded by authentic documents.

Likewise, there is no basis to consider the alliance of France with the North American colonies that proclaimed their independence from the United Kingdom as an act of intervention. [Gilbert du Motier, Marquis de] Lafayette set out for North America against the instructions of his government, exposing himself to severe penalties. The Versailles government waited an entire year before receiving Benjamin Franklin officially. It was only after Saratoga [1777] that it recognized the United States as an independent power. Still, it limited itself to signing a commercial treaty (February 8, 1778), and to secretly forming an alliance in case Great Britain were to break the peace with France, either in the form of direct hostility or by impeding commerce and navigation, against the provisions of international law and existing treaties between the two nations. This is the treaty, according to [Gaëtan de Raxis de] Flassan that did not come to life until war broke out between France and Great Britain. France did not, then, take up arms to support the emancipation of the North American colonies. Instead, it made common cause with them independently of the American question and in defense of its own rights, only after it took up arms against the United Kingdom. Furthermore, the recognition of a *de facto* government, or the making of a common cause with those fighting the same enemies, is not an intervention. What are we to say about the

16. Andrés Bello, International Intervention (1846–1847)

intervention of Venezuela and Buenos Aires in the emancipation of New Granada, Peru, and Chile? That is, the countries that in their war against Spain coordinated their operations with their brothers and neighbors, following the same principles and defending identical rights!

That an intervention may have once been beneficial proves nothing. The most wicked conquests may have improved the conditions of the vanquished, but this does not mean that a powerful state has the right to subjugate a weaker one on the pretext of seeking to make it happy. History shows very clearly what has been the true spirit of conquest, or interventions, justified by religious or beneficent motives. A people that does not become free and independent through their own efforts will rarely receive such gifts from foreign protectors.

El Mercurio blames the misfortunes of civil war torn Spain on non-intervention. What would a foreign army have done there other than exacerbate the conflict? With regards to tyrannized Poland, which is also on the list of victims of the same principle, *El Mercurio* forgets that the travails of this heroic people, and the political death of the country, are due precisely to *intervention*. It was intervention that fueled domestic strife; placed on its shaky throne unfit favorites; corrupted, enslaved, and dismembered Poland.

According to *El Mercurio* interventions in the ancient past were bad because their purpose was to destroy liberty. Modern interventions, inspired instead by the great interests of justice and the *good of the people*, are legitimate and beneficial. It would make a great difference, indeed, if there should be a supreme tribunal capable of judging the righteousness or appropriateness of the interventions. How good, also, if a moderating power existed that could keep the interventions within circumscribed and legitimate limits, preventing the abuses of power. *El Mercurio* sees abstractions with utter contempt, but its arguments are neither practical nor applicable. It shows a great ignorance regarding men and governments, when the paper gives the powerful the right to intervene in foreign affairs, albeit on the condition of consulting justice and appropriateness. By the nature of things, it is the powerful who decide between the just and the unjust, the appropriate and the pernicious. Generosity and magnanimity are not counted among the main political virtues. Leaders of governments would be ashamed to apply to their private lives the same rules they use in the conduct of the great national interests. These are political truths, however pedestrian and vulgar they might be, despite how much *El Mercurio* wants to insist that they are mere abstractions.

16. Andrés Bello, International Intervention (1846–1847)

III.

La Raison finit toujours par avoir raison. After so much debate, it now seems that we contenders agree. According to the last installment of *El Mercurio*, the question is purely a matter of words.

Our readers will recall that the issue was the Flores campaign. When *El Mercurio* assumed that a European government was providing support for the plan, it declared that we must oppose it, not exactly because it meant an intervention in the internal affairs of another state, but because it supported an unjust cause. We protested, then, the elevation of intervention to the status of a principle. We said that it granted the right to any power, a right not only unheard of until now but also universally rejected, to pass judgment on the internal matters of another state and then proceed to support with force that faction which it considered just, with or without foundation. In its answer, *El Mercurio* limited the principle somewhat: Powerful motivations must legitimize intervention, and great interests must demand it. And yet, according to *El Mercurio*, intervention was still a resource that nations could not forgo without a risk to their existence. The paper forgot, then, the *negative* intervention that it now proclaims. In its own words: "We want the adoption of this principle because nations can be assured that there will always be a response against aggression. Without the means to threaten weaker nations, world peace will be more secure. Intervention will be *negative*: It will not be good for aggression but good to prevent aggression."

Had *El Mercurio* limited aggression to this, it would have been unnecessary to contradict its notion of negative intervention, to which we subscribe. Let us suppose, as we believe, that the principle of international law recognized by all civilized nations indicates that a state cannot intervene in the domestic affairs of another. What would then be the consequences of this rule? Nothing less than the right to oppose intervention when a state decides to use it beyond the very rare, indeed exceptional cases, when it is legitimate. Otherwise, if such interventionist aggression would cause the indifference of other powers, what would the rule mean beyond a sense of duty and morality rather than law? If non-intervention is a duty, counter-intervention (the negative intervention of *El Mercurio*) becomes a right. When some powerful states involved themselves in the internal affairs of Poland, other states were able to oppose this violation. Stop there! they said, using the same words of *El Mercurio*: We will not allow this aggressive intervention.

16. Andrés Bello, International Intervention (1846–1847)

Despite this important modification of the argument first presented by *El Mercurio*, we observe some views in the last two articles that merit a response.

Firstly, what is the point about theoreticians raised by *El Mercurio*? That we shall not follow the opinions of [Hugo] Grotius, [Samuel] Pufendorf, and [Emmerich de] Vattel blindly? *Quid ad rem?* We have not cited any authority; it is *El Mercurio* that did so. We have not looked for any other support than reason and experience. We have exposed the danger of a principle that, given the scope that *El Mercurio* gives it, we regard as a dangerous tool in the hands of the powerful. That is why we have not invoked prestigious texts, but rather irrefutable observations extracted from human nature and its propensity, just like governments, to abuse power. *El Mercurio* objects that if they wanted to abuse, they could cite the principle of intervention, or else the right to wage war. But the latter only allows states to seek justice, not to meddle in the affairs of others. Why should we ourselves open the door to injustice? Why grant them a right they themselves are not looking for? Will we give a state the right to use force to get a secure or more comfortable border by arguing that denying it is useless? Or that they will always have a pretext to take the territory they want? This way of reasoning is unacceptable.

As *El Mercurio* knows, there are two types of international law treatises: theoretical and positive. Between them, there is the same difference as between an abstract theory of civil legislation and a civil code. In the former, the rules that nations should observe to live in peace and promote the general well-being of humankind are determined *a priori*. In the latter, the focus is on the rules that nations have agreed upon among themselves, and in which they limit their claims and the means to accomplish them. This does not mean that one should dismiss the importance of natural justice in the relations between states. What those agreed-upon rules mean is that the powerful states generally prevail, because the equality of nations in international law is a chimerical theory. There always was, is, and will be an oligarchy of states that promulgate this law. It does more: It enforces it. Even worse, divided legislatures can proclaim contradictory principles whereby weaker states adopt different policies for different countries. In any case, a positive international law must show the facts as they are.

Theoretical treatises have a different object; they aim for a different type of utility. They do not describe what *is* but rather what in the view of their authors *should be*. The fact that their doctrines vary so much warns

16. Andrés Bello, International Intervention (1846–1847)

us not to adopt them without scrutiny. And yet despite the differences that we can find in them, who will doubt that they have been beneficial to the world? They have led public opinion generally down the path of justice and the true interests of humankind. [Pellegrino] Rossi may want more specificity in their formulations, but this is impossible. Civil law itself can, among the legitimate means to reach an objective, approve some and prohibit others. It can fix a limit to rights that beyond a certain point cease to be such and become abuses. It can mitigate arbitrary actions by giving them a certain shape. In other words, civil law itself has not been able to eradicate from its articles the *more or less* that so upsets Rossi. What would then happen when two or more parties do not recognize a superior authority? What will an author do when he wants to describe the rights and obligations that natural justice imposes on contending parties? Who empowers him to do what nature, whose interpreter he claims to be, has not done? As a commentator of the eternal code of justice, will he determine and make precise that which is undefined and vague? Will he determine, for example, how many and which peaceful means of conciliation and agreement, in what order, and with what formalities, must be tried before appealing to the "judgment of God," and war? The selection and application of these means depend on an infinite variety of circumstances. Even if he could come up with a set of rules, what power would they have? There is nothing in sight that announces the proximity of an age when nations will agree on precise and uniform rules for their reciprocal relations. For as long as there is a divergence of interests, which is probably for as long as the world lasts, there will be conflicting doctrines. Consider, for example, a nation whose navy dominates the oceans. For such a nation enemy property covered by a neutral flag is a good prize, however much irate states proclaim the inviolability of the flag, assuming the right to protect enemy merchandise. Industry advances fast; political morality, barely. The decency of external formalities demonstrates the progress of modern nations. Intrinsic justice is what it has always been. Man constantly extends his power over physical nature. And yet, have his passions and appetites changed? What he has is more means to satisfy them, and to commit more injustices with impunity.

Positivist authors, it is true, sometimes lose their way trying to make practices fit principles, confusing what is with what should be. Theoretical authors, for their part, bend the doctrines too many times to account for practices. That is, both may contain erroneous notions. Such is the condition of the human mind in all the departments of knowledge. Here,

16. Andrés Bello, International Intervention (1846–1847)

a physicist establishes *a priori* a false principle to make the facts fit. There, another physicist reduces facts to inaccurate formulas and presents them as laws of nature. That such mistakes are more frequent in the moral and political sciences; that these sciences cannot develop their theorems with algebraic formulas; that because of the complex, delicate, and fleeting phenomena of the mind and will, they cannot offer precise and permanent results, all of this is an inherent defect of the matter, both necessary and unfixable. Wherever the defect comes from, has any human authority, however high, been able to prevail over reason?

El Mercurio flatters itself as having found a sufficient guarantee against abuses of power and against a force armed with the principle of intervention in its most dangerous form. It finds such a guarantee in "world opinion, manifested in parliaments, stock exchanges, clubs, popular organizations, periodicals, etc." Let us open our eyes and look at the facts. World opinion, so defined, is a hydra whose many heads proclaim true or false principles; generous or ignoble passions and interests that may or may not coincide with those of humanity. It can support monarchical legitimacy in Vienna or democratic omnipotence in Washington; universal suffrage here, socialism there; high tariffs to protect domestic manufactures, or low to protect national agriculture. Machinery promotes wealth and happiness, claim some; it brings misery to the people, say others. Everything is controversial, from first principles to ultimate consequences, even in matters of material interest, which are more susceptible to calculation and experience. Will the *world* be more constant and uniform in favor of a just cause in matters of foreign policy?

El Mercurio should go back to the beginning, the Flores campaign, and should address the following dilemma: If world opinion has not opposed such a scandalous attempt, the guarantee [against abuses of power] does not exist. If it has and its judgment has not been respected, the guarantee is impotent. *El Mercurio* is up in the clouds: It has no interest in what we are seeing and experiencing. We do not deny that world opinion recognizes justice, although more often after the fact. Has the world done justice to dismembered Poland? How is Poland? What has the empathy of the world done for that heroic people other than writing an honorable epitaph?

When we published our first article on intervention we had not seen, nor have we yet had the good fortune of examining the work by Rossi. However, *El Mercurio* has reproduced several passages. We are happy to find ourselves in complete agreement with this illustrious author. He

16. Andrés Bello, International Intervention (1846–1847)

does not recognize the right of armed intervention, except in extremely rare cases of present and imminent danger. With regards to unarmed intervention, we have not found a single word against it. In any event, such "intervention" is not properly *intervention*. Any government can stop communicating with another when it finds it convenient. Any government can legitimately offer counsel and good offices to two states that threaten or harass each other. All governments can provide mediation if belligerents request it. What it cannot do is to make intervention a matter of force against the will of one or both parties. Otherwise, there is no security or true independence except for the most powerful states.

17
JOSÉ ANTONIO SACO

The Political Situation of Cuba (1851)

José Antonio Saco (1797–1879), a native of Bayamo in Cuba, studied philosophy under the notable Félix Varela and succeeded him in the philosophy chair at the University of Havana.[1] He edited the journals El Mensajero Semanal *and the* Revista Bimestre Cubana, *where his writing against the slave trade caused his exile in 1834 – he only returned to Cuba for a brief period in 1860–1861. He traveled extensively in Europe collecting the documentation for his* Historia de la esclavitud *(1875–1879). He was elected to the Cortes in Spain but, after 1837, Cuba was excluded from representation there. Saco also became conspicuous for his opposition to the annexation of Cuba to the United States. The current selection was written in the wake of Narciso López's failed invasion of the island in 1851 and reveals a keen awareness of the international situation and the hard choices facing Cuba in the nineteenth century.*

I am not an alarmist, but I have a duty to tell the truth about Spain and Cuba (my fatherland). The future of Cuba looks clear now, but can we be sure that new tempests will not come to darken it? Will the defeat of the invaders [Narciso López and his troops] at Playitas, in the early morning of August 12 [1851],[2] be enough to consolidate the peace and future of

---

[1] From José Antonio Saco, *La situación política de Cuba y su remedio* (Paris, 1851), 473–499. (Editors' note)
[2] Narciso López de Urriola (1796–1851) was a Venezuelan-born royalist who moved to Cuba after the triumph of independence forces led by Simón Bolívar. López was rewarded with numerous military and administrative positions but by 1843 had turned against the

17. José Antonio Saco, The Political Situation of Cuba (1851)

Cuba? I see little more than a truce in our recent victory; we must use it to avert the external and internal dangers that threaten our island. The former danger is posed by the United States, and the latter by Cuban institutions. Both represent serious ills, but fortunately the remedy is easy enough to find that our motherland (Spain) can apply it any day.

There are two motivations that drive a portion of the United States to acquire Cuba: expansionism and slavery. Did they cease their attempts after the recent bloodshed? No. They are still there, and will return with more force at the first favorable opportunity.

In previous years, many Americans wished to acquire the territory from the North Pole to the Isthmus of Panama. Because this already vast territory seems to be insufficient for them, Americans have announced, in the press and in public assemblies, that they will conquer the entire New World. A country where such dangerous ideas are discussed is an immediate threat to its neighbors. Let us examine the territorial expansion of the United States. The first acquisitions were legitimate purchases: Louisiana from France, and Florida from Spain. However, they wickedly appropriated Texas. They also wanted to take Oregon, but fear of war with Great Britain stopped them. Subsequently, they launched an iniquitous war against Mexico, taking a great part of its territory. Lastly, they have tried Cuba, launching two invasions in the space of fourteen months. The schemes now under way against the unfortunate Mexican nation show how far the ambition of an out-of-control democracy can go.

The issue of slavery is even more pressing, because the Southern states have political and commercial interests in Cuba. Political, because they want to strengthen their position within the federal system: They want to not only absorb Cuba but also divide it into four states in order to secure eight more votes in the Senate. Commercial, because slave owners, no longer able to sell slaves in the Union, see Cuba as a new and large market

---

Spanish empire and worked with other Cubans for the annexation of the island to the United States. He organized the conspiracy known as "Mina de la Rosa Cubana" in 1847, which failed and led to his exile in the United States. He tried again in 1851 and landed in Pinar del Rio, expecting local Cuban support, but was soundly defeated by Spanish government forces. He was captured and executed on September 1, 1851. The involvement of Americans in the invasion led many Cubans to turn to Spain although looking for more autonomy and representation in the Spanish Cortes. Annexationist leanings did not go away, but for contradictory reasons: to either prolong slavery, or eliminate it after the American Civil War. See Tom Chaffin "'Sons of Washington': Narciso Lopez, Filibusterism, and US Nationalism, 1848-1851", *Journal of the Early Republic*, 1995, 15.1, 79–108. (Editors' note)

17. José Antonio Saco, *The Political Situation of Cuba (1851)*

for their dangerous merchandise. Under these circumstances, who can stop them? The US federal government, or the fear of a war with Spain?

The American government, by virtue of its organization, is weak, and made weaker by the dominant and intimidating influence of democracy. Demoralization is rampant, at least in some states; laws no longer command respect; the ambition to secure power, or retain it, leads even distinguished citizens to pander to the crowds to obtain favors and employment. Moreover, the American government is attempting to introduce a principle of public law in international affairs that is as strange as it is unacceptable. It seeks to prevent European powers from having a say in the Western Hemisphere, as if they did not legitimately possess colonies and had no territorial, political, or commercial interests. Such a government, as currently organized, and having such aims, cannot guarantee peace for Cuba. Neither President [Zachary] Taylor, nor Vice-President [Millard] Fillmore have promoted, at least ostensibly, the annexation of the island. But we have seen two attempted invasions in little more than a year. If this had happened under a moderate administration that wished, presumably in good faith, to avoid conflict with other nations, what could we expect from a new president who has his own ideas, or who is an instrument of others, regarding the acquisition of Cuba?

The fear of a war against Spain will not stop the ambition of the United States, either. Their extreme pride makes them believe that they are superior to all nations. Spain, recovering from her recent travails, receives no consideration, not even for the sake of her past glories. Americans think that it will be easy to defeat Spain. Although they are wrong, this mistake will not stop further aggressions. Located between the Atlantic Ocean and the Mediterranean Sea, and having the Canary and Balearic islands, as well as strategic positions in Gibraltar and the Philippines, Spain can do much damage to American trade. However, the United States could try to capture the islands of Annobon and Fernando Poo [Bioko, Equatorial Guinea], especially the latter because of its location by the Niger, off the coast of Africa. It could harass and possibly occupy Puerto Rico and, from California, the Philippines. With regards to Cuba, which is the core issue, its conquest would be the beginning and the end of the war. We must recognize that the United States has all the advantages.

The United States is situated close to Cuba, and has a fleet much stronger than ours. With resources close at hand, it can increase its forces rapidly. Spanish warships, facing immensely superior forces, will have to seek refuge in the island's ports, or be defeated in unequal combat,

17. José Antonio Saco, The Political Situation of Cuba (1851)

despite the courage of its sailors. In either case, the US would control the waters, blockade our ports, and invade Cuba. Let us be clear: It will be a large invasion. The United States has only 12,000 soldiers, but there are many natives and Europeans, in addition to peoples from the South and West, who are interested in conquering our Antilles.

It is very true that the Spanish government could respond with a desperate defense. However, the interruption of trade, the migration of families, capital flight, lack of funds to pay for the ordinary expenses of the island, the extraordinary expenditures of war, and the lack of reinforcements due to distance and the blockade will ruin Cuba in a few months, and make it vulnerable to invasions from the open coasts.

This will be the inevitable result of the war if Spain wages it *alone* against the United States. The invasion of Cuba could have a serious impact on the nations most interested in preventing it because they have their own colonies in the area: Great Britain and France. They share the same interests and dangers as Spain. It is imperative, therefore, that these nations help protect our island. This is not a new idea, as many distinguished Cubans have already advanced it. The European press has covered the matter, and the governments of those great nations want it. The US should contribute to this work of salvation and concord. To preserve the peace, a treaty is needed between France, Great Britain, and the United States, whereby none, or all together, should ever possess the island of Cuba. On the contrary, they should commit to preventing any other European or Western Hemisphere country from occupying it. In the context of such a treaty, Spain should not neglect the internal situation of Cuba. The island urgently requires administrative and *political* reforms. I am not suggesting that foreigners should solve our internal issues, but I would be very sorry if France and Great Britain abandoned the noble position of leadership they currently enjoy in the world. They should not help perpetuate those Cuban institutions that they have condemned in their own colonies.

Internal Dangers

These dangers come from Cuba's current institutions, which are despotic in all branches of public administration. The Cuban people have no legal protections beyond those that, out of prudence or integrity, the authorities are willing to provide. Could Cubans be happy with such an arbitrary form of government? No, a thousand times no. And yet, why did

17. José Antonio Saco, The Political Situation of Cuba (1851)

the revolts in Puerto Príncipe and Trinidad have no echo in other parts of the island? Why did they not join the invaders at Playitas, instead of showing their hostility to the intruders? Because Cubans are the enemies of revolution; because they are against annexations and abhor any type of foreign domination; because they hope to soon enjoy, along with Spain, a rational liberty. The noble and generous sentiments of the Cuban people toward the metropolis have put aside the grievances and injustices to reaffirm their inalterable loyalty. This is what the Cubans have just done, but it should not be concluded from this that they love, or are happy with, the despotism that oppresses them. As a Cuban who knows his compatriots very well I say *no*, a thousand times *no*. Today I can say this *no* with more conviction than ever because I have been persecuted as a revolutionary, and later accused of favoring annexation. And yet, I have opposed both the revolution and the annexation. I have written against them, and I will write again if necessary. Therefore, I can say without embarrassment that I am as much an enemy of revolution and annexation, as I am of the tyrannical institutions that oppress Cuba. It should be understood that most Cubans think as I do, even if fear silences them, or simply pretend the contrary.

Several arguments have been made to deny Cuba its well-deserved political liberty. I will refute each of them.

1st. *The political rights extended to the colonies by the October 15, 1810 decree of the Cortes of Cádiz, and by the Constitution of 1812, caused the independence of Spanish America. Therefore, to prevent Cuba from seeking it, political rights must be denied.*

I will respond to this by using the same argument: Cuba, Puerto Rico, and the Philippines were granted the same rights, and yet, they did not declare independence. Therefore, the concessions of October 15, 1810, and the Constitution of 1812, did not have the effects that are claimed. In fact, to attribute the independence of the colonies to the Cádiz Constitution is not only a blatant anachronism, but also a sophistic invention by the servile party to discredit, in Spain, the principles of liberty proclaimed by the constitution. Unfortunately, even the liberals used this fiction to reduce Cuba to slavery.

The idea of independence started at the same time as the conquest of the New World. Since then, all governments have feared it, thus committing the injustices against Columbus, and the suspicions and mistrust regarding [Hernán] Cortés. The civil wars in Peru, pitting the supporters of [Diego de] Almagro against those of [Francisco] Pizarro, led one of

17. José Antonio Saco, The Political Situation of Cuba (1851)

these groups to the point of becoming independent from the Crown of Castile, and fighting, weapons in hand, against the viceroy and his officials. In the past [eighteenth] century, Spain heard the cries of independence in various parts of the mainland colonies. [Francisco de] Miranda, along with 500 men, proclaimed independence, however unsuccessfully, when he invaded Coro in Venezuela. The French invasion of 1808 left the peninsula in chaos and without a government well before the Constitution of 1812. Even by September 24, 1810, when the constituent Cortes met, the fire of insurrection had spread all over Spanish America. Keep in mind, however, and make a note of it, that Cuba remained loyal to the metropolis despite this generalized fire. Cuba helped Spain with funds, and with the blood of her children.

In order to leave no doubt about the falsity of the argument I am refuting, I will invoke the authority of Count Toreno [José María Queipo de Llano], whose talent and patriotism, as well as his influence at the time and thereafter, will inspire confidence among peninsulars that no Cuban can hope to achieve. In the thirteenth book of his *Historia del levantamiento, guerra y revolución de España* [1835–1837], Toreno made clear that though there were some minor eighteenth-century antecedents of independence, the ties that united the colonies and the metropolis remained tight and strong.[3]

Toreno confirms that neither the decree of October 15, 1810, nor the Constitution of 1812, are responsible for the revolutionary crime of which they have been accused. However, his lack of courage to say the whole truth, or a partiality unworthy of a historian, made him say nothing about the principal motivations for independence. Another famous Spaniard, less rhetorical, but frank and concise, exposed the true causes of independence. When Spain recognized the independence of the United States, the Count of Aranda [Pedro Pablo Abarca de Bolea] anticipated the fate of the entire American continent. In a confidential report to Charles III in 1783, Aranda stated,

> I will not acknowledge the conclusions of some politicians, both national and foreign, who claim that Spain's control of the Americas cannot last. They say this because they believe that distant colonies will not remain tied to the metropolis for long. In the case of the American colonies, there are even stronger motives, namely,

---

[3] There follows a long and descriptive quotation of the well-known succession of events leading to independence. It has been omitted by the editors. (Editors' note)

17. José Antonio Saco, The Political Situation of Cuba (1851)

the difficulties of helping them from Europe in an emergency; the administration of viceroys and governors whose main motivation is to enrich themselves; the injustices they commit against an unhappy population; the distant location of central authorities and the courts where they need to file their complaints; the many years that it takes to settle a lawsuit; the vindictiveness that in the meanwhile they endure from their bosses; the difficulties of establishing the truth from such distances; the influence that their superiors have not only in their regions but also in Spain, the country they come from. These are the circumstances that make Spanish America unhappy, waiting for an opportunity to proclaim independence.

The opportunity was provided by the French invasion of 1808. Therefore, the independence of the Spanish American colonies was the result of the causes just mentioned, and not of the political concessions of October 15, 1810, or the Constitution of 1812.

2nd. *When Cuba was ruled by the constitution, there were disturbances during elections. To avoid them, Cuba must remain enslaved.*

The form of this argument implies that the whole period was one of disorder, when in fact it was confined to Havana toward the end of 1822. To fully understand the events, we must explain their causes.

It is well known that the 1812 Constitution is essentially democratic, and that while it lasted there was no electoral law. Moreover, Indigenous, and African races were totally excluded from political rights. The former disappeared a long time ago, and the latter never came even close to the voting places. It is important to mention this so that everyone understands that the alleged conflict had nothing to do with a clash between black and white people. The latter alone participated in the elections of 1822, to an extent never seen in the United States, or in the present French Republic. Property owners and honest people voted side by side with the dishonest and the criminal, not because of the constitution but because of the old vices introduced by despotism. Entire regiments voted en masse; crews from the merchant marine just arriving from the peninsula voted with false credentials, using addresses provided to them; and even school children, just twelve years of age, voted as well. Is it strange, then, that such chaotic elections should have provoked some disturbances? It is admirable, on the contrary, that there should have been so few. The Cuban people demonstrated prudence and the capacity to pass a most difficult test. A reasonable electoral law will produce the most satisfactory results.

17. José Antonio Saco, The Political Situation of Cuba (1851)

The Cádiz Constitution, did it not lead to greater abuses in Spain than in Cuba? And yet, have there been calls for an end to representative government, or to the death of all liberties? I do not expect that the metropolis will grant us all political rights at once. But I would be satisfied if property was considered as the basis to significantly increase the electoral rolls, in light of the wealth of Cuba today. An electoral college composed of not just property owners, but rich property owners, is the best guarantee for both Cuba and Spain. To deny us this small justice, on the grounds of the anarchical elections of the past, is an act that upsets the harmony that should exist between the colony and the metropolis.

3rd. *Cuba has prospered and become more enlightened under the current form of government. Therefore, it does not need political liberty.*

For the very same reasons, it should be free: The more enlightened it is, the more it knows its rights and hates tyranny. Being prosperous, it has more interests to defend, and requires political guarantees to protect its wealth.

The enlightenment and prosperity of Cuba have been acquired not because of despotism, but by the struggle against it. Is it not true that, had it been free, Cuba would be more enlightened and richer today? The enlightenment that we have is due to a considerable number of Cubans who have studied abroad; to others who have traveled either alone or with their families to Europe and elsewhere in the hemisphere, and many among them who have shared their knowledge upon their return. It also comes from trade with civilized nations, and from the instinct, or inner force, of societies that seek to improve their station regardless of obstacles. I will not say that the government has no role, because that would be unjust, and wrong. But it would be even more so to say that whatever enlightenment we have is due to despotism.

The material prosperity of Cuba is due to the fertility of the land, to the enslaved people that do the work, to the excellence of its products, and the prices they command in international markets. Three out of these four causes are independent of the government, and the one remaining – slavery – should have never existed because, however poorer without it, we would have fewer concerns about the future.

Does this prosperity reflect Cuba's actual wealth? A visit to some towns and fields shows that many are either far behind, or simply uncultivated. This is uncontestable evidence for anyone who seeks to contradict me.

Let us, however, concede that the material conditions of Cuba are in the most flourishing state. Can we conclude from this that Cuba is happy?

17. José Antonio Saco, The Political Situation of Cuba (1851)

The highest mission of a government cannot be reduced to such a small aim. There are other sacred duties that demand attention, and no country needs more political, social, and moral reforms than Cuba. Any further delay in introducing them will lead us to an abyss where we could all perish. The progress of modern societies, where Cuba has a part, has created new needs and new sentiments. In the past, Cuba may have been content with the ideas they inherited from their parents, but today they feel wretched because of the complete lack of liberty.

Those whose arguments seek to deprive us of liberty do not understand how much they help despotism. If the latter can advance enlightenment and greatness, why attack it? What ills follow from it? If it matters as much as liberty, why change the form of government? Nations that are dominated by absolutism must remain under its rule. Should they try to free themselves from such a happy situation they would be allegedly conspiring against their own best interests.

The material advancement of a country is not a sure sign of the quality of their institutions. Despotism cannot always prevent principles and influences of great vitality. In the Middle Ages, Venice grew territorially and commercially more than any other European nation. And yet, its citizens suffered under the horrendous tyranny of the Council of Ten and the State Inquisition. In our century, material progress has occurred in the middle of disorders in Piedmont, Lombardy, Tuscany, Naples, Russia, and other nations. Our own Spanish America, if we consider where it was at the time of independence, proves that peoples can improve their situation even under despotic institutions. If some of our peninsular brothers are convinced that material improvements are sufficient to make people who are ruled despotically happy, why do they not apply to themselves the same dose of happiness that they prescribe to Cubans? Why do they not ask for the ending of freedom of the press and assembly, close the parliament, and destroy at once the machinery of representative government? When tyranny ruled the metropolis, it would have been absurd for the colonies to expect principles of liberty. But after freedom has settled in the throne of Castile, it is a monstrous contradiction to keep Cuba under the obsolete institutions installed by the absolutist monarchs.

4th. *The old laws of the Indies are the true colonial legislation. With a few changes, they should be entirely satisfactory to Cuba. Therefore, no political novelties should be introduced.*

This is an old and repetitive argument, which I will refute with some of the reasons I have stated elsewhere.[4]

The political reforms demanded by Cuba are incompatible with the legislation of the Indies. The nine books of the *Recopilación de las leyes de Indias* do not add up to a political, civil, criminal, or any other type of code. As the name indicates, they are not part of a larger plan, but rather a collection of numerous laws dictated to respond to different circumstances in different parts of Spanish America over a period of almost two centuries. By the end of that period, there was such a multitude of licenses, ordinances, letters, and other documents, and such was the incoherence and confusion, that not even the governors knew what they had to command, nor the governed what they had to obey. To get out of this maze, a compilation was made of the documents scattered in the archives of the kingdom. But the collected laws were piled up without any system, so that instead of a simple and philosophical code, the result was a collection of everything, good or bad, that had been issued to rule Spanish America. Ever since the reign of Philip II, there was talk of a compilation, but incorporating significant changes. If this was seen as necessary in the middle of the sixteenth century, it would be even more so in the middle of the nineteenth. The laws of the Indies cannot be remade without destroying them, and the most effective way of destroying them is to start anew.

The compilation of the laws of the Indies, I should point out, was not made for Cuba, but for other parts of Spanish America. Spain had its eyes fixed on the gold and silver of the mainland, and thus sent the majority of the European population to the region. The four Antilles, populated during the late fifteenth and sixteenth centuries, were nearly abandoned. In addition to the loss of people and capital, they were forgotten by the government. Cuba only rarely appeared in the mountain of laws that compose the *Recopilación*. How can they be applied to a people whose interests and needs were not taken into consideration? Can it be said that they apply because Cuba is part of Spanish America, and therefore has similar circumstances that justify the same legislation? It would be easy to demonstrate that in such a vast area as Spanish America, one colony differs from the other considerably. But without entering into this discussion, which could lead us astray, let us simply state that the *Recopilación* refers

---

[4] In my letter to Mr. [Vicente] Vázquez y Queipo on the fiscal report, printed in Seville in 1847.

17. José Antonio Saco, The Political Situation of Cuba (1851)

specifically to the mainland colonies. The laws that apply to them could hardly be appropriate for Cuba. An important part had to do with the policing of Indigenous peoples, and the relations between this population and the Europeans. In Cuba, however, the Indigenous people perished more than two centuries ago. What was designed for an entirely different race cannot be applied to the current population of Cuba.

Even without these reasons, it would be unwise to govern Cuba with the laws of the Indies. What was thought appropriate for the happiness of Spanish America after the Conquest would be a fatal policy in Cuba today. The political, commercial, and moral conditions of Cuba have changed substantially. To condemn the island to live under the remains of the code of the Indies is tantamount to the perpetuation of slavery. The material prosperity of Cuba actually began with the abolition of several colonial laws. Its political importance, its moral dignity, require the abolition of the rest. There is no doubt that some of these laws speak highly of the government that introduced them, because their aim was to save the Indigenous people from the horrors of the Conquest. The majority, however, viewed from the perspective of trade, were designed to protect monopolies, and are therefore the enemies of progress. From the perspective of justice, they are so imperfect that in matters civil and criminal it is necessary to consult the codes of Castile. From the standpoint of culture, they are so far behind modern knowledge that they actually undermine the hopes for enlightenment. From the perspective of religion, they are sixteenth-century celebrations of intolerance and persecution. Finally, from a political perspective, they are barbaric and tyrannical, because they give frightening powers to the rulers.

5th. *Cuba has too many slaves. Therefore, it should not enjoy political liberty.*

Has domestic slavery, in the countries where it exists, ever been an obstacle to the enjoyment of political rights? This awful institution was generalized in the ancient world, even in the freest republics. The Greek republics were full of slaves and in Athens, the most flourishing of them all, the number of enslaved people exceeded that of citizens.

They were so numerous in Carthage that many owners had thousands of them. The republic used them in the galleys of war: The 350 vessels that fought against Rome in the First Punic War carried, according to Polybius, the astonishing number of 105,000 enslaved people.

Rome, the conqueror of the world, enslaved a considerable portion of the human race. And yet, in the midst of that huge population, citizens

17. José Antonio Saco, The Political Situation of Cuba (1851)

exercised the political rights that ensured their private liberty in the Senate, and in elections.

Venice, long before it lost its liberty, possessed slaves and sold them to various nations. Pisa, Florence, and Genoa did the same during the most glorious days of their liberty.

The United States of America enjoyed wide political and religious rights even when they had a large number of enslaved people. During colonial times, in some regions, there were more enslaved than free people. That was the case in Virginia, and especially South Carolina, where in 1740 there were three enslaved people per white person. Today, that republic has more than three million slaves, and though they are concentrated in the Southern states, and in some they outnumber the white people, no one has thought about curtailing the rights of the republicans in the United States, or in Europe.

Brazil has a representative government and a liberal constitution. And yet, both before and after having these institutions, the number of enslaved people was vastly superior to white people.

Let us examine the case of Cuba. According to the census of 1846, the number of white people was 425,767, while enslaved people numbered 323,759. I consider the latter number low, for there is one slave per white person. This represents a great contrast to the British and French Antilles, where the number of enslaved people is much higher. If in spite of this disadvantageous position the latter have enjoyed political rights, why should Cuba be entirely deprived of them?

6th. *The current institutions of Cuba maintain order and tranquility. Political reforms would bring unrest and eventually independence. Therefore, no alteration should be made.*

If this is the case, why is there no trust in the future? Why are capitalists taking all the money they can out of the island? How can one explain the frequent alarms, imprisonments, exile, invasions supported by Cuban discontent, uprisings in Puerto Príncipe and Trinidad, and the scaffolds where so many Cubans have been executed? This is all new to Cuba, and the policy that has had such bad results is an abominable one that will sooner or later bring about a catastrophe. If liberty reigned in Cuba, perhaps we could blame such events on immoderate actions. But when despotism rules, despotism is responsible for the greater ills that follow.

The idea of annexation comes from this despotism: Its fatal hands have sown the dangerous seeds on our soil. Having lost the hope of achieving political reforms through Spain, some started to expect liberty

17. José Antonio Saco, The Political Situation of Cuba (1851)

from North America. The dissemination of such ideas, both there and in Cuba, explains the recent events. The alarm caused in Cuba by the French Revolution could have been deadly to the metropolis, had it not dissipated quickly. However, the fundamental idea has not gone away, and will not, because the causes have not disappeared. The fear of annexation came from the fear of invasion; the fear of invasion led to the increase of naval and military forces; the increase of these forces led to new taxes and higher Cuban payments to Spain. The resulting discontent, combined with the complaints about the political system, have compounded the situation. However, the effects have been mistaken for the cause, leading to the conclusion that either annexation or independence are the only means to escape oppression. Give liberty to Cuba and the troubles will go away. Even *one hundred thousand bayonets* sent by the government will not strengthen Spanish control as much as political liberty could. I swear this as a Cuban who can see this truth in the hearts of Cubans.

Concessions are feared because they might lead to independence. What is not understood is that the current system is leading us to either a revolution or a conflict with the United States. If a revolution takes place, thousands of self-interested Americans will come to Cuba posing as helpers. These are real dangers, and will descend upon us sooner rather than later. If they are fatal to the child, so they will be to the parent. Independence, on the contrary, is absolutely impossible today, and nearly impossible in the future. In the unlikely event that it should happen in the far distant future, it might be advantageous to both the colony and the metropolis, because the common roots will remain, and commerce will flourish.

The label of independence has been attached to Cuba, but the events of 1851, do they not clearly demonstrate that the island does not have such inclinations? Does our coat of arms not state "always faithful"? Queen Isabel II of Spain, did she not validate this statement recently? Why, then, mistrust the Cubans? Loyal as they are, why are they in political chains? If they are not loyal, why flatter them with an undeserved praise?

The accusations, more or less loud, about independence leanings in Cuba come from the confusion between the mainland colonies and the island, whose circumstances are essentially different. The Spanish American colonies covered a vast surface from California to Patagonia, and from the Atlantic to the Pacific. But Cuba has a very small territory in the Antilles. The population of Spanish America was larger than in the metropolis, while the Cuban, in addition to being small, has a large

17. José Antonio Saco, The Political Situation of Cuba (1851)

proportion of peninsular Spaniards. Spanish America was protected by the distance from Europe, the lack of internal communications, the denseness of the forests, and the height of the mountains. Cuba, for its part, is closer to Spain, and, thanks to steam, even closer. The coast is open, and the small territory has an abundance of roads going in all directions. When the insurrection started in the vastness of distant mainland Spanish America, was there any way to stop it? If not even the power of Great Britain could have done it, what chance did an impoverished nation have, without an army or navy, in the aftermath of a bloody war against the captain [Napoleon] of the century? Smaller Cuba has even fewer resources for defense. The government can concentrate all its forces against an exposed enemy.

I will add three more reasons to the arguments I have already made about annexation:

1st. The Count of Aranda anticipated the conduct of the United States as well as the loss of all mainland Spanish America. But the idea that Cuba and Puerto Rico could become independent never crossed his mind. When he advised Charles III to divide Spanish America into three crowns (Mexico, Peru, and the rest of the mainland), he also advised him to retain Cuba and Puerto Rico in the northern area [of the Caribbean], and perhaps another island in the southern to keep the flow of Spanish commerce. Aranda considered the matter dispassionately, with a profound political sense, because he was convinced that Cuba could not be independent.

2nd. Now that Spain has a liberal government, chances are that it will become stronger. It has all the elements to become a great and powerful nation. Therefore, even if Cuba attempted, far into the future, to become independent, it would encounter a metropolis capable of subjugating even bigger and stronger colonies. This knowledge should be more than enough to prevent Cubans from embarking on a hopeless endeavor. Why, after gaining political liberty, would they risk their happiness? Who would want to break the sweet and beneficial bonds between parent and child?

3rd. The boundless ambition of the United States presents a formidable obstacle to the independence of Cuba because, even assuming that it is achieved, the island will quickly lose it. Without appropriate defensive forces, and without the support of the former metropolis, Cuba would fall victim to American rapacity. Under its claws, Cuba would lose its traditions, its nationality, and even its language.

17. José Antonio Saco, The Political Situation of Cuba (1851)

Having refuted the arguments of the enemies of Cuban liberty, I now ask the Cortes, the government, and the entire Spanish nation: Is it prudent and political to keep the tension between Cuban loyalty and aspirations for liberty? Is it good that they should remain unhappy when a neighboring country lusts for the possession of Cuba, and constantly tempts the country with the promise of free institutions?

Is it just, or politically smart, that people should pay so much money annually, and still lack the ability to have a say in how taxes are collected, and how the revenues are used?

Is it just, or politically smart, that even the richest, most influential, and best-educated person does not have the right to name a representative?

Is it just, or politically smart, that in the periods 1812–1814, and 1820–1823, Cuba had been granted the same rights as the metropolis under the constitution, and that, by Royal Decree of 1834, had been allowed to send representatives to the Cortes, only to subsequently take these rights away?

Is it just, or politically smart, that after being promised a government of *special laws* under the Constitution of 1837, namely, non-tyrannical laws that responded to Cuban needs, and having followed the spirit of Spanish institutions, Cuba should, fourteen years later, still be under the yoke of despotism?

Is it just, or politically smart, that while Spain has broken its chains and recovered its ancient liberty, Cuba (which is also Spanish) should not receive a single liberal concession?

Is it just, or politically smart, that while Spain is proud to be counted among free peoples, it should keep its favorite child, Cuba, enslaved?

Finally, is it just, or politically smart, that while the British and French Antilles have long enjoyed councils and colonial assemblies despite their smaller wealth, importance, and white population (with a larger number of enslaved people), Cuba should present such a painful contrast to the other islands in the same archipelago?

The government should open its eyes and save Cuba from the abyss. It should not entertain suggestions that, however well-intentioned, are as mistaken as they are dangerous. It should consider that, with a muzzled press, organizations that lack even the smallest popular representation, and with no channels to interpret the sentiments of Cubans, there is no way that the government will know the true opinions of the population.

17. José Antonio Saco, The Political Situation of Cuba (1851)

The government is currently in the dark and running straight into the abyss. I know that my opinion might not be trusted, but if the government considers the national interest, it will learn that my voice is impartial and friendly. Spain should rule, now and forever, in Cuba. For the rule to be a happy one, however, liberal institutions should be in place not only in the territory, but also in the hearts of the population. These institutions will be strengthened by a treaty with Great Britain and France which will ensure that Cuba will never fall into the hands of a foreign power, that it will be safe from danger, and will remain in the peaceful possession of the Queen of the Antilles.

Paris, October 28, 1851

18

JUAN BAUTISTA ALBERDI

International Society (1870)

Juan Bautista Alberdi (1810–1884) was originally from the province of Tucumán, in today's western Argentina.[1] Educated in Buenos Aires, Alberdi was part of the Generation of 1837, a literary salon highly influenced by European Romanticism. The increasingly dictatorial rule of Juan Manuel de Rosas forced the group to go underground and eventually to exile in neighboring Uruguay. After the siege of Montevideo in 1843, Alberdi went to Europe and settled subsequently in Chile. As a writer and political commentator, Alberdi was instrumental in the overthrow of Rosas and in the promulgation of the Constitution of 1853. Under the rule of Justo José Urquiza as head of the Argentine Confederation, Alberdi became a diplomatic representative in Europe. His alliance with Urquiza put him at odds with the Buenos Aires political establishment until he was invited to return in 1879. Respected but no longer influential, Alberdi decided to return to Europe, where he died. His most important work is Bases y puntos de partida para la organización política de la república Argentina, *which as the title indicates became the leading draft of the Constitution of 1853. Due to his experience in Europe, he was also a keen observer of international affairs. The selection included in this volume represents a strong argument in favor of a community of nations whose principal aim was the eradication of war, which he considered as a crime against humanity.*

---

[1] This chapter has been selected from *El crimen de la guerra* (Seville, 2017), 115–146. The editors did not translate the title of the section literally (*Pueblo-Mundo*) but interpret the meaning of the concept as "international society." While for the title of this chapter we have translated "Pueblo-Mundo" as "International Society", we have kept his references to "*pueblo-mundo*" and "*sociedad-mundo*" closer to his original by leaving a hyphen – "world-community" and "world-society." (Editors' note)

18. Juan Bautista Alberdi, International Society (1870)

I. The International Rights of Man

States are the preferred entities of international law. However, states are composed of persons and thus they are part of international law. It is not only the states that are part of humanity, but also the individuals that compose the states as members of society. In the last analysis, the individual person is the elementary unit of any human society. It follows that any right, be it collective or general, is in the end an individual right.

Accordingly, international law is an individual right, just as much as the state's. If it can be ignored or violated to the detriment of the individual or the state, the individual can claim the same protections as the state could. He who invokes international law seeks the intervention of international society, or the world, where the law's purpose is the defense of trampled rights. Hence, when one or many members of a state see their international rights violated, they can, as members of human society, claim the protections of international law even against their own governments.

When they ask for intervention, they do not ask in the name of the state: Only the government can speak in the name of the state. They ask in their own name, invoking the international law that protects their liberties, life, security, equality, etc.

This explains the right of the world to intervene in favor of the abolition of civil slavery, which is a crime committed against humanity. And considering that political slavery is but a variation of the confiscation of liberty, the day will come when it will be a cause for intervention, following international law, in favor of the victims of criminal governments.

There have been interventionist alliances such as the Holy Alliance. Why would alliances not be made to defend individual liberties and place them under the protection of the civilized world of which the individual is a member? The muse of liberty intuited such principles when [Pierre Jean de] Béranger welcomed the Holy Alliance of peoples.

II. The World-Community

The notion that there are two types of justice – one for the Romans and one for the juridical relations between Romans and Greeks (or other foreigners) – has led to the confusion that exists in the most important branch of the law. The progress of humanity has made international law the rule that governs the juridical relations among nations within the universal society that is called the civilized world.

18. Juan Bautista Alberdi, International Society (1870)

Matters become clearer and simpler thanks to the notion of a single and universal law. Indeed, what is the permanent objective anywhere? The individual, always the individual. Whether a person is viewed in isolation from others or as part of a mass, the law is the same, and its objectives likewise the same. That is why [Hugo] Grotius states that there are as many sources of litigation among persons as causes of war among peoples. The whole set of issues involving civil law matters coincides perfectly with those involving nations in international law. In effect, the purpose of all international legal actions is to defend one state's domains and rights from another state: to protect and recover what belongs to the injured party and punish the foreign state that is guilty of an offense against one's fatherland.

The peculiarity of international law resides in two great facts: First, that the individual person is represented by that society of which he is a member, as a political person who interfaces with another individual in the same situation. Second, that because of the absolute independence of that political entity called the state, there is no code or judge to decide on conflicts between states. Each state is simultaneously judge (or subject to be judged), lawyer, policeman, and executioner. It is not enough that a nation peacefully demands, in the name of reason, what claims to be its own in order to be heard. The other side may have no interest in listening to the claims or may in good faith believe the contrary. That a state lacks any justification for attacking or injuring another state does not prevent a conflict from taking place. Here, it is the power of the state that provides the reason of one to prevail against the error of another. Likewise, this is the only means to honor the right of one nation against the offense of another. However, in a conflict between individuals, the state is the judge. Such an impartial judge is lacking in the conflict between states because the people of different countries live in a state of nature. That is, isolated from, and independent of, any common and supreme authority other than their own. In the absence of a common judge (who by analogy should be the state-world that is humanity) each state is lawyer, soldier, and judge of its own case for the use of force. Such is the ultimately decisive reason in international conflicts: that is, the war that accounts for all actions in international law, either in civil or penal cases. This way of administering justice has the defect of leading to a war that destroys the issue instead of solving it. In fact, a procedure by which each litigant is part, witness, judge, and executioner does not deserve the name of justice. That sort of "justice" between individuals is called a crime. What then would be the case between nations? For as long as this situation lasts, the civilized world may proudly claim to have solved a thousand social injustices except the most important of all: the application of international justice. Since the day is nowhere in sight when sovereigns will submit to a universal power, the only way to escape this strange justice, which is analogous to crime, is to never enter into litigation. To inspire horror in this justice for beasts and savages, so unworthy of human beings, one must call any war a crime against humanity.

What reason cannot solve through discussion will not be solved by the sword. Far from being the last resort of the law, the use of force is the first step on the ladder of crime. Unless the contrary is proven, self-defense is presumed to be a crime because it is against human nature for someone to be both the interested party and the impartial judge of one's enemy. As a rule, war must be considered a crime, and most rarely a right. I prefer Cicero's definition rather than Grotius' as the more humane. War, says the former, is a conflict solved by means of animal force. Grotius believes that war is the card that a given party plays, not the action itself. It would be much better to assume that war is a quick and ephemeral action, just like the spontaneous reaction that violence provokes when directed against us. This is how war should be considered, as an exceptional act of self-defense. It cannot be seen as a normal state or situation because murder, theft, or arson cannot be construed as part of a durable system. War, in the form of supreme self-defense, should only be seen as an accident, or as a brief and isolated case, just like any criminal act committed against us. In short, if the crime of war cannot be a durable state of things, neither can war be waged in the name of justice, or punishment. Any war that lasts longer than the act that is invoked as a motive or pretext will soon degenerate into crime, and it is as such that it must be understood.

III. The Presumed Benefits of War

When war is considered as legal punishment of a criminal act, a belief follows in the beneficial effects on the education and improvement of humankind. This is in keeping with the beneficial influence that is attributed to ordinary penal law on the domestic education of a country. This is dubious, however, because oftentimes the punished is not the criminal, but the weak. The latter can be entirely innocent, but if he goes against a powerful criminal he will be vanquished and punished, even if he is not guilty.

A penal justice system where the judge and the executioner are the interested parties is monstrous. Far from being appropriate to educate humankind in what is good and honest, it only corrupts and destroys any notion of morality and justice. A punishment (i.e., a war to punish war or other offense) dictated by the impartial world would be characterized by the presumption of justice. But a punishment driven by interest, hatred, ambition, or envy is perverse, or at the very least unjustly disproportionate. From here it can be inferred that war considered from the most favorable perspective, that of penal justice, is radically incapable of improving and civilizing humanity.

Is there anything more absurd than to pretend that the extermination of millions of lives, the devastation of urban and rural areas, fires, ruins, deception, fraud, and desecration can be the means to educate and improve humankind? All justice by one's hand, or self-defense, is presumed to be a crime unless the contrary is proven. This rule of penal law is especially applicable to war. Even the most perfectly argued justification for war involves the presumption of a crime insofar as the aggrieved party takes justice into its own hands. The rule that in all wars both sides are right must be replaced by the following: Both are guilty until the world-community, the only qualified judge to produce a verdict, can deliver it based on the evidence, and its own legitimacy as a grand jury of nations.

The law of each state sentences as guilty those individuals who quarrel and hurt one another not only because by making themselves judges they evade the proper authorities, but also because the presumed justice that they adjudicate to themselves almost always involves an iniquity. In the same manner international law, which is founded on an identical principle, must condemn those states that resort to destructive violence to settle matters of honor or self-interest. Just like society vindicates the individual victim of a crime that hurts society as a whole, the world-society has every right to regard and condemn an offense to the rights of one state, as an offense against all.

IV. The Spontaneous Growth of Authority

A nation without a state, that is, a people without a common authority, exemplifies the world of Hobbes' war of all against all. Each man is his own judge as well as the judge of his adversary. War is his civil and criminal code, as well as his code of procedure. This is a state of ultimate barbarianism; it will become a permanent institution unless stopped by the emergence of a common authority that can settle differences. Such an authority lives alongside the formation of the state. It can even be said that its establishment represents the proper formation of the nation.

What occurs in the history of each state must also happen in the formation of the collective state that will eventually become the confederation of humankind. With the spontaneous formation of this association, and because of it, international institutions will emerge that will settle and regulate, in the name of the sovereign authority of a united world, the differences that are today left to the mercy of the passion and egotism of parties invested in the damage they can inflict on each other.

The establishment of courts in each state put an end to the quarrels and armed struggles that characterized the resolution of conflicts in the savage age. In the same manner, the necessary and inevitable establishment of a regular international law will end war. Today, war is a conflict decided by the more powerful or astute party. Nations will not achieve justice until humanity, as an impartial magistrate and judge, makes the decisions. This means those neutral states that are removed from the conflict: They will prevent or judge and then settle conflicts. Grotius has anticipated the advent of this institution as follows:

> And for this, as well as several other Reasons, it would be not only convenient, but somewhat necessary that Congresses of Christian States were held, where, by them who are no ways interested on one Side or other, the Differences of contending Parties might be made up; and that some Means were thought upon to oblige the Parties at Variance to accept a Peace upon fair and reasonable Terms.[2]

v. The World Organization

If there is ever a people fit to exercise self-government perpetually, that will be the composite of peoples called the society of nations.

Each nation is likely to govern itself as the world-community does, without common authorities. It is less likely that humanity will form a universal authority in the image of each nation. However, the absence of a common authority does not imply the absence of a common law; nor does the absence of law mean the absence of government. Proof of that is the notion of self-government: government without an authority. The

---

[2] Hugo Grotius, *The Rights of War and Peace*, 3 vols., ed. by Richard Tuck (Indianapolis, 2005), book II, chapter 23, part VIII. (Editors' note)

18. Juan Bautista Alberdi, International Society (1870)

practicality of this type of government is demonstrated by self-governing nations that adhere to international law in their foreign relations. The law reveals itself and applies to all who understand its necessity for the common good. Even those who do not comprehend this still submit to it for the sake of self-preservation. These are the people who will go on forever without a government, in the sense that the word "government" has for each individual nation. The society of nations will follow the same rule that applies to the members of a private association: Each one has the duty to respect the opinions of all. Thus, far from following the model of each individual nation, the society of nations will become the model to follow by each nation.

Accordingly, the absence of government does not imply the absence of law. The law exists regardless of the legislator. Once it has been acknowledged as such, it exists as the natural law of universal society. This is the essential condition for the existence of such a society. Only then is it possible for all members of the human family to achieve harmony, progress, and liberty. Those who subscribe to this international law are the free agents of a common and general law of existence. Just like the law of gravity presides over the physical world, international law presides over the world of nations. Its authority comes from the books that register the rules of manners and good society among individuals. Grotius, for example, is the Lord Chesterfield of nations. Treaties are the written rules of relations among nations. Such rules are preexisting and are contained in the books of moral science. They teach the principles of good behavior that allow nations to live peacefully. Thus, in a meeting of well-educated people, order is maintained without resort to authority. When it comes to nations, matters are different. It remains to be seen whether the harmony that can be achieved among nations will be the same if the society is composed of monarchical governments, however well educated, instead of governments that make no distinctions of rank or education. Will the democracies of the future be more capable of maintaining international order and peace than the monarchies of the past? Will the turmoil that is produced by domestic freedom be compatible with an unalterable international peace?

The United States, surrounded as it is by monarchies,[3] cannot solve this problem by example, because it is unclear whether what the country

---

[3] This reference suggests that the monarchies in question could include British Canada and Russian claims in the Western United States. (Editors' note)

has enjoyed is due to its own merits or to the restraint of its neighbors. South American democracies, for their part, have not followed the model of a private association composed of well-educated gentlemen.

VI. The Natural Organization

Nations, to become entities that govern themselves through common laws, do not need to form a confederation. Nor do they need to have a common authority that mirrors that of each state. Such a society already exists because of the natural law that explains the rise of each nation. It gathers further strength due to the need of each nation to collaborate with others to become richer, happier, stronger, and freer. As distances are bridged by the miraculous power of steam and electricity, the well-being of peoples is improved by commerce. This is the great international agent that unites, links, and locks mutual interests far better than all the diplomacy of the world. Nations get closer to the point of forming a single country.

Each new international railway is the equivalent of ten alliances; each foreign loan means that a border is knocked down. Three undersea cables have buried the Monroe doctrine without a fuss. The press facilitates the formation of an international public opinion that provides the governance that the world-community now lacks. The press is the light shed every day from one nation to the other. Without the help of the press, nations lose their sense of direction and no longer know where they are, or where they are going. The press points the way to liberty to the extent that it is based on the active contributions of society.

The presence of this judge who sees and judges everything without fear (because no one is stronger in the entire world) explains why criminal behavior by sovereigns becomes less and less practicable each passing day. How is a general power formed? By multiplying local powers. To become one, France divided provinces into departments. How to multiply the local powers that are the nations of the world-community? By dividing them into departments? No, just the contrary: by increasing the number of great nations composed of smaller ones. That is the natural tendency of humanity in a civilized age. When instead of five great states there are twenty, each one will be in a better situation. Hence, the fusion of states is not contrary to the formation of an international society whose power is increasingly democratic.

18. Juan Bautista Alberdi, International Society (1870)

VII. Human Nature

The great feature of modern democracy is international democracy; it heralds the arrival of world government. This means the sovereignty of the world-community as the guarantor of national sovereignty. If this king of kings, this sovereign of sovereigns, is not exercising sovereignty yet, it has it and is the highest supreme sovereignty on earth. The fact that it is not exercised today by an organized power does not negate that the world is the sovereign of sovereigns. Otherwise, there would be no sovereignty in any nation because no nation has, except nominally, the sovereignty of the people. As proof, it can be pointed out that when current sovereigns seek to justify their conduct to other states, they instinctively invoke the supreme judge of nations called humankind. This people-world and its sovereignty form and establish themselves by virtue of the natural laws that preside over the individual and collective development of man, fostering his indefinitely perfectible nature. The natural principle that has created each nation is the same that will give birth and formation to that ultimate and supreme nation of nations. This is the corollary, the complement, and the guarantee of the foundations of each nation, just like provinces, departments, districts, families, and cities are to each nation.

The notion of fatherland does not exclude that of world-community; that is, the idea that humankind can form a single society that is above, yet inclusive of, the component societies. The fatherland, on the contrary, is compatible with the existence of a large and diverse people made up of national fatherlands. In the same manner, the individuality of man is compatible with the existence of the state of which he is a member. National independence, in the world-community, will mean the liberty of the citizen-nation, just like individual liberty means the independence of each man within the state of which he is a member. Each man today has several fatherlands that help and sustain one another rather than fight each other. They include the province or locality of his birth or domicile; the nation, of which the province is a part; the continent, to which the nation belongs, and finally the world, of which the continent is a part. Thus, as man interacts and is increasingly capable of belonging to different realities, his whole and definitive fatherland, one worthy of him, becomes the whole earth. The sun never sets in his dominions.

VIII. The Biological Analogy

Nations tend to gravitate toward the formation of a single and great universal nation. This is what the still unwritten history shows us, and everyone sees. The law that drives nations in that direction is the natural law that has formed the diversity of nations that exist today. They will be component units of the aggregate or whole of the vast international body that encompasses the civilized part of humanity. To belong to this aggregate, to be a part of this body, will be both the pride and the basis for the civilization of each society. The law that will be common to all living beings will be that of evolution. This is how naturalists explain the formation, the structure or organization, and the purposes of the species.

The quality of "body" ascribed to a state, and the expression "social body," are far from rhetorical: They designate the reality of a natural fact. Hence, according to modern biologists and sociologists, one can regard the aggregate of nations as a single body of which each separate nation is an organ. This body is not yet formed, but proof exists that it is in the process of forming. The same law that has formed each of the nations will turn them into constitutive parts of the whole. The biological sciences have helped sociologists apply the laws of evolution to understand the creation, structure, and functions of the body called society. Why should it not help to understand the similar entity called the society of nations?

The role of biology in the study of international sociology will shed important new light on the science of international law. What is the vital condition of that great organism called international society, or world? As in any other body, it is the separation of organs performing particular tasks or functions, as well as their mutual dependence, that come together to play a larger role. The division of labor, on which life and the progress of work depend, applies not only to industry and commerce but also to all the elements of society. Such is the natural law of all living organisms because there is a physiological division of labor in the constitution of organized life, as [Henri] Milne Edwards has shown.

There is no organization but rather a shapeless mass where there is no separation of the parts belonging to a whole for the purposes of specialization and functional diversity. Nor where mutual dependence is lacking for the participation of parts in the larger life of the group. The human body would not be an organic unity without a variety of organs whose different functions contribute to the whole and are dependent on each other for their health and development. Each organ has a function and a

18. Juan Bautista Alberdi, International Society (1870)

special task — that is, a sphere, a role, a domain, and a jurisdiction within the body. They depend on one another for what each contributes to what they all need to live.

Such is the model of any individual, social, or international organization. The organizer of this model is the author of all properly constituted organisms, as well as the author and executor of the law called natural evolution. That is where all social bodies and all living beings come from. International law must look there for the origin, the true notion, and the sphere of the independence of each nation — also, the origin, nature, and limits of the mutual dependence between nations. The former, to produce well, more, and better; the latter, to move from what each nation has done in favor of its separation or independence, to what each requires from the other to satisfy the need to live well.

The independence or interdependence of each state requires both. Separately, they cease to be legitimate when they are no longer intrinsic and vital parts of the social organism called the civilized world. On the one hand, the absolute isolation of a given society is like an amputation performed on the social world. The killing of an organ is a threat to the entire organism. If the organ is a vital one, the body is exposed to imminent destruction. On the other hand, unlimited dependence means the destruction or death of the organism because a degree of separateness or division of labor are necessary for the reproduction of goods on the infinite scale that the perfectibility of man requires.

To make changes in the production and delivery of their respective specialties, the social units of the international body must be able to communicate with the same speed, ease, and safety as the organs of the biological body. In relations between states, the equivalent means of communication, unity, and vitality are free trade, railways, steam lines, and other forms of maritime contact. Also, the telegraph, the post office, currency, and ideas. Everything, in the end, that promotes solidarity in the collective existence of man. Human improvement will make society stronger as it brings together all members of the human species.

IX. Of Such Natural Laws

These natural laws of universal society ought to be studied not so much to be imposed by governments, as to implement the authority they are given by nature. They exist regardless of whether man believes in, or rejects, them. Societies have not been created by governments. Whether local, national, or universal, every society is the product of evolution or natural creation, whatever its form might be. The governments themselves are the products rather than the authors of this law. They are the natural condition as well as part of the social organism. The law of natural evolution can be obstructed in a thousand ways, but the most disastrous way, in general, is the policy of prohibition and protectionism. The latter ignores the organic role of the nation in the construction, or structuring, of the universal society of nations. By intending to turn the state into a whole being, when it is in fact an organ of the great international body, protectionism resembles a physiologist who seeks to liberate the head from the heart in the production of blood. To accomplish this task, the physiologist would sever the veins and arteries by whose means the head receives the blood from the heart. In its stead, he would give the head its own special heart. However, he would not be able to accomplish the latter feat after performing the previous. Death would follow this protectionist decapitation not only for the head, but also for the heart. That is to say, the death of the entire body. An organism is a state in which each organ is a citizen, a member, a constituting unit of the social world called the organic body.

X. International Law

Unless international law rests on the foundations of the internal law of each state, there will be nothing but permanent iniquity and disorder in the organization of the human species. And yet, the organization of the internal law of a state is the result of the existence of such a state, meaning the society of people ruled by a common legislation and government. The nations that compose humanity must form a type of society or unity so that their union can deliver a more or less common legislation and government. Such a work is now in progress due to the improvement of the human species, which is occurring everywhere on that home that is the earth.

This movement toward the unification or consolidation of the human species, in the various continents of the planet, is a stage in the life of humanity. Such a movement is the essential law that explains its vitality, development, and improvement. International law and its progress are not the cause of the human movement toward the general unity, but rather the inevitable consequence of its natural and spontaneous activity. What has occurred in the development of each state is also occurring in that entity that is emerging from all known nations. All societies precede,

18. Juan Bautista Alberdi, International Society (1870)

in their formation, the law considered as science and as legislation. Such precedence will lead to the improvement of society by preserving the living tradition and its legacy. Both life and international society must naturally precede the development of international law as a legislation and as a science. Everything that tends to bring together and unite nations is morally, intellectually, and materially conducive to the establishment of the international (and internal) law of the human species – that is, on the basis of the efficiency and impartiality that rests on the internal law of each state. This is the motivation that encourages every nation to form a great universal association prepared to submit to laws and a government common to all.

To the extent that any association expands, it undoubtedly becomes less capable of centralization. Centers, in other words, multiply. And yet decentralization is not incompatible with unity. Far from it: it complements the social order just as each biological organ has two lives – one local and one general.

International law will be an empty term unless there is an international authority that makes the law something alive and real. Otherwise, it will be like the civil code of a state that has no government and no civil authority: a catechism of morality or religion, like the rules of civility and good manners that we have today. In other words, it is a law that one acknowledges or ignores as one pleases. Each house, each family, each man would have to bear arms to protect his property, life, and liberty. Therefore, the task of international law is not so much to investigate principles and precepts, as to find the authority to promulgate and implement the law. Such an authority cannot exist, and will never exist, unless an association of all nations comes into being. Once united they will form a great and complex state as vast as humanity, or at least as large as the continents that comprise the earth, the common home of the human species.

Authority and association are facts: The former is the logical and natural product of the latter. A society can exist without a government, however badly, but a government cannot exist, well or badly, without a society or nation. In a society composed of all nations, authority will emerge automatically, as the very condition, natural and inevitable, of its existence. It will come from the need to establish and implement the law, which is what rules life in any human association. The question is whether such a society of nations exists today, even in an embryonic form, or not at all. A question even prior to that is, can the nations that encompass the human species form a single body, apart as they are, like dots in the immensity of

18. Juan Bautista Alberdi, International Society (1870)

our planet? The space that separates the peoples that compose the Russian empire is far greater than that of the states of Western Europe. If this is not an obstacle for the political union of Russia, why should it be for Western Europe? The proof that a society of civilized nations can exist and form a complex union is that it already exists, albeit in an incomplete form. A French person is socially and legally no different than a British one, compared to people living in a state of pure nature, like the barbarians of the Pampas or Araucania. The first pair is united by enough principles, interests, customs, and laws as to form a whole code. Or, what amounts to the same, a whole social and political order that can be considered as one body consisting of two. What I say of a French or a British person I extend to the individuals of all the nations of Europe. This society of societies has not yet come into being, but it will in a final form in the future. What is certain is that it will be more advanced than it has ever been by virtue of a natural law that compels all peoples to reach this stage of social and collective life, beginning with the family and culminating in humanity. The very science of international law, far from being the originator of the unity of nations, is but an expression and a product of it. Nations have not come together because of the advice of Alberico Gentili or Hugo Grotius, but rather because of their mutual interests, the path shown by reason, and the social essence of nations [*raza*]. The light of science has certainly contributed to the likelihood of this outcome. But more than international law *per se*, it is the contribution of those who have looked into the physical and moral sciences to find the means to bring people together to form the great association of the civilized world. These are the true makers of the unity of the human species, the true fathers and creators of international law, more so than the scholars and intellectuals who put in written form the laws that already exist. This is the law that creates and nurtures the life of all human associations.

Part VI.
Fin de Siècle

19
VALENTÍN LETELIER

The Tyranny and the Revolution (1891)

Valentín Letelier (1852–1929) was a Chilean educator, philosopher, and jurist who, after an assignment in Prussia in the early 1880s, contributed to the reform of the Chilean educational system, particularly through the creation of the teacher-training institute, the Instituto Pedagógico attached to the University of Chile.[1] A committed positivist and leader of the Radical Party, Letelier was a chaired professor of law who became rector of the University of Chile for two periods beginning in 1906. His principal works include Filosofía de la educación *(1892),* La evolución de la historia *(1900),* Génesis del Estado *(1917), and* Génesis del derecho *(1919). As a member of Congress, he joined the opposition to the government of José Manuel Balmaceda, signing the articles of impeachment that led to his arrest and exile in 1891, the year of the Civil War that ended with the victory of the congressional forces. The current selection provides Letelier's rationale for the opposition to Balmaceda and advances a passionate defense of the role of organized political parties in a democracy, the rule of law, and the meritocratic selection of public officials.*

The situation created by the tyranny [the government of José Manuel Balmaceda], in the area under its influence, shows how the oppressive regime, pretending to attack one social class, in the end attacked the republic as a whole. The accusation against the constitutionalists [the

---

[1] This essay comes from Valentín Letelier's *La tiranía y la revolución; o sea, relaciones de la administración con la política estudiada a la luz de los últimos acontecimientos* (Santiago, 1891), 3–54. (Editors' note)

221

19. Valentín Letelier, *The Tyranny and the Revolution (1891)*

Congress] of taking up arms to protect the interests of a monopolistic oligarchy was not only unjust but also absurd.[2]

States that are based on the principle of equality are not the same as states that are based on class divisions.

In states divided by class one of these classes can be oppressed while the other is free; one can be persecuted while the other is protected. We can see this in the history of the ancient world. In the Greek states, divided as they were into different classes, each one was completely independent. As a result, legislators did not pursue common rights, but rather class interests. There was a generalized prejudice, that one won when the other lost. Nothing could be given to the one without taking it away from the other. This explains why in some Greek republics, as noted by Aristotle, the oligarchs were compelled to swear, upon assuming a public post, that they would inflict as much damage as they could to the people.

In places where the principle of equality is paramount no one can be hurt without hurting everyone, nor take the rights of a few without taking them from all, nor conquering liberties for one without conquering them for the entire nation.

When the president of the Republic [of Chile] violated the legal order to become a dictator, he abandoned the rule of law and became a tyrant. As he lost all shame and exposed himself as such, the national sentiment was kindled in all hearts, from the highest to the lowest levels of society.

Tyranny gradually pervaded every layer of the social order. In three months, there was no Chilean, however poor, who did not see the absolute lack of guarantees, rights, and liberties in which we all found ourselves.

In Chile, no branch of government is allowed to raid and destroy property with the sole purpose of decimating the ranks of property owners; no one can suppress industrial liberty in order to prevent owners from making a living; above all, no one can bring back the barbaric use of torture to extract confessions from the imprisoned. And yet, the tyrannical government did all of this as if, by appropriating the sum of public authority, it had been endowed with a special faculty to violate the law, the culture, and the morals of our society. Tyranny did even more than this to

---

[2] The events here described by Letelier took place during 1891, when the Chilean Congress agreed to depose President José Manuel Balmaceda, thus precipitating the Civil War of that year. Defeated, Balmaceda took his own life while in asylum at the Argentine embassy in Santiago. (Editors' note)

19. Valentín Letelier, The Tyranny and the Revolution (1891)

elicit the hatred of the people because, without any warning whatsoever, it turned innocent activities into criminal acts.

Let me add that even if it had relied only on members of the oligarchic class, the revolution [of 1891] would still be just, patriotic, and deserving of victory.

Even if one concedes that the oligarchy did not have the support of the people, one must also acknowledge that the tyranny did not have it either. Whether they are few or many, political leaders must always sound the alarm when usurpation is under way. In societies such as the Chilean, where a wide gap exists between the political culture of the upper and the lower classes, the former should not wait for the support of the latter to defend their rights.

Once an abuse takes place one must immediately demand redress, whatever the reaction of others might be. It is for this reason that many citizens resisted the dictatorship without assessing the opinions of the wider public.

The opinion that matters in politics is not the opinion of the indifferent, nor of those whose ignorance or egotism prevents them from participating in public affairs. It is the opinion of those, whether few or many, who regularly show an interest in the honest performance of the government.

He who is born in a free society has the right to defend his liberty against the will of an entire people, and certainly against the will of one man. As far as I know, no one disapproved of Cato, who along with the oligarchs of Rome, rebelled against Caesar and received the resolute support of the people.

In an egalitarian republic all that can be demanded of the revolutionaries is that they launch their rebellion only when it is absolutely necessary. They should never do it with narrow aims in mind, or on behalf of a single individual, or to establish the dominance of one class. In the case of the Chilean Revolution, its causes, development, and effects, the civilized world understands that it was launched to restore the rule of law for the good of the people and in the interests of humanity and culture.

Up to this point I have been assuming that there is in fact an oligarchic class in Chile. That is what many foreigners assume who have only superficially studied the nature of Chilean society. And yet, it is easy to show that we do have a governing class that is constantly including some of the best minds in politics. We are not under the control of an oligarchy, meaning an exclusive and monopolistic caste.

19. Valentín Letelier, The Tyranny and the Revolution (1891)

I must recognize a fact that honors and distinguishes our public administration, namely, that public positions are far from being tied to a few families. They are the legal patrimony of all Chileans. This does not mean that the uneducated has the same chances as the educated of occupying a state post. Nor will I say that the wicked has more chances than an honest man.

In an oligarchic state, what are the political means a legislator can use to combat the class system? Is it not universal suffrage? This powerful instrument of leveling, which makes quantity prevail over quality, has been placed in the hands of the people.

At the same time, primary instruction, which is public, universal, and free, has been introduced by those who stand accused of seeking to control the administration and the government of the state. Primary education, however, is an elevating force, a means to bring the lower classes to the level of the higher.

If an oligarchy exists in Chile, it is not because the law has mandated a link between a few families and the administration of the state. Nor is it because the oligarchy has formed a monopoly. The actual reason is that the educated class, the class capable and worthy of conducting political and administrative affairs, is still too small. And matters of state cannot be entrusted to the unprepared without depriving the government of the more talented.

The actions of the government confirm every word I say.

To justify the usurpation and to promote resistance against the Congress, the dictatorship presented itself as anti-oligarchic, and announced its intention to bring the lower classes to the government. But despite the efforts to give a popular character to the ranks of the public administration, the dictatorship could not find men competent enough to replace those who were sacked.

Those identifiable persons who supported the tyranny were by and large recruited from the same governing class. The rest had no notion of administration and politics other than the art of defrauding the Treasury with impunity.

There was no honest man recruited from the lower classes who was not already involved in the finance and politics of the tyranny. They were called upon to replace the meritorious citizens who had become targets of persecution. The accomplices of despotism who entered politics ignored our old traditions of respect for the law. Those who joined the

19. Valentín Letelier, *The Tyranny and the Revolution (1891)*

administration abandoned the path of probity that was the legacy of public officials in the history of the republic.

The governing class cannot be replaced today without a serious blow to the state. In the long run, however, it can be enlarged through public education, universal suffrage, and industrial development.

Anyone who is truly capable of managing the duties of government has been or can be easily incorporated into it, on the same level as citizens of the highest social rank. The recently overthrown faction made a completely unnecessary, unjustified, bold, and criminal attempt to drive meritorious men away from the tasks of administration and politics.

Therefore, it cannot be said that the dictatorship was established to defend the rights of all, nor that the revolution was launched to preserve the monopoly of the few. Actually, the reverse is true: The dictatorship favored a clique of rapacious libertines, while the revolution was launched to restore to everyone, friend and foe, the rule of law.

This brief review of the devastating effects of tyranny demonstrates that a bad policy can disturb the whole of society, and break the machinery of administration, when despotism replaces liberty.

It occurs to me that, in the present situation, the first thing we need to do is determine how the reckless attempt at usurpation was born and developed, and from which the Chilean people are still trying to escape. By failing to understand the causes of tyranny we let it remain with us, spring back, and expose us to new evils.

We do not need to go too far back to place the origins of our misfortunes: the War of the Pacific [1879–1883[3]]. There was not much of a change in the legal system, but war meant an enormous concentration of power in the hands of the executive.

Thousands of citizens were pressed into service, and provisions were secured by means of coercion. Meanwhile, the press, the Congress, and public opinion failed to come to the defense of liberty and civil rights. On the contrary, they resolutely supported the authorities during this time of public commotion. The executive was thus substantially strengthened by the unanimous support for bringing the war to a successful conclusion.

---

[3] The War of the Pacific (1879–1883) pitted Chile against the alliance of Peru and Bolivia. It began as a dispute over mineral resources, borders, and taxes in the Atacama area, culminating in the victory and substantial territorial expansion of Chile. (Editors' note)

19. Valentín Letelier, The Tyranny and the Revolution (1891)

In order to understand the juridical side of this issue one must take into consideration that, from a scientific point of view, governments that by law have a larger number of faculties are not necessarily stronger, since none of these faculties can be used *against* society.

Strong governments are those that enjoy the greatest support from society. The adoption of extraordinary measures is legitimate only when the social body determines that absolute necessity requires it.

That is why the state of war, all things being equal, can lead to victory depending upon the degree of social cohesion, discipline, obedience, and unity. They all contribute to the political strength of governments, even if they go against the wishes of the governed, or the will of those who govern.

It is a principle of political science that in underdeveloped societies, where the state of war is permanent, their governments are autocratic. Industrial societies, for their part, tend to have more liberal governments: War takes place for purely accidental reasons.

In addition to the causes that changed the political character of our government, albeit without modification of the constitutional order, one must add the extraordinary weight of international affairs that, unknown to public opinion, made the government the ultimate arbiter of very important interests.

As it has long been observed, the conduct of foreign affairs, due to the necessary reserve that it requires, tends to concentrate power in the hands of the prince, thereby strengthening his position.

Many authors who have studied the formation of modern autocracies in Europe have pointed out that the establishment of foreign relations in the late Middle Ages made monarchs the arbiters of war and peace and, consequently, the masters of the fate of peoples, and the exclusive directors of political affairs.

Although on a different scale, the same phenomenon occurred in Chile as a consequence of the War of the Pacific. That is when the government controlled the agricultural sector by negotiating a deal on tariffs with Peru and Bolivia, and the nitrate interests through negotiations involving the region of Tarapacá.

The exorbitant growth of the national budget, with no private capital to match, turned the executive into a political power not seen since the times of [Bernardo] O'Higgins.

Never before had Chile seen such an enormous number of employees, contractors, manual workers, engineers, and architects whose income depended directly and exclusively on the Treasury.

19. Valentín Letelier, The Tyranny and the Revolution (1891)

Can any political independence be expected from a population that draws so heavily from the Treasury? How is the recipient of favors going to contradict the will of the giver? Those who are yet to receive those favors, will they want to irritate their potential provider?

To close this brief presentation of the main causes of dictatorship, we should not forget that the national misfortunes of recent times are the work of those habits of conquest and disrespect for the law that our military acquired during the years of occupation in Peru.

Before the War of the Pacific, our military boasted of their respect for institutions, public liberties, and civil authority. No one would have dared to involve them in an attempt against the constitutional order.

There are no habits more quickly lost by the military than those of discipline and respect for the rule of law, as when victory ensures their impunity and validates their disobedience. The victorious Chilean army was destined to become an instrument of oppression and tyranny in the hands of the first insolent master.

My purpose here is to extract the truth from the past to guide us into the future. It would be unworthy of my profession to hide the truth in order to save my friends from disappointment, or to antagonize my adversaries. Let us know this truth, open our eyes, and change course. It is the right path for a citizen of integrity and patriotism.

Accordingly, it would be absurd to ignore the fact that the first step toward the containment of public opinion was the attempt to dissolve the only political forces (other than the government and the church) that had some strength: organized political parties.

Under the pretext that parties are simple vehicles of ambition (negating all that liberalism represents in terms of independence and prestige), they have been attacked by the government. Also, and under the pretext that conservatism is opposed to progress, an implacable war has been waged against it, a war in which all weapons have been used, including fraud, forgeries, and vote-buying.

In truth, the effort to destroy political parties has been a threat to the republic. It clearly shows, in my view, that no other attempt reveals as clearly the lack of political sense that is ordinarily expected from public service.

One need not be a political science expert to understand that the existence of too many parties can be problematic. However, this is not always the case. Parties and factions are not the creation of *caudillos*: They emerge from social and political demands. A party that withdraws its support for

19. Valentín Letelier, *The Tyranny and the Revolution* (1891)

the government because it opposes its policies has as much of a right to exist as the oldest and most established party. These organizations are based on the diversity of ideas, and the confrontation between interests and ambitions is in the very nature of democracy. In a democracy, public positions that are not tied to a particular class help stimulate the participation of the citizenry. Until the science of politics becomes better known, there is little hope of stopping the proliferation of doctrines that lead to the proliferation of parties.

Despite the truth of these observations, the bulk of opinion is more inclined to support the party of government, which is viewed as successful, rather than the party of opposition, which is the party of the future. This is the opinion that supported the terrible policies of the government, the opinion that from the press and the assemblies hurled sarcasms and invectives to the independent men who resisted those policies.

Many citizens were driven by the error of thinking that political parties were the cause of all evils. They thought that if there was only one truth, so likewise there should only be one party of government. That is how they became the innocent accomplices of a perverse policy.

Given the current state of the science of politics, as some have pointed out, there are many views on government, and consequently, many parties. They add that even if several doctrines became a uniform one, there will still be legitimate but contradictory interests confronting each other. Democracy must stimulate such healthy antagonisms in order to motivate citizens to serve their country.

It was rather in vain that critics showed how there will always be a diversity of opinions to implement this or that principle. Even if all parties agree to merge into one, there is no reason to expect that either liberalism or the party of progress will become dominant enough to absorb the others, as the Radical Party once did, and might still do.

In spite of these just, reasonable, and incontrovertible observations, the destructive forces of government prevailed because of the triple support of special interests, ignorance, and ideology. The president of the republic, as a result, increased his dictatorial tendencies, and parties became less and less capable of stopping him.

After the defeat of tyranny [the revolution of 1891], the most logical steps are to direct our efforts to the strengthening of political parties; to motivate citizens to enroll in any of them, and to prevent some individuals who, under the pretext of their independence, seek to introduce

19. Valentín Letelier, The Tyranny and the Revolution (1891)

anarchy in our liberal environment. Above all, we need to remove the prejudices that promote hostility to the existence of political parties.

Lamentably, there are many who are involved in the opposite effort. It appears that we are condemned to never learn the lessons of experience. As soon as parties manage to agree on something, a murderous propaganda is unleashed to undermine them that takes advantage of ignorance to pursue the absolute extermination of parties, or go along with the dictatorship's policy to form one single political force.

The duty of public officials was no longer what the law defined, but rather the will of the president. They abandoned the character of honest officials to become docile servants of the citizen who occupied the presidential chair.

In my view, this has been the most blatant attempt to undermine our democratic institutions. The republican system differs from the absolutist precisely with respect to the role of public officials. In the first system, public employees are not required to do anything beyond what the law prescribes. In the latter, they are continuously subjected to the will of the prince, and must do whatever he wants.

Public officials, by law and by the nature of the republican system, can have their own opinions, join the party they like, and support whatever policy they wish.

The Revolution

The preceding remarks on the causes of dictatorship, and the means employed to make it stronger, demonstrate that a storm was in the making for a long time. How this happened had much to do with particular events, and the complicity of those who supported the policies of the previous decade.

The damage to our institutions has been so grave that it will require a long time, and the collaboration of all the political forces of the nation, to restore our public administration to its traditional functions.

To make my ideas clear I must make a distinction between *de facto* governments, and those based on the rule of law. The latter rest on a constitution to which they owe their existence, as well as the rigorous adherence to its articles in order to govern the republic. The former are the product of unusual circumstances, and will do anything to accomplish the aims of their establishment.

19. Valentín Letelier, *The Tyranny and the Revolution (1891)*

In Chile, a government of laws cannot use, and [President] Balmaceda's should not have used, public funds and the armed forces without the previous authorization of Congress.

A *de facto* government, however, in today's Chile or anywhere else in the world, can invest the state's funds and raise armies whenever one or the other project suits its own ends.

What the rule-of-law form of government cannot do because positive law prohibits it, the *de facto* type can because a state of war allows it.

Common sense counsels us not to apply the same arbitrary measures that led us to rebel [against President Balmaceda]. Governments should not follow a policy that awakens the lowest passions of the people, but rather one that dignifies and ennobles the national character.

For as long as the constitution granted extraordinary faculties to the president of the republic, it was possible to blame our institutions for the emergence of a dictatorship. But now, when this is not permitted, a new dictatorship will not come about unless it is in open defiance of our charter.

Once a political order has been validated by time, it cannot be changed overnight without some serious consequences. The best proof of the quality of institutions comes from peaceful rule over many years of progressive development, despite the uncertainties in the life of nations.

I do not claim that our political regime is perfect, nor deny that it has some more or less serious defects, nor dismiss the idea that it could be improved. I do consider it flawed and that the time has come to reform it. But we should not get too far ahead of where we were before the dictatorship, because no country should introduce laws for normal times when still under the influence of extraordinary events.

I believe, for example, that this is the time to introduce a considerable change in our administrative system: We should decentralize public services by means of the establishment of an independent municipal administration.

However, we should pay no attention to other calls for reform because they are either too recent, or rushed, to take root in the public spirit.

It may sound odd, but I say that our regime is better than any other in Spanish America. Institutions are not good or bad in the abstract: They are better or worse in comparison with others. Those of Chile are more adaptable to our social situation than the institutions of other nations.

It should be evident, then, that in order to avoid greater evils, such as those we have just escaped, we must change our customs rather than

19. Valentín Letelier, *The Tyranny and the Revolution (1891)*

change our laws. We will achieve better results by improving our politics instead of changing our institutions.

Along these lines, I have observed that our political corruption does not come from our laws but rather from our customs. Our electoral laws are as perfect as can be imagined, but our customs are as perverse as can be possible.

Our electoral laws have been designed to punish the abuses of authority as well as those of political parties. But compromised as our citizens are in some sort of vote-buying scheme, fraud, or abuse, there is no one left to enforce the law. In truth, it would be unfair to punish some while the rest maintain their corrupt practices.

The remedy to such ills, in my view, is the development of industry, which can place voters in a situation of relative independence. Also, the dissemination of primary education, especially civic education, to enlighten the minds of those who one day will exercise the right to vote.

However, such remedies are slow, and their effects take time. It will be necessary in the meantime to develop the public spirit of the electorate by convening assemblies where they can be taught their rights and duties, and impress upon them the dire consequences, especially for the lower classes, of corrupting the vote.

The previous points are made to show how wrong those who believe that there should be no politics in the future are, and that parties should disappear.

This will not happen, and ought not to happen. I truly believe that in the near future, barring some unforeseen setbacks, the needs of our country will require more administration than political action, and that our legislators will do a better job by honestly implementing the existing laws rather than dictating new ones.

It is evident that neither the government nor the Congress can exist without politics. The care and consolidation of order as well as the improvement of public services involve politics just as the development of our institutions does.

Without exception, anytime and anywhere on the planet, wherever a free people exist there will be political parties. And where political parties exist, there will be vitality, as well as unrest and struggles. Struggles are the means by which countries encourage the development of a legal culture.

The evils that are ordinarily blamed on parties are more imaginary than real. They come not from their existence, but rather from their not being sufficiently defined, characterized, and organized. Our duty is not to terminate them but to give them a new life. We should better end the so-called "independent" parties because they have not contributed anything as such, other than disturbances in the political development of the republic.

No one who loves democracy considers political conflict an evil, except when, in the absence of republican values, they become disorderly, or are inspired by egotism and carelessness.

A country that does not understand that public affairs matter to everyone is clueless when it comes to confronting the important issues of law. Only those democracies that are unprepared for liberty turn political conflict into an occasion for disturbing the public order.

The politics of respect for both the law and institutions, that is, a democratic politics that protects the life of political parties, and which tolerates political conflict, must be complemented by a foreign policy that consistently works for the maintenance and expansion of peace and friendship.

Countries should aim for happiness and virtue rather than greatness and power. Those who impose themselves by force are not as worthy of glory as those who rely on the influence of culture.

Let us assume that we can save any or all Spanish American countries from unrest and tyranny: We would not enjoy a single day of our triumph without tasting the bitterness of the fear of revolt.

But if we could show by example that happiness comes from respect for the law; if we could teach in practice how free men exercise their liberty; if we could offer a model of government that establishes order without restrictions to liberty, then we will have a legitimacy far higher than that of the conqueror. Chile would appear, before the eyes of the world, as truly a great country worthy of international respect.

20

MANUEL GONZÁLEZ PRADA

Our Indigenous Peoples (1904)

Manuel González Prada (Peru, 1844–1918), a poet and essayist, confronted the devastating defeat of his country during the War of the Pacific.[1] He analyzed the social underpinnings that in his view explained the lack of a unifying response to the conflict. Indigenous peoples and those of African descent, in particular, did not share the reasons for the war, or its objectives, and therefore held the key for the success or failure of Peru (at the time in alliance with Bolivia) in the campaign against Chile. His view was that the ruling establishment had failed to articulate a vision of the national interest, and he became a critic of it, embracing, while in Europe, anarchist views. His best-known works are Páginas libres *(1894) and* Horas de lucha *(1908) but his complete works did not appear until the 1980s, under the editorship of Luis Alberto Sánchez. The current text anticipated twentieth-century notions of Indigenismo. He had a lasting influence in the political and intellectual work of Víctor Raúl Haya de la Torre and José Carlos Mariátegui.*

The conquistadors and their descendants created a powerful system to subjugate and exploit the Indigenous peoples of the New World. Even if one considers the statements by Bartolomé de Las Casas to be exaggerated, it cannot be denied that the avaricious cruelty of the exploiters has brought the Indigenous peoples in some parts of America to near extinction.

---

[1] Selected passages from Manuel González Prada, 'Nuestros indios', *Latinoamerica. Cuadernos de Cultura Latinoamericana*, Mexico City, 29 (1978). (Editors' note)

20. Manuel González Prada, Our Indigenous Peoples (1904)

One must add what appears to be a law influencing our conduct: When an individual rises above the members of his class he often becomes their worst enemy. In the system of slavery, the most ferocious bosses were African themselves. Currently, the most hardened oppressors of the natives are Hispanicized Indians or Indians placed in a position of authority.

The true tyrants of the Indigenous masses are the mixed-race (*encastado*) men who use Indians to oppress and exploit other Indians. These men include the mestizos of the sierras and the mulattoes and zambos of the coast.[2] In Peru we see a form of ethnic domination: Aside from the very few white criollos, the population is divided into two unequally sized groups: the oppressive *encastados*, and the oppressed Indians. One hundred to two hundred thousand individuals oppress three million people.

There is an alliance and exchange of favors between the dominators in the capital and the bosses of the provinces: Just as the masters (*gamonales*) of the sierras serve as political agents to the bigwigs of Lima, the latter protect the *gamonales* who viciously abuse the Indians. Few social groups have committed as many iniquities and are as horrific as the Spaniards and the *encastados* of Peru. Revolutions and other disasters are nothing compared to the cold greed of these *encastados* in extracting the blood of the Indians. They have cared little about the pain and death they cause as long as they can extract a few coins from the abused. It is they who devastated the Indigenous population with their *repartimientos* and the *mitas*.[3] And yet, three to four hundred years of cruelty have not managed to exterminate the natives. They are obsessed with survival!

The viceroys of Peru condemned abuses and attempted to ensure the conservation, good treatment, and relief of our Indigenous peoples. The Spanish monarchs, following the urgings of their noble and Catholic souls, promoted humanitarian policies and supported those of the viceroys. Royal decrees brimmed with good intentions. However, while not knowing if the laws of the Indies were as high as Mount Chimborazo, we know for sure that nothing much changed, notwithstanding some isolated exemplary punishments. It could not have been otherwise: The exploita-

---

[2] Mulato, or mulatto, is a mixed-race person of white and black descent; zambo is a person of Indigenous and African descent; criollo is a white person born in Spanish America. (Editors' note)

[3] The *mita* is a rotational labor draft for work in the mines. The *repartimiento* was sometimes used as an allocation of Indigenous labor to various projects, or, as in Repartimiento de Mercancias, as the obligation to purchase European goods. (Editors' note)

20. Manuel González Prada, Our Indigenous Peoples (1904)

tion of the vanquished was expected at the same time that humanity and justice were demanded of the perpetrators. That is, that iniquities should be imposed humanely, and injustices be committed equitably. To end the abuses, it would have been necessary to abolish the *repartimientos* and the *mitas* or, in short, change the entire colonial regime. And yet, without the exploitation of the Indians, there would have been no revenues for Spain. The wealth shipped from the colonies to the metropolis was nothing more than blood and tears turned into gold.

The republic follows in the footsteps of the viceroyalty. Presidents proclaim the redemption of the oppressed and call themselves the protectors of the Indigenous peoples. Congresses enact laws that leave the Declaration of the Rights of Man far behind. Members of the cabinet issue decrees, write to the prefects, and name investigative committees, all with the noble purpose of assuring guarantees to the disinherited. But they are messages, laws, decrees, and notes confined to worn-out records. Lima's authorities issue definitive orders to the departments fully knowing that they will not be implemented; the prefects who receive the orders from the capital also know that there will be no consequences for the disobedience.

There is no shortage of purported sympathizers of the Indigenous people who act in the same fashion as the governments of the republic. The organizations created to defend the freedom of Indigenous peoples are little more than political tools hidden behind a philanthropic front. For these "redeemers" to act in good faith they would have to experience a moral transformation: to repent after taking the full measure of their iniquities; to commit to the delivery of justice; and to become men instead of tigers. This is hardly possible.

Do Indians suffer less under the republic than under the colonial domination? There may no longer be *corregimientos* or *encomiendas*, but there are coerced labor and the military draft.[4] What we do to them is enough to forever earn us the condemnation of humanity. We keep them in ignorance and servitude, humiliate them in the barracks, stupefy them with alcohol, force them to fight our civil wars, and from time to time we unleash on them massacres such as those at Amantani, Ilave, and Huanta.[5]

---

[4] *Encomienda* is an allocation of Indigenous peoples to a prominent conquistador or other Spanish settlers. The *corregimiento* is a territorial jurisdiction governed by a *corregidor*, an official appointed (and increasingly a purchased position) by the colonial government. (Editors' note)

[5] These massacres took place during the governments of Nicolás de Piérola in 1879–1881 and 1895–1899. (Editors' note)

20. Manuel González Prada, Our Indigenous Peoples (1904)

It is not official but nevertheless obvious that Indians have duties but not rights. Individual complaints are considered insubordination, and collective protests subversive attempts. While Spanish royalists killed the Indians who attempted to get rid of the conquistadors, we republicans exterminate them when they resist our onerous taxation, or when they tire of the iniquities inflicted by some local satrap.

Our form of government is a big lie, because a state where two or three million people are outside the rule of law does not deserve to be called a democratic republic. The Peruvian coast may enjoy a veneer of republicanism, but in the highlands rights are violated just like in feudal times. There are no courts or codes of justice: The *hacendados* (large landowners) and *gamonales* assume the role of judges and deliverers of sentences. Political authorities routinely support the rich and powerful rather than the weak and the poor. There are regions where justices of the peace and the governors are on the payroll of the *hacienda*. What governor, what prefect or subprefect would dare to confront an *hacendado*?

The *hacienda* is the sum of small plots stolen from their legitimate owners. The [Peruvian] boss imposes on his peons the authority of a Norman conqueror. He not only determines the appointment of governors, mayors, and justices of the peace, but he also arranges marriages, designates heirs, distributes funds, forces sons to pay the debts of their fathers and subjects them to a servitude that often lasts a lifetime. In short, the *haciendas* are kingdoms in the heart of the republic; the *hacendados* are autocrats in the land of a presumed democracy.

Is the dismal situation of our Indigenous peoples due to their lack of education? It is true that in many locations of the interior not a single person knows how to read and write. However, if by some miracle the illiterate should wake up tomorrow not just reading and writing, but possessing university diplomas, the Indigenous problem would not be solved: The proletariat of the unlettered would be succeeded by that of the bachelors and doctors. Even in the most civilized nations there are physicians without patients, lawyers without a clientele, engineers without buildings to work on, artists without followers, teachers without students, all forming the huge army of enlightened brains and empty stomachs. But in the land where the *haciendas* dominate the nation is divided between lords and servants.

Education often turns an impulsive brute into a reasonable and magnanimous person; it teaches him and illuminates the path he should follow to face the dilemmas of life. However, to identify the path is not

20. Manuel González Prada, Our Indigenous Peoples (1904)

sufficient. There must also be firmness and will. What is required is a strong sense of pride and rebelliousness rather than the obedience of the soldier and the monk. That is, finding one's own place rather than accepting the one that has been given. This is the right of every rational being.

Nothing changes the mentality of a person more radically than the ownership of some property: Shake off the slavery of hunger and you will prosper a hundredfold. By simply owning something the individual climbs several steps of the social ladder, because class is defined by the possession of wealth. In contrast to an aerostat balloon, what weighs more ascends more rapidly. To those who say that the solution is in schools, let us respond yes, but in schools *and* bread.

The Indian question is not pedagogical: It is economic and social. The situation can be improved in two ways. Either the heart of the oppressors softens enough to recognize the rights of the oppressed, or the latter rises to confront the former. Should Indians use the money they waste on alcohol and parties to invest in rifles and ammunition their condition would change: They would have the means to protect their lives and property. They would answer violence with violence, punishing the boss who steals their wool, the army that drafts them in the name of the government, and the hustler who robs their animals.

Let us not preach humility and resignation to our Indians, but rather pride and rebelliousness. What have they gained in three or four hundred years of patience and conformity? The fewer authorities they suffer, the safer they will be. There is a most telling fact: The farther communities are from the great *haciendas*, the more they enjoy their lives. The same happens in those communities less frequented by the authorities.

In sum, the Indigenous peoples will improve their situation through their own efforts, not through the supposed humanity of their oppressors. The latter will continue to be new Pizarros, Valverdes, and Areches.

21
ANDRÉS MOLINA ENRÍQUEZ

The Secret of Porfirian Peace (1909)

Andrés Molina Enríquez (1868–1940) was born in Jilotepec, Mexico.[1] A lawyer and journalist, his work as a public notary made him familiar with land-related conflicts during the Porfiriato (1876–1911). A leading spokesman for agrarian reform, Molina considered it necessary to resort to authoritarian means to control the conflicting interests that pervaded Mexican society; hence his apparent support for Porfirio Díaz's policies as well as the paternalistic approaches of revolutionary Mexico. He occupied several important technical government positions until his death in 1940. The current selection is taken from his Los grandes problemas nacionales, *which was in turn based on his articles for the periodical* El Tiempo. *As is the case with many other intellectuals of the period, Molina's analysis of social issues is laden with racial assumptions.*

General Porfirio Díaz's Personality at the Start of His Government

I am proud to have discovered the secret, and the main elements of General Díaz's politics, to which we owe our current state of peace. No one, I flatter myself, has done a better job, or devoted as many years to study, by means of direct observation, the sociology of our country. It is there

[1] From *Los grandes problemas nacionales* (Mexico, 1909). The editors use chapter 5 of the modern edition of this title (Mexico City, 2016), 107–128. (Editors' note)

21. Andrés Molina Enríquez, The Secret of Porfirian Peace (1909)

that we identify the inspired, fitting, and fortunate political approach of our current president.

I said elsewhere that the work of [Benito] Juárez was finished. The period that we call "integrative" should have ended, but the transition lasted artificially and precariously longer, until the Battle of Tecoac.[2]

The resistance that any strong power presents in order not to disappear artificially prolonged this period. It was a long time – nearly ten years – because Juárez's power, bolstered by two great revolutions, was strong. It was strong because it embodied a sense of nationality that was in turn rooted in the mestizo population. Once the republic was restored, his work, colossal though it may have been, was done. The new head of state had to be a different person.

The new leader had to be a mestizo himself, or otherwise he could have awakened the suspicions of the very group that founded and represented the true nationality. Still, it was important that he did not become the head of a political party solely composed of mestizos. The new man had to be above all political parties, or else he would not be able to control any of them. In order to do so, he had to build his prestige beyond parties. This is where the personality of General Díaz becomes central. He was the continuator of Juárez, [Melchor] Ocampo, [Juan] Alvarez, [Valentín] Gómez Farías, [Vicente] Guerrero, and the greatest of them all: [José María] Morelos. Díaz's mestizo background has been documented by Dr. Salvador Quevedo y Zubieta in his recent *Porfirio Díaz*, a book validated by General Díaz himself. It is also demonstrated by his personal habits and even his language, for instance in the pronunciation of the words *máiz*, and *páis*. The graduate [*licenciado*] Mr. Justo Sierra (in *México y su evolución social*) identifies the general as a mestizo as well. Díaz made his military career among the mestizo-supported liberals but was never the head of the party. His military persona was the foundation of his politics, although not in the way that a partisan fights for his fatherland. His true personality comes from the war against the [French] intervention and the empire rather than from the Three-Year War.[3] Both his military and political personalities are to be found in the honesty, activity, and probity

---

[2] A decisive battle (November 16, 1876) that paved the way for Porfirio Díaz's ascent to power. Díaz (1830–1915) dominated the government until 1911, when the Mexican Revolution began. (Editors' note)

[3] This is the civil war (1858–1860) that followed the liberal reform period and resulted in the triumph of Benito Juárez, who was later (1863) defeated by the French and Mexican forces that installed Maximilian of Austria as Emperor of Mexico. (Editors' note)

of the good administrator. This is the reason why, once the republic was restored, he had the triple prestige of fortunate warrior, hard-working patriot, and prudent administrator. Was he then the head of the Liberal Party, like Juárez? No, he was more than that. He could, therefore, control the Liberal Party, and that was the important point.

The Politics of Integration

It was necessary for the new leader to be above all parties, meaning all groups representing race and social action. Likewise, this integrative period required a new procedure. Actually, it was not new, but had been forgotten. During the period of disintegration – the viceregal authority that had somehow lasted until the end of [Agustín de] Iturbide's empire – the ties that bound society through coercive means, obligatory cooperation, and a military structure finally came apart. The new form of government made things worse, leading to anarchy. The federal organization of the republic was too weak to maintain internal order and could not defend the country from external threats. Rivalries, combined with the political, administrative, and economic difficulties of a new regime led by untrained personnel, toppled governments endlessly. Disorder brought the nation to the brink of destruction on more than one occasion. By that time [1830], there was only one person who understood the situation. Despite his great many errors, that person was [Lucas] Alamán, who was the true founder of our current political thought.[4] Had he the type of personality that avoided party politics, or had a good military career, including a prestigious performance in a foreign war, he would have known how to employ both the creole [criollo] population and the viceregal procedures to form a stable government. He almost did. Fortunately, these very societal tensions led to the predominance of the mestizo component that triumphed in the Ayutla Revolution.[5] During the period that we call "transition," mestizos, aided by new creoles, consolidated their power

---

[4] Lucas Alamán (1792–1853) was indeed a central figure in Mexican intellectual and political history. In addition to holding numerous public posts, he was the author of *Historia de Mexico desde los primeros movimientos que prepararon la independencia en el año de 1808 hasta la época presente* (1849–1852). For a complete biography, see Eric Van Young, *A Life together: Lucas Alamán and Mexico* (New Haven, 2021). See also above pp. 16–18. (Editors' note)

[5] The Ayutla Revolution (1854–1855) was launched in the State of Guerrero against the authoritarian rule of Antonio López de Santa Anna. This revolution started the liberal period known as La Reforma (1855–1857). (Editors' note)

21. Andrés Molina Enríquez, The Secret of Porfirian Peace (1909)

under Juárez's leadership and prepared the ground for the integrative period. General Díaz then launched his integrative politics, which is little more than viceregal politics adapted to the new circumstances. This is exactly what Alamán wanted to do but could not. It consists of concentrating enough authority to exercise coercion, and to compel cooperation in a truly military way. I call it integrative politics, which undoubtedly reflects the personality of General Díaz, but whose fundamental secret is the concentration of power. Díaz's addresses to his compatriots at the end of each of his administrations discreetly but clearly manifested this reality. As he literally said in his address corresponding to the period 1900–1904:

> We have eliminated the causes that kept the regions apart, in some cases hostile to one another. We have united them and made them cooperate. Experience has shown that there can be no nation unless there is a community of interests, feelings, and aspirations. There is no true fatherland where separation and antagonism prevail. For a long time, Mexico's federal ties were inconsistently maintained, except when the country was threatened by a foreign power. Under such circumstances, my government developed a national and patriotic program to consolidate the peace. That is to say, to make solid and permanent those ideals that were so rare in the past, building a definitive sense of nationality.

The Concentration of Power

The concentration of power encountered one main difficulty: the constitution and laws of the Reforma period. That is, the system of government established after independence and modified by the Three-Year War. Allow me to reproduce here a few lines I wrote in 1897 under the title *Notas sobre la política del señor general Díaz* [Observations on General Díaz's Politics]:

> Fortunately, General Díaz turned out to be a skillful politician. He understood very well that it was impossible to govern under the strict rule of those laws because they led to anarchy. He also understood that their sacred character made them untouchable, but found a way, like Augustus under similar circumstances. While respecting constitutional forms, he started to concentrate the power that had been fragmented throughout the governmental structures. Little by little he rescinded the right to elect governors as well as the right to elect lower functionaries, all without discarding a single electoral law, or

21. Andrés Molina Enríquez, The Secret of Porfirian Peace (1909)

suspending regular elections in any part of the republic. That is how he managed to command obedience. Likewise, he eliminated the prerogatives of the federal legislature, and did the same with each state legislature. He abrogated the prerogatives of the judiciary as well, himself, or his delegates, choosing all judicial functionaries. He had the governors do the same in each state, intervening directly in the rulings of judges at the federal and state levels. In sum, he concentrated all powers in the federal government, and especially in the hands of the president of the republic. The president and his cabinet formed a council similar to that of an absolutist sovereign.

It is thanks to this concentration of power that the great means of communication necessary for industrialization were established.

Concentration of power required the effective control of all parties, including those based on race and political action. To do so it was necessary to dominate them completely. This is where General Díaz has shown his genius, because this is an accomplishment without precedent in the history of humanity. As far as I know, there has never been, in one territory, such a combination of racial and regional distinctiveness on account of origin, stage of evolution, and participation in the distribution of wealth. It is quite difficult to unite such disparate elements, balance different interests, and introduce a sense of community that can help build a nation. All of this in the context of scarcity, and the lack of cooperation that followed the aftermath of a foreign war. However, the work is being done by means simple in appearance, but complex in reality. That is, meeting the needs of all while keeping the peace, and punishing without mercy anyone who disturbs it. Such procedures are by no means easy; we will see how difficult they have been, and how much political savvy has been required.

The Primary Engine behind the Policies of General Díaz

The procedures followed to satisfy different aspirations, however instinctive, clearly show a systematic approach that reveals a profound knowledge of the human heart in general, and the psychology of different groups in particular. Just like the humble fibers are woven to make a knot, General Díaz brought everyone together through ties of friendship. One can expect from a friend everything that he is capable of giving, depending on the degree of friendship as well as the status, personality, and means at his disposal. By the same token, there are related obligations

21. Andrés Molina Enríquez, The Secret of Porfirian Peace (1909)

on the part of he who asks for something. By virtue of this friendship – what Dr. Salvador Quevedo y Zubieta calls *amificación* in *El caudillo* – all elements of society have been able to ask for what they need from General Díaz. He, for his part, has granted all that they have asked for, but required proportional sacrifices. Mestizos have received all the material improvements they asked for (and more), but in return General Díaz asked them for the concentration of power as well as the sacrifice of their lives if necessary. Upper-class creoles have asked for less, so they have received less, but he has not asked them to sacrifice their lives. He has extended the benefits of his largesse to all, receiving some measure of sacrifice from everyone, making all wills to follow his own. Obviously, this has been done in accordance with the social ladder. All cabinet ministers and all governors are his friends. In the same manner, municipal presidents and political prefects are friends with the governors; city dwellers are friends with the municipal presidents; every political personality operates through ties of friendship. Ever since General Díaz assumed power his most important title has been that of *friend*. To me, this use of friendship as a powerful tool of social bonding is truly a sign of genius. Patriotism has never been a sufficiently clear or precise concept to help unite all social groups. The population has always been divided along the lines of race: As a result, each one has had its own goals. What one group considers patriotic, another regards as treasonous, and vice versa. Duty, which is a more abstract notion than patriotism, has been even less able to unite the population. However, friendship with a prestigious, feared, and admired personality has done what other qualities have not. Friendship has provided the basis for submission and obedience; it has overcome pride and stubbornness. Feelings of friendship toward General Díaz have not forced the different races and social groups to compromise: Each has continued to hold the same prejudices against the other. But at least, the sacrifices that each has had to make brought all of them closer together. When one group was forced to compromise with another, one could hear it say: "This is painful, but we will endure it because we are friends of General Díaz." Let us see how he has treated his friends.

General Díaz and the Mestizos

When the *integrative period* started, the mestizos had the highest expectations of material rewards. The Reforma had disappointed their hunger for riches and their thirst for pleasures. General Díaz saw himself

21. Andrés Molina Enríquez, The Secret of Porfirian Peace (1909)

as one of them and as part of the same race, nationality, and future. To fulfill their wants, he included items in the national budget. Prior to the Ayutla Plan,[6] the mestizos could be classified in four groups: peasants, employees, professionals, and revolutionaries. The last were his most important and loyal followers, that is, his friends. He gave them, and continues to give them, positions of trust – he made one of them president of the republic – positions that facilitate the concentration of power, and are essential for the functioning of authority. He has made them, and continues to make them, cabinet members, governors, heads of military areas, and commanders of the army. From the group of professionals and employees he has recruited, and continues to recruit, all the other members of his administration. From the group of *rancheros* he has recruited the officers of the army. Because he knows the mestizos well, General Díaz has let them take advantage of their positions to enrich themselves, and satisfy their ambitions and appetites. He knows very well how they continue to use their prerogatives in order to live a life of disorder and vice, but he lets them be. In fact, he helps them in their business, placing their friends and relatives in secondary yet important positions. He has placed them in the Senate and the diplomatic corps, where they hobnob with upper-class creoles. Lastly, he has tacitly authorized them to follow the same approach with their friends and subordinates. He went so far as to grant an amnesty to those who, out of anger or necessity, have resorted to banditry and perversity, or have committed other crimes. He called upon these men to join a rural police that has brought safety to the same areas that had been the site of their depredations. Unfortunately, not all mestizos could be financed, even though industrial development has extended employment to some of the poorer ones. There are still too many, especially in the agricultural sector, suffering hunger and want, and whose unrest could lead to disturbances.

 Mestizos are represented in the daily press, mostly tabloids, especially in the capital of the republic. These cheap and low-quality periodicals give shape and expression to all sorts of vague, disorderly, and confused aspirations. Also, to crude, passionate, and impulsive mestizo protests emerging from unmet demands.

---

[6] This is the plan, promulgated in March 1854, that outlined the objectives of the Ayutla Revolution against Santa Anna. (Editors' note)

21. Andrés Molina Enríquez, The Secret of Porfirian Peace (1909)

General Díaz and His Relations with Upper-Class and Clerical Creoles

These two groups had demands of their own. The upper-class creoles were divided between conservative and moderate creoles; the clerical group, between the ecclesiastical hierarchy and the *reaccionarios*, or supporters of the church. The conservative creoles had no other demand than keeping their property, which General Díaz was willing to concede.

The members of this last group have not taken an active part in politics, content as they are to use their wealth to influence, with more or less vigor, the official power. Their voice is heard in matters related to taxes and rural security. Nothing can be done on fiscal and administrative matters without their acquiescence. They keep agriculture in its current state of misery and ruin.

The moderate creoles are more active in public affairs, but in their own preferred way, that is, in the corridors of power. General Díaz has welcomed them and placed them in positions of honor, visibility, and representation, but has rarely granted them executive roles. They are usually counselors, congressmen, senators, diplomats, etc.

All upper-class creoles, conservative or moderate, are not at the center of national affairs. They are represented by the daily *El Tiempo* in Mexico City. This periodical is large, expensive, and considered somewhat rebellious by the church. It is antagonistic to the United States because of the differences in religion; it is the enemy of the new creoles and the mestizos because of their usurpation of church property; it is friendly to Europe for reasons of kinship. In a word, it represents well the interests of the upper-class creoles. In the past, when the division within this group was clearer, *El Tiempo* represented the conservatives, and *El Nacional* the moderates.

Among the clerical creoles, the hierarchy has ceased to become involved in politics, and has concentrated on their ministry. General Díaz has tried, and managed, to secure their good will and support by easing the laws of La Reforma, by honoring the high dignitaries, etc. The reactionary group lost all their social influence once the church lost its property. And yet, General Díaz has favored them with posts in the judiciary, the professoriate, etc. The main organ of the reactionaries is the daily *El País* in Mexico City.

General Díaz and the New Creoles, or, Liberal Creoles

This group, due to their service during the Intervention, has been among the hardest to please. They had already been favored, but they wanted, and obtained, more, in part because of their position in between the upper-class creoles, and the mestizos and Indians. More progressive than the upper-class creoles and the reactionaries, they have used their foreign heritage to bring their nations of origin to Mexico. They brought the capital that launched the infrastructure and stimulated all branches of production, from mining to industry. These contributions helped the consolidation of federal power, favored the economic development of the nation, improved trade, and provided a livelihood to the lower-class mestizos. To accomplish this, General Díaz had to open his purse because when it comes to economic issues the new creoles are just like the Spaniards in matters political: They demand special favors, monopolies, subsidies, taxation, all in the form of administrative concessions. General Díaz has made many of them immensely rich, and has promoted them to high posts in order to take advantage of their economic knowledge. But he has only exceptionally given them executive positions. Rightly so, in my opinion. They will never be as strong as the mestizos, nor have the same political orientation. In the daily press today, the new creoles are represented by *El Imparcial*, a periodical that equates national prosperity with that of the new creoles.

General Díaz and Indigenous Peoples

Among the Indigenous peoples, the *dispersos* deserved nothing but repression and punishment for their depredations.[7] General Díaz knew how to deal with them, but has always favored their assimilation regardless of their evolutionary stage. He has shown this in his dealings with the Kikapoos, demanding from them only the right to live in peace. Regarding two

---

[7] By *dispersos*, Molina Enríquez was most likely referring to Indigenous groups that were never fully incorporated into the colonial structure or the subsequent Mexican state, avoiding forced settlements and state and church authorities – more typically in northern Mexico. It is not easy to distinguish the other two groups mentioned below, *incorporados* and *sometidos*, but, by contrast with the *dispersos*, they can both be understood as being under some sort of control by the state and the church, and also as integrated into the Mexican labour market. We thank Alan Knight and Timo Shaefer for their help. (Editors' note)

21. Andrés Molina Enríquez, The Secret of Porfirian Peace (1909)

other groups, the *incorporados* and the *sometidos*, who formed four social action organizations –namely the lower clergy, army troops, communal property dwellers, and *jornaleros* – one can say that they were already far from the real or faked passivity that characterized their conduct during the colonial period. They started to make stern demands, and General Díaz has been attentive to them. He eased the laws of the Reforma so that the lower clergy Indians could celebrate their rites, occasionally allowing their semi-idolatrous Christianity to be manifested in festivals, processions, etc. He has recruited most of the revolutionary Indians for army service, paying them higher than regular wages. Those Indians not in the service have been hired to work in the great public projects, earning salaries close to those of the soldiers. The communal property Indians have been kept quiet by slowing down the division of land, and helping them in their disputes with the *hacendados* and governors. Finally, the Indigenous peons have seen their condition improved in exchange for the peace that has increased agricultural production and secured them permanent wages. There is no periodical representing Indigenous interests.

Unity and Strength in General Díaz's Character

The fiscal policy of General Díaz proves all the previous points. From the beginning, his government (not interrupted by the presidency of General [Manuel] González) was determined to make the share of salaries and public works an important part of the national budget. After so many years of bankruptcy, such a policy seemed insane, as more than a few, including the Finance Minister, told him. The response they received deserves to be recorded in history: "Peace above all, whatever the price." Peace, at that time, cost more money than was available. By means of various devices and loans, the Great Friend assisted his friends first and foremost, trusting that everything good would follow. He did that for about twenty years, displaying an incomparable spirit of enterprise, continuity of purpose, and foresight.

This policy was rich in results. When Mr. Matías Romero returned from the United States,[8] he admitted that income never matched expenditures,

---

[8] Matías Romero (1837–1898) was a lawyer and diplomat who also occupied finance positions in the governments of Benito Juárez and Porfirio Díaz. (Editors' note)

21. Andrés Molina Enríquez, The Secret of Porfirian Peace (1909)

but that only one more small sacrifice was needed to do so, in the form of new taxes. When he retired, he rendered one great service to the country by recommending Mr. José Yves Limantour as his successor,[9] who continued the fiscal policy that was just about to bear fruit.

These are the procedures of the Porfirian Peace, with General Díaz at the center. He has been a friend to all, asking in return that if he had been the cause of any trouble he should be told at once. He would try to fix the problem, but if he could not, he asked for patience. Should they start a revolution, they would no longer be friends, but mortal enemies.

In this respect, Díaz has opposed unrest, and treats it accordingly. He has vanquished his enemies in the same way that Louis XI and Richelieu did, the historical ones, not the Louis XI and the Richelieu of fiction and drama.

In practical terms, the work of concentrating power has consisted in the destruction of local lordships (*cacicazgos*) unwilling to be co-opted. Before the "integrative period" there were so many local powers that normal government was impossible. State governors supported by the central or federal government were *caciques* cut from the same cloth as [Santiago] Vidaurri. In turn, governors shared power with one or two individuals in each district, department, or canton. To them, one must add the heroes of our countless revolutions. Together, they challenged every single edict from our legal power. As a result, we had a complete paralysis of power and, with it, anarchy. Everyone knows this, but we must insist by mentioning a few examples after the Ayutla Plan. The cases of Vidaurri; [Jesús] González Ortega, when he was a member of the cabinet and tried to prevail over Juárez; the absolutist governors after the intervention; [Manuel] Lozada, and [Trinidad] García de la Cadena. It is certain that without the common danger posed by the Three-Year War and the Intervention, the Juárez government could not have functioned. Its vulnerability was evident in the period between the Battle of Calpulalpan[10] during the War of the Reforma and the arrival of the triple alliance [Spain, France, and Great Britain in 1862]. Without this threat, I repeat, the government would have fallen. One had to return to viceregal

[9] José Yves Limantour (1854–1935) served as Minister of Finance in the government of Porfirio Díaz from 1893 until 1911. He followed Matías Romero's agenda of increased foreign investment in Mexico and was a prominent member of the group of "*científicos*," or Comtean positivists, who supported Díaz. (Editors' note)

[10] This was the last battle of the War of the Reform (December 22, 1860), which resulted in the return of the liberals led by Benito Juárez to power in 1861. (Editors' note)

21. Andrés Molina Enríquez, The Secret of Porfirian Peace (1909)

procedures: The work of the concentration of power had to be done. In this respect, the status of General Díaz as a victorious warrior helped tremendously. Still, in order to concentrate power and maintain republican institutions, Díaz had to become an Augustus. He had to develop the same qualities of shrewdness, perseverance, energy, and even perfidy as well as cruelty that made the builders of modern France famous. Everyone who knows General Díaz in some depth, and has followed him and helped him in his efforts to achieve peace, can validate these remarks. As Justo Sierra stated in his book *México y su evolución social*:

> Many people have attempted to analyze the psychology of President Díaz. While he is not the apocalyptic figure described by Tolstoy, or the melodramatic tyrant of [Carlos O.] Bunge's narrative, Díaz is certainly an extraordinary man. However, they cite a serious deficiency: a certain contradiction within his will and determination. He makes quick decisions, followed by a deliberation that often changes, or nullifies, the initial will. This type of mind, usually found among Mexicans of mixed race (the great majority of the population), confirms his reputation for Machiavellianism and political perfidy (deceive in order to persuade; divide in order to rule). There is much to be said about this assessment, which is contrary to the qualities that everyone recognizes in the private man. And yet, they would be little more than defense mechanisms needed to handle multiple demands. The population uses them to deal with power. Mexicans have inherited from the Indigenous character, from colonial education, and from a permanent spirit of revolt, the habits of dissimulation and mistrust toward authority. What we criticize in others is probably a reflection of ourselves.

I do not agree that General Díaz has the deficiency claimed by Mr. Sierra. The contradictions in the will of the former are not real, only apparent. The mind and the will of everyone are intimately related, but act separately. A modern driver can reach a high speed because he knows that he can slow down by the simple act of hitting the brakes, and repeat the motion every time. He can do this because the will precedes the action. However, if a fast-moving pedestrian suddenly crosses the road, the driver may not have the time to avoid the danger. Why? Because the mind reacts immediately, but the action might be too slow.

The example just mentioned demonstrates that the mind is always ready to react to impressions. But the power to act is not always available. The mind needs a previous process of accumulation, both long and intense in proportion to the effort required. Once the energy is spent, a

21. Andrés Molina Enríquez, The Secret of Porfirian Peace (1909)

new process of accumulation begins in order to prepare for a new stimulus. It is amply demonstrated that a general who takes the offensive always wins, the reason being that he has previously accumulated the energy he needs to spend at the moment of battle. Should he remain in a defensive position, he will generate energy only when he is under attack. By that time, he will have lost his opportunity. This is why Francisco Bulnes, in his *El verdadero Juárez*, has stated that a defensive position in war always leads to defeat. The element of surprise is revealing: It is impossible to generate the energy that is necessary to prevent defeat. General Díaz always took the offensive, which means that he had to deploy enormous amounts of energy. He developed it, as is always the case, slowly. His superiority involved the capacity to generate more energy than most men, and thus the ability to spend it with the intensity or persistence that the situation required. His mind understands and then decides, but the decision does not involve immediate action. He calculates how to have an effect on the person in front of him. If he is a creole, Díaz will treat him with familiarity and trust; if he is a mestizo, with majesty and forcefulness; if he is an Indian, with kindness; if he is a foreigner, with attentiveness. Díaz may convey a decision, but he will take his time to make it. If the situation warrants it, he will accumulate a great deal of energy, and use it in more or less time, but always with overwhelming force. If the matter at hand is less important, the force will be applied proportionally, taking into consideration the obstacles that he may anticipate and wants to avoid. If the situation is minor, he will invest no energy at all. His reservoir of energy must be enormous, given his ability to maintain the peace for so many years, to balance the budget, and to accomplish the many things he has done, not by means of this or that person or situation, but by the sheer power of his will. Everyone understands that he possesses this energy: He who proclaims a revolution knows well that he will respond with equivalent repression. [Sebastián] Lerdo [de Tejada][11] lacked such energy, despite his considerable intelligence. In fact, the difference between a weak and a strong person is that the former blends decision and action. The intensity of the action will be proportional to the time it took to make the decision. In the case of the strong, the decision is not as relevant as the purpose of the action, which is important, lasting, and powerful. Naturally, the improvised words of General Díaz do not

---

[11] Sebastián Lerdo de Tejada (1823–1889) served as Minister of Justice in the government of Benito Juárez and was later president of Mexico (1872–1876). (Editors' note)

21. Andrés Molina Enríquez, The Secret of Porfirian Peace (1909)

always agree with his subsequent actions. It is perfectly explicable, then, that those who heard his words, and saw what they wanted to see, will feel cheated and will accuse the general of perfidy. But perfidy must be a part of the conduct of the great builders of nations because it is an instrument of demolition. Its use is justifiable when the object is not to destroy for the sake of destruction, but rather demolish in order to build. This determination is present in all great men, and General Díaz demonstrated it when he explained his political procedures and *accepted all responsibility*. This is the will that generates respect and obedience in the presence of majesty. The perfidy of which he is accused, that is, his likeness to Louis XI and Richelieu, has allowed him to advance his great work. His objectives have been to undermine the powerful, and to inflict punishment.

General Díaz has been efficient in breaking and deposing local lordships, and even more so in punishing the disturbers of the peace. He has punished the notable mestizos, heroes of our revolutions, with death. The lesser mestizos have seen imprisonment or abandonment, which for many has meant famine. The lowest mestizos have been treated with a shot in the back (*ley fuga*). The conservative creoles have seen their protections taken away; moderate creoles, sacking and indifference; upper-class clerical creoles, contempt for their rank and attacks against their dogma; reactionary creoles, irrelevance; new creoles, ruin and disfavor; lower-echelon Indigenous clergy, the rigors of the Reforma; Indigenous soldiers, the lash; communal property Indians, the devastation of their fields; Indigenous peons, the draft (*contingencia*). When it comes to punishment, Díaz has been implacable: death in every form; untold cruelties inflicted in the prisons – all the horrors ever seen in material punishments; and all the nuances of persecution, destitution, severity, indifference, contempt, and abandonment.

To compound the obstacles to his work, Americans have settled in the country in the last few years. This new racial group has proven to be very difficult to govern: It was in many ways obvious that in a context of economic development, and the prosperity of the new creoles, there would be an increasing number of foreigners as well as abundant capital. It was even more obvious that the majority should come from the United States, given the opening of communications with our northern frontier. Their influence is now being felt. Prior to the Reforma, the foreign element was relatively uniform, but now it is clearly divided into two groups: the European and the American. Europeans have been welcomed by the new creoles, and they have in turn joined them, due to the affinities of origin

21. Andrés Molina Enríquez, *The Secret of Porfirian Peace* (1909)

and character. The Americans, for their part, remain more independent, occasionally joining other groups, but without making any formal arrangements. The arrival of a new, strong, and expanding race could have met some resistance, making cooperation and harmony difficult. But this has not been the case because General Díaz is convinced of the impossibility of opposing it, and of the advantages of extending a warm welcome to the Americans. He has confronted the difficulties, as in his work for peace, by using the same tactics of friendship and enmity already discussed. At the present time, the American group is just one among many in the population of the republic. It is a group that avoids integration and regards other groups as inferior. Americans eschew contact with others, continue to speak their own language, and impose their nationality, their selectiveness, and their strength. We do not need to describe this group in more detail, as Americans are well known to us. They are represented in the press by the English-language *The Mexican Herald*, and in the Spanish-language *El Diario*.

The work of General Díaz, as can be seen, has been very complex, and his responsibilities very large. He is a unique man who has governed wisely in a nation composed of many distinct groups that represent different stages of evolution, from prehistoric to modern times. I believe, sincerely, that only rarely has human intelligence accomplished all that he has been able to do.

22
FRANCISCO GARCÍA CALDERÓN
Latin American Democracies (1912)

Francisco García Calderón (1883–1953) was one of the most prestigious Spanish American intellectuals during the first decades of the twentieth century, when he was considered "the best interpreter of the continent's realities."[1] *A Peruvian national, he was born in Valparaíso while his father (then provisional president of Peru) was held prisoner by the Chilean government following the negotiations that ended the War of the Pacific. The family returned to Peru in 1889, and settled in Lima, where García Calderón grew up. He studied philosophy and letters at the Universidad de San Marcos, graduating in 1903. He soon rose to prominence among a new generation of intellectuals, particularly when the Uruguayan José Enrique Rodó wrote the prologue of his first book* De litteris *(1904). García Calderón's early success was marred by the death of his father, and his own suicide attempt. In 1906, he moved with his mother and siblings to Paris, where he spent the next four decades of his life. From Paris, he continued his literary pursuits combined with diplomatic duties as the Peruvian government appointed him to various posts, including diplomatic missions in Paris, Brussels, and London. He authored several books on world affairs, edited the* Revista de América *(1912–1914), and wrote for Latin American newspapers such as* La Nación *in Buenos Aires. His book* Les démocraties latines de l'Amérique *(from where we have selected the passages of this chapter) was first published in French with a preface by the future French president Raymond Poincaré, in 1912. While some fragments of the book appeared*

---

[1] Originally published as *Les démocraties latines de l'Amerique* (Paris, 1912). The editors use selections from the Spanish version, *Las democracias latinas de América. La creación de un continente* (Caracas, 1979). The quote is from p. ix of Luis Alberto Sánchez's 'Prólogo' in García Calderón, *Las democracias*. (Editors' note)

253

22. Francisco García Calderón, Latin American Democracies (1912)

in Spanish in 1951, the first full Spanish version was published by the Biblioteca Ayacucho in Caracas in 1979.

Revolutionary doctrines arrived in Spanish America from France as purveyors of the ideal. The *Encyclopedia* [edited by Denis Diderot] provided the intellectual foundations for the Spanish American upheaval. The patricians of the old colonial cities became reconciled with Voltaire. They adopted the fundamental views of Rousseau, namely, the social contract, the sovereignty of the people, and the optimism that extends supreme rights to a human spirit not alienated by culture. Simón Bolívar read a copy of *The Social Contract* that once belonged to Napoleon and passed it on to a close friend. The great-sounding promises of democracy, sovereignty, human rights, equality, and liberalism fluttered like the pages of a sacred book in all patriotic tribunes. Masonic lodges worked secretly against Spanish and Portuguese power by promoting French humanitarian thought. It was at the Lautaro Lodge that San Martín and [Carlos María de] Alvear received their initiations. In Mexico, the York Lodge became a Jacobin club. Antonio Nariño, the precursor of Colombian independence, translated the [Declaration of the] Rights of Man in 1794. The Venezuelan [Francisco de] Miranda fought in the revolutionary French army, while the Peruvian Pablo de Olavide, a friend of Voltaire, participated in the convention debates. Raynal, Mably, and Condorcet had Spanish American disciples. Montesquieu was read at the universities as an antidote to the absolutism of the viceroys. Beccaria, Filangeri, and Adam Smith all had Latin American followers.

French ideas were not only dominant, but also exercised an irresistible influence on the fledgling democracies: They can be seen in the revolution, the terror, the Jacobin drive, the Girondins' eloquence, the dictatorship of the First Consulate, and the empire. The Mexican emperor [Agustín de] Iturbide imitated Napoleon. In Buenos Aires, there was a directorate just like in Paris; in Paraguay, consuls; [Bernardino] Rivadavia was a lone Girondin among the *gauchos*. In addition to French theories, the example of the United States was added: George Washington, and federalism, served as models for Spanish American statesmen. [Manuel] Belgrano elevated the first president of the United States to the status of a hero "worthy of the admiration of our time, and of the future generations: an example of moderation and true patriotism." He translated the *Farewell Address*, his favorite reading. Bolívar wanted to be the Washington of South America. One of the precursors of Brazilian independence,

22. Francisco García Calderón, Latin American Democracies (1912)

José Joaquim da Maia, met Jefferson in Paris and told him that his compatriots regarded "the American Revolution as the embodiment of their hopes and wished to receive the support of the United States." The first Spanish American constitutions incorporated this dual influence: They adopted federalism, imitated the political organization of the United States, and were inspired by French ideas. They destroyed the privileges of the nobility, and established the equality of the *castas*.[2] Despite the efforts of Bolívar and Miranda against federalism, the first Venezuelan constitution followed precisely that model. The Chilean constitution of 1822, and the Peruvian of 1823, gave a conservative role to the Senate, as in the North American republic. Chile [in the 1820s] established a federation as well. In Mexico and Central America, the federal principle dominated the constitutions of 1824 and 1826, respectively. The Argentine constitution of 1819 proclaimed "the declaration of American independence for the provinces of South America."

British influence was added to the French doctrines and the American example. Miranda and Bolívar admired the British political constitution and took it as a model. In 1818 Bolívar recommended the study of this constitution: "There you will find the division of powers, which is the only means to create a frank and independent spirit; freedom of the press, which is the best antidote against political abuses." His enthusiasm for Voltaire and Rousseau was tempered by the study of British procedures. At Angostura [1819], he defended the lifetime Senate, which was modeled after the House of Lords. He regarded the British executive power, namely, the sovereign and his cabinet, as "the most perfect model for a monarchy, an aristocracy, or a democracy."[3] The Cúcuta Constitution of 1821, which embodied the ideals of Bolívar, elicited the praise of the Marquis of Lansdowne: "It is based," he said, "on the two most solid and just principles," property and education. Miranda proposed to [William] Pitt a constitutional project based on British ideas: a lower and an upper chamber, although the latter would be composed of *caciques*[4] appointed

---

[2] "*Castas*" are various racial mixtures, up to sixteen of which were identified by the Spanish government. (Editors' note)

[3] See the Angostura Address in Simón Bolívar, *El Libertador: Writings of Simón Bolívar*, ed. by David Bushnell, trans. by Frederick H. Fornoff (Oxford, 2003), 44. (Editors' note)

[4] *Caciques* were appointed officials in the Inca Empire, usually on the basis of territorial divisions. The term continued to be used during the colonial and post-independence period to refer to local leaders. (Editors' note)

22. Francisco García Calderón, Latin American Democracies (1912)

by the hereditary Inca, as well as the Censors. This curious project mixed New World traditions with political forms borrowed from England. Spain also contributed to the development of revolutionary ideas. It united the Spanish American population through an overwhelming authority and brought the dispossessed together to fight for independence: "the despotic rigor of authority," wrote [Francisco] Bauzá, "united the heterogeneous population into one race."[5] In Spain itself, the Napoleonic invasion led to the creation of *juntas*, provisional representatives of the nation that substituted for the captive king. The principal *junta* proclaimed in 1808 that, "The American provinces are not colonies, but rather integral parts of the monarchy, enjoying the same rights as all other Spanish provinces."[6]

In 1810, the regency announced that "the fate of the Spanish American provinces no longer depends on ministers, viceroys, or governors: it is in your hands."[7] The constitution proclaimed by the Cortes in 1812, with the participation of American representatives, stated that "The Spanish union is not the patrimony of any one person or family: Sovereignty resides in the nation; the Cortes and the king together have the right to legislate."[8] Independence, national sovereignty, the idea of fatherland, and the functions of assemblies all arrived in these documents from the metropolis. At the same time, the struggle against pirates, against the British invasion of Buenos Aires, or the Dutch in Brazil, in addition to the influence of the land, all created a sense of nationality in Latin America. French, British, and Spanish ideas contributed to the still inchoate aspirations. Even before these ideas became established in universi-

---

[5] Francisco Bauzá, *Historia de la dominación española en el Uruguay*, vol. ii, p. 647.
[6] Here García Calderón seems to have given the wrong date. The citation is from a decree issued by the Junta Central in Sevilla on January 22, 1809, calling the Americans to vote for their representatives to the Junta. This was an important event in the independence process. See relevant citations of this decree in François-Xavier Guerra, *Modernidad e independencias* (Madrid, 1992), 135. A digital copy is available at www.memoriapoliticademexico.org/Textos/1Independencia/1809-RO-FVII-JCG-D.html (Editors' note).
[7] García Calderón is referring here to the 1810 instructions issued by the Consejo de Regencia, issued at the Isla de León, calling for elections to the Cortes in America and Asia. In the original: "vuestros destinos ya no dependen ni de los ministros, ni de los virreyes, ni de los gobernadores; están en sus manos." A digital copy is available at https://tinyurl.com/4ne6j7uc (Editors' note).
[8] This comes from the Cádiz Constitution, articles 2, 3, and 15; Constitución política de la monarquía española (Cádiz, 1812), 3 and 7, available at www.congreso.es/docu/constituciones/1812/P-0004-00002.pdf (Editors' note).

22. Francisco García Calderón, Latin American Democracies (1912)

ties and assemblies, the creole oligarchy discovered their ambitions for independence through both the periodical press and the *cabildo* (municipal council) meetings.

From 1818 until 1825, everything came together to favor independence: European revolutions, the role of British ministers, the independence of the United States, the excesses of Spanish absolutism, the constitutional doctrines of Cádiz on the one hand, and the romantic faith of the liberators on the other; the political ambitions of the oligarchy, the ideas of Rousseau and the *Encyclopedia*, and the hatred of the Spanish American populations for the viceroys and the inquisitors. All these elements combined created a lamentably divided world. The genesis of these republics was as heroic and brave as chivalric poems, but it degenerated until it became a game of selfish interests, and revolutionary pandemonium. Such, in short, is the evolution of Spanish America in the nineteenth century.

[Herbert] Spencer viewed human development as the invariable succession of two stages: military and industrial. [Walter] Bagehot opposed a primitive epoch of authority to a subsequent period of controversy. [Henry] Sumner Maine discovered a historical law: the transition from status to contract, from the regime imposed by despotic governments to the flexible organization established by the free will of the people. These three different formulas reveal the same principle of evolution. In the beginning, the martial and theocratic authority established the rituals, the customs, the dogma, and the laws. The sense of commonality was strong; individuals accepted without discussion, or critical distance, the fundamental rules of social life. Thereafter, history became the struggle between authority and liberty, the progressive affirmation of autonomous wills, and the emergence of a seditious and corrosive individualism.

In Spanish America, political development followed the same fundamental sequence. Invariably, we see the same military period followed by the civil or industrial. After independence, all Spanish American republics were militarized. Thereafter, the military sector was peacefully overthrown by the increasing prevalence of economic interests. At that time, civil influence prevailed. The military regime here was not theocratic, as in some European monarchies: The president did not embody the dual functions of religion and empire. The civil period was not necessarily a reaction against the church: It was neither anti-clerical nor radical. The revolution was simply a change of oligarchies from military to plutocratic.

22. Francisco García Calderón, Latin American Democracies (1912)

When Alexander the Great died, his generals competed for the possession of the provinces of Europe, Asia, and Africa like the spoils of an imperial banquet, and founded dynasties characterized by oriental decadence. In the same manner, Bolívar's generals dominated Spanish America for over half a century. [Juan José] Flores in Ecuador, [José Antonio] Páez in Venezuela, [Andrés de] Santa Cruz in Bolivia, and [Francisco de Paula] Santander in Colombia governed as the rightful heirs of the Liberator. As the shadow of this magnificent warrior spread over Spanish America, the *caudillos* took their place with the blessings of Bolívar. The monarchical principle was imposed on clueless men. The Liberator left us a Spanish American dynasty.

The war turned into civil wars and quarrels among generals vying for power. Once united by colonial life and by the struggle for independence, the fledgling nations separated from one another due to the influence of these warriors: Ecuador, Peru, and Bolivia in the name of Flores, [Agustín] Gamarra and [Ramón] Castilla, and Santa Cruz, respectively. A primitive sense of national identity emerged from the battlefields. The generals imposed arbitrary borders on the population. In Spanish American history, these men were artificers who impressed the multitude with parades as glittering as the massive Catholic processions – also, with their magnificent honor guards, decorations, and pomp. They called themselves Regenerators, Restorers, and Protectors.

The first period was turbulent, but also full of color, energy, and violence. The individual acquired an extraordinary prestige, just like during the heroic times of the Renaissance in Tuscany, the French terror, and the English Revolution. The heavy and bloody hand of the *caudillos* imposed a lasting shape on the amorphous masses. Ignorant leaders dominated Spanish America, and as a result the evolution of these republics was uncertain. Because of the lack of continuity, there was no history as such. A perpetual revolutionary *ricorso* threw off and brought back the same people with the same ideas and methods. The political farce was repeated over and over again: a revolution, a dictator, and a program of national regeneration. Militarism and anarchy became the universal forms of political development. Just like the European revolutions, dictatorship followed anarchy, and provoked immediate counter-revolutions. Spontaneous disorder was followed by formidable control. The French example appeared in a different scenario: The anarchy of the convention opened the door to Bonaparte's autocracy. Like the monarchs of feudal times, dictators overthrew both the *caciques* and the

22. Francisco García Calderón, Latin American Democracies (1912)

provincial generals: That is exactly what Porfirio Díaz, [Gabriel] García Moreno, and [Antonio] Guzmán Blanco did. Revolution followed revolution until the longed-for tyrant arrived to dominate the next twenty or thirty years of national life.

Autocracy brought material progress. This was the case of the dictatorships of [Juan Manuel] Rosas, Guzmán Blanco, [Diego] Portales, and Porfirio Díaz. The great *caudillos* abandoned any pretense of abstraction: Their realistic minds made them promote commerce, industry, immigration, and agriculture. By imposing a lasting peace, they stimulated the development of economic forces.

In the political and economic realm, dictators promoted a form of Americanism. They represented a new mestizo race, in addition to a territory, and a tradition. They were hostile to the influence of the church, to European capital, and to foreign diplomacy. Their fundamental functions, just like the modern monarchs after feudalism, were to introduce uniformity among the people, and unite the different social classes. Tyrants founded our democracy: They had the support of the people against the oligarchy, and of black people and mestizos against the nobility. They favored racial mixture, and liberated the enslaved.

The anarchy was as spontaneous as the Jacobin Revolution described by [Hippolyte] Taine. There was a hostile movement against order and civilization. That is why [José Gervasio] Artigas fought not only against the Spanish monarch, but also against both the Argentine Revolution and the Portuguese. He rejected any type of dependence: He was a patriot through the period of fragmentation and until death. [Martín Miguel] Güemes fought against both Spaniards and Argentines. The *caudillos* resembled the chiefs of the barbarian tribes: They stood for local autonomy, division, and chaos. [Domingo Faustino] Sarmiento compared the violent bosses of the sierras and the Argentine Pampas ([Ricardo] López [Jordán] and [Facundo] Quiroga) with Genghis Khan and Tamerlane. "Individualism was his essence, the horse his principal weapon, and the pampa his theater." The *montoneras*[9] were Tatar hordes, dark and devastating. Their leaders represented the essence of the continent: They were as deadly and rough as natural forces. Like the Yggdrasil, the mythical Scandinavian tree, they had their roots deep in the earth, and in the darkness of death. The general ideas of the period were simple. Political

---

[9] An irregular army, an early version of guerrilla warfare. (Editors' note)

22. Francisco García Calderón, Latin American Democracies (1912)

constitutions proliferated because of the belief in their efficacy. Congress was believed to be omnipotent, while governments were viewed with suspicion. Constitutions separated the branches of government, thereby weakening the executive to the point of irrelevance. They undermined authority by means of triumvirates, consulships, and *juntas*. The liberalism of the charters was remarkable: They generally established, following Montesquieu, three powers to secure political equilibrium; they recognized every theoretical freedom: those of the press and association, rights of property, and industrial and commercial liberty. They enshrined juries, popular petitions, universal suffrage, and, in sum, the entire republican ideal. They ratified Catholicism as the religion of the state, thus opening the gates to religious revolutions and factionalism, of either red or black stripes, in Latin American history. In some republics there were direct elections; in others, there were electoral colleges that appointed the president and the members of the legislature. From north to south, the institutions were democratic: They granted generous political rights. The judicial branch was independent, sometimes popularly elected, but generally chosen by the Congress. Judges often depended on the executive. Justice and the law remained inefficient. Finally, the president could not be reelected.

These constitutions imitated those of France and the United States, especially the democratic tendencies of the former, and the federalism of the latter. These charters were both hybrid and capacious. The presidentialist system was as real as that of the United States. Parliaments were prominent in the constitutional texts, but impotent in political practice to resist the pressures of the military. Revolutionary ideology, and the theory of the social pact, prevailed over flowery speeches.

The meaning of the civil wars varied significantly. They were waged in the name of a *caudillo*, in Ecuador; in the name of ideas, in Colombia; and either for or against the oligarchy in Chile. Multiple forces clashed in these nations. Revolution has been their common legacy. The races that populated the New World, either Indigenous or Spanish, were warrior races. It is their spirit that explains the prevailing disorder in the new republics. Castes and traditions were the enemies. The psychological instability of these uneducated populations opposed both discipline and authority.

Two groups, the military and the intellectuals (university-based in some cases), confronted one another since the origins of the republic. Sometimes they fought for power, but in some cases intellectuals collaborated with the generals. The learned doctors used questionable

22. Francisco García Calderón, Latin American Democracies (1912)

arguments to justify either dictatorship or revolution. Coto [Francisco Antonio] Paúl, a congressman from Venezuela, composed a lyrical elegy to anarchy in 1811.

The generals distrusted the lawyers, who represented the intellectual tradition of colonial times. Páez hated them as much as Napoleon hated the *Idéologues*. Under military rule, the learned doctors became the willing servants of the generals and the *caudillos*: They wrote constitutions and laws, providing a veneer of finesse to the coarse will of their bosses. To the violence of the latter, the learned ones responded with subtleties; to the ignorance of the despots, they answered with the scholastic formulas learned in Spanish [colonial] universities. Race war was added to the class war: mestizos against the national oligarchy, and the new middle class against the aristocracy of the capital cities. Indigenous populations continued to live in provincial cities unchanged since colonial times. The metropolises such as Buenos Aires, Lima, and Caracas continued to be Spanish and therefore alien to the rest of the country. Reformist ideas and exotic fashions and views arrived in the coastal areas, where the senses are quick and the will variable. The somber and sleepy sierras,[10] more American than the coastline to begin with, remained unimpressed by the luminous restlessness of the capital cities. That is how a multifaceted movement started: The lower classes opposed the colonial aristocracy; the provinces opposed the domineering metropolis; the mestizo sierra opposed the cosmopolitan coast. The provinces wanted autonomy, while the capital aspired to unity and monopoly. The metropolis was liberal and the sierra conservative. Politics may have changed names, but antagonisms prevailed. By pronouncing generalities, the bosses kept their deepest ambitions hidden: They defended [centralist] unity or federalism, a military or a civilian regime, Catholicism or radicalism. In Argentina, the provinces fought against the capital; in Venezuela, the mestizo middle class against the oligarchy; in Chile, the liberals against the property-owning *pelucones*;[11] in Mexico, the federalists against the monarchists; in Ecuador, the radicals against the conservatives; in Peru, the *civilistas*[12] against the military *caudillos*. Overall, one can discern a fundamental

---

[10] The cold Highland regions separated from the coast by the Cordilleras.
[11] *Pelucones* literally means "big wigs," a term used to refer to Chilean conservatives. (Editors' note)
[12] *Civilistas* refers to a civilians' party formed to oppose the succession of military governments since independence. (Editors' note)

22. Francisco García Calderón, Latin American Democracies (1912)

principle in these diverse confrontations: the struggle of two classes, the landowning against the landless and poor; the Spanish and the mestizos; the oligarchs and the generals. In sum, a democracy of barbarians.

The territory and traditions of each republic added some nuance to this pervasive struggle. In the Río de la Plata of the viceroys and intendants, the provinces enjoyed some autonomy: Federalism already had some foundations. Consequently, unity appeared to be an imposition from Buenos Aires, a city that had control over finances, customs, and which monopolized rents and credit. Chile, that long and thin slash of territory whose mountains impose a border of granite, had the conditions to become a unitary republic. There, the struggle between centralists and federalists did not last long. Unity was possible in the brilliant viceroyalty of Peru, because it had long been the center of a strong secular power. However, some aspects of this violent struggle remain confusing. In Ecuador, Peru, Venezuela, and Mexico, the coast and the sierras are antagonistic. Lima and Caracas are capital cities near the coast while Mexico City and Quito are located far inland. Military and civilians fought each other in Peru; conservatives and liberals in Ecuador; federalists and centralists in Venezuela and Mexico. Why did religious struggles, so cruel and lasting in Colombia, not take place in Bolivia or Argentina? To explain this variance, one must study the psychology of the different conquistadors (Castilian, Basque, Andalusian, Portuguese) and conquered races (Quechua, Araucanian, Chibcha, Aztec), as well as their mixture and the influence of the environment – tropical, temperate, coastal, sierra – on the different types of *mestizaje*.

These struggles were very confusing in some democracies because oligarchs were not always conservative, nor mestizos always liberal. There were reactionary autocracies, like Portales' in Chile, or liberal, like Guzmán Blanco's in Venezuela. In general, federalists were democratic and liberal, but some were conservative and authoritarian. The democrats of Peru were reactionary regarding religion, while in Chile they were radicals. The civilian regime in Bolivia was conservative under [Mariano] Baptista, and in Ecuador under García Moreno; it was liberal in Mexico under Juárez, and in Chile under Santa María and [José Manuel] Balmaceda. Militarism was radical under General [José Hilario] López in Colombia, and conservative under general Castilla in Peru. When political evolution followed logic, federalism, liberalism, and democracy launched revolutions that confronted dominant groups and elevated mestizos to the role of protagonists in a new epoch. Still, democratic society was created with great difficulty. It was opposed to the old classes,

22. Francisco García Calderón, Latin American Democracies (1912)

but slavery persisted, although somewhat modified by the liberal constitutions. The military class, which was opened to all, replaced the old nobility. By 1850, races increasingly intermingled thanks to the laws that liberated the enslaved. However, new economic interests presented difficulties to the new democracies. Revolutions, dictatorships, and anarchy have been the necessary legacies of an extinct era.

Politics moved away from ideological confrontations. Constitutional liberties acquired precision and efficacy. Plutocracies were formed that aspired to govern in spite of internal revolutions and external wars. Their rise was facilitated by an immigration that transformed society. National progress, which was anonymous and collective, advanced despite governments, because an industrious multitude replaced the energetic individualities of the military period. Heads of industry, merchants, and bankers removed the *caudillos* from the political scene. Valor used to be the ultimate distinction, but now individuals are judged according to their wealth. The scale of human values has changed: Education, foresight, and a practical sense are now the determining factors of success in industrial democracies. The upward social mobility of the new generations was launched by industry and commerce. They conquered the old aristocratic society. After a century of struggle against religious and class prejudice, modern nations have emerged.

Industrialization prevailed in the southern republics of Argentina, Uruguay, Chile, and even in tropical Brazil. Bosses were still strong in Bolivia and Peru, where parties continued to be highly focused on individuals, although their influence was not as decisive as in the previous thirty years. Anarchy and *caudillismo* prevailed in countries from Ecuador to Mexico, because political restlessness resisted the principle of authority. The long dictatorships of General [Cipriano] Castro, and of some Central American presidents, demonstrated that this form of government was the only one able to maintain the peace.

It is not possible to determine the historical moment when the Spanish American republics made the transition from a military to an industrial regime. The twilight of the *caudillos* was simply too long. It persisted even in Argentina, where economic life is as magnificent as it is diverse. In Peru, Bolivia, and Brazil there is an underlying militarism that can quickly destroy the work of civilian presidents. In these countries, in addition to Uruguay, presidential successions have occurred without revolutionary violence for ten years. However, can it be said that the half-century-long anarchy has disappeared completely?

22. Francisco García Calderón, Latin American Democracies (1912)

Political order was established slowly, in proportion to the development of wealth, immigration, and peace. The evolution of industry was the work of peace-making *caudillos*: General [José Manuel] Pando in Bolivia, General [Julio Argentino] Roca in Argentina, [Nicolás de] Piérola in Peru, [José] Batlle y Ordóñez in Uruguay, and, the greatest of them all, Porfirio Díaz in Mexico. Regarding the economy, this period of material progress was far superior to the first, that is, the time of fruitless revolutions. Politically, during this period, institutions improved and the constitutions acquired more strength. The legislature and the municipalities became more autonomous, thus balancing the omnipotent power of the executive during the military period. The prosaic years of industrialization pale in comparison to the previous decades when strong personalities gave history the intensity of tragedy. Death and destiny, as in the Italian Renaissance, were at stake. "The tyranny of the ancient Latin republics," wrote Jacob Burckhardt, "developed the individuality of the sovereign, the condottieri, to the highest degree." The historian then highlighted the equally personalistic character of the statesmen and popular leaders of Florentine history.[13] His analysis is applicable to the Latin American chiefs. Heroic audacity and masculine restlessness characterized the struggles of the *caciques*. Once the military cycle was spent, republics lost the sense of drama. Rather than writing the history of governments, we now need to study the economic evolution of nations, statistics, industry, and commerce. In a tragedy, the chorus, or multitude, becomes the principal protagonist: It takes center stage as both spectator and creator, while the old heroes who vanquished destiny and founded cities disappear.

Political change was reflected in the customs of the population and in the modernization of cities. The cosmopolitan irruption imposed a compact monotony: Interest became the main motivation for action; after constant war, peace finally settled in. Republics gained in wealth, but also in mediocrity. It was a time of transition, although we cannot yet see the main outlines of the future cities. Will Argentina and Brazil become as plutocratic as the United States? Chile copied the social organization of England: Will it suffer from the same demagoguery that afflicts the Saxon empire? The spectacle presented by the newly rich republics allows us to conclude that in revolutionary Latin America only four nations – Argentina, Brazil, Uruguay, and Chile – will become completely organized within a

---

[13] Jacob Burckhardt, *La civilisation en Italie* (Paris, 1885) I, 165 and ff.

22. Francisco García Calderón, Latin American Democracies (1912)

century. However, some old features of the race remain in these countries. As Gustave Le Bon stated, "the dead founded the race," and also, "the dead generations impose not only their physical constitution but also their thoughts: The forms of government matter very little."[14]

In the Latin American democracies, the "fundamental revolution" that politicians were so proud of has been useless. Under the republican veneer, the profound and ages-old Spanish legacy remains. The form varies but the soul of the race remains. Autocratic presidents replaced the viceroys. The old struggle between governors and bishops persists regarding the ecclesiastical *patronato*; so does the prestige of the doctors, as well as academic titles. The dominant group, heir to Spanish prejudices, views industry and commerce with contempt, and thrives on politics and agitation. Landowners remain as dominant as before the revolution. The immense dominions of the old estates explain the power of the oligarchy. Congresses have the same secondary role as the old *cabildos*. Catholicism continues to be the center of social life. The *pícaros* of Spanish literature, those proud and clever parasites, are still roaming the land.[15] Bureaucracy eats up the national income: About a century ago it was composed of voracious Castilians; today, it is filled with lazy Latin Americans. Despite the equality proclaimed by the constitutions, Indigenous peoples are still subjected to the implacable tyranny of the local authorities: the priest, the justice of the peace, and the *cacique*. The petty despots of Spanish colonialism have returned under a different guise.

Latin American democracies are therefore Spanish however much the elite claims to be inspired by French ideas. These democracies consist of pronouncements and anarchy; mestizo and leveling democracies where individuals sometimes assume a heroic significance, just like in [Thomas] Carlyle's biographies. These are medieval republics divided into factions and impenetrable family clans, governed by wealthy merchants. These are Greek republics, hostile to their own authorities, jealous of Aristides' virtue and Themistocles' wisdom, but without the passion for plebiscites that characterized Hellenic societies.

---

[14] Gustave Le Bon, *Les lois psychologiques de l'évolution des peuples* (Paris, 1900), 13 and 71.
[15] *Pícaros* are clever individuals who would do anything to gain social or financial advantage. In literature, the classic examples are *El Lazarillo de Tormes* and *Gil Blas*. (Editors' note)

23
CARLOS ARTURO TORRES

Idols of the Forum (1909)

Carlos Arturo Torres (1867–1911) was a journalist, teacher, and statesman.[1] *He was born in the Colombian town of Santa Rosa de Viterbo and studied in Tunja, Bogota, and the United Kingdom. After travels in Europe, he taught international law in Bogota, and founded such papers as* La Crónica, El Nuevo Tiempo, *and* La Civilización. *He was sent to diplomatic missions in France, England, and Caracas, where he died. He also served as minister of both treasury and finance. Undoubtedly,* Idola Fori *was his most influential work. He borrowed from Francis Bacon's* Novum Organum, *who discerned four "idols" that obstruct the truth, including the idols of the forum and the market.* Idola Fori *was originally published with a prologue by José Enrique Rodó, with whom he has often been compared, and with whom he shared ideas about history and culture. Torres' work, however, is more deeply grounded in politics, and shows his engagement with contemporary debates about the role of the state, major ideas about economic development, and the tension between individualism and collectivism.*

The Italian poet's dilemma, "renew or die," is the same dilemma confronting society, political parties, and people not only today, but at all times. The past, with all its experiences and memories, begins with each moment that passes. The future, likewise, starts in the present, hour by hour, as a projection of current activity. The slow gestation of life is

---

[1] *Idola Fori* was originally published in 1909. For the purposes of this collection, the editors use passages from the chapter "Hacia el futuro," included in *Obras de Carlos Arturo Torres*, vol. 1, ed. by Rubén Sierra Mejía (Bogota, 2001), 177–198. (Editors' note)

23. Carlos Arturo Torres, Idols of the Forum (1909)

not random, but determined by nature. We hear it repeatedly, that "we are at a time of transition," in reference to a particular period, as if any period was not one of transition. One generation has not yet finished its contributions when the next is already taking its own place, imagining that it has conquered it all without the aid of previous generations. This recurrent cycle of demolition, atonement, and rehabilitation is part of the human trajectory. It advances the collective work by leaving an authentic record of each generation's passage through history. This legitimate, necessary, and inevitable phenomenon shows that progress is not linear but rather a constantly changing process that gives us a true account of the development of civilization. This unceasing renewal and permanent adaptation constitute a law that cannot be infringed by those who aspire to life and success, or at least not to be left behind, lost and inert, on the way to human advancement.

The synthesis of the historical sense in the nineteenth century is the intense critique and the struggle for independence by both the spirit and the people. It means the emancipation of belief and commerce, of industry and thought, of individuals, classes, and nationalities; unlimited discussion and analysis, and liberation of all hindrances to human activity. This is the principle that resonates in the literature of ideas as a sustained *pein* that shatters all forms of absolutism in opinion, ethics, religion, science, philosophy, literature, and politics. The direction of the age that is just beginning is that of reconciliation and agreement. If we examine the evolution of ideas in one branch of knowledge, say, economics, we can see the unfolding of this sociological phenomenon. [David] Ricardo and the Manchester School showed how the interplay of individual self-interest and the functions of supply and demand had the effect of regulating and stimulating production and consumption. The unlimited expansion of individual initiative; exclusion of state intervention; and free exchange, work, and markets constitute the important revelation that Adam Smith communicated to the Western world. No aspect of social life had seen such a vigorous concept of independence and individualism. At the height of this cult of liberty and individual autonomy, which gave industry a tremendous impulse and accentuated the commercial hegemony of Great Britain during the halcyon days that followed the preachings of [Richard] Cobden, many believed that the absolute transformation of labor had come. The use of electricity, generated at a low cost, put small machines at the service of all. The future city could now be envisioned as a network of small autonomous factories managed by

23. Carlos Arturo Torres, Idols of the Forum (1909)

one individual who simultaneously served as owner, manager, and worker. This was the Ultima Thule of the liberal dream, the fabulous utopia of individualism and decentralization. The liberating concept of the British School undoubtedly contains great truths, but not the whole truth. It represented a powerful incentive to ideas and activities, a celebration of dignity, and a potent stimulus to the will. However, the exaggeration of these ideas generated a response tending to moderation and eventually rectification. Auguste Comte's philosophy already established a concept of society that placed some limits on individual initiative. Socialism went a step further by questioning the very essence of the belief in unlimited individual initiative. The scientific principle that [August] Weismann added to the Darwinian theory, according to which "the duration of life is governed by the needs, not of the individual, but of the species," provided a firm basis for understanding the social tendency: The individual absorbed by the masses equals democracy; the individual apart from and superior to the masses equals aristocracy; the individual integrated into the masses equals state socialism. British laws reveal the increasing influence of the state on areas that liberalism regards as the exclusive province of private industry and commerce.

Collective associations, trade unions, workers' funds, and all other forms of working-class solidarity designed to confront the trusts, the lockouts, and other kinds of capitalist response (denounced by Karl Marx but opposed today by [Eduard] Bernstein and the new German socialists) reveal a concept of association and society that supersedes the exclusively individualistic. The organization of strikes launched by occasional small groups that had no connection with each other became associations united by a common purpose and a sense of class solidarity. Today they are formidable movements that can stop all industrial activity in a particular location, and even put national life on hold. In response, capitalist ambition replaces the small workshops with the colossal factory, a city of slavery where workers are turned into machines that automatically obey a regimental discipline. The small stores are replaced by huge malls where the consumer finds everything at various prices. Large industries are concentrated in a sort of monopoly where the sanctions of the law amount to little: This is a disquieting development in the richest countries. Strikes and lockouts, collectivism and trusts, Knights of Labor and dynasties of wealth are all products of the same spirit of association, which cannot be farther apart from the individualism of the Manchester School. These are entirely opposite, but still related, forms of organization. When they

23. Carlos Arturo Torres, Idols of the Forum (1909)

reach their most extreme expression they will confirm [Gabriel] Tarde's law: "Opposite forces, unable to expand any further, will seek reconciliation following the laws of adaptation."

The study of those laws, like the laws of history, will prove that society cannot be changed in a day, as many revolutionaries would wish. In fact, violence will delay the realization of their ideals. The study will also demonstrate to the reactionaries that it makes no sense to try to prevent the necessary transformation of the institutions of the past. On the contrary, their blind insistence provokes and accelerates the transformations they resist, in the same way that their denial of justice provokes deadly revolutions that will make them the first victims. The gradual evolution of the relations between labor and capital has followed a very clear path: from a patriarchal to a servile regime; from a servile regime to salaried labor; from the latter to the collectivist project of cooperative work. As Gabriel Monod points out, it would be as insane to impose the collectivist utopia as to attempt to perpetuate the current conditions of wage labor. An understanding of this phenomenon could convince us all of the futility of trying to impede or precipitate an evolution that might be inevitable, although it is definitely not the product of either a revolution or a concession.

The most extreme forms of classical economics have been thoroughly contradicted. An interesting example can be found in the laws of the Brazilian state of São Paulo. When the coffee boom reached levels that threatened the value of the beans to the point of undermining the interests of various sectors of the economy, the legislators ignored the axioms of the scientific school by preventing the establishment of new plantations while officially, and therefore artificially, increasing the price of coffee. This blow against the free exercise of economic activity revealed, in the shape of a massive state intervention, a crisis of enormous proportions. This example shows how, in the typical spontaneous manner of natural phenomena, an equilibrium will be found between unlimited individual initiative and state intervention. Here emerges the true character of society, which is not just the sum, or aggregate, of individual interests, but rather something different and above it: the sense of nationality. The sociological process that moves from family to clan, from clan to community, and from community to province and nation shows the vigor of this last concept. In the future, when nationality reaches its own limits, perhaps we will see a new world order, whereby all nationalities will bring about a generously expansive concept of humanity. This process of expansion will be fulfilled, barring some sinister setbacks, without

23. Carlos Arturo Torres, Idols of the Forum (1909)

the Napoleonic principles of conquest and control, but rather through the Kantian ideal of justice and fraternity.

The concept that makes the state not only a political and geographical entity, but also a moral and international one, opens a field for the reconciliation of various economic systems, and represents perhaps the greatest concern of the contemporary era. The efforts today are geared to strengthening the collective potential, as well as the concept of the social, thereby stimulating national solidarity and the love of country. Each nation hopes to grow in international significance, in wealth, culture, might, and population. The Malthusian principle of population, which is suicidal from a sociological point of view, false from a biological one, and both suicidal and false from an economic perspective, has lost the prophetic aura that condemned the "degraded species" preached by the apostles of violence. Each people, each state should strive to develop their potential, strengthen their character, and assiduously cultivate the originality of their art, literature, philosophy, and science.

In the same way that there has been an English and a German philosophy, a Spanish and a Flemish school of painting, a French and an Italian literature, today there is an aspiration to establish a science for each nation, namely, an emphasis on original scientific research. Whatever the distinctive characteristics of a country might be, it is important to develop them to their fullest potential. This is a more productive endeavor than the servile imitation of foreign cultures. That is why the concept of love of fatherland prevails in well-established countries, especially over the spirit of factionalism.

In a global society, a nation can establish its right to the respect and consideration of others, not so much because of an overwhelming presence or material wealth, as for its capacity to inspire the love of its inhabitants. Under the superior criterion of reason, a citizen of Geneva has more right to be proud of their country than a subject of the tsar in imperial Russia. Greece possessed a civilizing force far greater than any empire in history. The love of one's country, therefore, must be cultivated with meticulous care and tenacity: It is the most efficient moral element, and the most productive way to develop the living forces of a nation. There can be no excuse for letting this love dim and decay, because it is precisely the cultivation of this sentiment, the rekindling of this love, that is the most powerful instrument to overcome prostration, and to restore debilitated energies. We must return to optimism; we must believe in our country, in its potential, future, and higher destiny.

23. Carlos Arturo Torres, Idols of the Forum (1909)

The concept of fatherland is not, as some have the audacity to say, a petty prejudice, an empty abstraction, a fool's mirage, or an invention by chauvinists. On the contrary, it is something very real: a community of very tangible and very positive interests. At the same time, it provides an ideal mix of tradition, aspirations, and feelings. It is all that we love, and all that loves us. It is the best and most permanent part of ourselves; the warm hearth of our homes, the cradle of our children, and the grave of our forebears. It is the valley of our past and the city of our future. Beware of people who have no love of country! The celebration of a religion of fatherland – the celebration of the centennial of independence is one good venue – contains the purest form of ethical teaching: It expands and illuminates in both time and space the principles of equity and eternal wisdom that come, above all, from the commandment to "honor thy father and thy mother."

All countries understand the importance of, and the need for, a glorious national tradition, so much so that if they have little of it, they magnify it; if they do not have it at all, they invent it. That is why [George] Washington is turned into a god, while William Tell is an invention. The former is a larger-than-life hero revered by the nation, and the latter a hero forged by popular tradition. The militia general, a patriot, and a man of probity, though lacking the spark of genius, is turned by the miraculous alchemy of love and gratitude into the eponymous hero of a continent: "first in war, first in peace." The legendary hunter, the unerring archer, endures in memory despite the corrosive critique that denies his existence. He becomes the sacramental symbol of an ideal. The collective adoration, which is an authentic manifestation of a collective need, creates a representative superhero from the traditions of each people. Such a hero embodies all that is good; he is the unique and mystical creation of a generous superstition from which nations trace their origins, their history, and their glory, like an irremovable [Mount] Horeb.

Fortunately, we are not in need of Aladdin's lamp of fantasy and legend to bring our heroes to existence and veneration: They are with us and have a stature that would be considered a legend if history did not confirm it. These effigies only need a pedestal that will make them visible from every point on earth. Let us build it!

To make our fatherland prosperous we must first remove the seeds of hatred, because hate produces nothing but devastation. We must then plant abundant ideas, virtues, and efforts as well as actual seeds. We shall cultivate the land as well as the spirit, for the present and for the future.

23. Carlos Arturo Torres, Idols of the Forum (1909)

When harvest comes, as a result of both our good will and the natural expansion of life, it will be a blessing just like the parable of the sower [Matthew]. Our heroes will then have a pedestal worthy of their stature. The centennial of our republic can provide the opportunity to reflect on our history and show that we have reached the age of maturity. In the same manner as positive religions have both an essential and a formal aspect (the dogma and the practice), so does the love of country, which is also a religion with a doctrine and a ritual. The latter is plausible and necessary as a way to express social sentiments. It involves the creation of viable and objective symbols that promote public respect for the best and purest of our traditions. This is the serious function of our civic festivities, our patriotic celebrations, and our monuments.

This concept of fatherland does not invalidate the ideal of human solidarity, not even at the stage of internationalism that constitutes a legitimate aspiration. On the contrary, the elevation of humanity to the level of a supreme sociological unity implies the vitality of the international elements that will be part of it, in the same way as a society of superior beings will be the most perfect of all. To become a part of this universal association requires, therefore, the highest degree of development of the national potentialities. This is the right and the duty of all peoples. The Spanish American republics were not invited to the first conferences on international peace. They had to grow in importance and in Pan American solidarity before they could receive an invitation reserved only for countries that had emerged as significant in the concert of nations. On the one hand, there is nothing more beautiful than the love for a great and just country that has emerged from the land and its people. On the other hand, there is nothing narrower or more reproachable than an exaggerated national pride. This is the lot of the jingoes and *chauvins* [chauvinists] who flaunt their presumed superiority, and become prone to imperialism and conquest. Internationalism represents the contrary, opposing a clear injustice and rightfully seeking social justice. And yet, it is still inclined to use questionable means and sanctions.

The great work of reparation of the greatest iniquities, when performed with love and justice rather than hatred and retribution, represents the highest expression of human development. It seems to me that modern pacifism in all forms, from [Jean] Jaurés to [Charles] Richet, from [August] Bebel to Morley, and before them [Percy Bysshe] Shelley, [Victor] Hugo, [Alphonse de] Lamartine, [Giuseppe] Mazzini, [Edgar]

23. Carlos Arturo Torres, *Idols of the Forum* (1909)

Quinet, [Emilio] Castelar, [Francesc] Pi y Margall, among other generous spirits, reconciles the labors of the past and the aspirations for the future. A remarkable bas-relief exhibited at the Grand Palais in 1905 displays the words Past, Present, and Future.[2] This symbol of life, which is as poetic as it is true, applies to today's mentality: The present is related to tradition, on the one hand, and the future, on the other. Heir to the past, laboring in the present, on the march toward the future, the triple meaning of this symbol brings together the unity of character and the creative impulse of initiative and sustained effort. It brings together the potential of three forces, applying the energies of the present to understand the past, and to build the systems of the future. History, as [Maurice] Maeterlinck has observed, is still far from overcoming the period of lost generations that will allow humanity to ascend to the higher and desired stage. More than a desire, it is the debt that the current generation owes to the future generations. It is a kind of parental obligation that cannot be ignored. The best means to reach this objective is to affirm, clarify, and propagate the concept of justice (the "profound virtue") by Alfonso of Castile [in the third of the *Siete Partidas*[3]] that both people and ideas should achieve. Contemporary thought, or rather the spiritual currents that dominate the present time, with all their rectifications, demolitions, and rehabilitations, is above all an instance of justice. This justice opens a generous horizon for the spirit, a path of light that emerges from the clash of contradictory human conceptions, and even from the debris of the most devastating cataclysms. The past should not be rejected, despite the incomprehension of iconoclastic revolutionaries, because this would be an unnecessary, even suicidal, demolition. Neither should the present be hostage to immutable traditions because that would mean paralysis, or death. Nor should it mean to deprive the future of the laws of causality, because such would be a morbid obsession, a delirium. This concept of justice, inspired by equity, discerns what is false or objectionable in some

---

[2] This refers to a bas-relief by an artist cited as "Frémieux," which shows a vessel carrying three women, one looking behind, another ahead, and the third, in the middle, concentrating on the task at hand, rowing. The editors have not been able to locate an image of this piece, or much information about the artist. It was also mentioned by José Enrique Rodó in the essay "Rumbos nuevos" (1910) included in *El mirador de Próspero* (1913). The Rodó reference is included in José Pedro Segundo and Juan Antonio Zubillaga, eds., *Obras completas de José E. Rodó*, 4 vols. (Montevideo, 1945–1958), IV, 31. (Editors' note)
[3] This is a reference to the third part of the *Siete Partidas*, the major legal corpus of thirteen-century Spain. (Editors' note)

23. Carlos Arturo Torres, Idols of the Forum (1909)

cherished ideals, and discards them without recrimination. However, it also rescues even the atom of truth that might exist in the most absurd beliefs, as well as the faintest ray of light that can be seen lurking in the depths of darkness. It kindles the fire in the homes of the future city, a fire that touches the heart with the miraculous virtue of sincerity. By joining inspiring effort, legitimate veneration, and fervent hope, justice, as in Frémieux's bas-relief, equips the human vessel for the explorations of the future.

William James and the followers of [Thomas] Carlyle and [Ralph Waldo] Emerson have eloquently propounded the idea that it is the men of genius – the heroes of thought or action – who have initiated the great movements of people and ideas. However, I believe that a lasting and fruitful concept emerges and triumphs only when the general ideas it embodies exist virtually in time, and float like invisible atoms of light in the atmosphere, where a brilliant mind will discover the essence of the system. Now more than ever there is a tendency that cannot be denied by anyone who follows the course of contemporary ideas. This is the strong tendency toward social equity, justice, and intellectual generosity. Also, the renaissance of idealism and the development of a superior awareness of humanity. If we should accept that this is the result of rethinking the scientific, philosophical, and political values of a more expansive culture, and a freer, more general, more daring and comprehensive critical thinking; if we should witness the restoration of discarded ideals, and the twilight of the *idola fori*; if, finally, we should notice the emergence of a superior and harmonious philosophy of hard work and hope, we should believe that the affirmation of the attitudes and mentality of the present generation is an important step toward the realization of a very high, but not impossible, ideal. Or at the very least it will help us find the way to it. The human mind, which is the primary directive force in society, becomes dominant as a result of a slow transformation of the moral energy of the masses, which is in turn a product of continuous education. This is the aim sought by the consistent popularization of those principles that will subsequently become facts, creeds, and institutions. As Albert Lafargue has put it, the fact emerges from the idea like life emerges from the seed. Those ideas that are today in the atmosphere will, I am sure of it, materialize because that is their optimal and necessary outcome. They must become the intellectual patrimony of the greatest number of people. They should turn into tangible realities so that the

23. Carlos Arturo Torres, Idols of the Forum (1909)

masses, for their part, support and sustain them, instead of obstructing or killing them with icy indifference. In this endeavor, every initiative, in word or deed, has the ultimate virtue of fecundity: In order for a truly collective, human, and universal idea to succeed, each individual mind must contribute its part, just like each wave utters the great voice, and joins the chorus of the ocean.

Selected Bibliography

What follows is not a comprehensive bibliography of the history of political thought in Spanish America, but a selection of titles to serve as a reading list companion to this volume. After some general references, its structure follows the order of the book, offering a few titles on the respective topics of each section, then adding selected primary and secondary sources for each author.

Selected General References

Aguilar Rivera, José Antonio. *Ausentes del universo: reflexiones sobre el pensamiento político hispanoamericano en la era de la construcción nacional, 1821–1850* (Mexico City, 2012).

Botana, Natalio R. *La tradición republicana: Alberdi, Sarmiento y las ideas políticas de su tiempo* (Buenos Aires, 1997).

Breña, Roberto. "Tensions and Challenges of Intellectual History in Contemporary Latin America," eds., *Contributions to the History of Concepts* 16.1 (2021).

Burke, Janet and Ted Humphrey. *Nineteenth-Century Nation Building and the Latin American Intellectual Tradition* (Indianapolis, 2007).

Chambers, Sarah and John C. Chasteen, eds., *Latin American Independence: An Anthology* (Indianapolis, 2010).

Collier, Simon. *Ideas and Politics of Chilean Independence, 1808–1833* (Cambridge, 1967).

Collier, Simon. *Chile: The Making of a Republic, 1830–1865: Politics and Ideas* (Cambridge, 2003).

Crawford, William Rex. *A Century of Latin American Thought* (Cambridge, Mass., 1961).

Davis, Harold Eugene. *Latin American Thought: A Historical Introduction* (Baton Rouge, 1972).

Davis, Harold Eugene. "The History of Ideas in Latin America," *Latin American Research Review* 3.4 (1968), 23–44.

Donoso, Ricardo. *Las ideas políticas en Chile* (Mexico City, 1946).

Selected Bibliography

Goldman, Noemí, Mariano Moreno, Juan José Castelli, and Bernardo Monteagudo. *Historia y lenguaje: los discursos de la Revolución de Mayo* (Buenos Aires, 2000).
Hale, Charles A. *Mexican Liberalism in the Age of Mora, 1821–1853* (New Haven, 1968).
Hale, Charles A. "The Reconstruction of Nineteenth-Century Politics in Spanish America: A Case for the History of Ideas," *Latin American Research Review* 8.2 (1973), 53–73.
Hale, Charles A. "Political and Social Ideas," in Leslie Bethell, ed., *Latin America: Economy and Society, 1870–1930* (Cambridge, 1989).
Hale, Charles A. *The Transformation of Liberalism in Late Nineteenth-Century Mexico* (Princeton, 2014).
Halperin Donghi, Tulio. *Letrados y pensadores: el perfilamiento del intelectual hispanoamericano en el siglo XIX* (Buenos Aires, 2013).
Jaksić, Iván and Eduardo Posada-Carbó. "Shipwrecks and Survivals: Liberalism in Nineteenth-Century Latin America," *Intellectual History Review* 23.4 (2013), 479–498.
Jorrín, Miguel and John D. Martz. *Latin American Political Thought and Ideology* (Chapel Hill, 1970).
Joseph, Gilbert M. and Timothy J. Henderson, eds., *The Mexico Reader: History, Culture, Politics* (Durham, N.C., 2022).
Lewis, Gordon K. *Main Currents of Caribbean Thought* (Baltimore, 1983).
Martz, John D. "Characteristics of Latin American Political Thought," *Journal of Inter-American Studies* 8.1 (1966), 54–74.
Morse, Richard M. *New World Soundings: Culture and Ideology in the Americas* (Baltimore, 1989).
Palti, Elías José. "The Problem of 'Misplaced Ideas' Revisited: Beyond the 'History of Ideas' in Latin America," *Journal of the History of Ideas* 67.1 (2006), 149–179.
Paquette, Gabriel. "The Study of Political Thought in the Ibero-Atlantic World during the Age of Revolutions," *Modern Intellectual History* 10.2 (2013), 437–448.
Romero, José Luis. *A History of Argentine Political Thought*, introduction and trans. by Thomas F. McGann (Stanford, 1963).
Safford, Frank. "Politics, Ideology, and Society," in Leslie Bethell, ed., *Spanish America after Independence, c. 1820–c. 1879* (Cambridge, 1987).
Stoetzer, O. Carlos. "The Importance of Classical Influences during the Spanish-American Revolutions," *Jahrbuch für Geschichte Lateinamerikas* 30.1 (1993), 183–226.
Véliz, Claudio. *The Centralist Tradition of Latin America* (Princeton, 1980).

Part I. On History

Colmenares, Germán. *Las convenciones contra la cultura: ensayos sobre la historiografía hispanoamericana del siglo XIX* (Santiago, 2006).
Halperin-Donghi, Tulio. *Ensayos de historiografía* (Buenos Aires, 1996).

Selected Bibliography

Krauze, Enrique. *La presencia del pasado* (Mexico City, 2005).
Maiguashca, Juan. "Historians in Spanish South America," in Stuart Macintyre, Juan Maiguashca, and Attila Pók, eds., *The Oxford History of Historical Writing*, vol. 4 (1800–1945) (Oxford, 2011).
Malerba, Jurandir. *La historia en América Latina: ensayo de crítica historiográfica* (Rosario, 2010).
Mitre, Antonio. *El dilema del Centauro: ensayos de teoría de la historia y pensamiento latinoamericano* (Santiago, 2002).
Schmidt-Nowara, Christopher. *The Conquest of History: Spanish Colonialism and National Histories in the Nineteenth-Century* (Pittsburgh, 2006).
Woll, Allen. *A Functional Past: The Uses of History in Nineteenth Century Chile* (Baton Rouge and London, 1982).

José Victorino Lastarria

Primary Sources

Lastarria, José Victorino. "Investigaciones sobre la influencia de la conquista y del sistema colonial de los españoles en Chile" (Santiago, 1844). Available at www.memoriachilena.gob.cl/602/w3-article-8207.html
Lastarria, José Victorino. *La América* (Ghent, 1865).
Lastarria, José Victorino. *Diario Político, 1849–1852* (Santiago, 1968).
Lastarria, José Victorino. *Lecciones de política positiva* (Paris, 1875).
Lastarria, José Victorino. *Recuerdos literarios* (Santiago, 1878) [English edition in Lastarria, *Literary memoirs* (Oxford University Press, 2000)].

Secondary Sources

Estudios sobre José Victorino Lastarria (Santiago, 1988) [essays by Alamiro de Avila Martel, Antonia Rebolledo Hernández, Luz María Fuchslocher Arancibia, Javier Barrientos Grandón, Norman P. Sacks, and Luis Oyarzún].
Jaksić, Iván. *El debate fundacional: los orígenes de la historiografía chilena* (Santiago, 2021).
Oyarzún, Luis. *El pensamiento de Lastarria* (Santiago, 1953).
Subercaseaux, Bernardo. *Lastarria: ideología y literatura* (Santiago, 1981).

Lucas Alamán

Primary Sources

Alamán, Lucas. *Disertaciones sobre la historia de la República Mexicana desde la época de la conquista que los españoles hicieron a fines del siglo XV y principios del XVI de las islas y continente americano hasta la independencia* (Mexico City, 1844).
Alamán, Lucas. *Historia de México desde los primeros movimientos que prepararon la Independencia en el año de 1808 hasta la época presente* (Mexico City, 1849–1852).

Selected Bibliography

Secondary Sources

Lira, Andrés. *Los imprescindibles: Lucas Alamán* (Mexico City, 1997).
Méndez Reyes, Salvador. *El hispanoamericanismo de Lucas Alamán, 1823–1853* (Toluca, 1996).
Plascencia de la Parra, Enrique. "Lucas Alamán," in Virginia Guedea, ed., *El surgimiento de la historiografía nacional* (Mexico City, 1997), 307–348.
Van Young, Eric. *A Life Together: Lucas Alamán and Mexico, 1792–1853* (New Haven, 2021).

Part II. Democracy, Constitutionalism, and Liberty

Adelman, Jeremy. "Liberalism and Constitutionalism in Latin America in the 19th Century," *History Compass* 12.6 (2014), 508–516.
Aguilar Rivera, José Antonio, Eduardo Posada-Carbó, and Eduardo Zimmermann. "Democracy in Spanish America: The Early Adoption of Universal Male Suffrage, 1810–1853," *Past & Present* 256.1 (2022), 165–202.
Gargarella, Roberto. *The Legal Foundations of Inequality: Constitutionalism in the Americas, 1776–1860* (Cambridge, 2010).
Loveman, Brian. *The Constitution of Tyranny: Regimes of Exception in Spanish America* (Pittsburgh, 1993).
Lynch, John. *Argentine Dictator: Juan Manuel de Rosas, 1829–1852* (Oxford, 1981).
Posada-Carbó, Eduardo, Joanna Innes, and Mark Philp, eds., *Re-Imagining Democracy in Latin America and the Caribbean, 1770–1870* (Oxford and New York, 2023).
Sabato, Hilda. *Republics of the New World: The Revolutionary Political Experiment in Nineteenth-Century Latin America* (Princeton, 2018).

Bernardo Monteagudo

Primary Sources

Monteagudo, Bernardo. *Memoria sobre los principios políticos que seguí en la administración del Perú, y acontecimientos posteriores a mi separación* (Lima, 1823). Available at https://sas-space.sas.ac.uk/7432/107/A00113.pdf
Monteagudo, Bernardo. *Peruvian Pamphlet, Being an Exposition of the Administrative Labours of the Peruvian Government* (London, 1823).
Monteagudo, Bernardo. *Ensayo sobre la necesidad de una federacion jeneral entre los Estados hispano-americanos, y plan de su organizacion* (Guatemala City, 1826).
Monteagudo, Bernardo. *El Censor de la Revolución*, reprinted in Museo Mitre, ed., *La prensa de la independencia del Perú* (Buenos Aires, 1910).
Monteagudo, Bernardo. *Escritos políticos* (Buenos Aires, 1916).

Secondary Sources

Iñiguez Vicuña, Antonio. *Vida de don Bernardo Monteagudo* (Santiago, 1867).
Lutz, Donald S. *The Origins of American Constitutionalism* (Baton Rouge, 1988).
Lynch, John. *San Martín: Argentine Soldier, American Hero* (New Haven, 2009).

McEvoy, Carmen. "El motín de las palabras: la caída de Bernardo Monteagudo y la forja de la cultura política limeña, 1821–1822," *Boletín del Instituto Riva Agüero*, Lima, 23 (1996), 89–139.

McEvoy, Carmen. "De la comunidad retórica al Estado-Nación: Bernardo Monteagudo y los dilemas del republicanismo en América del Sud, 1811–1822," in José Nun and Alejandro Grimson, eds., *Convivencia y buen gobierno: nación, nacionalismo y democracia en América Latina* (Buenos Aires, 2006), 59–86.

Montoya, Gustavo. "Pensamiento político de Bernardo Monteagudo, entre el autoritarismo y la democracia," *Investigaciones Sociales* 8 (2001), 93–95, 98–102.

The Political Faith of a Colombian

Primary Sources

Anonymous [un compatriota de Bolívar]. *Reflexiones sobre el poder vitalicio que establece en su presidente la constitución de la república de Bolivia* (Caracas, 1826).

Anonymous. *Fe política de un colombiano, o tres cuestiones importantes para la política del día* (Bogota, 1827). Available at https://archive.org/details/fepoliticadeuncooobogo

Anonymous. *Continuación de la fé política de un colombiano* (Bogota, 1827). Available at https://archive.org/details/continuaciondelaoovale

"Bolivar and the Bolivian Constitution," *The North American Review* 30.66 (Jan. 1830), 26–61.

Bushnell, David, ed.. *Simón Bolívar. El Libertador. Writings of Simón Bolívar* (Oxford, 2003).

Secondary Sources

Aguilar Rivera, José Antonio. "The Liberal Cloak: The Constant-De Pradt Controversy on Bolívar's Last Dictatorship," *Anuario de Historia de América Latina* 55 (2018), 84–107.

Bushnell, David. "The Last Dictatorship: Betrayal or Consummation?" *Hispanic American Historical Review* 63.1 (1983), 65–105.

Lynch, John. *Simón Bolívar: A Life* (New Haven and London, 2006).

Esteban Echeverría

Primary Sources

Echeverría, Esteban. "Symbolic Words (1837) (Excerpts)", in Natalio R. Botana and Ezequiel Gallo, eds., *Liberal Thought in Argentina, 1837–1940* (Indianapolis, 2013).

Echeverría, Esteban. *Dogma socialista de la Asociación Mayo, precedido de una ojeada retrospectiva sobre el movimiento intelectual en el Plata desde el año 37* (Montevideo, 1846).

Selected Bibliography

Echeverría, Esteban. *Obras completas de D. Esteban Echeverría: escritos en prosa con notas y esplicaciones por Don Juan María Gutierrez, con una noticia acerca de la vida del autor, juicios críticos ... y poesías laudatorias* (Buenos Aires, 1873–1874).

Secondary Sources

Betria, Mercedes. "El concepto de democracia representativa en Esteban Echeverría," *Acta Sociológica* 71 (2016), 145–165.

Gallo, Klaus. "Esteban Echeverría's Critique of Universal Suffrage: The Traumatic Development of Democracy in Argentina, 1821–1852," in C. A. Bayly and Eugenio F. Biagni, eds., *Giuseppe Mazzini and the Globalisation of Democratic Nationalism, 1830–1920* (Oxford and New York, 2008).

Halperin Donghi, Tulio. *Una nación para el desierto argentino* (Buenos Aires, 2025).

Katra, William H. *The Argentine Generation of 1837: Echeverría, Alberdi, Sarmiento, Mitre* (Madison, 1996).

Lynch, John. *Argentine Dictator: Juan Manuel de Rosas, 1829–1852* (Oxford, 1981).

Sosnowski, Saúl. "Esteban Echeverría: el intelectual ante la formación del estado," *Revista Iberoamericana* 47.114–115 (1981), 293–300.

Wasserman, Fabio Enrique. "Democracia, soberanía y razón: un ensayo sobre la igualdad y la desigualdad en el discurso de la Generación del 37," *Cuadernos del Instituto Ravignani* (October 2023), 109–152.

Florentino González

Primary Sources

González, Florentino. *Elementos de ciencia administrativa* (Bogota, 1840). Available at https://tinyurl.com/s4c6jzc9

González, Florentino. *Ensayo sobre la situación actual de los estados colombianos* (Bogota, 1848).

González, Florentino. *La federación en la Nueva Granada* (Bogota, 1852).

González, Florentino. *El juicio por jurados* (Buenos Aires, 1869). Available at http://bibliotecadigital.bibna.gub.uy:8080/jspui/handle/123456789/1304 11?mode=full

González, Florentino. *Lecciones de derecho constitucional*, 2nd edition (Paris and Mexico City, 1871).

Secondary Sources

Cardona Zuluaga, Patricia. "Florentino González y la defensa de la república," *Araucaria. Revista Iberoamericana de Filosofía, Política y Humanidades* 16.32 (2014), 435–458.

Colmenares, Germán. "Florentino González, el mentor," in Colmenares, *Partidos políticos y clases sociales* (Bogota, 1997).

Cucchi, Laura. "Las *Lecciones de derecho constitucional* de Florentino González en la Universidad de Buenos Aires (1869–1874): diseños políticos nacionales

y circulación transnacional de doctrinas en la construcción de los estados sudamericanos," *Revista de Historia Constitucional* 20 (2019).
Cucchi, Laura. "'Extranjeros al servicio de la libertad': los exilios de Florentino González y Manuel Bilbao en Buenos Aires (1868–1874)," in Adriane Vidal Costa and Elías Palti, eds., *História intelectual e circulação de ideias na América Latina nos séculos XIX e XX* (Belo Horizonte, 2021).
Mouchet, Carlos. "Florentino González, un jurista de América: sus ideas sobre el régimen municipal," *Journal of Inter-American Studies* 2.1 (1960), 83–101.
Rodríguez Guerrero, Ignacio. "Nota sobre las *Lecciones de derecho constitucional* de Florentino González," *Boletín Cultural y Bibliográfico* (Bogota) VIII.9 (1965), 1377–1383.

Justo Arosemena

Primary Sources

Arosemena, Justo. *Apuntamientos para la introducción a las ciencias morales y políticas por un joven americano* (New York, 1840). Available at https://tinyurl.com/bdfpz662
Arosemena, Justo. *Principios de moral política redactados en un catecismo i varios artículos sueltos* (Bogota, 1849). Available at https://tinyurl.com/32c7xzsk
Arosemena, Justo. *Estado federal de Panamá* (Bogota, 1855). Available at https://tinyurl.com/mvtkyw5y
Arosemena, Justo. *Estudio sobre la idea de una liga americana* (Lima, 1864).
Arosemena, Justo. *Estudios constitucionales sobre los gobiernos de la América Latina* (Paris, 1878), 2 vols., 2nd edition [3rd edition, 1888]. Available at https://tinyurl.com/tv75k3hy

Secondary Sources

Aguilar Rivera, José Antonio and Eduardo Zimmermann. "Democracy and Liberal Constitutionalism," in Posada-Carbó et al., eds., *Re-imagining Democracy in Latin America and the Caribbean, 1780–1870* (Oxford, 2023).
García, Hernán Alejandro Olano and M. C. Mirow. "Justo Arosemena Quesada (Panama and Colombia, 1817–96)," in M. C. Mirrow and Rafael Domingo, eds., *Law and Christianity in Latin America: The Work of Great Jurists* (London, 2021), 228–241.
González Marcos, Miguel. "Comparative Law at the Service of Democracy: A Reading of Arosemena's Constitutional Studies of the Latin American Governments," *Boston University International Law Journal* 21 (2003).
Otero, Ana María. "Catecismos ciudadanos y moral política en el siglo XIX colombiano. El caso de Justo Arosemena," in Eduardo Posada-Carbó, ed., *Malcolm Deas: historiador de Colombia: Ensayos en su honor* (Barranquilla, 2022), 168–195.
Reza, Germán A. "Un capítulo inadvertido del americanismo: el Segundo Congreso Americano de Lima y el liderazgo de Justo Arosemena (1864–

1865)," *Araucaria. Revista Iberoamericana de Filosofía, Política, Humanidades y Relaciones Internacionales* 41 (2019), 537–552.

Part III. Church, State, and Religion

Fernández Sebastián, Javier. "Toleration and Freedom of Expression in the Hispanic World between Enlightenment and Liberalism," *Past & Present* 211.1 (2011), 159–197.
Ivereigh, Austin, ed., *The Politics of Religion in an Age of Revival* (London, 2000).
Lynch, John. *New Worlds: A Religious History of Latin America* (New Haven and London, 2012), chapters 4–7.
Mechan, Lloyd J. *Church and State in Latin America: A History of Politico-Ecclesiastical Relations* (Chapel Hill, 1966).
Mijangos y Gonzalez, Pablo. *The Lawyer of the Church: Bishop Clemente de Jesús Munguía and the Clerical Response to the Mexican Liberal Reforma* (London and Lincoln, 2015).
Serrano, Sol. *¿Qué hacer con Dios en la República? Política y secularización en Chile, 1845–1885* (Santiago, 2008).
Serrano, Sol and Iván Jaksić. "Church and Liberal State Strategies on the Dissemination of Print in Nineteenth-Century Chile," in Iván Jaksić, ed., *The Political Power of the Word: Press and Oratory in Nineteenth-Century Latin America* (London, 2002).

Vicente Rocafuerte

Primary Sources

Rocafuerte, Vicente. *Ideas necesarias a todo pueblo americano independiente, que quiera ser libre* (Philadelphia, 1821). Available at https://sas-space.sas.ac.uk/7468/931/A00789.pdf
Rocafuerte, Vicente. *Bosquejo ligerísimo de la revolución de México desde el grito de Iguala hasta la proclamación imperial de Iturbide* (Philadelphia, 1822). Available at https://bdh-rd.bne.es/viewer.vm?id=0000080921&page=1
Rocafuerte, Vicente. *Ensayo político. El sistema colombiano. Popular, electivo, y representativo. Es el que más conviene a la América independiente* (New York, 1823). Available at https://sas-space.sas.ac.uk/7433/1147/A00798.pdf
Rocafuerte, Vicente. *Cartas de un americano: sobre las ventajas de los gobiernos republicanos federativos* (London, 1826), Available at https://bdh-rd.bne.es/viewer.vm?id=0000120318&page=1
Rocafuerte, Vicente. *Ensayo sobre tolerancia religiosa* (Mexico City, 1831). Available at https://sas-space.sas.ac.uk/7329/462/A00906.pdf

Secondary Sources

Aguilar, José Antonio. "Vicente Rocafuerte y la invención de la república hispanoamericana, 1821–1823," in Aguilar and Rafael Rojas, eds.,

El republicanismo en Hispanoamérica: ensayos de historia intelectual y política (Mexico City, 2002), 351–387.

Castrillón, Alejandro. "The Hemispheric Federalist Debate: The Literary Exchange between Juan Egaña and Vicente Rocafuerte," *History of Political Thought* XLII, 1 (2021), 131–156.

Mekum, Kent Bruce. "Practical Idealism in Vicente Rocafuerte (1783–1847), 'Un verdadero Americano, independiente y libre'," PhD thesis, University of Indiana, 1971.

Mills, Nick Dean. "Liberal Opposition in Ecuadorian Politics, 1830–1845," PhD thesis, University of New Mexico, 1972, chapter V, 122–152.

Rodríguez O., Jaime E. *El nacimiento de Hispanoamérica. Vicente Rocafuerte y el hispanoamericanismo, 1808–1832* (Quito, 2007).

Francisco Bilbao

Primary Sources

Bilbao, Francisco. "Sociabilidad chilena," in *El Crepúsculo*, Santiago, June 1, 1844. Available at www.memoriachilena.gob.cl/602/w3-article-71224.html

Bilbao, Francisco. *Revolución en Chile y los mensajes del proscripto* (Lima, 1853). Available at www.memoriachilena.gob.cl/602/w3-article-8491.html

Bilbao, Francisco. *La América en peligro* (Buenos Aires, 1862). Available at www.memoriachilena.gob.cl/602/w3-article-8492.html

Bilbao, Francisco. *El evangelio americano* (Buenos Aires, 1864). Available at www.memoriachilena.gob.cl/602/w3-article-8493.html

Secondary Sources

Lipp, Solomon. *Three Chilean Thinkers* (Waterloo, Canada, 1975).

Pike, Fredrick B. "Church and State in Peru and Chile since 1840: A Study in Contrasts," *The American Historical Review* 73.1 (1967), 30–50.

Spindler, Frank MacDonald. "Francisco Bilbao, Chilean Disciple of Lamennais," *Journal of the History of Ideas* 41.3 (1980), 487–496.

"Vida de Francisco Bilbao Escrita por Manuel Bilbao," in Manuel Bilbao, ed., *Obras completas*, vol. 2 (Buenos Aires, 1968), xi–clxxxv.

Wood, James A. "The Republic Regenerated: French and Chilean Revolutions in the Imagination of Francisco Bilbao, 1842–1851," *Atlantic Studies* 3.1 (2006), 7–23.

Miguel Antonio Caro

Primary Sources

Caro, Miguel Antonio. *Obras*, vol. 1, ed. by Carlos Valderrama Andrade (Bogota, 1962).

Caro, Miguel Antonio. *Estudio sobre el utilitarismo* (Bogota, 1869). Available at https://tinyurl.com/4nvvjwap

Caro, Miguel Antonio. *La unidad católica y la pluralidad de cultos* (Bogota, 1869). Available at https://tinyurl.com/552jn2dk

Selected Bibliography

Caro, Miguel Antonio. "Libertad de cultos," *El Tradicionista*, Bogota, November 28 and December 12, 1871; January 2, 1872. Available at https://bibliotecanacional.gov.co/content/conservacion?idFichero=138791

Secondary Sources

Deas, Malcolm. "Miguel Antonio Caro and Friends: Grammar and Power in Colombia," *History Workshop Journal* 34.1 (1992), 47–71.

Delpar, Helen. "Colombian Liberalism and the Roman Catholic Church, 1863–1886," *Journal of Church and State* 22.2 (1980), 271–293.

Ferrer, Gemma Bernadó. "Miguel Antonio Caro and the (Trans) Formations of Classical Tradition in Colombia," *Pnyx: Journal of Classical Studies* 1.1 (2022), 27–44.

Herrera, Eduardo and M. C. Mirow. "Miguel Antonio Caro Tobar (Colombia, 1843–1909)," in Mirrow and Domingo, eds., *Law and Christianity in Latin America: The Work of Great Jurists* (London, 2021).

Rodríguez García, José María. "The Regime of Translation in Miguel Antonio Caro's Colombia," *Diacritics* 34.3/4 (2004), 143–175.

Sierra Mejía, Rubén, ed., *Miguel Antonio Caro y la cultura de su época* (Bogota, 2002).

Part IV. Society

Appelbaum, Nancy P., Anne S. Macpherson, and Karin Alejandra Rosemblatt, eds., *Race and Nation in Modern Latin America* (Chapel Hill, 2003).

Davies, Catherine, Claire Brewster, and Hilary Owen. *South American Independence: Gender, Politics, Text* (Liverpool, 2006).

Gracia, Jorge J. E., ed., *Forging People: Race, Ethnicity, and Nationality in Hispanic American and Latino/a Thought* (Notre Dame, Ind., 2011).

Hodge, John E. "The Formation of the Argentine Public Primary and Secondary School System," *The Americas* 44.1 (1987), 45–65.

Larson, Brooke. *Trials of Nation Making: Liberalism, Race, and Ethnicity in the Andes, 1810–1910* (Cambridge, 2004).

Scott, Rebecca. *Slave Emancipation in Cuba: The Transition to Free Labor, 1860–1899* (Pittsburgh, 2000, 1st edition 1985).

Juan Antonio Manzano

Primary Sources

Autobiografía, cartas y versos de Juan Fco Manzano, con un estudio preliminar por José L. Franco (Havana, 1937).

Anonymous [Juan Francisco Manzano]. "Life of the Negro Poet," in *Poems by a Slave in the Island of Cuba, Recently Liberated; Translated from the Spanish by R. R. Madden, MD, with the History of the Early Life of the Negro Poet Written by Himself* (London, 1840).

Madden, Richard R. *Address on Slavery in Cuba* (London, 1840).

Selected Bibliography

Schoelcher, Victor. *Abolition de l'esclavage: examen critique du préjugé contre la couleur des Africans et des sang-mêlés* (Paris, 1841).

Secondary Sources

Burton, Gera. "Ambivalence in the Colonized Subject: The Counter-Discourse of Richard Robert Madden and Juan Francisco Manzano," PhD thesis, University of Missouri-Columbia, 2002.

Cánovas, Rodrigo. "Juan Francisco Manzano, esclavo. Autobiografía (1835): reimpresiones de lectura," *Mapocho. Revista de Humanidades* 94, Santiago (2024).

Luis, William. "Introducción," in William, ed., *Juan Francisco Manzano. Autobiografía del esclavo poeta y otros escritos* (Madrid, 2007), 13–69.

Molloy, Sylvia. "From Serf to Self: The Autobiography of Juan Francisco Manzano," *Modern Language Notes* 104 (1989).

Mullen, Edward J. *The Life and Poems of a Cuban Slave: Juan Francisco Manzano, 1797–1854* (New York, 2014).

Schulman, Ivan A. "Introduction," in *Autobiography of a Slave by Juan Francisco Manzano. A Bilingual Edition* (Detroit, 1996), 5–38.

Mariano Otero

Primary Sources

Otero, Mariano. *Ensayo sobre el verdadero estado de la cuestión social y política que se agita en le República Mexicana* (Mexico City, 1842). Available at www.loc.gov/item/05014593/

Otero, Mariano. *Obras*, ed. by Jesús Reyes Heroles, 2 vols. (Mexico City, 1967).

Otero, Mariano. *Considerations on the Political and Social Situation of the Mexican Republic. 1847*, trans. and ed. by Dennis E. Berge (El Paso, 1975).

Otero, Mariano. 'Individual Vote in the Constituent Congres', in José Antonio Aguilar Rivera, ed., *Liberty in Mexico. Writings on Liberalism from the Early Republican Period to the Second Half of the Twentieth Century* (Indianapolis, 2012), 207–241.

Varios mexicanos [Mariano Otero]. *Consideraciones sobre la situación política y social de la República Mexicana, en el año 1847* (Mexico City, 1848). Available at https://bdh-rd.bne.es/viewer.vm?id=0000047359&page=1

Secondary Sources

Boyd, Melissa. "The Political Career and Ideology of Mariano Otero, Mexican Politician (1817–1850)," PhD thesis, University of St. Andrews, 2012.

Guardino, Peter. *The Dead March: A History of the Mexican–American War* (Cambridge, Mass., 2017).

Hale, Charles A. "The War with the United States and the Crisis in Mexican Thought," *The Americas* 14.2 (1957), 153–173.

Reyes Heroles, Jesús, "Estudio preliminar," in Otero, *Obras*, vol. 1, 9–190.

Selected Bibliography

José María Samper

Primary Sources

Samper, José María. *Apuntamientos para la historia política i social de la Nueva Granada desde 1810, i especialmente de la administración del 7 de marzo* (Bogota, 1853). Available at https://tinyurl.com/yezbuxmn

Samper, José María. *Ensayo aproximado sobre la jeografía política i estadística de los ocho estados que compondrán el 15 de sepiembre de 1857, la Federación Neo-Granadina* (Bogota, 1857). Available at https://tinyurl.com/yr36ub6a

Samper, José María. *Ensayo sobre las revoluciones políticas y la condición social de las repúblicas colombianas (Hispano-Americanas) con un apéndice sobre la orografía y la confederación granadina* (Paris, 1861). Available at https://tinyurl.com/wxyzu4h3

Samper, José María. *Historia de una alma: memorias íntimas y de historia contemporanea, 1834 á 1881* (Bogota, 1881). Available at https://tinyurl.com/mrx68j2y

Secondary Sources

D'Allemand, Patricia. "Quimeras, contradicciones y ambigüedades en la ideología criolla del mestizaje: el caso de José María Samper," *Historia y Sociedad* 13 (2007), 45–63.

Halperin Donghi, Tulio. "El nacimiento del intelectual hispanoamericano en el testimonio de José María Samper," in *Letrados y pensadores* (Buenos Aires, 2013), 349–380.

Hinds Jr., Harold Earl. "José Maria Samper: The Thought of a Nineteenth-Century New Granadan During His Radical-Liberal Years, 1845–1865," PhD thesis, Vanderbilt University, 1976.

Langebaek, Carl. "La obra de José María Samper vista por Élisée Reclus," *Revista de Estudios Sociales* 27 (2007), 196–205.

Juana Manso

Primary Sources

Manso, Juana. "La emancipación de la mujer," *Album de Señoritas: Periódico de Literatura, Modas, Bellas Artes y Teatros* 1.1, Buenos Aires (January 1, 1854). Available at https://tinyurl.com/35hyv742

Manso, Juana. *Compendio de la historia de las Provincias Unidas del Río de la Plata, desde su descubrimiento hasta la declaración de su Independencia el 9 de Julio de 1816* (Buenos Aires, 1862). Available at https://tinyurl.com/5yyn3c7y

Anales de la Educación Común, Buenos Aires, 1858–1875. Available at www.juanamanso.org/obras/anales-de-la-educacion-comun/

Selected Bibliography

Juana Manso's works are available in digital versions at www.juanamanso.org/obras/

Secondary Sources

Area, Lelia. "El periódico *Álbum de Señoritas* de Juana Manso (1854): una voz doméstica en la fundación de una nación," *Revista Iberoamericana* 63.178–179 (1997), 149–171.

Basdeo, Stephen and Luiz F. A. Guerra. "Juana Manso's *Mistérios del Plata* (1852) and a Global 'Mysteries' Tradition," *Victorian Popular Fictions* 4.2 (2022), 128. Available at https://doi.org/10.46911/TCWH4587

Davies, Catherine, Claire Brewster, and Hilary Owen. "Juana Manso (1819–1875): Women in History," in Davies et al., *South American Independence: Gender, Politics, Text* (Liverpool, 2006).

Peard, Julyan G. "Enchanted Edens and Nation-Making: Juana Manso, Education, Women and Trans-American Encounters in Nineteenth-Century Argentina," *Journal of Latin American Studies* 40.3 (2008), 453–482.

Rodríguez, Laura Graciela. "La educación de las mujeres según Domingo F. Sarmiento y Juana P. Manso: de la costura y el bordado a la escuela graduada (Buenos Aires, 1858–1878)," *Saberes y prácticas. Revista de Filosofía y Educación* 8.1 (2023), 1–121.

Martina Barros

Primary Sources

Barros Borgoño, Martina. Translations of "La esclavitud de la mujer" first appeared serialized in the *Revista de Santiago* 11, Santiago (1872–1873), 297–325, 512–531, 773–787, and 909–921. Her "Prologue" was published under a "Sociology" section in *ibid.*, 297–325.

Barros de Orrego, Martina. *Recuerdos de mi vida* (Santiago, 2023).

Undurraga, Lucrecia viuda de S. "Ensayo sobre la condición social de la mujer en Chile," and "Algunas observaciones sobre la educación de la mujer," *Sud-América*, Santiago (August 25 and September 25, 1873).

Secondary Sources

Botting, Eileen Hunt and Sean Kronewitter. "Westernization and Women's Rights: Non-Western European Responses to Mill's Subjection of Women, 1869–1908," *Political Theory* 40.4 (2012), 466–496.

Errázuriz Tagle, Javiera. "Discursos en torno al sufragio femenino en Chile, 1865–1949," *Historia* 38.2, Santiago (2005), 257–286.

Maza Valenzuela, Erika. "Liberals, Radicals, and Women's Citizenship in Chile, 1872–1930," Helen Kellogg Institute for International Studies, Working Paper 245 (Notre Dame, 1997).

Stabili, María Rosaria. "El sexo de la ciudadanía: las mujeres y el sufragio en el Chile liberal (1875–1917)," in Bárbara Potthast and Eugenia Scarzanella, eds., *Mujeres y naciones en América Latina. Problemas de inclusión y exclusión* (Madrid, 2001), 135–159.

Part V. Spanish America and the World

Ferrer, Ada. *Cuba: An American History* (New York, 2021).
McLynn, Francis James. "Consequences for Argentina of the War of Triple Alliance 1865–1870," *The Americas* 41.1 (1984), 81–98.
Schmidt-Nowara, Christopher. *Empire and Antislavery: Spain, Cuba, and Puerto Rico, 1833–1874* (Pittsburgh, 1999).
Sexton, Jay. *The Monroe Doctrine: Empire and Nation in Nineteenth-Century America* (New York, 2011).

Andrés Bello

Primary Sources

Bello, Andrés. *Principios de derecho de jentes* (Santiago, 1832). Available at https://libros.uchile.cl/561
Bello, Andrés. "Intervención internacional," *El Araucano*, Santiago, December 18, 1846, January 8 and February 5, 1847.
Bello, Andrés. *Obras completas*, 26 vols. (Caracas, 1981–1984).
Selected Writings of Andrés Bello, ed. by Iván Jaksić (Oxford, 1997).

Secondary Sources

Dawson, Frank Griffith. "The Influence of Andrés Bello on Latin American Perceptions of Non-intervention and State Responsibility," *The British Yearbook of International Law* (1986), 253–315.
Fawcett, Louise. "Between East and West: Latin American Contributions to International Thought," *The International History Review* 34.4 (2012), 679–704.
Jaksić, Iván. *Andrés Bello: Scholarship and Nation-Building in Nineteenth-Century Latin America* (Cambridge, 2001).
Obregón, Liliana. "Completing Civilization: Nineteenth-Century Criollo Interventions in International Law," PhD thesis, Harvard University, 2002.

José Antonio Saco

Primary Sources

Saco, José Antonio. *Paralelo entre la isla de Cuba y algunas colonias inglesas* (Madrid, 1837). Available at www.loc.gov/resource/scd2015.00158179489/?st=pdf&pdfPage=3
Saco, José Antonio. *La situación política de Cuba y su remedio* (Paris, 1851). Available at https://bdh.bne.es/bnesearch/detalle/2170049

Saco, José Antonio. *Obras*, 2 vols. (New York, 1853). Available at https://ufdc.ufl.edu/UF00074013/00002/citation

Secondary Sources

Chaffin, Tom. "'Sons of Washington': Narciso López, Filibustering, and US Nationalism, 1848–1851," *Journal of the Early Republic* 15.1 (1995), 79–108.
Cruz-Taura, Graciella. "Annexation and National Identity: Cuba's Mid-nineteenth-century Debate," *Cuban Studies* 27 (1998), 90–109.
Opatrný, Josef. "José Antonio Saco's Path toward the Idea of 'Cubanidad'," *Cuban Studies* 24 (1994), 39–56.
Schmidt-Nowara, Christopher. "The Specter of Las Casas: José Antonio Saco and the Persistence of Spanish Colonialism in Cuba," *Itinerario* 25.2 (2001), 93–109.
Whalen, Wickie Burton. "José Antonio Saco, Cuban Reformer, 1797–1879," PhD thesis, University of Miami, 1970.

Juan Bautista Alberdi

Primary Sources

Alberdi, Juan Bautista. *The Crime of War*, trans. by C. J. MacConnell (London and Toronto, 1913). Available at https://ia801504.us.archive.org/33/items/crimeofwar00albe/crimeofwar00albe.pdf
Alberdi, Juan Bautista. *Bases y puntos de partida para la organización política de la república Argentina*, ed. by Francisco Cruz (Buenos Aires, 1915).
Alberdi, Juan Bautista. *El crimen de la guerra* (Seville, 2017).

Secondary Sources

Adelman, Jeremy. "Between Order and Liberty: Juan Bautista Alberdi and the Intellectual Origins of Argentine Constitutionalism," *Latin American Research Review* 42.2 (2007), 86–110.
Davis, Harold. "Juan Bautista Alberdi, Americanist," *Journal of Inter-American Studies* 4.1 (1962), 53–65.
Jacobini, H. B. *A Study of the Philosophy of International Law as Seen in Works of Latin American Writers* (The Hague, 1954).
Mayer, Jorge M. *Alberdi y su tiempo* (Buenos Aires, 1963).
McLynn, Francis James. "Consequences for Argentina of the War of Triple Alliance 1865–1870," *The Americas* 41.1 (1984), 81–98.

Part VI. Fin de Siècle

Arciniegas, Germán. *Latin America: A Cultural History*, trans. by Joan MacLean (New York, 1967), especially chapter XVI "Del utilitarismo al positivismo," 378–403.

Selected Bibliography

Kilgore, William J. "The Development of Positivism in Latin America," *Inter-American Review of Bibliography* 19 (1969), 23–42.
Woodward, Ralph Lee, ed., *Positivism in Latin America, 1850–1900: Are Order and Progress Reconcilable?* (Lexington, Mass., 1971).
Zea, Leopoldo. *Dos etapas del pensamiento en Hispanoamérica: Del romanticismo al positivismo* (Mexico City, 1949).
Zea, Leopoldo. ed., *Pensamiento positivista latinoamericano*, 2 vols. (Caracas, 1980).

Valentín Letelier

Primary Sources

Letelier, Valentín. *La tiranía y la revolución; o sea, relaciones de la administración con la política estudiada a la luz de los últimos acontecimientos* (Santiago, 1891). Available at https://tinyurl.com/yz38ambf

Secondary Sources

Barría Traverso, Diego. "Positivism, Evolutionism, and Public Administration: The Work of Valentín Letelier (1886–1917)," *Administrative Theory & Praxis* 39.4 (2017), 275–291.
Jaksić, Iván. "Valentín Letelier: The Influence of Positivism on Chilean Educational Thought," *Pensamiento Educativo* 46.1 (2010), 117–132.
Lipp, Solomon. *Three Chilean Thinkers* (Waterloo, Canada, 1975).

Manuel González Prada

Primary Sources

González Prada, Manuel. "Discurso en el Politeama," Casa de la Literatura Peruana, facsimile, Lima, 1888. Available at https://repocaslit.minedu.gob.pe//handle/123456789/1018
González Prada, Manuel. "Nuestros indios," *Latinoamerica. Cuadernos de cultura latinoamericana*, Mexico City, 29 (1978).
González Prada, Manuel. *Free Pages and Other Essays: Anarchist Musings*, ed. by David Sobrevilla (Oxford, 2003).

Secondary Sources

Basadre, Jorge. "Ubicación histórica de González Prada," in Basadre, *Perú: problema y posibilidad* (Lima, 1994).
Plaskacz, Bohdan. "Manuel González Prada and Prince Peter Kropotkin – Aristocrats Turned Anarchists," *Études Slaves et Est-Européennes/Slavic and East-European Studies* 15 (1970), 83–92.
Sobrevilla, David. "Introduction," in Manuel Gonzalez Prada, *Free Pages and Other Essays: Anarchist Musings*, ed. by David Sobrevilla (Oxford 2003).

Ward, Thomas Butler. "Manuel González Prada: Devoted Follower or Insubordinate Partisan of August Comte?" *Revista Hispánica Moderna* 44.2 (1991), 274–279.

Andrés Molina Enríquez

Primary Sources

Molina Enríquez, Andrés. *Los grandes problemas nacionales* (Mexico City, 1909). Available at https://archive.org/details/losgrandesprobleoomoli/page/n5/mode/2up

Secondary Sources

Brading, David. *Prophecy and Myth in Mexican History* (Cambridge, 1984).
Kourí, Emilio, ed., *En busca de Molina Enríquez: cien años de Los grandes problemas nacionales* (Mexico City, 2009). Available at https://doi.org/10.2307/j.ctvhnob22
Shadle, Stanley Frank. "Mexican Land Reformer: Andrés Molina Enríquez and the Mexican Revolution," PhD thesis, University of California, Santa Barbara, 1990.
Tenorio Trillo, Mauricio. "Del mestizaje a un siglo de Andrés Molina Enríquez," in Emilio Kourí, ed., *En busca de Molina Enríquez: cien años de Los grandes problemas nacionales* (Mexico City, 2009).

Francisco García Calderón

Primary Sources

García Calderón, Francisco. *Latin America: Its Rise and Progress* (London, 1916). Available at https://tinyurl.com/4un9kvyb
García Calderón, Francisco. *Las democracias latinas de América* (Caracas, 1979). Available at https://biblioteca-repositorio.clacso.edu.ar/handle/CLACSO/15331

Secondary Sources

Colombi, Beatriz. "Una ciudad letrada extraterritorial: escritores hispanoamericanos en París en el fin–de–siglo," in Pamela M. Graham, ed., *Migrations and Connections: Latin America and Europe in the Modern World* (New Orleans, 2012).
Sánchez, Luis Alberto. "Prólogo," in García Calderón, *Las democracias latinas de América. La creación de un continente* (Caracas, 1979).

Selected Bibliography

Carlos Arturo Torres

Primary Sources

Torres, Carlos Arturo. *Idola Fori* (Valencia, 1909). Available at https://bdh-rd.bne.es/viewer.vm?id=0000080266&page=1

Torres, Carlos Arturo. *Obras*, 2 vols. (Bogota, 2001).

Secondary Sources

McDaniel, Shawn. "The Paradoxes of (Anti-)Imperialism: Race, Religion, and Resistance in the Latin American 'Arielista' Essay, 1898–1921," PhD thesis, City University of New York, 2013.

McDaniel, Shawn. "Arielista Elitism and Geopolitical Exigencies in Post-War Colombia, 1902–1910," *CiberLetras: Revista de Crítica Literaria y de Cultura* 29 (2012).

Sierra Mejía, Rubén. "Estudio preliminar," in Torres, *Obras*, vol. 1, xix–lxii.

Index

absolutism, 197, 257, 267
Alamán, Lucas, 16–18, 240, 241
Alberdi, Juan Bautista, x, xxx, xxxi, 205–218
anarchism, xxxiii
anarchy, 47, 240, 258, 263
Argentina, xiv, xxxii, 85, 88, 155, 205
   Album de Señoritas, 156
   Anales de la Educación Común, 155
   Association of Young Argentina (1837), 44, 47, 54, 60
   Constitution of 1853, xvii, xxx, 205
   El Nacional, 162
   La Nación, 253
Aristotle, 73, 75, 76
Arosemena, Justo, xviii, 72–90
Asia, 77
atheism, 113, 117
Ayen, Duke of (Jean de Noailles, 7th Duke of Ayen), 65, 68, 71

Bacon, Francis, 50, 266
Balmaceda, José Manuel, xxxii, 221, 230, 262. *See also* Chile
Barros Arana, Diego, 163
Barros Borgoño de Orrego, Martina, xxvii, 163–173
Bello, Andrés, ix, x, xi, xxviii, xxix, 62, 151, 177–188
Bentham, Jeremy, 88, 109, 120
Bilbao, Francisco, xx, 102–108, 151
   "Sociabilidad Chilena," xx
Bolívar, Simón, x, xiv, xv, 31, 254, 255
Bolivia, xiii, xiv, xxxiii, 84, 233

Bossuet, Jacques-Bénigne, 105, 107
Brazil, xviii, xxvi, 84, 86, 87, 155, 200
   O Jornal das Senhoras, 155
British and Foreign Anti-Slavery Society, xxiii, 127
Buckle, Henry Thomas, 169, 170
Bulnes, Manuel, 5
Bustamante, Carlos María, xii

Caro, Miguel Antonio, xxi, 109–123, 146
Castelar, Emilio, 273
Catholic Church, xx, xxi, xxvi, 102, 105, 109, 115, 119, 122, 156
Catholicism, xviii, xxi, xxii, 79, 101, 102, 104, 106, 107, 112, 114, 115, 116, 119, 260, 261
Central America, xvii, 85, 87
Chile, x, xiii, xxii, xxvii, xxviii, 12, 84, 85, 87, 102, 179, 230, 233, 260
   Constitution of 1833, 230
   El Censor de la Revolución, 23
   El Mercurio, xxviii, 178–188
   Radical Party, 221
Cicero, 40, 76, 208
citizenship, 49, 56
Colombia, xiv, xviii, xxi, xxv, xxxvi, 33, 36, 84, 85, 87, 114, 116, 118, 120, 146, 260
   Constitution of 1886, 109, 146
   Constitution of Cúcuta (1821), 36, 255
   Diario de Cundinamarca, 123
   El Nuevo Tiempo, 266
   El Tradicionista, xxi, 109
   Gaceta de Colombia, 31

Index

Colombia (cont.)
  La Civilización, 266
  La Crónica, 266
commerce, 95, 148, 149, 180, 199, 201, 212, 214, 215, 259, 260, 267
Comte, Auguste, xxxiii, 76, 268. *See also*, positivism
constitutionalism, xii, 84, 88, 150, 255, 265
  constitutional government, 27, 63, 69, 260
  Ocaña convention, xv, 31
corregimientos, 235
Cortés, Hernán, 22, 193
Cousin, Victor, 96
Crawford, William Rex, ix
Cuba, xxii, xxiii, xxvi, xxix, xxx, xxxi, 127, 128, 155, 189–204
  El Mensajero Semanal, 189
  Revista Bimestre Cubana, 189
custom, 49, 50, 59, 74, 80, 89, 140, 141, 148, 156, 163, 230, 264

Darwin, Charles, 268
Del Monte, Domingo, xxii, 127
democracy, xii, xiv, xvi, xxv, xxvii, 23 n. 5, 25, 28, 30, 47, 48, 49, 51, 53, 54, 55, 57, 58, 59, 60, 82, 83, 107, 149, 150, 191, 212, 213, 221, 228, 232, 262, 268
despotism, 30, 87, 117, 152, 156, 193, 195, 196, 197, 200, 224
Díaz, Porfirio, xxxiv, 238–252, 259
Dominican Republic, xx
Donoso Cortés, Juan, 105, 106

Echeverría, Esteban, xvi, 44–61
Ecuador, xv, xix, 84, 93, 177, 178, 260
education, xvii, 50, 66, 68, 69, 111, 112, 139, 142, 160, 162, 167, 171, 172, 208, 231, 236, 263, 274
  Catholic, 104, 140
  popular, xxvii, 120, 161–162, 224
  public, 27, 67, 81, 95, 117, 122, 155, 225
Egaña, Juan, xix
elections, 119, 120, 195, 196, 231
Emerson, Ralph Waldo, 274
encomienda, 79, 235
equality, 27, 45, 47, 50, 52, 53, 57, 61, 110, 206, 222, 254, 265
Europe, xx, xxiv, xxv, 35, 37, 81, 93, 110, 145, 147, 148, 151, 152, 153, 156, 178, 181

Holy Alliance, 180, 206
  revolutions of 1848, 102
evolution, 214, 215, 216, 242, 257

factionalism, 46
federalism, 28, 29, 122, 254, 255, 260, 261, 262
Ferdinand VII, 82, 93, 150, 153
Flores, Juan José, xxviii, 93, 178, 179, 181, 184, 187, 258. *See also* Ecuador
France, 22, 74, 81, 83, 121, 150, 182, 193, 204, 212
fraternity, 47, 270
freedom, 29, 30, 33, 54, 102, 160, 170. *See also* liberty; rights
  democratic, 50
  individual, xxxiii
  of association, 122, 197, 260
  of conscience, 110
  of education, 121, 170
  of the press, 39, 41, 42, 104, 121, 138, 197, 260
  of religion, 109–123
French Doctrinaires, xi, xvi
French Revolution, xii, 38

Gamarra, Agustín, 258
García Calderón, Francisco, xxxv, xxxvi, 253–265
general will, 39
Godoy, Manuel (Prince of the Peace), 82
González, Florentino, xvii, xviii, 62–71
González Prada, Manuel, xxxiii, 233–237
government, 63, 70, 74, 75, 78, 100, 111, 116, 143, 180, 206, 210, 211, 217, 226, 260
Gran Colombia. See Colombia
Great Britain, xxviii, 29, 81, 87, 104, 181, 182, 192, 204, 266
Grimke, Frederick, 62, 65–66, 67, 69
Grotius, Hugo, 185, 207, 208, 210, 211, 218
Guizot, François, 76

Hale, Charles A., viii
Haya de la Torre, Víctor, 233
Herder, Johann Gottfried, x, 8
Herrera, Antonio de, 17
Hildreth, Richard, 73
historiography, xii, 16–18
Hobbes, Thomas, 73, 77, 209

Index

humanity, 153, 181, 185, 186, 209, 212, 214, 223, 235, 242, 269, 273, 274
Humboldt, Alexander von, 17, 147, 148

immigration, 121, 259, 263, 264
independence, xi, xxxi, 12, 18, 78, 85, 86
Indigenismo, xxxiv, 233
individualism, 267, 268
industry, 56, 59, 76, 79, 95, 96, 97, 98, 99, 101, 123, 145, 157, 160, 186, 214, 225, 231, 242, 259, 260, 263, 264, 267
inequality, 75, 80, 98, 167
international relations, 52
Italy, 81, 94, 112
Iturbide, Agustín de, 93, 240, 254

Jacobinism, xiii, 23 n. 4, 34, 259
James, William, 274
Juárez, Benito, 239, 240, 241, 262
justice, 45, 46, 74, 97, 98, 144, 158, 171, 206, 207, 209, 235, 260, 270, 272, 273, 274

Kant, Emmanuel, 270

labor, 267, 268, 269
Laboulaye, Édouard, 76
Lamennais, Hugues-Felicité de, xx, 102
Las Casas, Bartolomé de, 79, 233. *See also* Spanish Conquest
Lastarria, José Victorino, ix, x, xi, xxxii, 5–15, 151
law, 45, 49, 50, 51, 54, 59, 89, 97, 156, 208, 217, 224, 260, 267
civil, 56, 72, 81, 185, 186, 207, 217
common, 115
constitutional, 56, 74
criminal, 72
international, xxviii, xxix, xxxi, 181, 184, 185, 206, 207, 210, 214, 216–218
laws of the Indies, 80, 198, 199, 234
natural, 46, 50, 55, 74, 118, 211, 212, 213, 214, 218
penal, 56, 72, 88, 208
positive, 45, 46, 55, 115
Roman, 81
rule of, xxviii, 24, 44, 82, 83, 86, 105, 166, 221, 222, 223, 225, 227, 229, 236
Siete Partidas, 273
Letelier, Valentín, xxxii, xxxiii, 221–232

liberal democracy, 44
liberalism, xxi, 62, 94, 109, 120, 200, 228, 254, 260, 262, 268
liberty, xii, xxxii, xxxvi, 7, 9, 10, 27, 39, 40, 41, 42, 43, 46, 47, 48, 52, 53, 56, 61, 63, 70, 77, 82, 85, 87, 96, 97, 98, 99, 100, 105, 108, 112, 118–119, 120, 150, 158, 206, 211, 212, 213, 225, 232, 257
commercial, 95
individual, 79, 200. *See also* rights
political liberty, 51, 79, 85, 94, 95, 202
Lieber, Francis, 63
life, 46, 54, 206, 237. *See also* liberty; property; rights
Locke, John, 73
López, Narciso, xxx, 189
López, Vicente Fidel, xii
López de Santa Anna, Antonio, 153
Loyola, Ignatius of, 104, 106

Machiavelli, Niccolò, 77
Madame de Staël, 41
Madden, Richard R., xxii, xxiii, 127. *See also,* Manzano, Juan Francisco
Mann, Mary Peabody, xxv
Manso, Juana, xxv, xxvi, xxvii, 155–162
Manzano, Juan Francisco, xxii, 127–135
Mariátegui, José Carlos, 233
Martí, José, x
Marx, Karl, 268
Mazzini, Guiseppe, 272
mestizaje, xxxiv, 262
Mexico, xvii, xx, xxii, xxiv, xxix, 16–17, 85, 87, 238–252
constitution of 1824, 136
El Imparcial, 246
El Nacional, 245
El País, 245
El Tiempo, 238, 245
federal system, 94, 136, 242
French intervention, xx, xx, xxi, 239, 246, 248
Liberal Party, 240
nationality, xxxiv, 239, 241, 244, 252
Reforma, 240, 241, 243, 245, 247, 248, 251
revolution of 1910, xxxiv
The Mexican Herald, 252
Treaty of Guadalupe Hidalgo, 136, 137 n. 2
US–Mexican War (1846–1848), 144, 145, 190

Index

Michelet, Jules, xx
military (and militarism), 80, 87, 146, 227, 257, 258, 262, 263
Mill, John Stuart, xvii, xxvii, 62, 65, 66, 71, 163, 165, 170
   On Liberty, 163, 164
   The Subjection of Women, 163, 167
Miranda, Francisco de, 194, 254, 255
mita, 234, 235
Mitre, Bartolomé, xii
Molina Enríquez, Andrés, xxxiv, xxxvi, 238–252
monarchy, 85, 180, 181, 211
monopoly, 80, 81
Monteagudo, Bernardo, xiii, xiv, 21–30
Montesquieu, xiv, 73, 254, 260
   Spirit of the Laws, 24
Montt, Manuel, xx, 5
morality, 56, 60, 76, 89, 94, 95, 96, 112, 141, 160, 184, 186, 209, 217
Mosquera, Tomás Cipriano, xvii
Muñoz, Juan Bautista, 17

Napoleon, 82, 202, 254, 258
Napoleon III (Louis-Napoleon Bonaparte), xxi, xxxiii, 70
nationalism, xxiv, xxxiv, 72
nature, 96, 97, 267
New Granada, xv. *See also*, Colombia
Newton, Isaac, 170, 173
Núñez, Rafael, 109

O'Higgins, Bernardo, 226
order, xxviii, xxxii, xxxvi, 43, 85, 87, 100, 211, 218, 231, 232, 240. *See also* liberty
Orrego Luco, Augusto, xxvii. *See also* Barros Borgoño de Orrego, Martina.
Otero, Mariano, xxiv, 136–145

Panama, xxxvi, 31 n. 1
Paraguay, 87
peace, 210
Pérez Rosales, Vicente, ix
perfectibility, 6, 10, 11, 15, 53, 83, 213
Perú, xiii, xiv, xxxiii, xxxv, 23, 24, 25–30, 84, 93, 227, 233, 253
   civilista party, 261
Philippines, 191, 193
philosophy, 54, 59, 105, 267, 270

Pizarro, Francisco, 22, 193, 237
political economy, 97
political parties, 221, 227, 228, 229, 231
politics, 54, 59, 73, 75, 78, 81, 172, 223, 231, 266, 267
Pope Pious IX, xxi, 105, 106, 109
Porfiriato. See Díaz, Porfirio; Mexico
Portales, Diego, xx, 262
Portugal, 78, 80, 81, 82, 180
positivism, xxxvi
   Comtean, xxxii, 5. *See also* Comte, Auguste
   Religion of Humanity, xxxii
printing press, 153
progress, xxxii, 47, 52, 154, 156, 158, 161, 211
property, 25, 39, 46, 54, 55, 57, 63, 64, 88, 111, 186, 237, 245, 260
protectionism, 216
public opinion, 89, 94, 95, 212, 225, 227
Puerto Rico, xxii, xxx, xxxi, 191, 193, 202
Pufendorf, Samuel, 185

Quinet, Edgar, xx, 7, 102, 273

race, 80, 87, 136, 139, 140, 144, 148, 154, 199, 242, 243, 260, 263
   African, 86, 195, 234
   Creole, 79, 81, 82, 234, 240, 243, 244, 250, 251
   Indigenous, xxxiv, 78, 79, 86, 140, 199, 233–237, 246–247, 250, 260, 261, 265
   mestizo, xxv, 234, 240, 243–244, 245, 246, 250, 251, 259, 261, 262, 265
rationalism, 103
reason, 55, 103, 107, 108, 158, 159, 166, 185, 187, 207, 208, 218
religion, 49, 52, 54, 59, 75, 95, 96, 100, 141, 150, 180, 199, 217, 245, 267, 272. *See also* Catholic Church; Catholicism
   Anglicanism, 156
   Christianity, 94, 95, 99, 100, 115, 152, 167, 247
   clergy, 49, 100, 101, 140, 141, 145
   Mormon, 112, 115
   natural, 99
   Protestant, xxvi, 101, 114, 115
   religious fanaticism, 104, 105, 138, 142;
   freedom, xxii, 94, 95, 104, 109–123;
   intolerance, 80, 105, 110; toleration, xx, 93–101, 110, 113, 114, 115
repartimientos, 234, 235

Index

representation, 39, 122, 203
representative democracy, xviii, 70
representative government, xv, xxvi, 32, 38, 43, 66, 68, 196, 197, 200
representative institutions, xxviii
republican government, 53, 229, 235
republicanism, xxi, 85, 102, 232, 260
Ricardo, David, 267
rights, 43, 222, 225, 263
   Declaration of the Rights of Man, 235, 254
   individual, 45, 54, 78, 85, 206
   of association, 45, 55
   of petition, 41, 42, 121, 122, 260
   of suffrage, 42, 117, 122
   political, 172, 173, 196, 200
   social, 172
Rivadavia, Bernardino, 44, 254
River Plate, xv, xvi, xxv, 22. *See also* Argentina
Robertson, William, 17
Robespierre, Maximilien, 34
Rocafuerte, Vicente, xix, 93–101
Rodó, José Enrique, 253, 266, 273 n. 4
Rosas, Juan Manuel de, xvi, xxvi, 44, 104, 153, 205, 259. *See also* Argentina
Rossi, Pellegrino, 186, 187
Rousseau, Jean-Jacques, 23, 40, 77, 131, 254, 255, 257

Saco, José Antonio, xxix, 189–204. *See also* Cuba
Samper, José María, xxiv, xxv, 146–154
San Martín, José, xiii, xiv, 21
Santa Cruz, Andrés de, 178, 258
Santander, Francisco de Paula, 258
Sarmiento, Domingo Faustino, x, xxvi, 155, 259. *See also* Argentina
science, 53, 73, 74, 75, 86, 98, 157, 158, 164, 165, 170, 218, 267, 270
   mathematical, 96
   natural, 169
   physical, 77, 96
   political, 75, 76, 77, 83, 120, 121, 187, 226, 228
   social, 75, 166
security, 46, 206
separation of church and state, xxii, 146
Sierra, Justo, 239, 249
Sismondi, Simonde de, 11, 13
slave trade, 156, 181

slavery, xxii, 76, 87 n. 6, 105, 127, 190, 196, 199, 234, 263
Smith, Adam, 254, 267
socialism, 268
Society of Equality, 102. *See also* Bilbao, Francisco; Chile
sovereignty, 35, 37, 54, 55, 56, 58, 213
   popular, 55, 69, 106, 254
Spain, xxviii, xxix, 28, 48, 49, 50, 51, 80, 81, 82, 87, 112, 142, 143, 150, 151, 154, 180, 183, 192, 194, 196, 200, 202, 235
   Constitution of 1812, 193, 194, 195, 196, 256
   Constitution of 1837, xxx, 203
   Cortes, xix, 189, 193, 203
   Council of Regency, 256
   French invasion, 194, 195. *See also* Napoleon
   legacy, 52, 264
   legislation, 78, 197
   reign of Charles III, 194, 202
   reign of Ferdinand and Isabella, 95
   reign of Isabella II, 201
   reign of Philip II, 144, 198
Spanish colonial system, 13, 33, 138, 153
Spanish Conquest, 12, 18, 78, 79, 105, 153
Spanish–American War (1898), xxxii, 143
Spencer, Herbert, xxxiii, 257
suffrage, xvii, 62–71, 146, 172, 187, 224, 225, 260
   Argentina, xvii
   France, xvii
   Mexico, xvii
   New Granada, xvii

taxation, 67, 80, 95, 145, 201, 236, 246
theocracy, 103, 106
Tocqueville, Alexis de, xxiii, 54, 73
Torres, Carlos Arturo, xxxv, xxxvi, 266–275
Tracy, Destutt de, xxi, 120, 121
tyranny, 222, 223, 224

United States, xiii, xxv, xxvi, xxviii, xxxvi, 28, 29, 66–67, 104, 110, 114, 115, 116, 145, 161, 162, 182, 194, 200, 201, 202, 211, 245, 251, 254, 260
   Civil War, 115
   expansionism, 190
   federal government, 190–191
   Monroe doctrine, xxx, 212

Index

Urquiza, Justo José, 205. *See also* Argentina
Uruguay, xxvi, 155, 205
utility, 97, 100, 185
utilitarianism, xxi, 109, 117

Varela, Félix, 189
Vattel, Emmerich de, 185
Venezuela, xv, xxviii, 31, 84
    Constitution of 1811, 29 n. 8
    Gazeta de Caracas, 177
virtue, 49, 94, 95, 98, 140, 141, 232
Voltaire, 131, 255

war, 179, 180, 208–209, 226
War of the Pacific (1879–1883), xxxi, xxxiii, 225, 226, 227, 233, 253
War of the Triple Alliance (1864–1870), xxxi
Washington, George, 254, 271
women, 155–160
    education, xxvii, xxviii, 155
    emancipation, xxvi, xxvii, 166
    suffrage, 70–71

Yanes, Francisco Javier, 31

CAMBRIDGE TEXTS IN THE HISTORY OF POLITICAL THOUGHT

Titles published in the series thus far

Aquinas *Political Writings* (edited and translated by R. W. Dyson)
Aristotle *The Politics and The Constitution of Athens* (edited and translated by Stephen Everson)
Arnold *Culture and Anarchy and Other Writings* (edited by Stefan Collini)
Astell *Political Writings* (edited by Patricia Springborg)
Augustine *The City of God against the Pagans* (edited and translated by R. W. Dyson)
Augustine *Political Writings* (edited by E. M. Atkins and R. J. Dodaro)
Austin *The Province of Jurisprudence Determined* (edited by Wilfrid E. Rumble)
Bacon *The History of the Reign of King Henry VII* (edited by Brian Vickers)
Bagehot *The English Constitution* (edited by Paul Smith)
Bakunin *Statism and Anarchy* (edited and translated by Marshall Shatz)
Bartolus of Sassoferrato *Political Writings* (edited and translated by George Garnett and Magnus Ryan)
Baxter *Holy Commonwealth* (edited by William Lamont)
Bayle *Political Writings* (edited by Sally L. Jenkinson)
Beccaria *On Crimes and Punishments and Other Writings* (edited by Richard Bellamy; translated by Richard Davies)
Bentham *A Fragment on Government* (edited by Ross Harrison)
Bernstein *The Preconditions of Socialism* (edited and translated by Henry Tudor)
Bodin *On Sovereignty* (edited and translated by Julian H. Franklin)
Bolingbroke *Political Writings* (edited by David Armitage)
Bossuet *Politics Drawn from the Very Words of Holy Scripture* (edited and translated by Patrick Riley)
Botero *The Reason of State* (edited and translated by Robert Bireley)
The British Idealists (edited by David Boucher)
Burke *Pre-Revolutionary Writings* (edited by Ian Harris)
Burke *Revolutionary Writings* (edited by Iain Hampsher-Monk)
Caliphate and Imamate: An Anthology of Medieval Muslim Texts on Political Theology (edited and translated by Hassan Ansari and Nebil Husayn)
Cavendish *Political Writings* (edited by Susan James)
Christine de Pizan *The Book of the Body Politic* (edited by Kate Langdon Forhan)
Cicero *On Duties* (edited by E. M. Atkins; edited and translated by M. T. Griffin)
Cicero *On the Commonwealth and On the Laws* (edited and translated by James E. G. Zetzel)
Comte *Early Political Writings* (edited and translated by H. S. Jones)

Comte *Conciliarism and Papalism* (edited by J. H. Burns and Thomas M. Izbicki)
Condorcet *Political Writings* (edited by Steven Lukes and Nadia Urbinati)
Constant *Political Writings* (edited and translated by Biancamaria Fontana)
Dante *Monarchy* (edited and translated by Prue Shaw)
Albert Venn Dicey *Writings on Democracy and the Referendum* (edited by Gregory Conti)
Diderot *Political Writings* (edited and translated by John Hope Mason and Robert Wokler)
The Dutch Revolt (edited and translated by Martin van Gelderen)
Early Greek Political Thought from Homer to the Sophists (edited and translated by Michael Gagarin and Paul Woodruff)
The Early Political Writings of the German Romantics (edited and translated by Frederick C. Beiser)
Emerson *Political Writings* (edited by Kenneth S. Sacks)
The English Levellers (edited by Andrew Sharp)
Erasmus *The Education of a Christian Prince with the Panegyric for Archduke Philip of Austria* (edited and translated by Lisa Jardine; translated by Neil M. Cheshire and Michael J. Heath)
Fénelon *Telemachus* (edited and translated by Patrick Riley)
Ferguson *An Essay on the History of Civil Society* (edited by Fania Oz-Salzberger)
Fichte *Addresses to the German Nation* (edited by Gregory Moore)
Filmer *Patriarcha and Other Writings* (edited by Johann P. Sommerville)
Fletcher *Political Works* (edited by John Robertson)
Sir John Fortescue *On the Laws and Governance of England* (edited by Shelley Lockwood)
Fourier *The Theory of the Four Movements* (edited by Gareth Stedman Jones; edited and translated by Ian Patterson)
Franklin *The Autobiography and Other Writings on Politics, Economics, and Virtue* (edited by Alan Houston)
Gramsci *Pre-Prison Writings* (edited by Richard Bellamy; translated by Virginia Cox)
Guicciardini *Dialogue on the Government of Florence* (edited and translated by Alison Brown)
Hamilton, Madison, and Jay (writing as 'Publius') *The Federalist with Letters of 'Brutus'* (edited by Terence Ball)
Harrington *The Commonwealth of Oceana and A System of Politics* (edited by J. G. A. Pocock)
Hegel *Elements of the Philosophy of Right* (edited by Allen W. Wood; translated by H. B. Nisbet)
Hegel *Political Writings* (edited by Laurence Dickey and H. B. Nisbet)
Hess *The Holy History of Mankind and Other Writings* (edited and translated by Shlomo Avineri)

Hobbes *On the Citizen* (edited and translated by Michael Silverthorne and Richard Tuck)
Hobbes *Leviathan* (edited by Richard Tuck)
Hobhouse *Liberalism and Other Writings* (edited by James Meadowcroft)
Hooker *Of the Laws of Ecclesiastical Polity* (edited by A. S. McGrade)
Hume *Political Essays* (edited by Knud Haakonssen)
Jefferson *Political Writings* (edited by Joyce Appleby and Terence Ball)
John of Salisbury *Policraticus* (edited by Cary J. Nederman)
Kant *Political Writings* (edited by H. S. Reiss; translated by H. B. Nisbet)
Ibn Khaldūn *Political Thought* (edited by Gabriel Martinez-Gros; translated by Anna Bailey Galietti)
King James VI and I *Political Writings* (edited by Johann P. Sommerville)
Knox *On Rebellion* (edited by Roger A. Mason)
Kropotkin *The Conquest of Bread and Other Writings* (edited by Marshall Shatz)
Kumazawa Banzan *Governing the Realm and Bringing Peace to All below Heaven* (edited and translated by John A. Tucker)
Lawson *Politica Sacra et Civilis* (edited by Conal Condren)
Leibniz *Political Writings* (edited and translated by Patrick Riley)
Lincoln *Political Writings and Speeches* (edited by Terence Ball)
Locke *Political Essays* (edited by Mark Goldie)
Locke *Two Treatises of Government* (edited by Peter Laslett)
Loyseau *A Treatise of Orders and Plain Dignities* (edited and translated by Howell A. Lloyd)
Luther and Calvin on Secular Authority (edited and translated by Harro Höpfl)
Catharine Macaulay *Political Writings* (edited by Max Skjönsberg)
Machiavelli *The Prince, Second Edition* (edited by Quentin Skinner and Russell Price)
Joseph de Maistre *Considerations on France* (edited and translated by Richard A. Lebrun)
Maitland *State, Trust and Corporation* (edited by David Runciman and Magnus Ryan)
Malthus *An Essay on the Principle of Population* (edited by Donald Winch)
Marsiglio of Padua *Defensor minor and De translatione Imperii* (edited by Cary J. Nederman)
Marsilius of Padua *The Defender of the Peace* (edited and translated by Annabel Brett)
Marx *Early Political Writings* (edited and translated by Joseph O'Malley)
Medieval Muslim Mirrors for Princes: An Anthology of Arabic, Persian and Turkish Political Advice (edited and translated by Louise Marlow)
James Mill *Political Writings* (edited by Terence Ball)
J. S. Mill *On Liberty and Other Writings* (edited by Stefan Collini)
Milton *Political Writings* (edited by Martin Dzelzainis; translated by Claire Gruzelier)

Montesquieu *The Spirit of the Laws* (edited and translated by Anne M. Cohler, Basia Carolyn Miller and Harold Samuel Stone)
More *Utopia* (edited by George M. Logan and Robert M. Adams)
Morris *News from Nowhere* (edited by Krishan Kumar)
Nicholas of Cusa *The Catholic Concordance* (edited and translated by Paul E. Sigmund)
Nietzsche *On the Genealogy of Morality* (edited by Keith Ansell-Pearson; translated by Carol Diethe)
Paine *Political Writings* (edited by Bruce Kuklick)
William Penn *Political Writings* (edited by Andrew R. Murphy)
Plato *Gorgias, Menexenus, Protagoras* (edited by Malcolm Schofield; translated by Tom Griffith)
Plato *Laws* (edited by Malcolm Schofield; translated by Tom Griffith)
Plato *The Republic* (edited by G. R. F. Ferrari; translated by Tom Griffith)
Plato *Statesman* (edited by Julia Annas; edited and translated by Robin Waterfield)
Political Thought in Portugal and Its Empire, c.1500–1800 (edited by Pedro Cardim and Nuno Gonçalo Monteiro)
The Political Thought of the Irish Revolution (edited by Richard Bourke and Niamh Gallagher)
The Political Thought of Nineteenth-Century Spanish America (edited by Iván Jakšić and Eduardo Posada-Carbó)
Price *Political Writings* (edited by D. O. Thomas)
Priestley *Political Writings* (edited by Peter Miller)
Proudhon *What is Property?* (edited and translated by Donald R. Kelley and Bonnie G. Smith)
Pufendorf *On the Duty of Man and Citizen according to Natural Law* (edited by James Tully; translated by Michael Silverthorne)
The Radical Reformation (edited and translated by Michael G. Baylor)
Rousseau *The Discourses and Other Early Political Writings* (edited and translated by Victor Gourevitch)
Rousseau *The Social Contract and Other Later Political Writings* (edited and translated by Victor Gourevitch)
Seneca *Moral and Political Essays* (edited and translated by John M. Cooper; edited by J. F. Procopé)
Shundai *Writings on Political Economy* (edited and translated by Peter Flueckiger)
Sidney *Court Maxims* (edited by Hans W. Blom, Eco Haitsma Mulier and Ronald Janse)
Sorel *Reflections on Violence* (edited by Jeremy Jennings)
Spencer *Political Writings* (edited by John Offer)
Stirner *The Ego and Its Own* (edited by David Leopold)

Emperor Taizong and ministers *The Essentials of Governance* (compiled by Wu Jing; edited and translated by Hilde De Weerdt, Glen Dudbridge and Gabe van Beijeren)
Thoreau *Political Writings* (edited by Nancy L. Rosenblum)
Tönnies *Community and Civil Society* (edited and translated by Jose Harris; translated by Margaret Hollis)
Utopias of the British Enlightenment (edited by Gregory Claeys)
Vico *The First New Science* (edited and translated by Leon Pompa)
Vitoria *Political Writings* (edited by Anthony Pagden and Jeremy Lawrance)
Volney *The Ruins and Catechism of Natural Law* (edited and translated by Colin Kidd; translated by Lucy Kidd)
Voltaire *Political Writings* (edited and translated by David Williams)
Weber *Political Writings* (edited by Peter Lassman; edited and translated by Ronald Speirs)
William of Ockham *A Short Discourse on Tyrannical Government* (edited by Arthur Stephen McGrade; translated by John Kilcullen)
William of Ockham *A Letter to the Friars Minor and Other Writings* (edited by Arthur Stephen McGrade; edited and translated by John Kilcullen)
Wollstonecraft *A Vindication of the Rights of Men and A Vindication of the Rights of Woman* (edited by Sylvana Tomaselli)

For EU product safety concerns, contact us at Calle de José Abascal, 56–1°,
28003 Madrid, Spain or eugpsr@cambridge.org.

www.ingramcontent.com/pod-product-compliance
Ingram Content Group UK Ltd.
Pitfield, Milton Keynes, MK11 3LW, UK
UKHW022312240426
470365UK00021B/600